THE OTTOMAN AGE OF EXPLORATION

THE Ottoman Age OF EXPLORATION

Giancarlo Casale

OXFORD
UNIVERSITY PRESS
2010

OXFORD
UNIVERSITY PRESS

Oxford University Press, Inc., publishes works that further
Oxford University's objective of excellence
in research, scholarship, and education.

Oxford New York
Auckland Cape Town Dares Salaam Hong Kong Karachi
Kuala Lumpur Madrid Melbourne Mexico City Nairobi
New Delhi Shanghai Taipei Toronto

With offices in
Argentina Austria Brazil Chile Czech Republic France Greece
Guatemala Hungary Italy Japan Poland Portugal Singapore
South Korea Switzerland Thailand Turkey Ukraine Vietnam

Published by Oxford University Press, Inc.
198 Madison Avenue, New York, New York 10016

www.oup.com

Library of Congress Cataloging-in-Publication Data
Casale, Giancarlo.
The Ottoman age of exploration / Giancarlo Casale.
p. cm.
Includes bibliographical references and index.
ISBN 978-0-19-537782-8
1. Turkey—History—16th century.
2. Indian Ocean Region—Discovery and exploration—Turkish.
3. Turkey—Commerce—History—16th century.
4. Navigation—Turkey—History—16th century. I. Title.
DR507.C37 2010
910.9182'409031—dc22 2009019822

5 7 9 8 6 4

Printed in the United States of America
on acid-free paper

FOR MY SEVERAL PARENTS

Ne revādur ki bir bölük Etrāk
Hind'e varmış gibi ticāret ide,
Ya'nī kim re's-i māl-i cüz'īden
Nef'-i küllī bulub riyāset ide?

Is it right that a bunch of Turkish bumpkins
Should engage in commerce as if gone to India?
That from a very small capital
They should make huge gains and become exalted persons?

—MUSTAFA ĀLI, *Counsel for Sultans* (1581)

ACKNOWLEDGMENTS

Some years ago, shortly after graduating from my PhD program, I presented my mother with a copy of my dissertation. In retrospect, this was probably a cruel thing to do. But she dutifully spent several hours slogging through its pages, until finally, after closing the back cover and looking up with an encouraging smile, she said, "Well, the acknowledgments are definitely my favorite part!"

For the record, it is my sincere hope that most readers of the present work will not be of the same opinion. Still, I have to admit the wisdom in Mom's words, for there are few parts of the writing process quite so gratifying as the chance to acknowledge the long list of debts accumulated over many years of hard work.

So let me begin by thanking someone who is sadly no longer with us: the late and much lamented Şinasi Tekin, who lived just long enough to see me safely exit the hallowed halls of Harvard University with diploma in hand. Since then, in my vainer moments, I have sometimes imagined that the experience of sharing with me some of his vast knowledge of the Ottoman Turkish language was exactly how Şinasi Bey had hoped to spend his golden years—although my generally appalling performance in his classes suggests rather the opposite view. In any case, I am certain that had it not been for his limitless patience, wisdom, and good humor, the book before you would quite simply have never been completed.

Similarly, a special and all-too-rarely acknowledged debt of gratitude is owed to my academic advisor, Cemal Kafadar, who more than a decade ago dragged me, kicking and screaming like a beardless *devshirme* recruit, into the strange and terrifying world of Ottoman history. It is only recently, having survived the ordeal, graduated from the palace school, and gained a comfortable appointment for myself in the provinces, that I am finally in a position to appreciate my time spent with him.

Many other individuals have contributed to my research in ways they may not even realize. Salih Özbaran, through his many pioneering books and articles on the history of Ottoman-Portuguese relations, has been a continual source of inspiration throughout my work, although we met in person on only one brief occasion. In a more hands-on fashion, Gary Shaw and Bruce Masters of Wesleyan University, Wheeler Thackston and James Hankins of Harvard, and Hakan Karateke, now of the University of Chicago, have all been mentors to me and, throughout the years, tireless advocates.

My colleagues from graduate school, especially Selim Kuru, Dimitri Kastritsis, Aaron Shakow, Ilham Khuri-Makdisi, Aslı Niyazioğlu, Erdem Çıpa, Bruce Fudge, T. J. Fitzgerald, Rachel Goshgarian, Emine Fetvacı, and Nicolas Trépanier, all served as constant intellectual companions and occasional dance partners (or, in some cases, the reverse) during my most formative years of work on this project. Naghmeh Sohrabi, another member of this group, gets a special line of acknowledgment all her own, since on a previous occasion she failed to receive one and made me pay dearly for the omission. Also included in this category, in an ex officio capacity, is my longtime friend Chris Woods, despite (or perhaps because of) the laudable suspicion with which he generally views academic life.

During my time in the field as a research fellow in Istanbul, I was equally fortunate to benefit from the guidance of many selfless archivists and librarians, particularly Ahmed Kılıç of the Başbakanlık State Archives, Gülendam Nakipoğlu and Zeynep Çelik of Topkapı Palace Library, Ülkü Altındağ of the Topkapı Palace Archives, and Havva Koç at the Istanbul Archaeology Museum, as well as the entire staff of Süleymaniye Library. In addition, Tony Greenwood of the American Research Institute in Turkey provided both hospitality and timely institutional support on more than one occasion; Mahmut Ak of Istanbul University kindly shared his expert knowledge of Ottoman geography; and Tarig Noor, now of the University of Khartoum, proved endlessly patient in helping me confront the horrors of *mühimme* paleography. Meanwhile, Louis Fishman was my perpetual partner in crime, both at the archives and in many of Istanbul's less reputable nocturnal establishments, as was Pino Cossuto. Steve Bryant and Joseph Logan were also regulars at the nocturnal establishments, although during the daytime, our paths tended to diverge. For similar reasons, I would also like to express my appreciation and deep affection for all Istanbul-based members of both the Çıpa and Griffin families.

During my much briefer stay in Portugal, the staffs of the Biblioteca Nacional, the Torre do Tombo Archives, and the Lisbon Fulbright Office were all extraordinarily helpful. An enormous debt of gratitude is also owed to Jorge Flores, Isabel Miranda, Andre Cuckov, and Sarah Watson.

Since arriving at the University of Minnesota in 2005, I have been blessed to find myself in the most supportive environment a young scholar could hope for. I am particularly grateful to Carol Hakim, Michael Lower, Carla Rahn Phillips, Jim Tracy, M. J. Maynes, Eric Weitz, Marguerite Ragnow, and Bali Sahota. The University of Minnesota also provided me with generous institutional support, including a McKnight Summer Research Fellowship in 2006, a single-semester leave in the fall of 2007, a Grant-in-Aid for Faculty Research from fall 2007 to spring 2009, and a fellowship at the Minnesota Institute for Advanced Study in the fall of 2008.

An embarrassing number of other institutions, both private and public, also contributed generous financial support for my research. These include Harvard's Weatherhead Center for International Affairs, the Social Science Research Council, the American Research Institute in Turkey, the Fulbright-Hayes fellowship program, the Institute for Turkish Studies, the National Endowment for the Humanities, and the Koç Research Center for Anatolian Civilizations.

Esteemed colleagues at several outside institutions were kind enough to read drafts of various versions of this manuscript and to provide me with invaluable feedback. These include Sanjay Subrahmanyam, Walter Andrews, Daniel Headrick, Alex Snell, Hardy Griffin, and two anonymous readers from Oxford University Press. In addition, Rebecca Moss, Scott Lesh, and Felipe Rojas helped me prepare the illustrations that appear in this book, and my research assistant John Wing (now Prof. Wing of the College of Staten Island) prepared the maps. I am equally grateful to my editor Susan Ferber, for all of her wise advice and attention to detail. All remaining errors in the text, of which I am sure there are too many to count, are naturally mine alone.

Before concluding, I must also say a word about my dizzyingly complicated family, whose convoluted and mercurial organization has played no small part in informing my understanding of sixteenth-century Ottoman court politics. Yet through it all, each of its individual members has displayed unfailing confidence in me, even when I had none in myself, and loved me always, as I love all of them. In this sense, no matter how dispersed across the globe or divided into rival households they may find themselves in the future, for me they will always be united between the pages of this book.

Finally, I would like to thank Sinem Arcak for things too numerous and too personal to enumerate here. But most of all, I thank her for making Minnesota, quite contrary to all conventional wisdom, the warmest home I have ever had.

CONTENTS

MAPS AND ILLUSTRATIONS

MAPS

ILLUSTRATIONS

A NOTE ON SOURCES

One of the most daunting obstacles to studying the history of Ottoman overseas exploration is the scarcity of the kind of relevant and easily accessible sources that inform more traditional studies of Ottoman political history during the early modern period. For a number of reasons discussed in more detail in the following pages, most contemporary Ottoman chronicles and narrative histories pay very little attention to events in the Indian Ocean, focusing instead on developments in the imperial capital and the core areas of the empire in the Balkans and in Asia Minor. While there are, to be sure, some notable exceptions to this trend, in general the historian is forced to look elsewhere for sources with enough information to allow a satisfactory reconstruction of events.

One important alternative is provided by Ottoman archival documents. These are very rich for the second half of the sixteenth century, and in this book, I have made particularly heavy use of the *Mühimme Defterleri* collection of the Başbakanlık State Archives in Istanbul. These "Registers of Important Affairs" are essentially day-to-day, verbatim records of the sultans' outgoing correspondence with their own provincial officials, as well as with visiting dignitaries from abroad and with foreign heads of state. Most remain unpublished, but they are well catalogued and relatively complete from the mid-1560s, and even before this date, they survive in fragmentary form.

When available, I have also made generous use of the sultan's incoming correspondence, although regrettably, this is a body of evidence that survives in a much more haphazard state of conservation than the outgoing correspondence preserved in the *mühimme* registers. Of the documents still extant, some are housed in the archives of Istanbul's Topkapı Palace Museum; others, especially the sultans' epistolary exchanges with foreign leaders, are preserved in bound volumes of hand-copied letters known as *münşe'ātnāmes*, today scattered in a number of different manuscript collections.

Alongside these archival documents, another important body of evidence for this study is a group of Turkish-language works that until now have been underutilized as historical sources: cosmographies, geographies, maps, travel narratives, and other original examples of sixteenth-century Ottoman discovery literature. While these often contain very little in the way of information about specific dates or events, they prove extremely useful for reconstructing the worldview that Ottoman leaders used as they devised a blueprint for imperial expansion. And since these works and their authors actively shaped this Ottoman worldview as much as they reflected it, in my narrative they also appear as protagonists of the story in their own right.

In addition, I have relied heavily on a number of texts in languages other than Ottoman Turkish, at least to the extent that my own linguistic capabilities have made possible. Of these, perhaps the most important are several copious, multivolume published collections of administrative, ecclesiastical, and diplomatic correspondence from the Portuguese *Estado da Índia*. These have been supplemented by the works of contemporary Portuguese chroniclers (of which the multivolume *Décadas* of Diogo do Couto have proven especially valuable), by unpublished documents from the Torre do Tombo Archives in Lisbon, and by a variety of other Western sources, ranging from Venetian and French consular reports to narratives of travel by European visitors to both the Ottoman Empire and the Indian Ocean.

Finally, the significance of contemporary sources in Arabic and Persian should by no means be discounted, although my woefully inadequate knowledge of these languages has led me to make unabashed use of modern translations whenever possible. I have also used English editions of Ottoman Turkish sources in a few cases when they are available. All other translations are my own, with the original text in most instances appearing in the footnotes. In a few places, I have made translations from French translations of Arabic sources rather than from the original, which is also indicated in the notes.

THE TRANSCRIPTION SYSTEM EMPLOYED IN THIS BOOK

The transcription of Ottoman Turkish into the Latin alphabet is a perpetual problem for historians. No system is entirely satisfactory, and the one I have chosen is, I fear, even less so than most. For the sake of legibility, I have elected not to fully transcribe Ottoman Turkish proper names, instead writing them in their closest approximation to modern American English spelling. Against many people's better judgment, I have also decided not to use any characters from the Modern Turkish alphabet to clarify pronunciation, since for non-Turkish speakers, these tend to make things more confusing, rather than less so. The only exception has been made for the Turkish "ğ" or "soft g," a silent letter with no real English equivalent or even approximation. As for place-names, in similarly unsystematic fashion I have used the most common English spelling, or in the few cases where none exists, its closest equivalent according to standard English pronunciation.

By contrast, titles of works in Ottoman Turkish and extended citations of Ottoman Turkish text (appearing mostly in the footnotes) I have rendered in full transliteration. The system employed is the following: ا - ā, ب - b, ت - t, ث - s̱, پ - p, ج - c, ح - ḥ, خ - ẖ, چ - ç, د - d, ذ - ẕ, ر - r, ز - z, ژ - j, س - s, ش - ş, ص - ṣ, ض - ż, ط - ṭ, ظ - ẓ, ع - ʿ, غ - ġ, ف - f, ق - ḳ, ك - k or ñ, ل - l, م - m, ن - n, ه - h, و - v or ū, ي - y or ī, ء - ʾ

Short vowels are rendered using the modern Turkish alphabet: a, e, ı, i, o, ö, u, ü.

LIST OF ABBREVIATIONS

A.N.T.T. Lisbon, Arquivo Nacional da Torre do Tombo.

APO Rivara, J. H. da Cunha, ed., *Archivo Portuguez-Oriental.* 6 vols. in 10 parts. Nova Goa: Imprensa Nacional: 1857–1877.

CALENDAR OF STATE PAPERS Public Records Office. *Calendar of State Papers and Manuscripts Relating to English Affairs Existing in the Archives and Collections of Venice.* 38 vols. Great Britain: Public Records Office, 1939–1947.

CARTAS João de Castro, *Cartas de D. João de Castro.* Edited by Elaine Sanceau. Lisbon: Agencia Geral do Ultramar, 1955.

CDP *Corpo Diplomatico Portuguez.* 15 vols. Paris: J. P. Aillaud, 1846.

DA Couto, Dogo do. *Da Ásia.* Lisbon, 1777. [vols. 10–24 of 24 volume *Da Ásia de João de Barros e de Diogo do Couto.*] Note: Because Couto's text is a multivolume work that exists in numerous variant manuscript versions and in many partial published editions, I have chosen not to give citations by volume and page number, as these vary widely between versions. Instead, citations appear according to the internal organization of the work by *década*, book, and chapter.

DOCUMENTA INDICA Joseph Wicki, ed. *Documenta Indica.* 11 vols. Roma: Institutum Historicum Societatis Iesu, 1948–1994.

DP Rego, António da Silva, ed. *Documentação para a história das missões do Padroado Português do Oriente.* 12 vols. Lisbon: Ministério das Colónias, 1948–.

DUP *Documentação Ultramarina Portuguesa*, Lisboa: Centro de Estudos Históricos Ultramarinos da Junta de Investigação do Ultramar, 1960–1973.

EI^2 *The Encyclopaedia of Islam. New Edition.* 1954–.

FS Faria e Sousa, Manuel de. *Ásia Portuguesa.* Translated by Isabel Ferreira do Amaral Pereira de Matos, 6 vols. Porto, 1956.

GAVETAS *As Gavetas da Torre do Tombo.* 8 vols. Lisbon: Centro de Estudos Históricos Ultramarinos, 1960–1977. Note: Citations here appear according to the original classification by *gaveta*, file, and document, rather than the volume and page numbers of the published version.

MD Istanbul, Başbakanlık Devlet Arşivi, *Mühimme Defterleri* [Prime Ministry's State Archives, *Registers of Important Affairs*].

PM Rego, A. da Silva and T.W. Baxter, eds. *Documentos sobre os portugueses em Moçambique e na Africa central, 1497–1840.* 9 vols. Lisbon: Centro de Estudos Storicos Ultramarinos, 1962–1989.

SÃO LOURENÇO Sanceau, Elaine, ed. *Collecção de São Lourenço.* 3 vols. Lisboa: Centro de Estudos Históricos Ultramarinos da Junta de Investigação do Ultramar, 1973–.

T.S.M.A. Istanbul, Topkapı Sarayı Müzesi Arşivi [The Archive of the Topkapı Palace Museum].

T.S.M.K. Istanbul, Topkapı Sarayı Müzesi Kütüphanesi [The Library of the Topkapı Palace Museum].

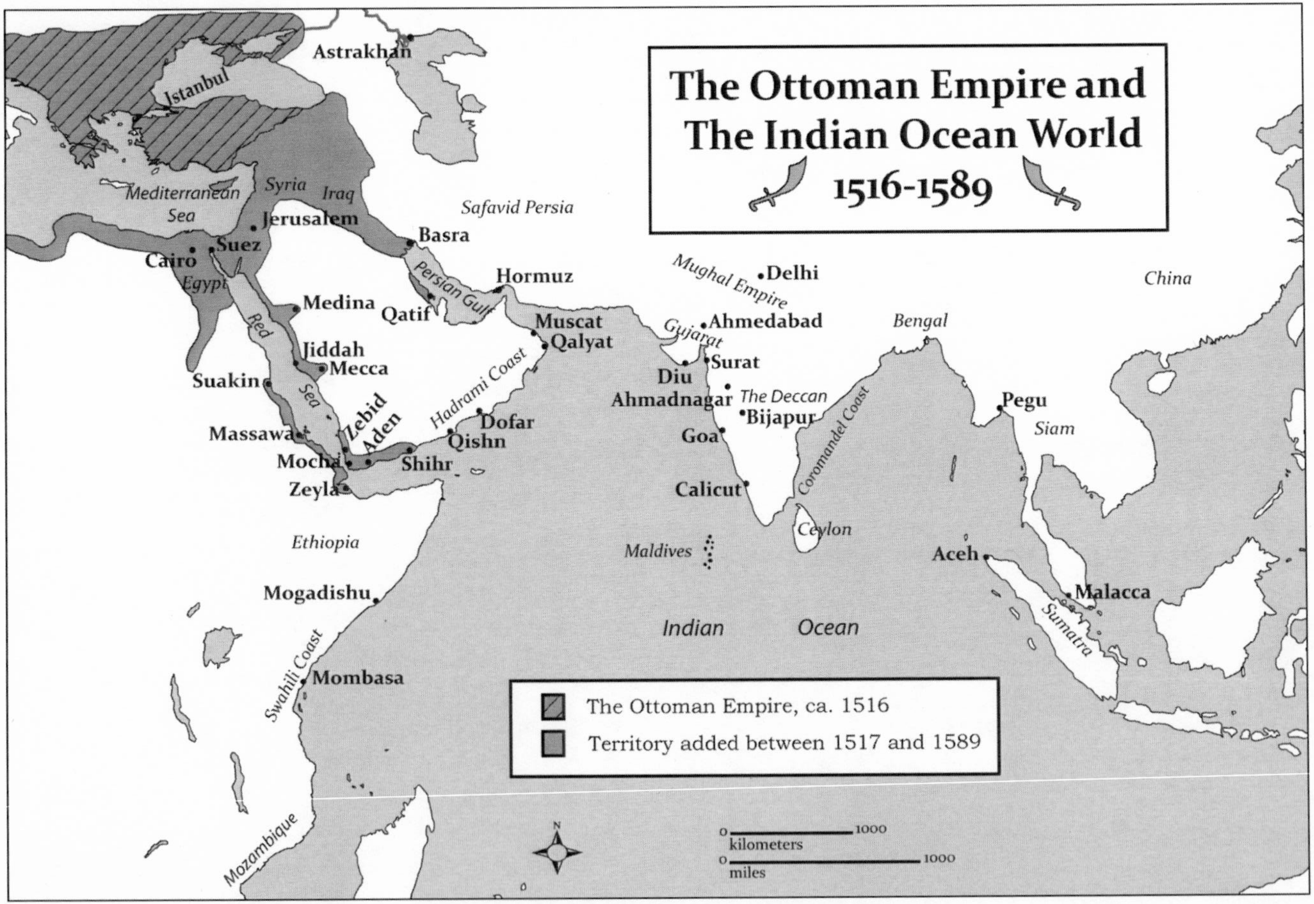

MAP 0.1 The Ottoman Empire and the Indian Ocean world, 1516–1589

THE OTTOMAN AGE OF EXPLORATION

Introduction

AN EMPIRE OF THE MIND

Imagine, just for a moment, that the Ottoman Sultan Mehmed the Conqueror never captured the city of Constantinople. Instead, suppose that Emperor Constantine Palaeologos and the ragtag remnants of his Byzantine army managed, against all odds, not only to save their capital on that fateful Tuesday in 1453 but also, during the following decades, to reoccupy all of the lands in the Balkans and Anatolia that had once constituted the core of their empire.

Now imagine that the dawn of the sixteenth century witnessed an even more startling rise in this empire's fortunes, as victorious Byzantine legions marched ever further, conquering provinces like Syria and Egypt that had been lost to them for centuries and, later, spreading into such distant and unfamiliar lands as Yemen, the Sudan, and the Horn of Africa. Then, from these advanced bases, imagine that Byzantine fleets began to conduct patrols of the Indian Ocean, to organize massive expeditions against enemy strongholds in Hormuz and Gujarat, and to send crack military teams to support their allies in places as remote from one another and from the imperial capital as Indonesia and the Swahili Coast.

Naturally, such prodigious military expansion would be accompanied by equally impressive advances in other fields. Thus, picture a Byzantine treasury that began to use the spice trade to move beyond its traditional reliance on agriculture, dispatching commercial agents to the markets of India and Sumatra and organizing regular convoys of state-owned ships to bring pepper and cloves to the spice bazaars of Egypt. Meanwhile, back in Constantinople, imagine the growth of a new group of Byzantine intellectuals who, inspired by these far-flung successes and bankrolled by the city's burgeoning imperial elites, began to cultivate an interest in the rapidly developing sciences of cartography and geography. In short, imagine a sixteenth-century Byzantine Age of Exploration.

If such a Byzantine state had actually existed, how might scholars in our own day characterize its growth? Here, as historians, we are now on slightly firmer ground. For although our imaginary Byzantine state was never to be, there is a substantial body of real-world scholarship that examines the delicate connection between late Byzantine intellectual life (during a period sometimes known as the Palaeologan Renaissance) and the development of Renaissance humanism in the West.[1]

Judging from the direction taken by such works, it seems clear that a comparison between the accomplishments of our sixteenth-century Byzantine explorers and those of their contemporaries from Western Europe would be an obvious one, providing inspiration for an endless series of scholarly questions about their relative similarities and differences. "Why were the Byzantines so uninterested in the New World?" one virtual historian might ask. "How important were the religious and linguistic differences that divided them from the West?" might ask another. "Was the contemporaneous nature of Byzantine and Western expansion just a coincidence?" might ask a third. But regardless of the ways in which these individual questions might be framed, researchers of all stripes would naturally take up the challenge of incorporating Byzantine history into the larger story of European global exploration.

So what about the Ottomans? It just so happens that the Ottoman Empire accomplished in the real world of the sixteenth century every one of the things that the virtual Byzantines accomplished only in our imagination. Yet astonishingly, no serious attempt has ever been made to portray these Ottoman achievements as part of the larger story of physical expansion abroad and intellectual ferment at home that characterized Western European history during precisely the same period.[2] Herein lies the central question of this book. Stated simply, it asks: "Did the Ottomans participate in the Age of Exploration?" The answer, also stated simply, is yes.

DEFINING OTTOMAN EXPLORATION

There are few historical subjects that have aroused passions for as long, and for as many reasons, as the European Age of Exploration. Despite a vast and constantly growing literature dedicated to it, scholars continue to disagree widely about its origins, its scope, and its ultimate consequences. But if the phenomenon remains one that can be defined in any number of ways, for the purposes at hand the problem need not be so complicated. This book therefore focuses on a few key aspects of European expansion that are both generally agreed upon and directly relevant to the Ottoman case.

The first of these is the relative isolation of Western Europe during the period directly preceding the earliest voyages of discovery. During the first half of the fifteenth century, a time when Muslim merchants could travel virtually unobstructed from Morocco to Southeast Asia, and navigators from Ming China could boast of enormous naval expeditions reaching as far west as Hormuz, Aden, and Mombasa, Western Europeans remained almost totally confined, both physically and intellectually, to a small slice of the world bounded by the North Atlantic and the Mediterranean.[3] Even as late as the eve of Columbus's first voyage, European knowledge of other world regions continued to be based on a handful of sketchy medieval travelers' accounts and a few dusty maps and geographical texts only recently recovered and translated from ancient Greek.[4] In this sense, European exploration was possible in large part because Europeans had so much more of the world left to explore.

At the same time, however—and rather ironically, considering this state of isolation—a second distinguishing characteristic of European exploration is the audacious political ideology that accompanied it. To illustrate this, no better example exists than the famous Treaty of Tordesillas, signed in 1494 between the crowns of Portugal and Spain under the sacred auspices of Pope Alexander VI. According to its terms, the two Iberian powers agreed to nothing less than a partition of the entire extra-European world, with each side claiming the right to conquer and rule all lands within its own hemisphere and to maintain exclusive control over its navigation and maritime trade. The sweepingly global scope of this agreement, combined with the explicit connection it drew between state power and maritime commerce, established a prototype for a new kind of overseas empire that would redefine European political discourse for centuries to come. And yet, at the time that the Treaty of Tordesillas was signed, neither Portugal, nor Spain, nor any other European nation controlled so much as one square inch of territory (or even a single ship) anywhere in Asia or the New World. History may offer other examples of rulers who have staked claims to universal dominion on a similarly tenuous basis, but rarely have these claims anticipated real-world success in such an unexpected and innovative way.[5]

Of course, if European powers were willing to indulge these improbable aspirations, this was in part thanks to a pair of recent but critical technological advances that permitted exploration and colonial expansion on a scale previously unimaginable: firearms and the oceangoing sailing ship. Strictly speaking, the former was not a Western innovation, as the military uses of gunpowder were by no means entirely unknown outside Europe before the sixteenth century. Still, the widespread use of handguns and the casting of heavy iron and bronze artillery bores were technologies perfected in the West. And when combined with the carrack, an innovative type of sailing vessel ideally suited to long-distance navigation and, more important, to mounting large numbers of cannon on board, firearms provided Westerners with the perfect military tool for fulfilling their dreams of empire. By the turn of the sixteenth century, their heavily armed sailing ships had developed into veritable floating fortresses, allowing the Spanish and Portuguese to use the sea to project their power abroad as never before.[6]

Finally, alongside these considerations of technology and political ideology, the last and perhaps most recognizably European component of the Age of Exploration is the distinctive cultural and intellectual transformation that accompanied it. Coinciding with the spread of Renaissance humanism and with the invention of the movable-type printing press, the explorations ushered in a period of intense Western intellectual ferment, as the flood of new information from abroad inspired Europeans to undertake a comprehensive reevaluation of their traditional understanding of the world and their own place within it. Intellectually speaking, much of what is understood today as Western civilization can thus be seen as an immediate by-product of the European voyages of discovery.[7]

In broad lines, then, these are the four characteristics of sixteenth-century European expansion that constitute the basic definition of the term Age of Exploration in this book: a starting point of relative geographic and cultural isolation, the subsequent development of expansive political ideologies focused particularly on trade routes and maritime navigation, innovation in a few key areas of military and naval technology that made overseas expansion possible, and an unprecedented intensification of intellectual interest in the outside world.

But how does this definition relate to the specific experience of the Ottoman Empire during the sixteenth century? This book argues that Ottoman expansion shared, to varying degrees, all of these essential traits of European exploration—an assertion that will no doubt come as a surprise to those accustomed to thinking of the Ottoman Empire in quite different terms: at first as the primary *obstacle* to exploration and later as its principal *victim*. After all, a suspicious reader may ask, isn't it common knowledge that both the Spanish and the Portuguese envisioned their overseas ventures as a logical extension of the Crusades? Isn't it also true that the establishment of a Portuguese trading empire in the Indies came at the expense of Muslim merchants? And didn't this, over the *longue durée*, permanently marginalize the economy of the Islamic world?[8]

Yes and no. On the one hand, even if historians continue to debate the long-term economic consequences of early Iberian expansion, there is little doubt that Muslim merchants did indeed bear the brunt of the notoriously violent early Portuguese efforts to seize control of the Indian Ocean spice trade. But on the other hand, there is an important distinction to be drawn between Muslims and Ottomans—a distinction without which the Ottoman Empire's true place in early modern history cannot be properly understood.

Specifically, it is an essential tenet of this book that before the Age of Exploration began, the Ottoman Empire had virtually no meaningful contact with the Indian Ocean—a part of the world that was, despite a deeply rooted indigenous Muslim presence, nevertheless as remote and unfamiliar to the Ottomans as it was to contemporary Europeans. Prior to the sixteenth century, Ottoman scholars were almost totally ignorant of the history and geography of the Indian Ocean, Ottoman statesmen lacked even a rudimentary knowledge of its resources and its political economy, and the empire's trade with the region, while not insignificant, was largely carried out by intermediaries. In this respect, the situation of the Ottoman Empire at the turn of the sixteenth century was not substantially different from that of Portugal or Spain: it was a newly consolidated and rapidly expanding state, but one whose intellectual, political, and economic horizons were still firmly encompassed by the Mediterranean basin. Indeed, this condition of relative isolation would last even longer for the Ottomans than it would for their European rivals, ending only with the Ottoman conquest of Egypt in 1517—a full twenty years after Vasco da Gama's triumphant circumnavigation of the Cape of Good Hope.

Once the Ottomans finally did establish a toehold in this previously unknown part of the world, however, they rapidly began to reorient themselves, take stock of the region, and develop a new set of imperial ambitions that were particularly suited to its oceanic vastness. And crucially, the Ottomans soon learned that competition from Europeans (or, more precisely, from the Portuguese) actually made the fulfillment of these ambitions *easier* rather than more difficult, by providing a foil against which the House of Osman could radically redefine the terms of sovereignty and legitimacy throughout the Islamic world.

Using the conquest of Egypt as a pretext, after 1517 the Ottomans began to assert a new kind of transcendent authority over all the Muslims of the Indian Ocean, as they claimed for their dynasty the titles of Caliph and Protector of the Holy Cities previously associated with the Egyptian Mamluks. These two titles, despite an ancient pedigree in Islamic legal parlance, had long been devoid of any overt political significance and for centuries had been invoked only for vague motives of ceremony and prestige. But after the arrival of the Portuguese in the Indian Ocean—and their establishment of a naval blockade that restricted, for the first time in history, maritime access to the holy cities of Mecca and Medina—these titles acquired a new political currency that the Ottomans proved adept at exploiting. Thanks to their efforts, by the second half of the sixteenth century, the Ottoman sultan's rank as supreme leader of the Sunni Muslim world was, at least on a theoretical level, generally recognized throughout maritime Asia. In other words, in a quintessentially Islamic response to the claims of universal dominion outlined in the Treaty of Tordesillas, the concept of a Universal Caliphate became a fixture of the political discourse of international Islam to an extent not seen since the early Abbasid Empire in the ninth and tenth centuries.[9]

How, in practical terms, were the Ottomans able to accomplish this? In a manner again strikingly similar to the experience of the Iberian powers, the Ottomans owed much of their success to their privileged access to the most advanced military technology of the day. The superiority of Ottoman artillery, for example, proved crucial during the conquest of Egypt, and even more so in subsequent conflicts in

Yemen and Ethiopia where such weaponry was virtually unknown prior to Ottoman intervention. Later, the Ottoman state played an equally instrumental role in disseminating firearms throughout the wider Indian Ocean, where its ability to supply far-flung allies with artillery, cannon founders, and other forms of military expertise added a practical punch to the already considerable cachet of Ottoman dynastic prestige.[10]

Meanwhile, at sea, evidence suggests that the Ottomans began to experiment with tall-sided sailing ships similar to those employed by the Portuguese, although these never took more than a supporting role in naval operations.[11] More important, Ottoman seamen were able to adapt traditional galley technology to the special conditions of the Indian Ocean, and by mid-century had grown confident enough to launch a string of predatory corsair attacks targeting Portuguese shipping. Eventually, such attacks proved so effective at undermining the Portuguese maritime blockade that the Ottomans were able to appropriate the lion's share of the transit trade in spices previously carried in Portuguese ships around the Cape of Good Hope.

Moreover, as the volume of this trade steadily increased, the Ottoman state also devised an array of new techniques for extracting profit from it. In the provinces bordering the Indian Ocean, fiscally minded administrators experimented with new taxation policies to coordinate traffic through the competing routes of the Red Sea and the Persian Gulf, thereby maximizing revenues from both. And in the Red Sea, the state itself became an active participant in trade by organizing a regular convoy of ships that imported state-owned spice cargoes from Yemen and resold them in Egypt at a handsome profit. Farther afield, Ottoman commercial agents were established in remote trading centers like Hormuz, Calicut, and Aceh and contracted business for the imperial treasury in these overseas markets as well. Together, these initiatives amounted to a comprehensive strategy for controlling Indian Ocean trade, which over time proved more than a match for the Portuguese Estado da Índia.[12]

Finally, the Ottoman Age of Exploration was, like its European equivalent, defined as much by cultural and intellectual expansion at home as by economic and territorial expansion abroad. Early on, this was a phenomenon stimulated chiefly by patronage from the imperial court and shaped by the influx of information from Europe about the spectacular discoveries of Western explorers. But as the century progressed, Ottoman travelers began returning from overseas with their own first-hand accounts of adventures in the East, while more sedentary scholars busied themselves with the translation and dissemination of previously neglected geographical works in Arabic. All of these different types of sources were, in time, combined in a number of new, distinctively Ottoman maps, atlases, and geographical treatises that profoundly transformed the Ottoman worldview and played a crucial role in shaping the Ottomans' ideological and strategic objectives as they competed with their imperial rivals from the West.[13]

EXPLORATION, GLOBAL POLITICS, AND THE PROBLEM OF EUROCENTRISM

In the following pages, each of these remarkable parallels between Ottoman and European overseas expansion is explored in greater detail. But at the outset, it must be stressed that although a comparative framework informs the underlying issues raised by this book, *The Ottoman Age of Exploration* is at its heart a narrative rather than a comparative history. As such, it is written from an Ottoman perspective, and remains thoroughly focused on the actions of the Ottomans themselves. Its chapters are organized chronologically, each covering a period of between ten and twenty years and together providing a comprehensive account of a century of Ottoman contact with the world of the Indian Ocean. And throughout this narrative, the emphasis is on politics, with each chapter highlighting the role of individual political actors and the factions to which they adhered, while integrating into this political story a discussion of the most important texts, maps, and other sources of information that guided them on both practical and ideological levels.

Through this basic narrative approach, *The Ottoman Age of Exploration* seeks to introduce a new concept of "global politics" into the study of early modern Ottoman history. By detailing the ways in which a developing Ottoman worldview translated into concrete strategies for imperial expansion overseas, it demonstrates that the Ottomans of the sixteenth century were able to act as protagonists of the first order in creating a newly integrated world system of competing imperial states. In so doing, this book contributes to the developing scholarly literature on the history of the discoveries on multiple levels. Most basically, it presents a stark empirical challenge to interpretations of sixteenth-century political history that portray European empires as the only states capable of engaging in politics at anything more than a regional level. But in even more general terms, *The Ottoman Age of Exploration* also aims to open a new area of dialogue between two dominant but still largely separate trends in recent scholarship on the early modern world as a whole: one firmly grounded in the study of the Western intellectual tradition, and the other quite self-consciously opposed to it.

Of these two trends, the former can be loosely classified under the rubric of encounter studies, a field that blends the disciplines of history and literary theory in a way first popularized through the study of narratives of travel in the post-Columbian New World.[14] More recently, encounter studies has broadened its gaze to include almost any intellectual artifact of Europe's interaction with the Other during the late medieval and early modern periods, ranging from examples of Western geography, cartography, and narrative history to painting, epic poetry, and even works of philosophy and legal theory.[15]

Through a critical reexamination of all of these diverse images and texts, encounter studies has immeasurably deepened our understanding of the Age of Exploration in two fundamental respects. First, it has documented the very profound extent to which Europe's interaction with the outside world was, from the European perspective, conditioned by the preexisting intellectual traditions of the medieval and Renaissance West. Second, it has revealed the extremely complex ways in which this very process of engagement was a formative experience in the development and consolidation of Western civilization at the most elementary level. But what encounter studies does *not* do is reveal very much about the world independent of its representation by Westerners. This is a lacuna that is sometimes easy to overlook, since the subject matter of "encounters" is, at least superficially, so seemingly cosmopolitan. But in the end, by focusing almost exclusively on European authors and European texts, the discourse of encounter studies is still an inherently Eurocentric one, even as it attempts to frame its discussion within the most global and expansive of intellectual settings.[16]

The same cannot be said of the self-styled world historians, an opposing camp of scholars who, over the past few decades, have dedicated themselves to developing narratives of human history that consciously avoid any Eurocentric bias. Instead, world historians have intentionally focused on phenomena unbounded by geographically or culturally specific categories of analysis, ranging from transfers of technology and the spread of infectious disease to patterns of migration and the consolidation of relationships of global economic dependency. In the process, they have produced a body of work of a truly remarkable creativity and explanatory power, employing a range of methodologies and a diversity of perspectives so broad as to defy easy description. Still, whether they frame their arguments in terms of "strange parallels," "great divergences," "guns, germs, and steel," or any of the other superbly original paradigms of world history crafted in recent years, all such works can be said to share the same basic appeal: an ability to explain the development of the global human community in a way that is completely independent of the narrative of Western civilization.[17]

The problem, however, is that by consciously avoiding any direct reference to culturally specific trends, texts, or intellectual movements—as well as the politics they reflected and engendered—world historians have succeeded in taking much of the human element out of their story. And while this would count as a serious limitation for almost any period of history, it is especially so when dealing with the early modern world. For all its problematic implications, the history of global exploration in the sixteenth century remains one of the most compelling human stories of all time. Through their willingness to sacrifice it before the altar of inclusiveness, world historians have therefore paid a very high intellectual price.[18]

How, then, do we reconcile these two conflicting visions of the early modern past? *The Ottoman Age of Exploration* proposes one possible solution, by integrating the kind of expansive intellectual history practiced by students of global encounters with the more inclusive grand narratives of world historians. Through its twin focus on politics and culture, it provides an example of a non-Western state whose encounter with the outside world was experienced as a discovery precisely because it involved the same delicate interplay of political ambition, economic self-interest, and intellectual inquisitiveness characteristic of the European Age of Exploration.[19] This does not imply, however, that the Ottoman experience of discovery was always identical to its European equivalent or that it is relevant to the broader history of the early modern world only to the extent that it was similar. Rather, it suggests that the experiences of both Ottomans and Europeans were part of a larger interactive process, in which each side formulated ambitious plans for global expansion that followed the same underlying logic, even as the particulars of their respective imperial projects diverged in important ways.

A case in point is the Ottoman Empire's oft-lamented "failure" to explore the Atlantic or to establish colonies in the New World as Europeans did. In most existing literature on the subject, this is a piece of evidence routinely pointed to as proof that the Ottomans lacked both an awareness of the discoveries and an inclination to participate in them.[20] But this book, rather than asking why the Ottomans never explored the New World, begins with an altogether different question: Why would they even wish to in the first place? As every schoolchild knows, Columbus himself set sail for the west not to discover a new continent (whose very existence he repeatedly tried to disprove) but in search of an alternate route to the Indies. In much the same way, the Portuguese explorers who discovered Brazil did so accidentally while on their way to India, since only by sailing far into the Atlantic could they find winds that would carry them past the southern tip of Africa. Even as late as the seventeenth century, numerous Dutch, English, and French expeditions to North America were similarly undertaken in search of an elusive Northwest Passage to the Orient.

Hence, from the perspective of their own times, the Ottomans' lack of involvement in the Western Hemisphere can hardly be considered a manifestation of collective failure. Instead, it was a logical reflection of the fact that, unlike for Europeans, the New World for them was not on the way to India. As a result, once they had successfully conquered Egypt (a prize for which the Spanish and Portuguese would have gladly traded all their claims in the Americas), the Ottomans quite reasonably took advantage of the Red Sea and Persian Gulf to gain access to the treasures of the East, rather than vainly searching the Atlantic for a shorter route that simply did not exist.[21]

With the benefit of a half millennium of hindsight, of course, we know just how valuable the New World was one day destined to become. But at the dawn of the Age of Exploration, this future was far from obvious, and it therefore serves as a very poor standard for evaluating the relative success of the Ottoman imperial project. By comparison, a much fairer (and certainly less anachronistic) set of criteria are those laid out by the Ottomans' contemporaries and rivals in the sixteenth century. First among these was Admiral Afonso de Albuquerque, the redoubtable founder of the Portuguese empire in maritime Asia, who stated in the most explicit terms exactly what he hoped to achieve as he set out for the Indies: cut off maritime traffic through the Red Sea, seize control of the Indian Ocean's lucrative trade in spices, use the profits from this trade to finance the invasion and conquest of Mamluk Egypt, and ultimately liberate Jerusalem for the honor of Christendom and the glory of the Portuguese Crown.[22]

If we assume, as the evidence presented in this book suggests, that the contemporary Ottomans shared a similar set of goals—and if we keep in mind that, at the dawn of the Age of Exploration, they were no closer to achieving them than were the Portuguese—then the Ottomans' accomplishments during the course of the sixteenth century seem very impressive indeed. Despite a precocious Portuguese start, by century's end it was not they but the Ottomans who had conquered a weakened Mamluk state, the Ottomans who controlled the bulk of the transit spice trade between the Indian Ocean and the Mediterranean, and the Ottomans who held Jerusalem (and Mecca and Medina as well) for the honor of Islam and the glory of the House of Osman. In this sense, it is no exaggeration to declare the Ottomans victors in the opening round of history's first truly global struggle for dominance. This book is an attempt to tell their story.

One

SELIM THE NAVIGATOR

1512–1520

At first glance, few historical figures seem less ripe for comparison than the Infante Dom Henrique of Portugal and the Ottoman Sultan Selim I. Dom Henrique, or Henry the Navigator as he is popularly known, has been traditionally portrayed as both a pious Christian devoted to serving the Church and a remarkable visionary almost single-handedly responsible for laying the foundations of future European maritime expansion. Founder of the legendary school of navigation at Sagres; generous benefactor of mathematicians, astronomers, and cartographers; and sponsor of the first genuine voyages of overseas exploration, Dom Henrique has achieved, in the centuries since his death, the status of a bona fide cultural hero of Western civilization. Meanwhile Selim I, better known as the infamous Selim the Grim, seems the very picture of an oriental despot. Autocratic, arbitrary, and unscrupulous, Selim was a bloodthirsty tyrant who would stop at nothing, not even armed rebellion against his own father, in a relentless quest to fulfill his ambitions of conquest. How could two such men, so strikingly different and not even contemporaries, ever be compared in a meaningful way?

In fact, fertile ground for comparing these two imposing figures does exist, but requires looking beyond the familiar textbook caricatures of their lives. In the case of Dom Henrique, this task is made easier thanks to recent revisionist accounts that portray him, rather than a visionary or a saint, as a much more prosaic figure with a set of goals and aspirations firmly rooted in the ideals of chivalry and crusade shared by his contemporaries. According to this view, Henry began his career with no master plan for Portuguese overseas expansion. Contrary to his reputation, he was not a learned man, nor even one who was particularly interested in navigation. The numerous voyages of "exploration" he famously sponsored (but never participated in) can be more accurately described as freelance expeditions by slave raiders and privateers. And the school of nautical science he is credited with founding at Sagres seems never to have existed at all, except perhaps in the minds of nineteenth-century historians.[1]

None of this, however, is meant to imply that Henry's accomplishments were anything less than revolutionary. It may be true that he organized naval expeditions to the Atlantic only as a means of employing his vast retinue of retainers, that these exploits occupied only a small fraction of his attention and resources, and that he subsequently set about the exploitation of the West African coast only in a vain attempt to raise funds for another holy war against the Muslims of Morocco. But even so, Henry's ambition, his powers of organization, and the considerable human and economic resources at his disposal ultimately pushed his followers toward the pursuit of an entirely new set of goals in a new area of the world. And once the Portuguese had established themselves in West Africa through Henry's coaxing, the direction of future expansion was clear to all, and the road to India lay open before them.[2]

Thus, whatever Dom Henrique's original motivations may have been, their eventual consequences were of a magnitude hard to exaggerate, and it is precisely in this realm of unintended consequences that the achievements of Henry and Selim are most directly comparable. As in the case of Dom Henrique's expeditions to western Africa, Selim's motivations for conquering Egypt in 1517 remain equally hazy, and if he did have a master plan, it seems likely to have involved using Egypt's resources for a renewed attack against Shah Ismail in Iran rather than any clearly defined aspirations in the direction of India. Nevertheless, the breadth of Selim's ambition, like that of Dom Henrique, led him to consider possibilities for profit and future expansion that were unimaginable to his predecessors. Once the Ottomans found themselves masters of the Nile and protectors of the holy cities of Mecca and Medina, they, too, found the prospect of exploiting wealth from the spice trade to champion the cause of God and country both obvious and irresistible.

This chapter explores the ways in which the opening of a direct Ottoman sea route to the Indies during Selim's reign closely corresponded, in its general contours, with a similar process that had already taken place in Portugal during the fifteenth century. For the Ottomans, as for the Portuguese before them, this was a process that included three principal components: first, a growing awareness of the cultural and physical geography of an area of the world that was previously almost totally unknown to them; second, a rising interest in the economic potential of trade with the East, most noticeable with reference to the spice trade; and third, the articulation of an entirely new set of political ambitions and imperial claims to universal sovereignty that would shape the course of future expansion. In order to fully appreciate this parallel development, however, it is first necessary to consider the ways in which both the Ottomans and the Portuguese, in the decades before their history of contact with the Indian Ocean had even begun, shared a similar intellectual preparation for the dawning Age of Exploration.

EUROPEAN CARTOGRAPHY AND ARABIC GEOGRAPHY: THE BACKGROUND TO DISCOVERY

Portugal, in common with the rest of Western Europe, suffered throughout the Middle Ages from an acute lack of information about the outside world—a condition graphically illustrated by the numerous surviving medieval *mappaemundi*, all of which betray a profound ignorance of the Indian Ocean and, indeed, of the entire world outside Europe and the Mediterranean basin (Figure 1.1). In most respects, in fact, the practical value of these early "world maps" is so slight that they are better understood as ideal representations of the medieval Christian universe rather than as attempts to depict the world realistically. In practice, this meant that even when travelers occasionally brought back new information from abroad, it had almost no effect on this cosmically based worldview.[3] As a result, by the late fifteenth century—when large numbers of European explorers began to arrive in the Indian Ocean for the first time—they still understood it in almost completely mythical terms or, as the French medievalist Jacques Le Goff has colorfully described it, "as a repository of dreams, myths, and legends for the medieval mentality...the *hortus conclusus* of an Eden in which raptures and nightmares were mixed."[4]

To a very large extent, the history of the discoveries is the story of Europe's emergence from the state of intellectual otherworldliness graphically represented by these *mappaemundi*. Beginning in the fifteenth century, as more and more explorers returned from voyages overseas, scholars were forced to reconcile enormous amounts of new empirical information about the globe with an increasingly inadequate medieval cosmology. And since this process coincided with the flowering of Renaissance humanism (a scholarly movement that was itself deeply committed to undermining the intellectual traditions of medieval Europe), the result was a new Western awareness of the outside world and a profoundly changed understanding of Europe's place within it.[5]

Such developments present a sharp contrast to the situation in the contemporary Arabic-speaking world, where the scholarship of Arab geographers—who had enjoyed an intimate familiarity with other world regions (and especially the Indian Ocean) from the very earliest centuries of Islamic history—could undergo no such radical transformations. Indeed, nowhere was an awareness of this yawning deficit of knowledge capital more painfully present than among the early Portuguese explorers, who during the course of their discoveries faced repeated reminders of their comparative intellectual backwardness in the face of Islam's cosmopolitan world civilization. Vasco da Gama, for example, might never even have reached India had he not been guided there from the African coast by an experienced Arab

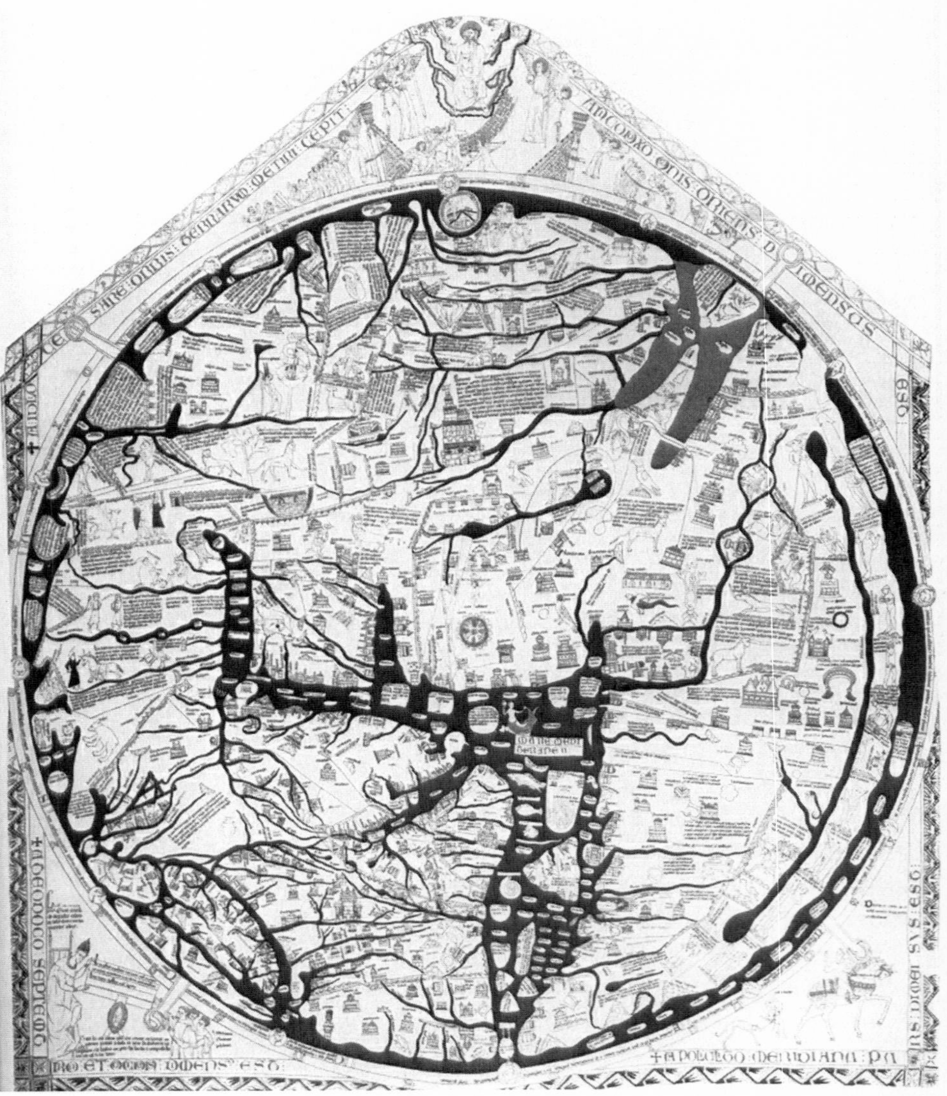

FIGURE 1.1 The Hereford Mappamundi, c. 1290, one of the most famous world maps of Europe's late medieval period. Its image is centered on Jerusalem, with the Indian Ocean represented as the thin dark strip along the upper right-hand edge. Photograph courtesy of the Hereford Mappa Mundi Trust, Hereford, England.

pilot. And when, after an epic voyage of more than 12,000 miles, he and his men finally did arrive in the subcontinent, they were astonished to be met in the harbor of Calicut by two North African Muslims, both of whom could understand Portuguese.[6] Even as late as the 1510s and 1520s, by which time the Portuguese were busy building a maritime empire clear across the Indian Ocean, they still relied heavily on Arabic sources when compiling charts and maps of the region.[7]

In short, it was impossible for Arab geographers to discover the Indies in the same way as Europeans since they had already known about them—and been a part of them—for centuries. But was the same also necessarily true of the Ottomans? Because the Ottoman Empire is generally classified as an Islamic state, most modern scholars have simply assumed that the Ottomans, too, must have been well acquainted with the achievements of Arab geographers from a very early date.[8] But considering the almost total lack of detailed modern studies on the subject, such an assumption remains unsubstantiated by any direct empirical evidence. To be sure, there is no absence of early works of Arabic geography in the libraries and manuscript collections of modern Istanbul. Many of these, in fact, are so old as to predate the founding of the Ottoman state itself by several centuries. Yet until more is known about these manuscripts and the circumstances under which they were acquired, it remains an open question how many of them were actually available to Ottoman scholars during the fourteenth and fifteenth centuries, and how many were brought back from the Arab lands only much later, following the conquests of the 1500s.[9]

For the time being, what can be said with certainty is that, at least with reference to the Indian Ocean, the Ottomans were decidedly *un*familiar with the relevant Arabic geographical corpus. A review of the inventories of several major Ottoman manuscript collections shows that a surprising number of well-known and widely circulated Arabic works on the geography of the Indian Ocean seem to have been completely unknown in Ottoman learned circles prior to the sixteenth century.[10] There is no sign in any Ottoman collection, for example, of any of the important early travel narratives or itineraries by authors such as Ibn Khurdadhbih, Abu-Zayd al-Hasan, or Ibn Jubayr, while al-Biruni's classic *Kitāb al-Hind* ("Book of India") exists only in a single, undated version from which no copies or translations seem to have ever been made.[11] It also seems extremely unlikely that any Ottoman in this period read the early-fourteenth-century travel narrative of Ibn Battuta, even though this celebrated author is unique in having provided firsthand accounts of both India and the Ottomans' native Anatolia during the course of his extensive journeys.[12] And although Marco Polo and later Portuguese explorers are known to have consulted nautical charts of the Indian Ocean that were drafted by local Muslim navigators, there is no evidence that any such maps ever reached Istanbul.[13]

Indeed, from the entire classical Arabic geographical corpus, there are barely a handful of works that we can confidently conclude were copied and circulated among Ottoman scholars prior to the sixteenth century. Of these, the only one that seems to have been generally well known was Zakariyya al-Kazvini's *'Acā'ib al-Maḫlūḳāt* ("The Wonders of Creation"), a half-fanciful thirteenth-century encyclopedia of zoology, botany, and cosmography of extremely limited practical use as a geographical text.[14] By contrast, Ibn Majid, the Arab navigator and contemporary of Vasco da Gama, tells us that he consulted more than forty different works while compiling his famous guide to sailing on the Indian Ocean. Perhaps unsurprisingly, his text, too, was unknown to the Ottomans until the 1550s.[15]

Further evidence for this general trend can be measured by the rate at which relevant geographical texts were translated into Turkish, an important gauge of the breadth of audience a given work could reach. Here the figures are stark indeed: from the fourteenth century, just one such translation exists; from the fifteenth, only two; and all three of these are translations of the very same work: al-Kazvini's "Wonders of Creation" described above.[16] Thus, despite the lack of detailed scholarly literature on this subject, all of the available evidence points to just one conclusion: with the possible exception of a very small circle of madrasa scholars trained in international centers of learning like Tabriz or Cairo, the Ottomans before the sixteenth century had virtually no access to the classical corpus of Arabic texts about the geography of Indian Ocean.[17]

Given this state of affairs, and considering the relatively high level of sophistication of Arab geographers at this time, one might expect the Ottomans to have been even less interested in works by geographers and cartographers of the contemporary West. Yet surprisingly, Ottoman scholars seem instead to have been quite well informed about the principal developments in European geography and cartography during the fourteenth and fifteenth centuries. Of these, the first important development was a new kind of terrestrial map, the portolan chart, which began to make an appearance in the maritime trading centers of southern Europe around the end of the thirteenth century. In a marked departure from the earlier cartographic traditions of medieval Europe, portolans were designed as practical tools to be used in navigation and, as a result, were the first maps since classical antiquity that attempted to systematize mathematically the presentation of terrestrial space.[18] Furthermore, although the oldest maps of this type appear to be of Genoese origin, surviving portolans from numerous countries indicate that their use quickly spread throughout the Mediterranean basin, from Catalonia and the Maghreb in the west to the lands of the Ottoman Empire in the east (Figure 1.2). Today, some of the best examples of fifteenth-century portolan charts are found in Ottoman manuscript collections, including a map by the Majorcan master Johannes de Villadestes (1428)[19] and charts in Arabic by Ibrahim al-Katibi (1413–4)[20] and Ibrahim al-Mursi (1461).[21]

One important limitation of portolan charts is that, because they were used as navigational tools, they typically depicted only the Mediterranean basin itself and included few terrestrial details beyond the coastlines and sea routes of immediate interest to seamen. The same was not true, however, of a new type of world map (commonly known as "Catalan" world maps) in which the Eurasian landmass, Africa, and the Indian Ocean all began to appear in a somewhat realistic and

→

FIGURE 1.2 The Portolan Chart of Ibrahim al-Katibi, c. 1413, is virtually indistinguishable from contemporary European portolans except that the meticulously labeled series of place-names along the coasts (too small to be distinguished here) are written in Arabic rather than Latin script. Source: Topkapı Palace Museum Library, Istanbul, Hazine Ms. 1823.

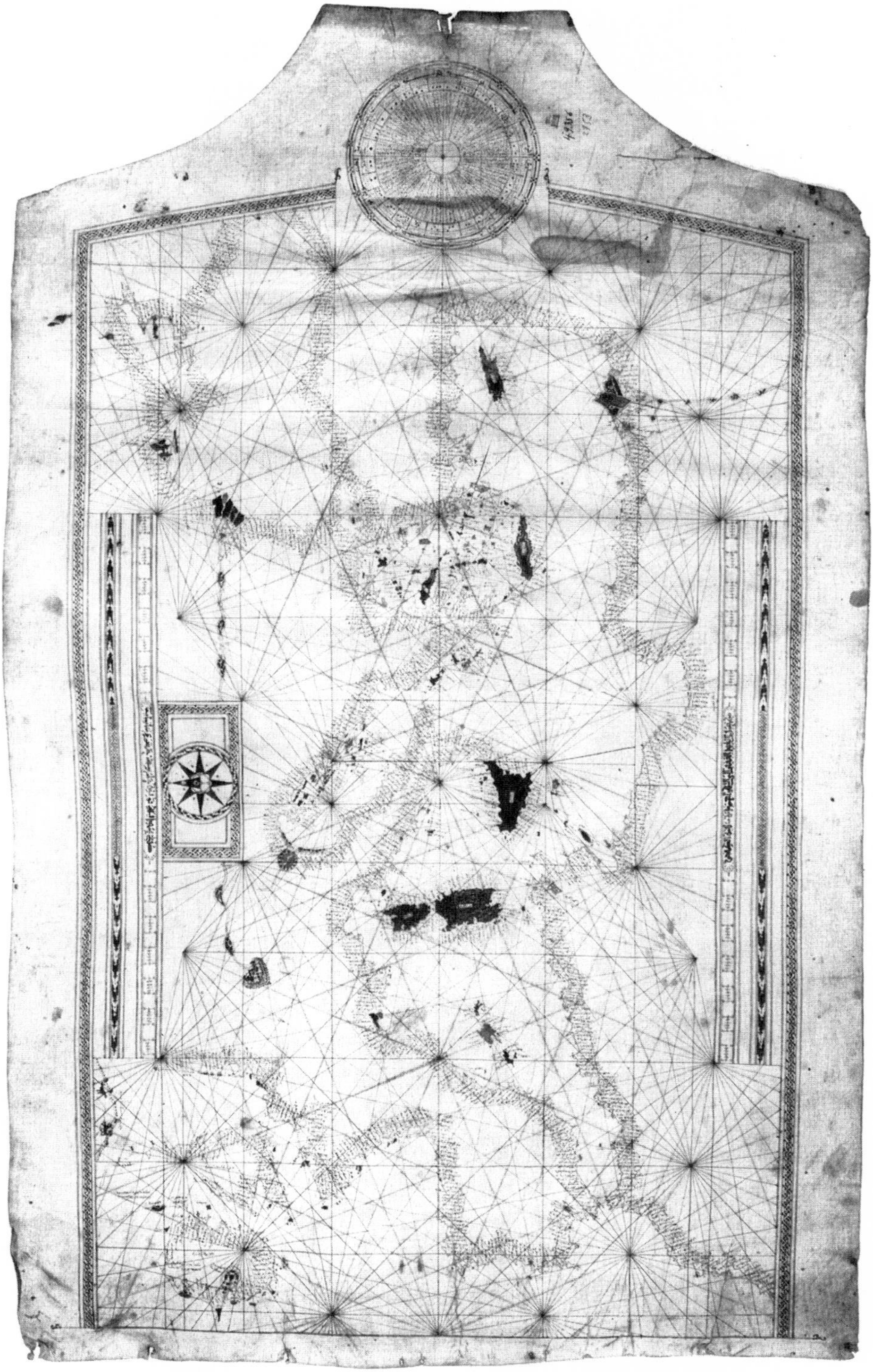

recognizable form. The earliest of these, dating from the late fourteenth century, were produced on the island of Majorca, an important center both for the production of portolan charts and for the translation of Arabic atexts into Latin.[22] Subsequently, their production became more widespread, centered in Italy, and once again there is evidence that the Ottomans followed their development with considerable interest. The map collection of Istanbul's Topkapı Palace library, for instance, includes fragments from two such world maps, one a very early Catalan production from the 1370s, and the other a more richly detailed Venetian work, dating from around 1450, that represents the most mature stage of this mapmaking tradition.[23]

The third major advance of European cartography during the pre-Colombian era was sparked by Italian humanists' recovery of classical geographical texts from the ancient world, including the works of Strabo, Pliny the Elder, and most important, Ptolemy.[24] Chronologically, the beginning of this process dates to the year 1400, when the famous humanist Palla Strozzi had a version of Ptolemy's *Geographia* brought from Constantinople to Florence. With his encouragement, and under the direction of the Byzantine scholar Manuel Chrysolorus, a Latin translation of the text was begun in 1406 by Jacopo Angeli da Scarperia, and a translation of the maps themselves followed a few years later. By mid-century, no fewer than four schools of cartographers were engaged in the reproduction of the *Geographia* and its maps, and in 1477 one of these versions became the first map to be published in printed form as an engraving.[25] By the 1480s, literally thousands of copies of Ptolemy's maps were being published and disseminated throughout Europe, and such was the prestige and authority of these classically inspired images that they rapidly superseded all "older" types of world maps.[26]

Significantly, this process was mirrored almost exactly in the Ottoman Empire, thanks to the patronage of Sultan Mehmed II (d. 1481) during the middle decades of the fifteenth century.[27] Of the several examples of Ptolemy's *Geographia* today extant in Ottoman collections, the oldest is an undated Byzantine manuscript, probably from the late 1300s, that passed into Mehmed's possession following his conquest of Constantinople in 1453. A few years later, in 1465, he commissioned the Byzantine scholar George Amirutzes of Trabzon to undertake a translation of the work from Greek and later is even said to have ordered a copy of one of its maps to be reproduced as the central image woven into a silk carpet.[28] At the same time, Mehmed also sought out contemporary Italian reproductions of the *Geographia*, including an original copy now at the Topkapı library (dated 1481 and including thirty color charts) of the printed edition by the Florentine humanist Francesco Berlinghieri.[29] As an indication of how closely Mehmed had followed Berlinghieri's work, the Topkapı copy also features a personal dedication to the sultan from the scholar, although it apparently failed to arrive in Istanbul until just after the sultan's death in 1481 (Figure 1.3).[30]

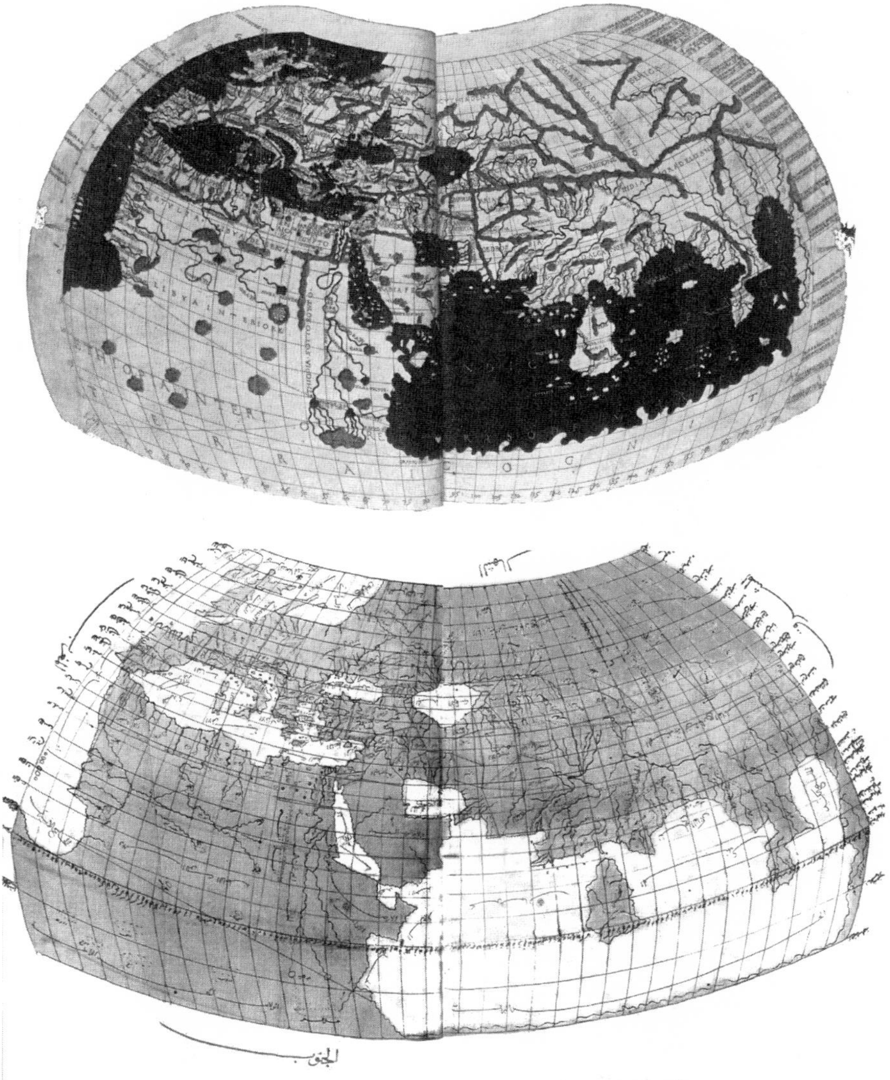

FIGURE 1.3 Two examples of fifteenth-century Ptolemaic world maps from the reign of Mehmed the Conqueror. At the top (a) is a world map from the copy of Francesco Berlinghieri's published Ptolemaic atlas that he presented to Mehmed in 1481. Below (b) is the same image from an earlier Arabic translation of Ptolemy's *Geographia*, commissioned independently by the sultan and completed by George Amirutzes in 1465. Source for figure 1.3a: Topkapı Palace Library, Istanbul, Gİ. Ms. 84, 37–38. Source for figure 1.3b: *Coğrāfyā-yı Baṭlamyūs*, Süleymaniye Library, Istanbul, Ayasofya Ms. 2610, fol. 7. (Note: shading in figure 1.3b is computer enhanced.)

Thus, on the eve of the great discoveries of the sixteenth century, the Ottoman Empire was in a singular position. An Islamic state on the verge of a series of conquests that would bring it into direct contact with the Muslim civilization of the Indian Ocean, it was nevertheless almost totally ignorant both of this region itself and of the numerous works in Arabic that were dedicated to it. Instead, the Ottomans were largely dependent on the same sources of information about the outside world available to Europeans: portolan charts, "Catalan" world maps, and Ptolemaic geographies. Without question, these were primitive resources for understanding the Indian Ocean when compared with contemporary Arabic works like Ibn Majid's *Kitāb al-Fawā'id fī Uṣūl al-Baḥr wa'l-Ḳawā'id* ("Guidebook to the Principles of Navigating the Sea"). Yet until the sixteenth century, they defined the worldview of the Ottomans to the same extent as those of explorers from Portugal and Spain.

From a certain perspective, of course, there should be nothing particularly surprising about this. To take an analogous example, no one would expect navigators or learned men from late medieval Scandinavia to be intimately familiar with Genoese or Venetian portolan charts simply because they were made by fellow Christians. Quite naturally, the lands of the Baltic had their own intellectual traditions and a shared set of practical concerns that were distinct from those of southern Europe, so even if individual pilgrims, merchants, or church officials traveled from one place to the other, it would be unreasonable to assume that because of this the two regions had access to exactly the same body of knowledge about the world. In the same way, the early Ottomans were part of the cosmopolitan community of the late medieval Mediterranean and shared a basic understanding of the world that was common to its people. As such, the Indian Ocean at the turn of the sixteenth century remained for them a remote and unfamiliar place—although with the world-conquering aspirations of Sultan Selim the Grim, all of this was about to change.

OTTOMAN GEOGRAPHY DURING THE REIGN OF SELIM THE GRIM

Like his conquering grandfather Mehmed II, who had proven so instrumental in stimulating early Ottoman interest in Ptolemaic maps and other forms of classical scholarship, Selim was a tireless empire builder whose ambitions led him to cultivate a natural interest in geography. Under his direction, the established Ottoman practice of seeking out the latest cartographical productions from western Europe continued unabated.[31] And perhaps even more important, Selim's reign witnessed, for the very first time, the emergence of a group of totally original Ottoman geographical works, distinguished both by their lack of any direct foreign precedents and by their obvious focus on the world beyond the shores of the Mediterranean.

One example of just such a work is the Ottoman merchant Ali Akbar's *Ḫitāynāme* ("The Book of Cathay"), a firsthand account of a voyage from Iran to China that was composed and presented to Selim in 1516.[32] This text, used extensively by later

Ottoman geographers such as Katip Chelebi and Ebu Bekr Behram ad-Dimashki, provided its readers with information about the history, culture, and politics of contemporary China at a level of detail unmatched by European sources for nearly a century.[33] Moreover, it was composed in exactly the same year as another important Ottoman text, the anonymous *Vāḳıʿāt-ı Sulṭān Cem* ("Events in the Life of Prince Jem"). Like the "Book of Cathay," this work, too, was a firsthand account of travel abroad, detailing the peregrinations of Selim's deceased uncle Jem during his many years spent in exile in Rhodes, France, and Italy after losing a contest for the Ottoman throne to Selim's father, Bayezid II. Written from the perspective of a member of Jem's personal entourage, the text ranks as the earliest known narrative of travel in Europe ever to be composed in Ottoman Turkish.[34]

Meanwhile, with specific reference to the Indian Ocean, the most important geographer to emerge under Selim's patronage was without question Piri Reis (or "Captain Piri"), the celebrated Mediterranean sea captain and cartographer.[35] Piri's famous world map of 1513, his earliest extant work and the only one known to have been completed during Selim's reign, has unfortunately survived only in a fragmentary form.[36] The extant portion, perhaps a quarter of the original, displays the Atlantic Ocean and its shores, including (most notably) the Caribbean and a long stretch of the South American coastline (Figure 1.4). This fact, combined with its surprisingly high technical quality—comparable to the very best European maps of the day—has helped the map to achieve a status as one of modern Turkey's most recognizable cultural icons (even for a time appearing on the Turkish ten-lira banknote). Because of its relatively early date of composition, it has also inspired numerous less-than-scholarly "theories" about the Ottomans discovering America before Columbus, and in one case, even of having received aerial photographs of its coast from visiting extraterrestrials![37]

For our purposes, however, the historical accident that the sole surviving fragment of this map happens to depict the *western* hemisphere is relevant only insofar as it distracts us from the real issue at hand: the explicit connection between the map's creation and Sultan Selim's plans for expansion in the *eastern* hemisphere. This is apparent from Piri's later writings, which allow a partial reconstruction of the missing portions of his map, and which make it clear that the Indian Ocean (and *not* the New World) was the main focus of the work.[38] Additionally, we know that Piri personally presented his map to Sultan Selim in Cairo, only shortly after Selim's first victorious entrance into the city in 1517.[39] This is important because of the traditional connection between Egypt and the Indian Ocean, but also because Sultan Selim is known immediately thereafter to have opened direct negotiations with the Indian potentate Muzaffar Shah II of Gujarat about a possible joint strike against the Portuguese in Goa.[40] Hence, however enthralling the surviving portion of Piri Reis's map may be for audiences today because of the information it contains about the New World, it was probably (and for precisely the same reason) also the portion least interesting to Sultan Selim. Indeed, it may even owe its survival to this very

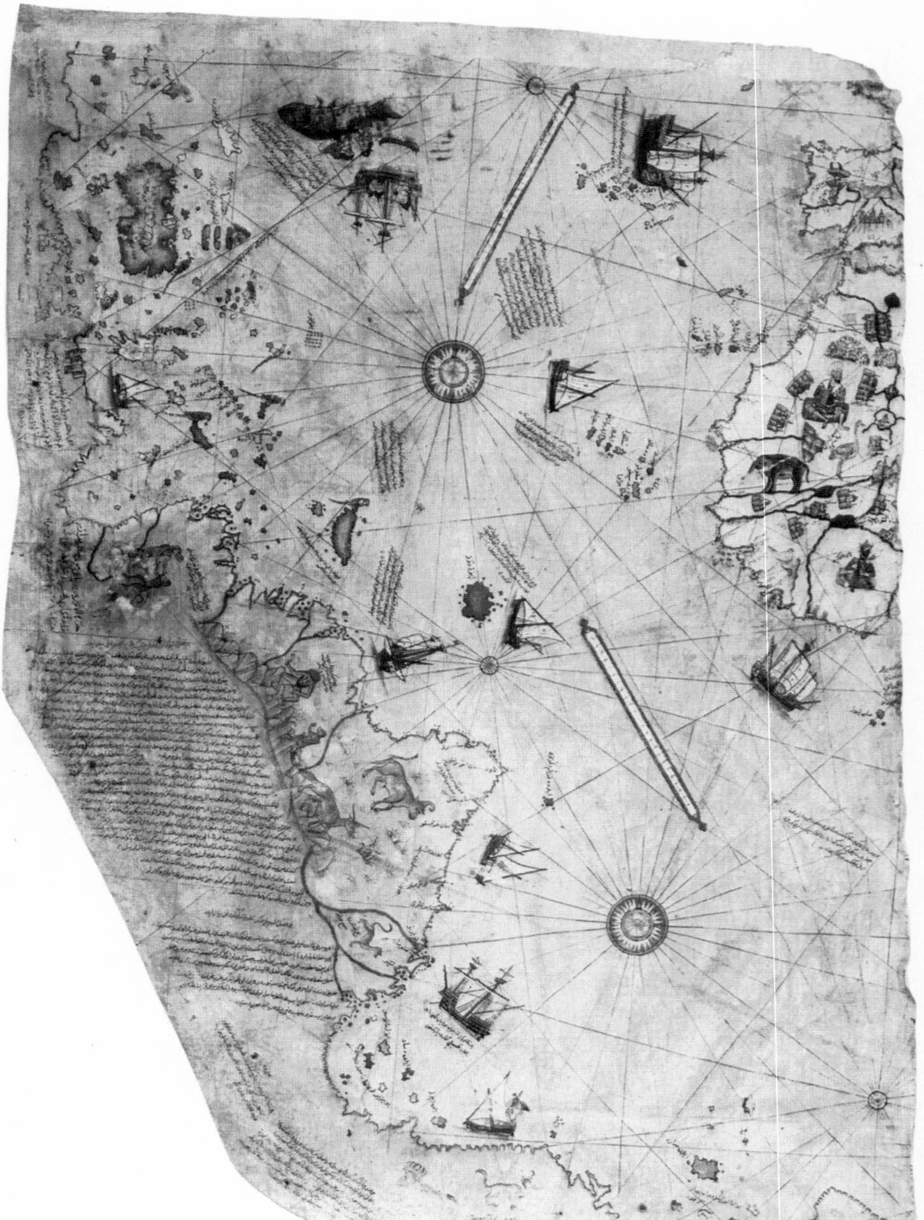

FIGURE 1.4 The surviving fragment of Piri Reis's world map of 1513. Spain and West Africa appear to the upper right; the coast of Brazil to the lower left. Source: Topkapı Palace Museum Library, Istanbul, Revan Ms. 1633.

fact, having been intentionally separated so that Selim could make more convenient use of the main body of the map as he began to develop a strategy for the Indian Ocean.[41]

None of this, however, changes the basic fact that Piri Reis's map marked the beginning of a new era in the history of Ottoman cartography. The author's notes on the map's margins indicate that he consulted nearly two dozen different works while compiling it, including eight Ptolemaic maps, four separate Portuguese sea charts, and an "Arabic chart of India"—the first recorded instance of such an Arabic source from the Indian Ocean having reached an Ottoman scholar. Piri also apparently had access to an original sketch map of the Americas from Columbus's third voyage to the New World, and even personally interviewed a Spanish prisoner who had previously served as a crew member on one of Columbus's expeditions. All of this bears witness to a true sea change in the Ottomans' understanding of the world, and the author himself offers us a taste of this period's heady atmosphere of intellectual excitement, boasting: "I have made maps in which I was able to show twice the number of things contained in the maps of our day, having made use of new charts of the Chinese and Indian Seas which no one in the Ottoman lands had hitherto seen or known."[42]

Yet even as we admire the revolutionary content of Piri's map, we must carefully guard against the temptation to see it as a sui generis masterpiece that was somehow unrepresentative of the larger Ottoman cultural milieu in which it was created.[43] As should by now be clear, there was nothing fundamentally new or unique about Piri Reis's comfortable familiarity with Western scholarship, since by the sixteenth century Ottoman cartographers already enjoyed a long-established tradition of producing maps according to Western prototypes. Piri Reis's work was therefore new and exciting not because of the provenance of his sources per se but rather because of the radically expanded breadth of the information that these Western sources provided. Alongside the conquest of Egypt, which physically brought the Ottomans into contact with a vast and previously unknown region, his map thus awakened his compatriots to a whole new universe of possibilities for conquest and imperial expansion.

SELIM, THE SPICE TRADE, AND THE CONQUEST OF EGYPT

Against this exhilarating intellectual background, we can pinpoint the true beginning of the Ottoman Age of Exploration to Sultan Selim's decision to invade the territories of the Mamluk empire in 1516. This was a move with overwhelmingly important consequences for later Ottoman history, doubling the size of the empire in a single year and solidifying the Ottomans' status as the most powerful state in the Islamic world. Yet surprisingly, it is also a decision whose motivations still remain, nearly five hundred years after the fact, shrouded in a thick veil of mystery. Was it intended as a preemptive strike against Selim's archrival Shah Ismail of Iran, designed to deprive him of a potentially powerful Egyptian ally? Was it instead a political gambit to shore up Selim's legitimacy on the domestic front, by appropriating the prestigious religious centers of Jerusalem, Mecca, and Medina? Or was it merely the first step in a much grander strategy aimed at pulling the Indian Ocean into the Ottoman orbit and seizing control of the spice trade from the newly established Portuguese Estado da Índia?

Probably no single factor can fully explain Selim's decision, and even a considerable element of chance may have lain behind the immediate political conditions that brought his army first into Syria and then to Egypt. Still, it seems extremely likely that an interest in the spice trade played at least some role in drawing Selim to the banks of the Nile.[44] And although it remains an elusive goal to determine exactly how and under what circumstances this came about, at least one fact is clear: just as Ottoman geographic knowledge of the Indian Ocean had begun to grow in the years leading up to the conquest of Egypt, so, too, did Ottoman merchant communities begin to establish their first direct commercial ties with the region.

Curiously, much of this growing commercial contact seems to have been the responsibility of just one man: a former slave by the name of Malik Ayaz, who served the sultans of Gujarat as governor of the important Indian seaport of Diu during the first decades of the sixteenth century. Regrettably, not nearly enough is known about this intriguing and enigmatic figure, whose origins and early career are almost totally obscure and who is variously described in contemporary sources as a Tatar, a Persian, a native of Dubrovnik, and even a Russian.[45] But whatever his heritage and regardless of his original mother tongue, he appears to have been fluent in some form of Turkish, and there are enough hints in the historical record to suggest that he may also have spent a considerable period in the Ottoman Empire prior to his arrival in Gujarat.[46] Most notably, Malik Ayaz was regularly referred to by the Portuguese as a "Rumi," a word typically used in the sixteenth-century Indian Ocean to denote Turkish-speaking Muslims from the Ottoman Mediterranean, and he was similarly described in at least one Indian chronicle as having a particular fondness for "Rumi specialties" at his dinner table.[47] Moreover, as governor of the port city of Diu—the epicenter of Indian transit trade with the Red Sea, Persian Gulf, and Mediterranean—Malik Ayaz found himself surrounded by a large community of fellow Rumi merchants, and his connection to this group was strong enough that during his tenure the city was commonly referred to as "the port of the Rumis."[48]

Since Malik Ayaz was also a merchant in his own right, with substantial private trading concerns in the Red Sea, he naturally emerged as an advocate of this group's interests in the face of Portuguese aggression. In the years following the first Portuguese incursions into Indian waters at the turn of the sixteenth century, he had been instrumental in convincing Kansuh Gawri, then the reigning sultan of Mamluk Egypt, to intervene in defense of Muslim shipping. And subsequently—at least for a time—he had actively collaborated with the Mamluk admiral Hussein al-Kurdi, whose fleet sailed from Egypt to India in 1507. By March of the following year, their coordinated efforts bore tangible fruit when a combined Indian and Egyptian armada defeated the main Portuguese fleet off the coast of Chaul, capturing or killing scores of Portuguese, including Dom Lourenço de Almeida, the viceroy's son.

Before long, however, Malik Ayaz and his Rumi constituents began to lose confidence in Hussein, who despite his skills as a naval commander proved to be an imperious and untrustworthy ally. Already by 1509, in fact, Malik Ayaz had grown so suspicious of Hussein's intentions that he withdrew his support on the eve of a critical sea battle off the coast of Gujarat—a decision that led to the almost total destruction of the Mamluk fleet at Portuguese hands.[49] Following this debacle, Hussein al-Kurdi managed to return safely to Egypt, and in 1515, he set sail from Suez with a second and even larger Mamluk fleet. But his actions during this second campaign served only to confirm Malik Ayaz's worst suspicions. Rather than following his orders from Cairo, which had called for the fleet to proceed directly to India for a renewed engagement with the Portuguese, the chronically insubordinate admiral instead diverted his entire force to Yemen, where he set about conquering its principal cities in a brazen attempt to establish a personal fiefdom.[50] Muslim observers throughout the region were scandalized, especially after Hussein bombarded the independent port city of Aden just as the merchant fleet from India was preparing to sail home with the yearly monsoon.[51]

Thereafter, it seems that Malik Ayaz and the Rumi merchants of Gujarat decisively shifted their allegiance away from the Mamluks and toward the Ottomans, finally convinced that the former were either incapable or unwilling to properly defend their interests.[52] And suggestively, this final break between Hussein al-Kurdi and the merchants of the Indian Ocean took place less than a year before the beginning of the Ottoman Sultan Selim's invasion of Mamluk lands. Might certain Rumi merchants with ties to Malik Ayaz have played a role in coaxing Selim into action?

Admittedly, there is little explicit evidence in either Egyptian or Ottoman sources of a direct connection between solicitations from these merchants and Selim's decision to invade.[53] But the contemporary Egyptian chronicler Ibn Iyas, who makes frequent mention of the activities of Rumi merchants in Cairo, does give vent to a general feeling of suspicion and hostility toward them in his writings. He reports, for example, that just after news of the Mamluk Sultan Kansuh Gawri's death at Selim's hands reached Cairo, rumors began to spread that the army's new recruits were planning to storm out of their barracks, set fire to the central Khan Khalili market, and massacre Rumi merchants who were conducting business there. When this plot was uncovered, the soldiers justified their intentions by saying: "These merchants are in cahoots with the Ottomans, and insulted the good name of our master upon hearing of his death."[54]

Subsequently, the Mamluk authorities in Cairo ordered a large number of merchants rounded up on charges of divulging state secrets, and according to Ibn Iyas "several Ottoman spies were discovered" as a result of the investigation.[55] To be sure, at least some of these "spies" were likely victims of simple anti-Ottoman hysteria at a time when Selim's forces were rapidly converging on the Mamluk capital. But the impression that the allegations against them contained at least a grain of truth was soon reinforced by the actions of Selim himself. Once securely established in Cairo following the final defeat of the Mamluk army, one of his first acts as the new ruler of Egypt was to order the arrest and execution of Hussein al-Kurdi, the insubordinate Mamluk admiral whose behavior had so antagonized the merchants of the Indian Ocean. Then, to fill Hussein's vacated post as governor of the port of Jiddah, Selim appointed an Azeri merchant, Kasim Shirvani, who immediately wrote letters to Malik Ayaz and his sovereign Sultan Muzaffar Shah of Gujarat informing them of Selim's conquests.[56] Alas, the former of these two letters has not come down to us, but the latter includes, in addition to details about Selim's battlefield victories in Egypt and the Levant, a specific promise that the Ottoman fleet would soon come to the aid of beleaguered Muslim merchants in India. According to the text:

> The Twenty ships that were previously constructed by the Circassians [Mamluks] are currently in Jiddah, and His Imperial Majesty [Selim], who is the refuge of the Sultanate and whose heart is that of Solomon—may God Almighty assist him!—has ordered fifty more ships to be constructed. If God so wills, with numberless troops he will soon undertake to push these perfidious troublemakers towards a destiny of blackness, and [with his troops] whose effect is like that of a tempest, he will cast them, soldier by soldier, to the winds of annihilation...then there will be safety and security.[57]

This momentous proclamation was met with an explosion of enthusiasm by members of the Muslim merchant community in Gujarat—and with an equal measure of dismay by the administrators of the Portuguese Estado da Índia. Malik Ayaz's reply to Selim, sent in late 1518, expressed joy at the sultan's message and included both a detailed account of recent Portuguese provocations and a plan to oust them from India by means of a joint Indo-Ottoman naval operation.[58] Conversely, an urgent message dispatched by the Portuguese Viceroy Afonso de Albuquerque to Lisbon around the same time alerted the Portuguese king about the possibility of an imminent Ottoman invasion of India, and warned him about the electrifying effect this was having on the resident Muslim population. Noting that conditions in the subcontinent had been completely tranquil at the time of his departure for Malacca two years previously, he wrote: "Now, with this news of the Ottomans, I have returned to find everywhere in rebellion. Your Highness should take note of what it will mean to have the Ottomans for neighbors, given the reputation they enjoy in these parts."[59] Similarly, another Portuguese official, Aires da Gama, wrote to Lisbon in the following year advocating immediate military action against Gujarat, since "Diu is waiting for the Ottomans with open arms" and "the merchants there now control the entire trade with Mecca, and do nothing but go back and forth in their ships."[60]

Meanwhile, as these battle lines were being drawn across the Indian Ocean, Selim was also busily engaged on the Mediterranean front, where he took steps to reassure the traditional European customers for spices in Egypt that opportunities for trade would in no way be undermined by his recent conquests. Accordingly, he issued an imperial edict to Dubrovnik reconfirming the trading privileges that city's merchants had enjoyed under the Mamluks,[61] and likewise sent word to Venice that he "desired the friendship of the Venetians, and at the start of his new administration [in Egypt] was trying to increase commercial traffic in that province both for the particular use and benefit of its subjects and in the interest of public revenues."[62] Within months, Venetian and other European merchants in Egypt (who under the Mamluks could rarely travel further inland than Alexandria) were openly buying and selling in the spice markets of Cairo.[63]

Such measures notwithstanding, it would be a mistake to make too emphatic an argument about the sophistication of the Ottomans' approach to the spice trade at this early date. At a time when the Portuguese "Grocer King" Manuel I was already pursuing, as a fundamental goal of his imperial strategy, an innovative "crown monopoly" of the Indian Ocean pepper trade, the Ottoman state's commercial role under Selim was still limited to the collection of transit tariffs through Egyptian ports, much as it had under the preexisting regime of the Mamluks.[64] Only later, under Selim's successors, would the Ottoman state become more directly involved in the spice trade in a manner roughly analogous to Dom Manuel's "pepper monopoly." But although this system would take several more decades to emerge and develop into its mature form, Selim nevertheless paved the way by establishing a precedent for state policies that were responsive to commercial interests in a way that Mamluk policies had never been. And equally important, Selim's willingness to engage with the complex and geographically extensive network of Indian Ocean trade also had more immediate political consequences, inspiring him to radically reformulate the basis of his claims to imperial legitimacy in a direct parallel with the imperial project of the Portuguese crown.

PARALLEL DEVELOPMENT OF PORTUGUESE AND OTTOMAN CLAIMS TO UNIVERSAL SOVEREIGNTY

Prior to the reign of Selim's grandfather Mehmed II, whose dramatic conquest of the city of Constantinople in 1453 had transformed the Ottoman state into an empire in the fullest sense, early Ottoman sultans had based their claims to legitimacy on historical origins as frontier *gazis*, or warriors of the faith engaged in a holy struggle against the infidels of Byzantium.[65] In this respect, they were not substantially different from the early kings of Portugal, who were known as "athletes of Christ" and claimed a special role as the champions of Christendom in the rough-and-tumble frontier regions of medieval Iberia.

Then, during the course of the fifteenth century, the Portuguese were able to gradually secure several footholds in Morocco and eventually extend their reach as far as the coast of West Africa—a region never before visited by any European. In recognition of this success, the papacy provided the Portuguese with a series of bulls granting them exclusive rights to the navigation and conquest of all newly discovered regions in the Atlantic and along the coast of Africa. By the end of the century, once the Cape route to India had been opened, these same papal bulls were reinterpreted by the Portuguese crown as the juridical basis for its aspirations in the Indian Ocean as well.

The essence of these dramatically expanded Portuguese claims was embodied in the new imperial title that Dom Manuel assumed immediately following Vasco da Gama's triumphant return from India in 1499: "King of Portugal, Lord of Guinea, and Lord of the Conquest, Navigation and Commerce of Ethiopia, Arabia, Persia and India." It should be emphasized, however, that since Dom Manuel assumed this title at a time when he possessed not so much as a single ship anywhere in the Indian Ocean, this title represented a theoretical ideal rather than a realistic description of his authority.[66] And as later events would show, it was never Dom Manuel's intention to actualize this claim by directly abrogating the sovereignty of individual kings in India or anywhere else in the east. Instead, he hoped not to replace these local, preexisting rulers, but rather to be recognized as their superior, a "king of kings" or emperor, whose authority transcended the physical possession of any specific territory.[67] As a result, despite a long string of military successes across maritime Asia during the following decades, neither Dom Manuel nor any of his successors ever changed this royal title, always maintaining the pretense that their authority extended universally across all of the Indies, not just the specific territories under their immediate control at any given time.[68] Thus, as the Portuguese historian Antonio Vasconcelos de Saldanha has described it, "For the first time in history the title of Portugal's kings corresponded not with an effectively controlled geographical space, but rather to a 'political space' based in a powerful juridico-political fiction, which was the result of diplomatic conventions and legitimized by the authority of the Pope."[69]

How does this model of "universal empire" compare with the situation in the contemporary Ottoman state? Remarkably, despite all of the obvious differences between the political cultures of the Ottoman and Portuguese realms, in several fundamental respects Saldanha's description appears as applicable to the imperial claims advanced by Selim in 1517 as those advanced by Dom Manuel in 1499. If Dom Manuel became "Emperor" upon Vasco da Gama's return from India, Selim, too, marked his triumphant entrance into Cairo by assuming the prestigious title "Protector of the Holy Cities" (*Ḫādım al-Ḥaremeyn*), a mantle that had previously belonged to the Mamluk sultans. Subsequently, he arrested al-Mutawakkil, the last puppet "caliph" of the Abbasid family still resident in the city, and appropriated for himself this title as well. Although earlier sultans, most notably Selim's grandfather Mehmed, had also occasionally flirted with the idea of styling themselves as "caliph," it was only at this point that the claim began to resonate with other Muslim rulers in the international arena.

Then, armed with these new credentials, Selim began to actively promote himself as a universal Islamic ruler whose sovereignty, especially with regard to the Indian Ocean, extended far beyond the borders of the areas under his physical control.[70] As early as 1518, in a piece of official diplomatic correspondence (addressed to the ruler Shirvan Shah), Selim included among his many titles lordship over Arabia, Yemen, Ethiopia, and even Zanzibar, although at the time he commanded no military forces at all beyond the Red Sea port of Jiddah.[71]

Certainly, none of this posturing would have meant much had Selim's claims been simply ignored by the local powers in the Indian Ocean. But most rulers in the region seem to have taken them very seriously indeed. As soon as news of Selim's conquests reached Mecca, for example, the reigning sharif sent his son to Cairo to pay personal homage to the sultan and present him with the keys to the holy cities, after which Selim duly reconfirmed him in his position.[72] A few months later, an envoy arrived from the Emir of Aden, who likewise swore allegiance to Selim and begged forgiveness for having supplied a visiting Portuguese fleet with provisions and local pilots earlier in the year.[73] Shortly thereafter, Malik Ayaz's letter also reached Istanbul, in which he explicitly addressed the Ottoman sultan as "Caliph on Earth."[74]

Thus Selim, like his contemporary Dom Manuel of Portugal, had begun to build consensus for a claim to an entirely new kind of imperial sovereignty—one that corresponded not with an effectively controlled geographical space, but rather with an expansive extraterritorial political space defined through the language of Islam's juridically based universalism. And by no means coincidentally, in both the Portuguese case and the Ottoman case, this new claim referred to the *same* political space: the trading world of the Indian Ocean, which Muslims and Christians alike now recognized not only as a sphere of economic exchange but also as a battleground of competing imperial ideologies.

By 1519, Selim had even begun to take the first concrete steps toward enforcing this new claim, by organizing a small armed naval expedition to Yemen under the command of the seasoned corsair Hussein al-Rumi.[75] Although the sultan's unexpected death in 1520 would force this expedition to be called to a halt, the newly expanded scope of Ottoman ambitions was by this point clear to all and would continue to move forward even without his leadership. By appropriating the authority and prestige that resulted from control of the holy cities, Selim had set his successors on a collision course with the Portuguese for control of the Indian Ocean and provided them with enormous political and diplomatic resources to draw from in the approaching conflict. Never before had two powers challenged each other more directly in such a wide-ranging global theater.

CONCLUSION: THE OTTOMANS AND THE "ISLAMIC TRADITION"

The tendency to view the "Islamic world" as a timeless, undifferentiated whole has a long tradition in Western scholarship.[76] With specific reference to the history of

Ottoman expansion in the Indian Ocean, it is also a tendency exacerbated by available sources from the period, whose authors (both Portuguese and Indian Muslims alike) rarely made a careful distinction between the Ottomans and Mamluks.[77] As a result, most modern studies based on these sources have naturally seen the Mamluk naval campaigns in the early part of the century and the Ottoman operations in the decades that followed as all part of a single, continuous, and undifferentiated historical process.

But in reality, there was a huge difference between the Mamluk Sultanate and the Ottoman Empire, for it was the Mamluks—and the Mamluks only—who had a vested interest in the spice trade before the arrival of the Portuguese in India.[78] This is not to deny that a certain number of Ottoman sailors and gunners served as private mercenaries in the Mamluks' Indian Ocean fleet prior to 1517; under Selim's father, Bayezid II, this fleet had even received limited logistical support (in the form of artillery, supplies of lumber, and possibly a few sea captains) directly from the Ottoman government.[79] But there is simply no evidence to suggest that Bayezid played any direct role in organizing this fleet or directing its activities, and his shipments of supplies were in any case discontinued by Selim shortly after his accession to the throne.[80] In fact, the main body of "Ottomans" who volunteered for service in the Mamluk navy during Selim's reign (a force of some two thousand Levantines under the command of the Mediterranean corsair Selman Reis) seem to have enlisted expressly against his wishes. This is evident from the fact that, following Selim's conquest of Egypt, he promptly summoned their commander to Cairo and ordered his arrest—apparently less than pleased to find so many of his subjects in Mamluk service.[81]

Clearly, then, Selim was by no means a collaborator or even a silent partner in the Mamluk Sultanate's feeble attempts to defend Muslim shipping from the Portuguese before 1517. As such, since the Portuguese blockade of the Red Sea was firmly in place long before Selim arrived on the scene, the oft-repeated accusation that he "failed to defend" the Indian Ocean trade routes following his conquest of Egypt makes little sense.[82] The Mamluk dynasty may well have suffered (and ultimately even collapsed) as a result of Portuguese incursions. But for the Ottomans under Selim, the spice trade can in no way be considered a "lost" source of revenue that the sultan was unable to protect. Rather, it represented a great future opportunity to exploit an untapped and potentially vast source of wealth.

In time, subsequent generations of Ottoman statesmen, merchants, and adventurers would indeed exploit this opportunity to the fullest. But the magnitude of such an undertaking required a substantial gestation period before any of their efforts could bear fruit. After all, the Portuguese had allowed nearly a decade to elapse between their first voyage around the Cape of Good Hope in 1488 (under Bartolomeu Dias) and Vasco da Gama's follow-up expedition to India in 1497. By comparison, the Ottomans were even later arrivals to the Indian Ocean, so it should hardly come as a surprise that they, too, assumed the same methodical pace in pursuing their economic and political goals in the region.

At the same time, when considering the longer term consequences of Selim's reign, it is also important to appreciate the continuing vitality of Egypt as a magnet of world trade long after the arrival of the Portuguese in the Indian Ocean. Despite extensive and seemingly conclusive evidence to the contrary, it remains a stubbornly entrenched belief among many modern historians that the Portuguese Cape route to India was inherently faster and cheaper than any alternative and therefore permanently superseded the traditional transit route through Egypt and the Red Sea.[83] The Portuguese of the time, however, were under no such illusions. As contemporary records make clear, they were well aware of the superiority of the traditional Egyptian route, such that Egypt and the Holy Lands remained at the very center of their strategic calculations throughout the early decades of the sixteenth century. By their own admission, in fact, early Portuguese strategists hoped not to permanently *bypass* Egypt by means of their blockade of the Red Sea, but rather to pave the way for an *invasion* of Egypt by weakening the Mamluks' access to customs revenues and raising money for themselves in the process. Once this was accomplished, and once Egypt itself lay firmly within their grasp, the spice trade would be allowed to return naturally to its traditional routes, and the tenuous and expensive network of Portuguese bases in the Indian Ocean would be rendered superfluous and abandoned.[84]

Stated in these terms, the entire first period of Portuguese expansion thus appears to be a risky, desperately complex, and ultimately failed attempt to achieve, over the course of several decades, what Selim had accomplished by 1517 after only a few short months of military campaigning. In time, control of Egypt and the Holy Lands would give the Ottomans an enormous strategic advantage over the Portuguese—an advantage whose importance would become ever more obvious as the century unfolded. "Selim the Navigator" thus provided his countrymen with the keys to maritime Asia. He left to his successors the task of opening the door and entering the vast new world that lay before them.

Two

IBRAHIM PASHA AND THE AGE OF RECONNAISSANCE

1520–1536

The year 1520 marks the beginning of the very long reign of Suleiman the Magnificent, widely considered (both then and now) the grandest and most powerful sultan in the history of the Ottoman state. For all his undeniable accomplishments, however, Suleiman's carefully cultivated reputation deserves to be treated with a certain degree of skepticism, for in one sense the forty-six years of his rule mark the start of something new and decidedly unmagnificent in the history of the Ottoman dynasty: an extended period during which the influence of viziers, advisors, and members of the royal household rose precipitously, eventually to such an extent that they began to undermine the authority of the sultan himself. To understand politics during Suleiman's reign, therefore, requires pulling the focus away from the sultan in order to accommodate a wider political playing field. From 1520 on, a constantly shifting cast of characters, including grand viziers, provincial governors, and even ladies of the imperial harem were consistently more active in shaping the empire's policies than anyone sitting on the throne in Istanbul.[1]

What were the reasons for such a dramatic change in Ottoman political culture? At the risk of oversimplification, much of the responsibility probably lies with the delicate character of Suleiman himself. Unlike his fearsomely autocratic father, the young sultan seems to have suffered throughout his life from a compulsive need for intimacy, and he formed a series of intense personal relationships that he allowed to guide his decisions as head of state. The most obvious—and notorious—example of this tendency is his passionate love for the slave girl Roxelana (later "Hurrem Sultan"), whom he married in flagrant violation of all dynastic protocol, and who later became one of the empire's most influential power brokers. But even before this, when Suleiman was still in the flower of youth and barely settled on the throne, he had already given in to this gentler side of his nature by showering favor on his childhood friend and boon companion Ibrahim, whose meteoric rise in the 1520s is inextricably linked with the beginning of the second phase of the Ottoman Age of Exploration.[2]

IBRAHIM PASHA'S RISE TO POWER

According to contemporary accounts of his origins, Ibrahim Pasha was born a subject of the Republic of Venice in the Epiran town of Parga. Taken captive by pirates at the age of six and sold as a slave to an elite household only shortly thereafter, he is said to have met the future Sultan Suleiman when the two were still in their teens. One popular story about their first encounter, widely circulated in later years, maintains that Ibrahim initially caught the prince's attention by virtue of his beautiful violin playing. True or not, it is certain that the two became fast friends. Ibrahim was therefore presented as a gift to Suleiman by his former owner, and the two spent the rest of their adolescence together at the provincial capital of Manisa, where Suleiman completed his princely education.

When Suleiman ascended to the throne in 1520, Ibrahim accompanied him to Istanbul, initially taking up residence in the Sultan's private quarters and frequently spending the night in the same room with him—something virtually unheard of in the tightly controlled world of the Ottoman imperial palace. Then, in the following year, Ibrahim began construction of a mansion of his own built in close proximity to the grounds of Topkapı Palace, so that he could still remain nearby when not physically in Suleiman's presence. During these years, the two were so inseparable that Ibrahim was described by a Venetian official then resident in Istanbul as "the heart and breath of the Sultan."[3]

In a time and place where access to the sultan's person translated almost directly into unadulterated political power, this unusually close relationship was by itself enough to make Ibrahim one of the most influential individuals in the Empire. But Suleiman also sought to advance Ibrahim's career through more formal channels as rapidly as he could. Already at his accession to the throne, he had appointed Ibrahim to the post of head falconer, and he promoted him repeatedly in the years that followed. Then, in 1523, after easing his father's aged advisor Piri Mehmed out of office, the sultan ordered Ibrahim (now Ibrahim Pasha) to replace him as grand vizier—making him in name, as well as in fact, the titular head of the Ottoman civil and military administration. For good measure, he also appointed Ibrahim Lord of Lords of Rumelia (the most coveted governorship in the empire), and a few months later, in a ceremony celebrated with spectacular pomp in the capital city, he married him off to a bride from among Istanbul's most highly placed families.[4]

All of this was bound to antagonize the more entrenched members of the Ottoman establishment, who normally expected the sultan to observe unwritten but rather strict rules of seniority when making decisions about promotions to the empire's highest offices. In particular, the very senior Ahmed Pasha, who under Piri Mehmed had served as Suleiman's second vizier, felt (with considerable justification) that the grand vizierate rightly belonged to him or at least to someone of equal experience. The young sultan's decision to promote Ibrahim instead, who was at the time only in his late twenties, was thus a bitter pill for Ahmed to swallow. As a sop for his wounded pride—and perhaps also as an excuse to send him away from the capital city—the sultan nominated him as governor of Egypt and dispatched him to Cairo. Unfortunately, Ahmed refused to accept this new status quo, and shortly after reaching the banks of the Nile, he raised the banner of rebellion. Suleiman responded by assembling a large fleet and appointing Ibrahim as its commander to sail to Egypt and deal with the crisis personally.[5]

Ahmed Pasha's rebellion and Ibrahim's subsequent campaign to reconquer Egypt for the sultan are of central interest to our story for two reasons. First and most obviously, Egypt was the crucial link between the Indian Ocean and the Ottoman Empire, and its conquest in 1517 was what had first awakened Suleiman's father, Selim, to the possibilities of maritime expansion to the southeast. The sudden loss of the province now completely severed this link, showing just how tenuous the Ottomans' connection to the world of the Indian Ocean remained more than five years after the initial conquest of Egypt. But at the same time, Ahmed's rebellion also had the very positive consequence of bringing Ibrahim Pasha to the banks of the Nile, an experience that would provoke a response in the young and ambitious pasha very similar to that of his conquering predecessor, Selim the Grim. Soon enough, Ibrahim, too, would begin to dream of building an empire in the Indian Ocean, even while realizing that his countrymen in the early 1520s still suffered from an acute lack of reliable information about the region.

IBRAHIM PASHA'S RECONNAISSANCE CAMPAIGN

On the military front, Ibrahim made short work of Ahmed's rebellion, having overseen his execution within just a few weeks of his first arrival in the province.[6] As was soon to become clear, however, the most important campaign that Ibrahim was destined to fight during his time in Egypt was not against Ahmed's rebellious troops but against the Portuguese—and was to be waged not with soldiers and artillery but rather with maps and geographical texts.

In truth, this campaign of reconnaissance began even before the grand vizier had arrived in Egypt, as Ibrahim's flagship during his passage from Istanbul to Rhodes was commanded by none other than the navigator and cartographer Piri Reis, the same man who had traveled to Cairo and presented Sultan Selim with his famous world map in 1517.[7] According to an account in Piri Reis's later writings, he and the pasha first made one another's acquaintance during this voyage, when Ibrahim saw Piri consulting nautical charts to plot a safe course. Immediately intrigued, he asked for a demonstration of how they were used, and thereafter, the two men talked regularly about navigation, cartography, and the science of the sea.[8]

It would be hard to overstate the long-term implications for the Ottoman Age of Exploration of this chance encounter at sea, for upon their safe arrival in Egypt, Ibrahim commissioned Piri Reis to complete an expanded edition of the work he had consulted during their sea passage: his recently completed atlas and navigational guide, the *Kitāb-ı Baḥrīye* ("Book of the Sea").[9] In its final form, as presented to the sultan in 1526, this magisterial work constituted an intellectual contribution of such groundbreaking importance that it is even today considered the single greatest masterpiece of Ottoman geography and cartography ever produced.[10]

However, while most modern readers of the "Book of the Sea" have been drawn first and foremost to its rich and comprehensive descriptions of the Mediterranean (particularly since these are accompanied by several dozen masterfully executed and beautifully illustrated maps), the portion of the work of the most immediate interest to Ibrahim Pasha was probably its lengthy introductory section, which was not included in Piri's earlier edition and, in fact, contains no information at all about the Mediterranean. Instead, this lively text, composed in rhyming verse and written in clear, layman's language, counts as the first original work in Ottoman Turkish to contain specific and detailed information about the geography of the Indian Ocean. Consisting of an updated textual summary of Piri's earlier world map, but with new sections describing the history of Vasco da Gama's circumnavigation of Africa, Columbus's discovery of the New World, and the technical advances that had made these voyages possible, the work was above all designed to convey a sense of the monumental importance of the discoveries in both intellectual and political terms.

Such was the significance of the "Book of the Sea" that, had Ibrahim Pasha accomplished nothing else during his years as grand vizier, his commissioning of the book would by itself have been enough to seal his reputation as a patron of science and learning. But Piri Reis's masterpiece was just one of several similar works that became available to the Ottomans during the mid-1520s as a direct result of Ibrahim Pasha's efforts. Another example, in its own way just as extraordinary, is a chart of Magellan's circumnavigation of the globe attributed to the official Portuguese court cartographer, Pedro Reinel (Figure 2.1). A historic work, it contains both the original record of the discoveries made by Magellan in the Western Hemisphere and the most up-to-date information (as of 1519) from Portuguese voyages in East Africa and Southeast Asia. It is also significant from a technical standpoint as the earliest known example of an equidistant polar projection on a terrestrial map, a technique not employed regularly until the 1560s.[11]

Perhaps the most remarkable characteristic of this map, however, is the simple fact that it is today in the collection of Istanbul's Topkapı Palace library. A document with such sensitive information would have been considered a precious state secret by the Portuguese authorities and, under normal circumstances, would have been kept in the tightly guarded archives of Lisbon's Casa da Índia. Indeed, as a result of

FIGURE 2.1 Pedro Reinel's world map with south polar projection, c. 1519 (water damaged). Source: Topkapı Palace Museum Library, Istanbul, Hazine Ms. 1825.

this habitual secrecy, there are virtually no other official Portuguese maps from the decade of the 1520s known to have survived to modern times.[12] The Ottomans' acquisition of this particular map thus ranked as an intelligence coup of the first order, and was doubtless the result of an epic tale of international cloak-and-dagger espionage about which we regrettably know almost nothing. We can surmise, however, that Ibrahim Pasha—whose keen interest in geography and cartography was commonly remarked upon by foreign diplomats—almost certainly played a central role.[13] No other Ottoman official had comparable financial or diplomatic resources at his disposal, and none enjoyed such a vast array of contacts in important Western centers of trade and espionage, particularly Venice.[14] Although it is only speculation, the most likely scenario seems to be that Ibrahim acquired the map by means of Venetian intermediaries, and probably with the help of Antonio Pigafetta, a prominent explorer originally from the northern Italian town of Vicenza. Pigafetta, who had personally participated in the first leg of the Magellan expedition, had abandoned the mission and returned to Italy (via Lisbon) by 1524, the same year as Ibrahim's Egyptian campaign.[15]

Ibrahim's third major contribution to the advancement of Ottoman geographical knowledge is by comparison much better documented, involving his resuscitation of the shattered career of the naval commander Selman Reis (or "Captain Selman"). This storied Ottoman seaman, originally from the Aegean island of Lesbos, had entered Mamluk service in the years prior to the Ottoman conquest of Egypt and had actively participated in the last Mamluk naval expedition to the Indian Ocean in 1515. Thereafter, he had heroically defended Jiddah from a Portuguese attack in 1517, only a few months before the final collapse of the Mamluk regime. But then, immediately following the Ottoman conquest of Egypt—and apparently because he had signed on for military service with the Mamluks against the wishes of Sultan Selim—he was arrested, sent to Istanbul, and imprisoned for disloyalty.

His biography after this point becomes somewhat hazy, although he seems to have been released from prison upon Selim's death in 1520, after which he returned briefly to Yemen as a private soldier of fortune.[16] By the time Ibrahim Pasha arrived in Egypt in 1524, Selman was back in Cairo, but still officially out of favor and languishing in obscurity. Fortunately for the corsair's tarnished reputation, the grand vizier realized that, whatever his past transgressions, Selman's experience made him uniquely qualified to supply information about the current situation in the Indian Ocean. He therefore ordered the corsair to travel once more to Jiddah and inspect the derelict Mamluk fleet still stationed in its harbor. On his return, he was to report back to Ibrahim with an inventory of the available vessels and artillery in Jiddah and provide advice about how best to refurbish this fleet and put it to use.[17]

Selman's report, which was submitted to the grand vizier in 1525, differs from all earlier Ottoman documents relating to maritime Asia in that it was based, at least in part, on firsthand experiences of travel in the region.[18] Although concise (106 lines of text), it describes in varying detail all of the major areas of the Indian Ocean littoral, from the Swahili Coast, Ethiopia, and Yemen to the Indian subcontinent and the Indonesian archipelago. Throughout, it takes careful note of the economic resources of various areas, their general level of technological development, and the ease with which they could be conquered and held by Ottoman forces.

One particularly striking element of Selman's prose is the extent to which it echoes both the tone and the content of reports brought back by European explorers at precisely the same time. When describing Ethiopia, for example, Selman writes:

> The capital of the province of Abyssinia is in fact called Bab al-Muluk, the infidels of which are bare-footed and weak footmen with wooden bows and shields made of elephant hide. Yet these people are dominant in that country for there is no one to put up

> resistance against them. God knows best, but I say that it would be easy to take not only the town called Tabarah [on the Nile] with a thousand men . . . but also the entire province of Abyssinia.[19]

Thus, in much the same way as the letters of Christopher Columbus or Afonso de Albuquerque, Selman's report included specific recommendations about imperial policy alongside raw data about exotic human and physical geography. And although it proposed Ethiopia as a particularly promising venue for future expansion, the text also advocated the military occupation of Yemen and the Swahili Coast for similar reasons, and likewise suggested that the Portuguese strongholds of Hormuz, Goa, and Malacca were also vulnerable and should all be considered as possible future targets.

Every one of these recommendations would, in one way or another, be put into practice by Ottoman statesmen in the decades to come. Selman's report is thus the closest approximation to a blueprint for future Ottoman expansion in the Indian Ocean, enabling Ibrahim Pasha to take the first concrete steps toward establishing a real Ottoman presence in the region. But before he could do so, he still needed to consolidate Ottoman rule in Egypt itself, in order to ensure that the province's administration was secure enough to serve as a launching pad for further expansion overseas.

IBRAHIM PASHA'S ADMINISTRATIVE REFORMS IN EGYPT

Ibrahim remained in Egypt for the better part of a year, during which he oversaw a full review of all of Egypt's laws, administrative norms, and customary rules, with a special eye for those related to revenues, tax collection, and the redistribution of resources.[20] These were then modified, codified, and collectively promulgated as the *Ḳānūnnāme-i Mıṣır* ("Law Book of Egypt") of 1525.[21] The primary objective of this law book was to bring Egypt more firmly under the heel of the imperial bureaucracy in Istanbul, and as such, its promulgation introduced important changes to various aspects of the administrative and fiscal apparatus of the province.

Many of the law book's most significant innovations relate to the tax regime governing trade, particularly the spice trade, in both Egypt itself and in the Red Sea. Overall, it appears that Ibrahim, while maintaining an obvious interest in securing revenues for the state, aimed to reorganize the existing tax system to make it more favorable to the interests of private merchants.[22] Among the most important changes that he instituted was the permanent abolishment of coercive Mamluk import and export quotas that had required merchants to buy or sell (at extortionate rates) a predetermined quantity of pepper through state agents.[23] Instead, the new Ottoman regulations now mandated that all commodities passing through Egyptian customs houses, including pepper and other spices, should be taxed at the same rate: the traditional 10 percent *ʿöşr* ("dime tax") stipulated by the sharia. Ibrahim also overhauled the mechanism of tariff collection, which had been plagued by corruption and arbitrary taxation during the last years of Mamluk rule.[24] In Alexandria and Cairo, he reorganized customs houses as tax farms whose proceeds were sent directly to the provincial government, while the outlying collection centers of Jiddah and Suakin were placed under the control of appointed officials (known as *emīns*) who were mandated to divide the revenues from these ports equally between the Egyptian treasury and the Sherif of Mecca.

Taken as a whole, these reforms amounted to a comprehensive "market-based" restructuring of the state's regulation of the transit spice trade, designed to accommodate the interests of private merchants and to limit state interference as much as possible. Ibrahim realized that the uncompromising and exploitative Mamluk system, based on the expectation that there was no real alternative to the trade routes under Mamluk control, was untenable now that the Portuguese had opened the Cape route and established themselves in the Indian Ocean. The pasha thus tried to create a trading environment more favorable to private spice merchants, so that they would continue to trade in Egyptian ports despite the high risk of attack from Portuguese patrols. At the same time, Ibrahim clearly hoped to maximize the flow of revenue from this trade to the imperial treasury by limiting corruption and reaffirming the state's rights in a few key areas. His establishment of *emīns* in the customs houses of Jiddah and Suakin, for example, reclaimed for the Egyptian treasury its rightful share of the receipts of these ports, which had been exclusively controlled by the Sharif of Mecca since the collapse of the Mamluk regime in 1517.[25]

A provincial budget from 1527 gives a sense of the overall importance of these revenues for Egypt's finances following Ibrahim Pasha's reforms. According to official figures, tax revenues from the four principal ports of Alexandria, Suez, Suakin, and Jiddah (excluding the portion designated for the Sharif of Mecca), amounted to 17,731,964 *akçes* out of a provincial aggregate of 116,538,994.[26] This calculates to just over 15 percent of the total, a significant figure considering that, in the same year, the total customs revenues of the Portuguese Empire (including tariffs on land transport) was only 11.5 percent.[27] The figure is even more impressive given that it was achieved in the mid-1520s, the golden years of the Portuguese anti-Muslim maritime blockade when organized defense of the Red Sea had virtually collapsed. There is, in fact, no other multiyear period during which Portuguese attacks against Muslim shipping to and from the Red Sea were more successful than the years from 1517 to 1525.[28] Yet at the end of this period, customs receipts in Egyptian ports remained a principal source of revenue for what was by far the empire's richest province. Trade-based revenues thus presented themselves as an area with obvious growth potential for the state. And for Ibrahim Pasha, the best way to capitalize on this potential was also obvious: having successfully removed internal impediments to trade through a series of administrative reforms, he must arm a fleet and eliminate the external threat posed by the Portuguese at sea.

THE FIRST OTTOMAN EXPEDITION TO YEMEN

In his report delivered to Ibrahim Pasha in 1525, the corsair Selman Reis had included two critical observations that seem to have made a particular impression on the grand vizier. First, he had warned that the holy cities of Mecca and Medina were completely defenseless against Portuguese attacks, since the old Mamluk fleet lay derelict and abandoned in Jiddah. As he put it, "One cannot escape from painful feelings when one sees these ships and arms lying idly, while one hears about the successes of the accursed Portuguese in those lands of India."[29] But even more alarmingly, Selman had speculated that it was only a matter of time before the pace of Portuguese attacks would intensify and threaten not only the holy cities but also the safety of Egypt itself. He therefore urged the grand vizier to refurbish the fleet in Jiddah as quickly as possible, before the Portuguese had a chance to strike again (Figure 2.2). "It has been solely out of fear that these ships and guns might be sent against them," he wrote, "that the Portuguese have not yet entered the sea of Tor [and attacked Egypt]. But if they hear that these ships are not operational and lack crews they will inevitably come with a big armada for, apart from these ships, there is nothing here to deter them."[30]

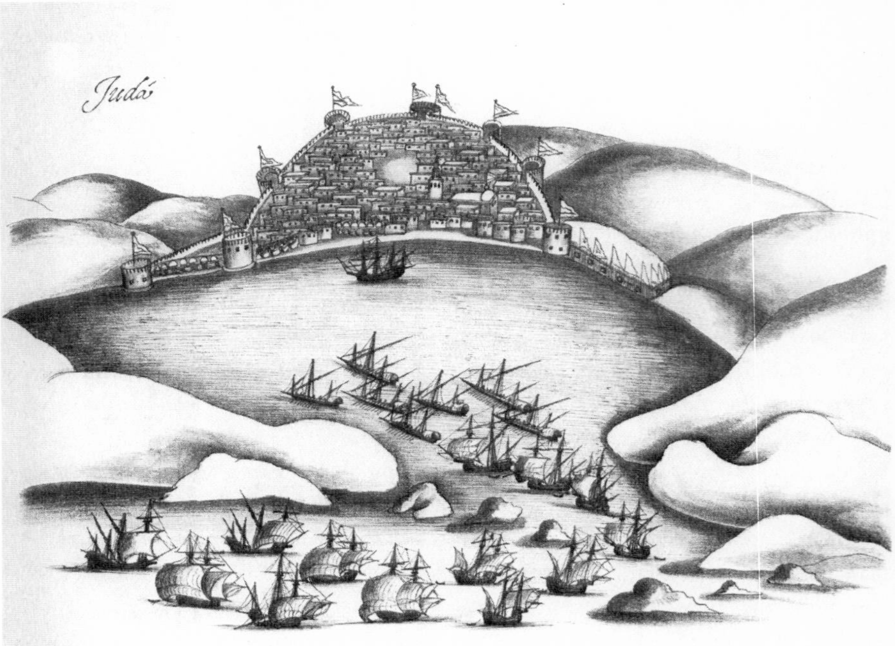

FIGURE 2.2 A contemporary view of Jiddah, the principal maritime entry point for the holy cities of Mecca and Medina, during the Portuguese attack of 1517. Source: Gaspar Correia, *Lendas da Índia* (Lisbon, 1858–1864).

These turned out to be prophetic words. In the same year that Selman wrote them, a Portuguese fleet penetrated deep into the Red Sea and devastated Muslim shipping, burning or capturing a total of twenty-six merchant vessels in just a few weeks of campaigning. Clearly, the Jiddah fleet would have to be rebuilt. But this, as Selman was quick to point out, was only a point of departure. Once the Ottomans had a fleet at their disposal, he urged Ibrahim to think not only defensively but also offensively, by training his sights on the land of Yemen to the south. As Selman described it, Yemen was "a land with no lord, an empty province. It would be not only possible but easy to capture, and should it be conquered, it would be master of the lands of India and send every year a great amount of gold and jewels to Istanbul."[31]

There could be little doubt that the corsair knew of what he spoke, having already campaigned extensively in Yemen during the failed Mamluk naval expedition of 1515, and again for a brief period in the early 1520s. Indeed, by the mid-1520s most of Yemen's territory had fallen into the hands of a fractious band of Levantine and Circassian mercenaries left behind from the last Mamluk expedition there, whose rapacious misrule of the province had become notorious. According to one local chronicler, Yemen during these years was "in a state of incessant anarchy and discord, during which there was nothing but spurted blood, violated hearths, spoiled goods and spilled tears."[32] Even worse, the incessant infighting of these warlords had left them constitutionally incapable of putting up a united front against the Portuguese, as the devastating raid of 1525 had shown all too clearly.[33]

Under such circumstances, Ibrahim Pasha was therefore easily convinced that bringing Yemen under direct Ottoman control was not only a lucrative project in and of itself, but also the only way to permanently secure the Red Sea from future Portuguese attacks. Acting quickly, he ordered nineteen galleys from the derelict fleet in Jiddah to be brought to Suez and refurbished, appointing Selman Reis as their admiral.[34] Additionally, he mustered a fighting force of some four thousand volunteer infantry and placed them under the command of Hayreddin al-Rumi, another experienced veteran of the last Mamluk naval campaign and a long-time associate of Selman.[35] Then, before leaving Cairo and returning to Istanbul in the fall of 1525, Ibrahim Pasha's last act was to appoint a replacement for himself as governor of Egypt.

The pasha's choice for this exalted position, a wizened eunuch by the name of Hadim Suleiman, may have seemed at the time an unlikely (and temporary) successor to the young and dynamic Ibrahim.[36] But this portly product of the sultan's household was an administrator of no small experience, and despite his emasculated condition, he was also a veteran of numerous major military campaigns, including the recent Ottoman conquest of Rhodes (1522). Although already more than seventy years old at the time of his appointment, he would outlive the grand vizier by more than a decade and in time emerge as the leading proponent of Ottoman expansion to Yemen and beyond.

For the moment, the new governor's primary responsibilities were to keep the grand vizier informed of the progress of Selman's expedition and to provide logistical support for his mission from the Ottoman arsenal in Suez.[37] Under his supervision, Hayreddin al-Rumi and Selman Reis fully outfitted their fleet and left Egypt in late 1526, heading first for the port of Jiddah, where they stopped to subdue an armed band of Levantines who had taken control of the harbor and customs house.[38] This accomplished, they continued on their way south, landing the bulk of their forces at the port of Mocha near the mouth of the Red Sea in January 1527.

From there, the two Ottoman commanders led their army into the Yemeni interior and began to demand the submission of the various independent warlords of the region, whose resistance soon coalesced around a certain Mustafa Beg, the ruler of Zebid since 1523 and an old adversary of Selman Reis.[39] Over the course of the next year, Selman and Hayreddin fought Mustafa repeatedly, always getting the better of him, and in September 1527, they defeated his forces definitively. Mustafa was captured and beheaded, his troops were dispersed, and the Ottomans were left undisputed masters of almost all of coastal Yemen.[40] The only major holdout was the emir of the port city of Aden, who stubbornly refused to open his gates to the Ottoman forces, although he did agree to have the sultan's name read in his congregational mosque every Friday and to strike coins in his name.[41] Satisfied by this public (if only partial) display of submission to Istanbul, Selman then headed for the island of Kamaran, just inside the Bab al-Mandab at the mouth of the Red Sea, where he set up a permanent naval base and appointed his nephew, Mustafa Bayram, as its commander. From here, Selman also established a customs house and announced that henceforth all ships traveling from India would be required to stop and pay transit fees.[42] For the first time, the Ottomans had gained control of trade at both ends of the Red Sea.

YEMEN AS "MASTER OF THE LANDS OF INDIA"

In his original report to Ibrahim Pasha in 1525, Selman Reis had boldly predicted that with the Ottoman conquest of Yemen, "the total destruction [of the Portuguese] will be inevitable, for one of their fortresses is unable to support another and they are unable to put up a united opposition."[43] And by all appearances, his rapid string of successes did have an immediate demoralizing effect on the Portuguese: In 1527, for the first time in more than a decade, no Portuguese fleet visited the Red Sea—the admiral Lopo Vaz de Sampayo choosing instead to stay in Goa out of fear of the Ottoman presence in Yemen.[44]

Equally important, with no Portuguese deterrent to discourage them, various Muslim leaders began to approach the Ottomans with proposals for collaboration or requests for help. Early in 1527, the Vizier of Hormuz sent Selman a letter (later intercepted by Portuguese spies) in which he asked for military assistance in liberating his island from Portuguese rule.[45] Some months later, the Zamorin of Calicut (who had united the Muslim corsairs of the Malabar coast and forced the Portuguese to abandon a fortress there in 1524) likewise sent an embassy exhorting the Ottomans to send a fleet to India.[46] Meanwhile, the corsair Mamale, who was the head of the neighboring south Indian Muslim community of Cannanor, pioneered an important new transoceanic spice route from Sumatra through the Maldives. This route allowed merchants for the first time to entirely bypass Portuguese India and sail directly to the Red Sea from the spice islands of Indonesia.[47] As a result, by 1528 Portuguese patrols as far away as Sumatra were encountering Muslim merchant ships defended by armed escorts of Ottoman mercenaries.[48]

Within two years of the Ottomans' arrival in Yemen, a vast nexus of forces from across the Indian Ocean thus appeared to be coalescing under the Ottoman banner into a concrete anti-Portuguese alliance. Selman's claim that whoever controlled Yemen would be "master of the lands of India" seemed to be proving truer than anyone could have expected. And yet, in a cruel reversal of political fortunes, it was precisely at this moment of heady success that the two Ottoman commanders, Selman Reis and Hayreddin al-Rumi, fell into a bloody personal dispute. In surprisingly short order, their rivalry would undo all the gains of the previous year and make any larger scale coordination with Muslims overseas an impossibility.

YEMEN SINKS BACK INTO ANARCHY

This sudden souring of Selman's fortunes could not have come as a complete surprise, for it was hardly the first time in the corsair's volatile history that hard-won gains had been undone by his prickly character. A decade earlier, during the Mamluk campaign of 1515, his relationship with the Mamluk commander Hussein al-Kurdi had been marred by bitter personal animosity that had ended only with Hussein's death (possibly at Selman's hands) in 1517. Similarly, when Selman returned to Yemen as a mercenary in the early 1520s, he had quickly run afoul of the local ruler of Zebid, another veteran of the Mamluk expedition, and was forced to flee back to Egypt, practically as a fugitive.[49]

This time around, Selman's troubles began over a jurisdictional dispute with Hayreddin al-Rumi, when the latter demanded that he withdraw from the mainland and return to his island base in Kamaran on the pretext that, as admiral, he had no authority over Hayreddin's land forces. When Selman refused, insisting that he alone was supreme commander of the expedition, his rival hired some disgruntled Levantine cutthroats to eliminate him. Surprising Selman in his war tent (according to one account, while he was playing a round of chess), they surrounded him and stabbed him to death, bringing the corsair's career and his life to a bloody end in September 1528.[50]

Subsequently, Hayreddin was to suffer a similar fate with little chance to enjoy the fruits of his treachery. Following Selman's assassination, the corsair's nephew Mustafa Bayram, who was also a senior officer of the fleet, rallied his uncle's forces, hunted down Hayreddin, and ordered his execution. Then, declaring himself Selman's successor, Mustafa Bayram briefly attempted to reestablish control over Yemen on his own. Despite his best efforts, however, the political situation continued to deteriorate, and he was soon forced to abandon the mainland. Gathering his most trusted men and the remaining artillery pieces and supplies, Mustafa retreated to his uncle's naval base on the island of Kamaran, and Yemen began once more to descend into lawlessness.[51]

As news of Selman's death and his nephew's retreat spread across the sea lanes, the situation in the wider Indian Ocean region began to deteriorate as well. By the end of 1528, the Portuguese once more found the courage to dispatch a fleet to the Red Sea and captured eight large merchant vessels and forty-four small ones in the space of just a few weeks.[52] The following year, they sent an even larger fleet, which, in addition to stalking Muslim merchants at sea, threatened to establish permanent Portuguese control in parts of Yemen itself. This fleet's commander, Eitor da Sylveira, first sailed to the southern Arabian port of Shihr, whose ruler he pressured into conceding trading privileges to the Portuguese. He then attacked Mustafa Bayram and the remaining Ottoman forces in their base of Kamaran, forcing them to abandon the island and flee. Finally, Sylveira headed for Aden, where the local emir (the same ruler who had refused to open his gates to Selman in 1527) now agreed to become a vassal of the King of Portugal, to pay the Portuguese a tribute of ten thousand *ashrafis* a year, and to prevent any ships under Aden's jurisdiction from traveling in the direction of Mecca.[53] Worse yet, upon Sylveira's departure, he left behind a permanent garrison of forty Portuguese soldiers, who took possession of the citadel and insisted on participating in the emir's weekly procession to the mosque, ostentatiously brandishing their swords, muskets, and other weapons before a scandalized local population. As a local chronicler later complained:

> This was a reprehensible act committed by the lord of Aden. The jurists found fault with him, but he would not listen. The reason why he perpetrated such an act was his fear of the Turk entering his town. But upon my life his judgment erred, the measure was a bad one, and he angered his lord, the Exalted Almighty.[54]

Thus, almost as quickly as it had begun, the Ottomans' first tentative foray into the world of the Indian Ocean ended ignominiously. Internecine fighting within the Ottoman leadership had been the root cause, but as the accommodation between the Portuguese and the Emir of Aden had shown, there were also limits to the cooperation that the Ottomans could expect from other Muslim rulers. Moreover, even before setting out, the Ottomans must have suspected that Selman's fighting force was barely adequate for the task at hand. The vessels under his command were nothing more than hastily refurbished derelicts from the abandoned Mamluk fleet, and his four thousand "fighting men" cut such a poor figure as they first set sail from Egypt that they were described by one contemporary as "a pack of vagrants and young libertines without any experience."[55]

But even in the face of this considerable list of liabilities, Selman Reis had very nearly succeeded in establishing a permanent Ottoman foothold in Yemen. In the process, he had managed (however temporarily) to deny the Portuguese access to the Red Sea, to establish Ottoman control of the maritime trade from India, and to demonstrate the Ottoman dynasty's potential for building alliances throughout the Indian Ocean. Observing events from afar, both the young grand vizier Ibrahim Pasha and his aged lieutenant Hadim Suleiman had thus learned a great deal from the mission even in failure, and would soon begin preparations for a second and much more serious attempt to project Ottoman power abroad.

Such was the contribution of Selman Reis to the Ottoman Age of Exploration. But although the blustery corsair breathed his last in 1528, his story does not quite end even here. For his followers, under the command of his nephew Mustafa Bayram, still had their own important contribution to make to the Ottoman Age of Exploration.

MUSTAFA BAYRAM ARRIVES IN INDIA

Following the Portuguese attack on their naval base in Kamaran in 1529, Mustafa Bayram and the remaining loyal members of Selman's expeditionary force fled to the port of Shihr on South Arabia's Hadrami coast, nearly a thousand miles from the nearest Ottoman supply center in Jiddah. Exactly why they chose this distant outpost, rather than simply returning to Ottoman Egypt, is unclear. But despite the remoteness of their refuge, they nevertheless seem to have remained in contact with both Hadim Suleiman in Cairo and with other members of Selman Reis's family still in Istanbul.[56] Then, apparently with the blessing of Ottoman authorities in Egypt, they left Shihr and set sail for the port of Diu in northwest India, arriving there in the winter of 1531.[57]

Mustafa's arrival in Diu revived and deepened the link between this Gujarati port and the Ottoman Empire that had first been established during the reign of Sultan Selim. In fact, Gujarat's ruling sovereign in 1531, Sultan Bahadur, was the son of Selim's old correspondent Sultan Muzaffar Shah II, and Diu's local governor, Bahaulmulk Tughan, was none other than the son of Malik Ayaz, the former head of Gujarat's Rumi merchant community. Just as important, Mustafa Bayram and his men could not have reached Diu at a more critical juncture: just days before the Portuguese Admiral Nuno da Cunha was to launch a major attack on the city by sea. Under such circumstances, the Gujaratis welcomed the timely Ottoman arrivals as a godsend, and Bahaulmulk Tughan immediately invited Mustafa Bayram's men (some six hundred Ottomans and more than a thousand Arab auxiliaries in all) to assume full responsibility for the defenses of Diu. This they did, extracting heavy casualties from the besiegers with barrages from the large guns they had brought with them from Yemen, and disrupting the Portuguese siege by mining the fortifications outside the citadel with powder charges. Within just a few days, collaboration between the Ottomans and local Gujarati forces had put the Portuguese to a rout—the first "transoceanic" victory in Ottoman history.[58]

As news of this triumph spread, memories of Selman Reis's recent failure in Yemen were erased, and the House of Osman's reputation as the most powerful and dynamic Muslim dynasty in the Indian Ocean was reaffirmed. Even the recalcitrant Emir of Aden, who had so scandalously agreed to become a Portuguese vassal in 1529, now declared for the Ottomans and ordered all forty members of the small Portuguese garrison left behind in his city arrested and put in chains.[59] In Gujarat itself, a grateful Sultan Bahadur bestowed gifts and titles on Mustafa Bayram and invited his men to remain in Gujarat and enter his service permanently. Bahadur's terms were generous, and in the end, nearly all of Mustafa's men chose to accept his offer and stay.[60]

Since Bahadur's kingdom lay at the geographic and commercial center of the vast Indian Ocean network of trade and navigation, this group of Ottoman émigrés was destined to play a pivotal role in Indian affairs in the years ahead. Although their leader, Mustafa Bayram, later defected to the Mughals, the remaining members of his entourage who enlisted in Bahadur's service quickly emerged as maritime Gujarat's new ruling elite.[61] As such, they would drive the political life of the sultanate for the next generation, all the while maintaining close professional, mercantile, and even family ties with members of the Ottoman establishment in Istanbul and Egypt.[62] In practice, these Rumi émigrés founded what amounted to an informal but permanent Ottoman colony in the very heart of the Indian Ocean trading world.

THE ABORTED EXPEDITION OF 1531 AND THE OTTOMAN CONQUEST OF IRAQ

Meanwhile, from the imperial centers of Istanbul and Cairo, Ibrahim Pasha and Hadim Suleiman had already begun to plan their next move. In the wake of Selman Reis's ephemeral success in Yemen, they were more determined than ever to build a powerful Ottoman navy in the Red Sea. But this project, so obviously essential to their long-term goals in Yemen and beyond, was fraught with logistical difficulties, since the almost total lack of forests in Egypt and Arabia meant that timber and other naval supplies had to be shipped in from the northern Mediterranean and then transported overland to Suez at enormous expense. This necessity threatened to raise the cost of building a Red Sea fleet to prohibitive levels, permanently handicapping Ottoman efforts to use the sea to project their power abroad.

Ibrahim Pasha and Hadim Suleiman's solution to this problem is a testament to just how ambitious they had become. If there was no direct maritime link between the Mediterranean and the Red Sea, then they proposed to build one themselves, by reopening the ancient canal (closed since pharaonic times) between the Nile and the

Red Sea port of Tor. Already in 1529, Luigi Roncinotto, a Venetian resident in Egypt, reported having seen in the desert between the Nile and Tor several teams of engineers and more than twelve thousand workmen engaged in an attempt to reopen this ancient canal "so that the caravels loaded with spices might come from India to Alexandria, and from there to Constantinople."[63]

Roncinotto maintained that a channel some twenty miles long had already been opened at the time of his writing. By the following year—as reports of ongoing progress continued to circulate—speculation about the canal was dominating political discussions even in Paris, amid rumors that the Ottomans would seek a peace with Charles V in Europe in order to devote themselves entirely to a coming naval campaign in India.[64] Then, in November 1531, the Portuguese envoy to Venice forwarded an intelligence dispatch from Egypt (confirmed by documents in the Ottoman archives) reporting the construction of a massive fleet in the Ottoman arsenal in Suez, composed of some sixty war galleys of various sizes, as well as twenty supply ships. In the most urgent terms, the report also suggested that the departure of the fleet was imminent, that Hadim Suleiman Pasha had been nominated as its commander, and that three thousand men were ready to accompany the expedition.[65]

This same Portuguese report also provided valuable information about the decision-making process behind these truly herculean preparations, based in part on economic considerations and in part on concerns about Ottoman dynastic prestige. On the economic side, the report confirmed that 1531 had been a particularly effective year for the Portuguese blockade of the Red Sea. According to Venetian merchants in both Beirut and Alexandria, spices had become so scarce in those ports that they had been forced to load their ships with beans and wheat instead. Because of this, two Muslim converts from prominent Venetian families, Giovanni Contarini "Cacciadiavolo" and Francesco Giustiniani, had been invited by Ibrahim Pasha to the Imperial Divan:

> And it is said that they are providing the Sultan with everything he needs to know about how to prepare a fleet to send to the Red Sea, and that because of them he is now very knowledgeable about the Kingdom of Portugal and the capabilities of its king to such an extent that the Sultan is now preparing an even larger force than he previously intended.[66]

At the same time, the report also indicated that the sultan, while concerned about the security of the spice route, had been particularly enraged by news that the Portuguese had raided the coast of Arabia near Jiddah: "and that according to what is being said, the armada which he is now preparing is more for the defense of Mecca than any other objective."[67] Clearly, the desire of the sultan to maintain his prestige as "Defender of the Holy Cities" and to protect the interests of merchants had now converged, and a solid consensus about the future direction of Ottoman policy was the result.

Or was it? Despite all of the chatter in European sources (until as late as 1531) about ongoing work on the canal, in reality excavations were called off shortly after they had begun, as mounting costs and technical difficulties made the project look unfeasible. Preparations for the Suez fleet appear to have continued somewhat longer and do seem to have been nearly complete by the end of 1531. But then, rather mysteriously, these preparations were called off as well, and the fleet's supplies, munitions, and artillery were abruptly transferred from Suez to the Mediterranean. Hadim Suleiman Pasha and his three thousand men were then sent to Syria, where they were ordered to begin preparations for an entirely different operation: a land campaign against the Safavids in Iraq.[68]

Neither Ottoman nor European sources reveal solid reasons for this abrupt about-face. Modern historians, for lack of a better explanation, have been tempted to see it as a "turning away" from the Indian Ocean or, in more sociological terms, as a sign that the fundamentally "land-based" Ottoman state was naturally more inclined to employ its resources in a land campaign whenever the opportunity presented itself.[69] This explanation, however, seems very difficult to reconcile with the central role played throughout the process by Ibrahim Pasha, who was responsible both for the decision to invade Iraq and for the earlier Ottoman naval buildup in the Red Sea. Given the grand vizier's history of interest in the Indian Ocean, his many efforts to gather information about the region, his close contacts with the Venetian merchant community in Istanbul, and his unprecedented influence with the sultan during these years, it hardly seems plausible that a structurally ingrained "land-based bias" was really behind his sudden change of heart.

This is not to deny that, under normal circumstances, a perceived threat from the Portuguese was unlikely to preoccupy Ibrahim (or indeed any Ottoman grand vizier) more than a conflict with the Safavids, the Ottomans' closest and most powerful neighbors. But in this particular case, a significant amount of evidence suggests that the strategic imperatives behind a land campaign against the Safavids and a sea campaign against the Portuguese were not as separate as they might otherwise appear. To begin with, Ibrahim Pasha had known since at least 1525 that the Portuguese had made contact with the Safavid ruler Shah Tahmasp and were hopeful of creating an openly anti-Ottoman alliance with him. In fact, the same Ottoman official who had first warned Ibrahim Pasha about these Portuguese-Safavid negotiations (Husrev Pasha, who at the time was governor-general of Diyarbakir on the Safavid frontier) was shortly thereafter transferred to Egypt, where he was responsible for overseeing the preparations for Hadim Suleiman's fleet.[70]

Equally significantly, 1529 had witnessed the first Portuguese intervention in the western Persian Gulf, where a small fleet from Hormuz had raided and burned several coastal settlements in order to punish Emir Rashid, the independent ruler of Basra, for refusing to hand over an escort of fifty Ottoman mercenaries in his service.[71] Tensions there continued to rise in the following year, when a number of armed Muslim merchant vessels from Calicut successfully evaded Portuguese patrols around Hormuz and reached Basra safely, prompting the Portuguese to retaliate by launching an attack against the island of Bahrain.[72] Shortly thereafter, the Portuguese sent another fleet to the mouth of the Red Sea.[73]

As a result, by 1531 Ibrahim Pasha was becoming increasingly aware that the Portuguese posed a threat from the Persian Gulf as well as from the Red Sea, meaning that their naval power could be conceivably combined with Safavid land forces in a coordinated strike against the Ottomans. As Daniello De Ludovisi, the *bailo* or official Venetian representative in Istanbul, described it at the time: "The King of Portugal is now taken into consideration by the Sultan . . . with regard to the affairs of the Indies both because of the help that he can provide to the Safavids by means of that route, and because of the campaign which the Sultan himself hopes to undertake to destroy Portuguese seapower in those parts."[74]

From this perspective, there are therefore ample grounds for interpreting Ibrahim Pasha's decision to redirect forces from Suez to Iraq not as a "turning away from the Indian Ocean," but rather as an attempt to broaden the empire's involvement in the region to include the Persian Gulf in addition to the Red Sea. Ottoman diplomatic activity immediately following the conquest of Iraq, which was completed in 1534, certainly lends support to this view: within just three months of Sultan Suleiman's first entrance into Baghdad, at a time when he, Ibrahim Pasha, and Hadim Suleiman were all still in residence there, Emir Rashid of Basra was ordered to send his son to Baghdad for an imperial audience, where he formally swore allegiance to the sultan and, on the emir's behalf, agreed to recognize submission to the Ottoman state by striking coins and reading the Friday sermon (*ẖuṭbe*) in Suleiman's name. The emirs of the gulf states of Bahrain and Katif also followed suit, and nominal Ottoman suzerainty was thereby confirmed over the entire western Persian Gulf. A new, northern maritime frontier had been established with the Portuguese.[75]

CONCLUSION: THE END OF RECONNAISSANCE

Both for Ibrahim Pasha personally and for the Ottoman Age of Exploration as a whole, the lightning conquest of Iraq in 1534 was a tipping point. For the pasha, the victorious campaign was without question the crowning achievement of his career—but one that would also lead, hardly more than a year later, to his sudden and dramatic downfall. In the flush of victory from the capture of Baghdad in November 1534, and apparently intoxicated by his own seemingly limitless power, the grand vizier dared to refer to himself in a piece of official correspondence as "he who stands in the place of the sultanate." This was the first of several apparently unauthorized transgressions that would give his enemies at court, in collaboration with those inside the imperial harem, the leverage they needed to slowly but surely undermine Suleiman's confidence in him.[76]

Ibrahim's position deteriorated steadily in the following months, despite his continued success on the war front in Persia following his victories in Iraq. According to some, the nail in Ibrahim's coffin was driven home by the sultan's beloved Roxelana, who could tolerate for only so long the place in Suleiman's heart that he continued to occupy.[77] In early 1536, only weeks after his glorious return to Istanbul from more than two years on the eastern front, he was invited for the last time to visit the palace. And there, in the wintry cold of an Istanbul March, the sultan ordered his childhood friend's summary execution.[78]

Thus ended the brilliant but strangely incomplete career of Ibrahim Pasha. Had he lived, there seems little doubt that he would have continued to push for a major Ottoman maritime offensive against the Portuguese, for which his accomplishments up to 1536 had served merely to lay the groundwork. But even though these larger ambitions were cut short by his death, the grand vizier had nevertheless achieved much during his thirteen years in power. In 1523, when Ibrahim had first been promoted to the grand vizierate, the Ottomans had no operational fleet in the Red Sea, had virtually no reliable information about conditions in the Indian Ocean, and had even briefly lost control of Egypt. They were, for all intents and purposes, in the same position they had been in before the conquests of Selim the Grim in 1517. But by 1536, conditions had been so dramatically transformed as to be almost unrecognizable. Ottoman rule in Egypt was on a firmer footing than it had ever been before, and its administration had been revamped to accommodate the interests of Indian Ocean merchants. The arsenal in Suez was fully operational, and the Ottoman fleet had staged a successful (albeit temporary) occupation of Yemen. Iraq was also occupied, and a new front had opened with the Portuguese in the Persian Gulf. Diplomatic ties had been established with Muslim powers across the Indian Ocean (from the Malabar corsairs to the straits of Hormuz), as had an informal colony of Ottoman émigrés in Gujarat. And perhaps most important, the Ottomans had gained access to the most up-to-date intelligence on the Indian Ocean and could draw on the experience of a cadre of advisors and policy makers (including Hadim Suleiman, Piri Reis, "Cacciadiavolo" Contarini, and Francesco Giustiniani), all of whom had an intimate familiarity with the workings of the region.

In this sense, Ibrahim Pasha's grand vizierate can best be understood as an age of reconnaissance rather than an age of conquest. At the time of Ibrahim's death in 1536, Hadim Suleiman's fleet in Suez lay only half-built, Yemen remained stubbornly outside Ottoman control, and Portuguese power at sea was still largely unchallenged. But patiently and determinedly, Ibrahim Pasha had successfully built a platform for projecting Ottoman power abroad. And within just two years of his demise, a massive Ottoman fleet would sail from Suez and permanently redraw the political landscape of the Indian Ocean world.

Three

HADIM SULEIMAN PASHA'S WORLD WAR

1536–1546

Ibrahim Pasha's death left the empire with a gaping power vacuum. For nearly a decade thereafter, no other Ottoman figure would dominate affairs of state as Ibrahim had during his years in office. But of all the various contenders for power during the period from 1536 to 1544, the one who came closest to qualifying as the empire's new leading statesman was Ibrahim's deputy, Hadim Suleiman Pasha. In itself, this reveals just how central the Indian Ocean had become for Ottoman political life. Unlike Ibrahim, who had grown interested in the Indies only after achieving supreme power through the sultan's favor, Hadim Suleiman was able to advance through the ranks of the Ottoman hierarchy primarily as a result of his involvement in the empire's efforts to establish a presence in the Red Sea and the Persian Gulf. By 1541, after leading an expedition to India and, in the process, successfully conquering Yemen, he was promoted to the grand vizierate—the first case in Ottoman history in which the Indian Ocean became a springboard for attaining the empire's highest office.[1]

None of this, however, would have been easy to predict in the immediate aftermath of Ibrahim's execution. Indeed, to most political observers at the time, Hadim Suleiman must have seemed the most unlikely of candidates for the greatness that awaited him. A eunuch since childhood, grotesquely overweight, and already more than eighty years old in 1536, he was reportedly so decrepit that he could barely move under his own power. And in addition to these distasteful physical attributes, Hadim Suleiman also enjoyed a reputation for ruthlessness and cruelty bordering on the sadistic, which seems to have made him universally disliked even by his closest colleagues and associates. As one roughly contemporary Ottoman author put it: "Although he had been the personal slave of the sultan, he had apparently learned nothing from his master except to spill blood on the slightest pretext."[2]

Despite this formidable list of liabilities, by the time of Ibrahim Pasha's death Hadim Suleiman had served with considerable distinction in a number of important senior offices, most notably as the governor-general of Egypt—an experience that left him incomparably qualified to direct Ottoman policy in the Indian Ocean. During his years in Cairo, the pasha had been responsible for providing logistical support for Selman's expedition to Yemen, for overseeing the abortive attempt to build a canal from the Nile to the Red Sea, and for developing the Ottoman arsenal in Suez. In 1531, he was even tapped to be the admiral of the new Ottoman fleet in the Red Sea, until the outbreak of war with the Safavids led to his transfer to Syria later that year.

Hadim Suleiman had played an equally prominent role in Ibrahim Pasha's ongoing efforts to gather intelligence about the Indian Ocean, collaborating closely with other leading advisors on Portuguese affairs such as "Cacciadiavolo" Contarini, Francesco Giustiniani, and Selman Reis. He was even an avid collector of maps and a cartographer in his own right, compiling navigational charts of the Indian Ocean so authoritative that they continued to be consulted by Ottoman officials well into the 1580s.[3] And just as important, Hadim Suleiman's years of service in Egypt had brought him into close contact with the enterprising Rumi community associated with the corsair Selman Reis. After Selman's death in 1528, when most of these Rumis fled to India and took up employment with Sultan Bahadur of Gujarat, he was therefore able to tap these contacts to keep himself well apprised of events both in Yemen and throughout the larger Indian Ocean world.

Hadim Suleiman's relationship with one member of this group was to prove particularly important for the subsequent formulation of his Indian Ocean policies. This was a man known by the name of Hoja Safar, a former slave of Selman Reis originally from the port city of Otranto in southern Italy. The early career of this singular individual, like so many of his fellow Rumi cohorts, is obscure, and the circumstances under which he entered Selman's service, converted to Islam, and eventually gained his freedom are unknown. By the time of Selman Reis's expedition to Yemen in 1526, however, Hoja Safar could be counted among Selman's most trusted lieutenants, and played a key role in avenging Selman's death by helping to hunt down and kill his assassins.

Thereafter, he had accompanied Selman's nephew Mustafa Bayram and his Rumi entourage to their new home in India. And in 1534, the year in which Mustafa Bayram left Gujarati service and defected to the Mughals, Hoja Safar was chosen to replace him as the new titular head of Gujarat's Rumi community. Accordingly, Sultan Bahadur awarded him the title Khudavend Khan and granted him extensive land holdings that included the strategic port cities of Surat and Diu.[4] Three years later, when Bahadur was betrayed by the Portuguese and assassinated in an ambush at sea (under circumstances described in more detail later), Hoja Safar was still at his side, fighting bravely against his assailants until the bitter end and sustaining several serious injuries. In fact, on this occasion, he very nearly suffered the same fate as his master, only narrowly escaping with his life by jumping ship and swimming a considerable distance to shore.[5]

Throughout all of these dramatic events, extending over more than a decade and ranging from the Middle East to India, Hoja Safar was able to maintain a lively long-distance correspondence with Hadim Suleiman Pasha, thereby bringing the political worlds of the subcontinent and the Ottoman Empire closer together than they had ever been before. Eventually, this relationship would provide a pretext for Hadim Suleiman to directly intervene in the affairs of Gujarat, stoking the smoldering rivalry between Ottomans and Portuguese into a global conflagration.

BETWEEN MONGOLS ON LAND AND INFIDELS AT SEA: THE REIGN OF BAHADUR OF GUJARAT

Understanding how this conflict emerged requires stepping back a few years to follow the erratic career of Sultan Bahadur of Gujarat, who ruled his kingdom during a troubled decade stretching from the death of his father Muzaffer II in 1526 to his own demise in 1537. Bahadur's reign is of particular importance because, more than any other Gujarati sultan of the sixteenth century, he harbored a consistent interest in maritime affairs, traveling frequently by sea and pursing an active policy of commissioning ships for both military and commercial purposes. From the very earliest years of his reign, he also strove to develop the port of Diu into a powerful naval base as well as a trading center, an effort successful enough in its early stages to have provoked a Portuguese attack in 1531.[6]

Bahadur was able to fend off this attack only thanks to the fortuitous arrival from Yemen of Mustafa Bayram and his Rumi fleet, an experience that led him to completely reorient his foreign policy around the concept of a strategic partnership with the Ottomans. As early as 1532, in fact, he sent an embassy to Ottoman Egypt with the help of his new Rumi retainers.[7] And in 1533, he used another group of these Rumis to develop ties with the Muslim corsairs of Calicut, who were already engaged in their own attacks against Portuguese shipping, and heavily invested in the project of reviving maritime trade to the Red Sea.[8]

In the midst of all of these efforts to establish Gujarat as a naval power, however, Bahadur also began a misguided campaign of expansion on land that dragged him into conflict with the Mughal Emperor Humayun. This, too, in its own way, was related to the Rumi presence in his camp, for it seems to have been Bahadur's confidence in the powerful artillery of his new Ottoman gunners that had first emboldened him to provoke a war with the mighty Mughals. But whatever its rationale, the move proved to be a tragic miscalculation, as Bahadur was first outmaneuvered by Humayun, then weakened by the treacherous battlefield defection of Mustafa

Bayram, and finally defeated and put to flight by the Mughal army in March 1535. Militarily depleted and politically isolated, Bahadur had no choice but to take refuge in Diu, and from there, in desperation, he turned to his erstwhile adversaries the Portuguese for help. In October 1535, with the Mughal army still closing in, Bahadur signed a humiliating treaty with the Portuguese viceroy Nuno da Cunha, handing over to the Portuguese the control of Diu's customs house, giving them permission to build a fortress in Diu's harbor, and promising to sever all of his kingdom's relations with the Ottoman Empire in exchange for a promise of immediate military support.[9]

For the Portuguese, who had spent much of the previous decade scheming unsuccessfully for control of Diu, this treaty was celebrated as a diplomatic coup of the first order. But Bahadur, who had no intention of giving up his dreams of turning Gujarat into a seaborne power, seems to have regarded it, at best, as a temporary agreement, and had begun taking steps to force its abrogation even before it had been ratified. Already in the summer of 1535, probably at the instigation of Hoja Safar, Bahadur had placed his treasury and all the women of his household in the charge of Asaf Khan, a trusted official, and sent them to safety in Mecca.[10] From there, he instructed Asaf Khan to send an envoy to Istanbul and persuade the Ottoman authorities to intervene on his behalf by restoring Diu to Bahadur's control.[11]

The envoy chosen for this mission, Umdet al-Mulk, arrived in the Ottoman capital in the fall of 1536. Presenting the sultan with a fabulously expensive girdle of jewels and many other sumptuous gifts, he pleaded with him to relieve the people of Gujarat from, as he put it, the twin scourges of "Mongols by land and infidels by sea."[12] To cover the expenses of the campaign, he offered to hand over Bahadur's entire state treasury, valued at the stunning sum of "two hundred and fifty chests containing one million two hundred and seventy thousand and six hundred measures of gold."[13] This windfall, combined with news in the spring of 1537 that Bahadur had been treacherously murdered by the Portuguese, was enough to convince the sultan of the need to intervene. Hadim Suleiman Pasha, at the time serving as the governor-general of Rumelia, was promptly reassigned to Egypt, promoted to the rank of vizier, and given orders to begin preparing for a naval invasion of India.[14]

HADIM SULEIMAN BUILDS A GLOBAL ALLIANCE

Once in Egypt, the pasha began planning for his expedition through a combination of aggressive intelligence gathering and sophisticated diplomacy. His first step was to send discreet messages about his plans to Sultan Badr, ruler of the strategic port city of Shihr on the Hadrami coast of Arabia, who responded by having a number of Portuguese merchants in his territory arrested and sent to Egypt as an official gift.[15] Twenty-five of these Portuguese prisoners were then personally interrogated by Hadim Suleiman, and two of them, identified by the pasha as the most knowledgeable and cooperative, were sent on to Istanbul. There, his trusted advisor Francesco Giustiniani managed to convince one of them, a Jewish convert to Christianity named Diego Martins, to embrace Islam and collaborate with the Ottomans. After a brief interview with the sultan, Giustiniani then escorted Martins back to Egypt, where the two assisted Hadim Suleiman in planning the particulars of the expedition.[16]

Meanwhile, in Gujarat, Hoja Safar was also preparing for the impending Ottoman offensive. From his base in Surat, he sent a letter to Hadim Suleiman in which he urged the pasha to make the fortress of Diu his primary military target, promising to provide any help necessary for the campaign. According to a Portuguese paraphrasing of his letter:

> [Hoja Safar] asked that the fleet be sent directly to India and land at the island of Diu, where it would be very easy to capture the [Portuguese-held] fortress there since he would provide all necessary assistance. And since [Diu] is the center of all the maritime trade routes of India, from there war can be made against all the principal strongholds of the Portuguese at whatever time desired, none of which would be able to resist. The Portuguese will thus be expelled from India, trade will once again be free as it has been in times past, and the route to Muhammed's sacred residence will once again be safe from their depredations.[17]

With cooperation from Hoja Safar thus assured, Hadim Suleiman was now ready to begin a wider diplomatic effort to co-opt Muslim powers on every side of the Indian Ocean for his offensive. He started by sending his lieutenant, Solak Ferhad (or "Ferhad the left-handed"), on an embassy to the Muslim-held ports of Yemen and the Hadramaut. Here, however, Ferhad met with only mixed success. In Zebid, he received a decidedly lukewarm reception from Nakhoda Ahmed, the local strongman, who openly questioned the wisdom of Hadim Suleiman's plans. And in Aden, even more dramatically, the reigning Emir ibn Daud fled the city before Ferhad's arrival, refusing to meet with the Ottoman delegation at all.[18] In Shihr, on the other hand, Sultan Badr showered the Ottoman delegation with gifts and compliments, ordered Sultan Suleiman's name to be henceforth read in the Friday sermon (*h̲uṭbe*), and sent Ferhad on his way "in a grateful mood, and full of praise for the honor, chivalrous treatment and consideration which he had received on the part of Sultan Badr towards him."[19] Finally, before heading back to Ottoman territory, Ferhad's delegation crossed the Arabian Sea to the horn of Africa, where he received similar expressions of support from the powerful Emir of Zeyla, Ahmed Grañ al-Mujahid.[20]

Upon Ferhad's return to Egypt, Hadim Suleiman's next step was to establish relationships with much more distant powers, including some who had never before enjoyed formal contacts of any kind with the Ottoman state. Most impressively, we learn from the account of the contemporary Portuguese traveler Fernão Mendes Pinto that the pasha sent to the distant Sultanate of Aceh on the southeast Asian island of Sumatra a team of "hand-picked men" from Egypt "under the command of a Turk by the name of Hamad Khan."[21] Pinto's account also includes a stern warning to the Portuguese, delivered to him in Malacca by a visiting ambassador from one of Aceh's local rivals for power, about the conditions under which Hadim Suleiman had agreed to send this force. According to this envoy:

> [The Ottomans sent these troops to help the Sultan of Aceh] gain naval supremacy of the Malacca strait and cut you [the Portuguese] off, as his people openly boast they will, from all your spice commerce with the Banda and Molucca islands, and block all your trade routes to China, Sunda, Borneo, Timor and Japan. Those are the conditions of the pact, as we have learned, that he has just signed with the Grand Turk, with the intermediary of his nephew [*sic*] the Pasha of Cairo, who has filled him with hopes of receiving all kinds of assistance.[22]

There are, admittedly, some interpretive challenges relating to this passage. Pinto himself did not arrive in Malacca until 1539, a full year after the completion of Hadim Suleiman's expedition to India. And because his account indicates that Hamad Khan and his men also arrived in Sumatra only in early 1539, some historians have raised doubts about whether this force of Ottoman soldiers was really sent by Hadim Suleiman Pasha directly from Egypt or was merely a "fortuitous windfall" of mercenaries who reached southeast Asia independently, after the pasha's withdrawal from Diu in 1538.[23] In the absence of corroborating sources, this question will probably never be answered with certainty. But Pinto does state quite explicitly that the Ottoman force came directly "from the straits of Mecca."[24] And if we assume that Pinto really was in Malacca in June 1539, as he says he was, then a close inspection of the chronology of his narrative suggests that mercenaries from the siege of Diu could have reached Sumatra before him only with the greatest difficulty.[25]

Furthermore, Pinto maintains that Hamad Khan and his men reached Aceh "in the four ships he [the Sultan of Aceh] had originally sent [to the Red Sea] with a cargo of pepper."[26] This suggests a connection between Ottoman military support for the Acehnese and a developing relationship between Hadim Suleiman and the Mappilla corsairs of Calicut. As has already been noted in the previous chapter, the opening of a direct sea route between Aceh and the Red Sea via the Maldives had been an innovation of these Mappilla corsairs in 1527, and by the 1530s, as many as eight ships a year were regularly sent to Jiddah along this route. During these years, the Mappilla leader Pate Marakkar also amassed a large offensive fleet of some fifty light fustas and several thousand men (including a thousand harquebusiers and four hundred pieces of artillery), with which the corsairs began to attack the Portuguese in the Sea of Ceylon in 1537.[27]

Although very little direct evidence exists, it seems extremely likely that this Mappilla offensive off the coast of south India was directly coordinated with Hadim Suleiman's preparations in Egypt, as well as with the start of nearly simultaneous military operations in Aceh. The most probable scenario seems to be that Hadim Suleiman, encouraged by envoys sent from Pate Marakkar and the Zamorin of

Calicut sometime in 1537, dispatched Hamad Khan to Aceh at the same time as his own departure for India, with orders to harass Portuguese ships and, if possible, assist in an attack on the Portuguese fortress of Malacca. This hypothesis is supported by the fact that Aceh's fleet did besiege Malacca shortly after Hamad Khan's arrival there, following Sultan Ala'ad-din Ri'ayat Sjah's seizure of power in a palace coup against his brother in the summer of 1539.[28]

Thus, by the spring of 1538, as Hadim Suleiman's own fleet neared completion in the arsenal of Suez, the pasha had managed to construct an enormous transoceanic coalition, linking Istanbul with allies across the entire breadth of the Indian Ocean from Shihr and Gujarat to Calicut and Sumatra. It was arguably the most geographically extensive alliance ever assembled—one that could hardly have been conceived of more than a few decades earlier. As a final piece of this intercontinental puzzle, Hadim Suleiman took advantage of political developments in the Mediterranean to further extend the geographical range of his planning. Using the Ottomans' declaration of war against Venice in 1537 as a pretext, he impounded all of the Venetian merchant vessels in Egypt and impressed their crews into service in his own fleet.[29] With his forces in Suez augmented by hundreds of Venetian gunners, pilots, and skilled craftsmen, he was finally ready to set sail for India.

THE OTTOMAN EXPEDITION OF 1538

Although Hadim Suleiman's expedition to India has attracted surprisingly little attention from modern scholars, it was by almost any measure an undertaking of truly astounding proportions. Suleiman's armada, consisting of nearly seventy vessels in all, was the largest that had been seen in the Indian Ocean since the legendary fleets of the Chinese admiral Cheng Ho more than a century earlier.[30] Moreover, with a total crew approaching ten thousand individuals, his force dwarfed contemporary Portuguese fleets, probably equaling the population of all the colonies of Portuguese Asia combined.[31] Even by the more formidable standards of warfare in the Mediterranean, the pasha's armada was massive, ranking in its day as one of the largest Ottoman fleets ever assembled. And all of this was accomplished despite the total absence of forests in Egypt and Arabia, meaning that every plank used in its construction was shipped to Egypt from elsewhere in the empire and then hauled overland to the arsenal in Suez across more than a hundred miles of desert.

And yet, as carefully planned and as extravagantly financed as his 1538 campaign undoubtedly was, in the end it still fell short of achieving all that Hadim Suleiman had hoped. Most disappointingly, the pasha's collaborative efforts with his far-flung allies failed to produce their intended result: off the Coromandel coast, Pate Marakkar's fleet of Mappilla corsairs was destroyed by the Portuguese months before Hadim Suleiman had even left Suez; in Southeast Asia, the Acehnese attack on Portuguese Malacca was likewise repulsed; and in Gujarat, Ottoman operations were plagued by poor cooperation between Hadim Suleiman and his local allies, eventually compelling the pasha to lift the siege of Diu and retreat empty-handed to Yemen.

Still, it should not be forgotten that, at least at Diu, victory was to elude the Ottomans by only the slenderest of possible margins. When Hadim Suleiman finally gave the order to lift the siege in September 1538, after an epic six-week struggle to take the city, the Portuguese garrison inside Diu's fortress was virtually moribund, having completely run out of munitions and with no more than forty soldiers still healthy enough to bear arms.[32] According to the Portuguese chronicler Diogo do Couto, during the closing days of combat, "the situation was so precarious that any outside observer would have surely guessed that all was lost."[33]

Why, then, when the capture of Diu seemed all but inevitable, did Hadim Suleiman choose an ignominious retreat? Most surviving accounts of the siege, which are nearly unanimous in their condemnation of the pasha, attribute his decision to cowardice, arguing that he had been frightened by rumors of a Portuguese relief force on its way from Goa. But while there may be some element of truth to this view, it also seems clear that the pasha was facing mounting resistance to his siege even from his own local allies. For this reason, the Ottoman retreat from Diu—in contrast to the reverses suffered by the pasha's allies in Sumatra or the Sea of Ceylon—should be considered first and foremost a political rather than a military defeat.

This by no means exonerates Hadim Suleiman from all personal responsibility for his failure. Time and again during the course of the siege, the same man who had been so adept at constructing grand alliances from a distance proved at close range to be a far less capable statesman and diplomat. His demeanor throughout the campaign is universally described in both Muslim and Christian accounts as imperious, deceitful, and prone to sudden and violent fits of rage. And his extremely advanced age and unsavory physical appearance must also have been a factor, for as a grotesquely fat octogenarian eunuch, he hardly fit the image of a mighty conquering hero around which the Muslims of India could be inspired to rally their forces.

Such flaws in the pasha's character, however, only served to exacerbate a series of preexisting political challenges that were based not so much in a lack of leadership as in a resistance among some Indian Ocean Muslims to the very idea of Ottoman ascendancy in the region. Indeed, trouble of this kind had begun for Hadim Suleiman even before he had set sail from Egypt, when Emir ibn Daud of Aden had refused to receive his envoy Ferhad in 1537. Although downplayed by the pasha at the time, this was an affront with all the makings of a major diplomatic crisis, since Aden was the most strongly fortified port on the entire Yemeni coast and had a history of hostility to the Ottomans (and friendly relations with the Portuguese) stretching back at least two decades. Because of Aden's strategic importance, Hadim Suleiman well knew that he could not simply bypass the city on his way to India, for to do so would leave his supply lines dangerously exposed throughout the rest of his mission. But at the same time, he also knew that a lengthy conflict with the emir could jeopardize the success of his coordinated attack on Diu, which was an equally unacceptable alternative.

With no good options, the pasha's solution upon his arrival in Aden while en route to India had been to act with a characteristic combination of duplicity and brutality: first feigning friendship and inviting the emir aboard his flagship for a formal reconciliation; then abruptly ordering him bound and hanged by the neck from the ship's yardarm, while a contingent of janissaries was sent ashore to take possession of Aden's citadel (Figure 3.1).[34] Without firing a shot, Hadim Suleiman had thus taken control of a strategic port that had previously eluded the grasp both of the Mamluks and of Selman Reis before him. But he had done so at a heavy cost to his own reputation, for news of his treachery spread fast and far and convinced more than one potential Indian ally that the pasha was simply not to be trusted.[35] This became obvious to the pasha himself just a few weeks later, when the vanguard of the Ottoman fleet reached the coast of India and sent an embassy to the powerful Muslim ruler Adil Khan in the Deccan, offering to help him conquer Goa from the Portuguese in exchange for logistical support during the siege of Diu. Adil Khan refused, declaring that in light of recent events in Yemen, "he would rather be a friend of the Portuguese, who had taken Goa from him, than of the Grand Turk who promised to restore it."[36]

Nor did things get any easier for the pasha once his troops had finally disembarked in Diu. There, as expected, he was welcomed by Hoja Safar's contingent of Rumis and several thousand more troops sent by Bahadur's son Mahmud, the new sultan of Gujarat.[37] But in Hadim Suleiman's first meeting with Ulu Khan, Sultan Mahmud's commander-in-chief, the pasha reportedly treated his counterpart with such disdain that he was rumored to have mistaken him for one of Hoja Safar's personal servants.[38] Hadim Suleiman denied this, insisting in his own account that it was Ulu Khan who had first insulted him by refusing to even greet him with a friendly "selam aleykum."[39] But Ulu Khan nevertheless reported the affront to Sultan Mahmud, thereby arousing his sovereign's suspicions to such an extent that when Hadim Suleiman's envoy reached Mahmud's court a few days later with the gift of a robe of honor, Mahmud angrily refused the gift, responding with the terse message that a servant who presents a robe to a sultan "does not understand his rank."[40] Hadim Suleiman was deeply offended, so much so that, according to one contemporary source, upon hearing this news he flew into a blind range and exclaimed, "when that vizier came to see me, I should have solved things by having him hung by the neck!"[41] From that moment, he was said "to harbor nothing but hatred for that king and his viziers."[42] The feeling, apparently, was mutual, and shortly thereafter Mahmud ordered the withdrawal of all of his forces from Diu and a unilateral retreat to the interior.[43]

Virtually all surviving accounts of this breakdown in Ottoman-Gujarati relations agree that it was a critical factor in the ultimate failure of the siege of Diu. Hajji ad-Dabir, the author of the nearly contemporary "Arabic History of Gujarat," summed

FIGURE 3.1 The city of Aden, built inside the crater of an extinct volcano, ranked among the most heavily fortified port cities in maritime Asia. Source: Georg Braun and Franz Hogenburg, *Civitates Orbis Terrarum*, vol. 1 (Cologne, 1572).

up Hadim Suleiman's shortcomings with these words: "Had he been courteous, he would have received what he desired, but he was harsh and obstinate. Nor was anyone inclined towards him or on conciliatory terms with him. He therefore accomplished nothing."[44]

Even so, there is a sense in which this diplomatic fracas—however instrumental Hadim Suleiman's behavior had been in provoking it—was also symptomatic of a more profound shift in Gujarati politics, which can be said to have claimed the pasha as a hapless (if not entirely innocent) victim. Here it should be remembered that when Sultan Bahadur had originally invited the Ottomans to intervene in the affairs of Gujarat three years before, he had just suffered a humiliating battlefield defeat at the hands of the Mughals and was on the verge of voluntarily surrendering the city of Diu to the Portuguese. At that desperate moment, an alliance with Istanbul must have seemed to Bahadur as the only reasonable chance he had of preserving his throne. But in the intervening three years, there had been great changes afoot: Bahadur himself had been treacherously killed by the Portuguese, the Mughals had unexpectedly retreated to Delhi, and the new sultan, Bahadur's son Mahmud, now had little desire (or incentive) to invite yet another foreign occupying force into his country.

All of this raises the possibility that the appearance of Mahmud's army at Diu in 1538 may well have been arranged merely to avoid a public loss of face with the Ottoman commander. As Mahmud must have suspected, Hadim Suleiman, having invested so much in the campaign, was unlikely to simply return Diu's fortress to its previous ruler should he manage to capture it. So it seems more than plausible that the young sultan was, from the beginning, eager to find any convincing pretext to back out of an alliance inherited from his father, and for which he himself had never displayed any particular enthusiasm.

Along these same lines, we can also detect signs of a growing rift within the upper echelons of Mahmud's court, which appears to have become increasingly divided between Hoja Safar's pro-Ottoman Rumi elite (openly favored during Bahadur's reign) and the province's more traditional indigenous warrior aristocracy, headed by Ulu Khan. As a relatively weak ruler who was still barely an adolescent at his accession to the throne, Sultan Mahmud seems to have fallen under the sway of this latter group, who resented the Rumis as interlopers and—following the battlefield defection to the Mughals of Mustafa Bayram in 1535—increasingly saw their loyalty to the sultan as suspect.[45] Even worse, since these Rumis were themselves originally Ottomans and had been instrumental in bringing Hadim Suleiman to Diu in the first place, members of Ulu Khan's more indigenously rooted faction feared that an Ottoman victory over the Portuguese would only serve to further entrench Rumi power in Gujarat. Suggestive of such anti-Ottoman sentiments, Hadim Suleiman would later accuse Ulu Khan of openly favoring the Portuguese over his own troops during the siege and describe him as "a man so deeply in the clutches of the infidels that he no longer knew his own religion."[46]

On the battlefield, the practical result of this complex web of internal rivalries was that forces loyal to Hoja Safar and his contingent of Rumis remained at the pasha's side and continued to cooperate with the Ottomans throughout the siege of Diu, but without support either from Sultan Mahmud or from any other local Muslim power. And as the weeks wore on, casualties mounted, and stocks of gunpowder and provisions were depleted, even the relationship between Hadim Suleiman and Hoja Safar began to fray.[47] For this reason, the pasha's decision to lift the siege and withdraw at precisely the moment that victory seemed within reach must be seen as more than simply the result of his cowardice or lack of judgment. Instead, it was a move forced on him by an absence of clear alternatives and by an increasingly isolated diplomatic position. Having lost most of his Indian allies through a combination of his own clumsy diplomacy and circumstances beyond his control, Hadim Suleiman could no longer be sure of his ability to keep possession of Diu even if he managed to conquer it. Rather than risking the remainder of his forces in such a dubious venture, he decided that the best course of action was to return to Yemen and, at the very least, consolidate his position there.[48]

THE CONSOLIDATION OF OTTOMAN POWER IN YEMEN

However controversial Hadim Suleiman's decision to retreat from Diu may have been, the final Yemeni chapter of his expedition proved an unequivocal success.

Heading first for the Hadrami port city of Shihr, whose ruler, Sultan Badr, had remained a faithful Ottoman ally throughout the campaign, the pasha used the power of his fleet to help Badr extend control as far up the coast as Dofar, and conferred on him the title of Ottoman *sancak begi* ("Lord of the Standard") in return for an annual tribute of ten thousand *ashrafis* payable to the treasury in Egypt.[49] Then, after reinforcing the Ottoman garrison in Aden, he overthrew Nakhoda Ahmed, the independent ruler of Zebid, and established Ottoman control over Ta'izz and Mocha as well.[50] Finally, before heading north to perform a pilgrimage to Mecca and return to Istanbul, he introduced a formal Ottoman administrative structure to all of coastal Yemen, placing Mustafa al-Neshar, a son of the former Grand Vizier Biyikli Mehmed Pasha, in charge of the province.[51]

By almost any standard, this consolidation of Ottoman power in Yemen served as ample compensation for the embarrassment of Hadim Suleiman's hasty retreat from Gujarat. By 1538, Diu probably ranked as the most heavily defended fortress in all of the Estado da Índia. But even for the Portuguese, its strategic significance paled in comparison with control of the Red Sea, which could be guaranteed only by establishing a military presence in Yemen. In fact, nearly a decade earlier, on the eve of the first abortive Portuguese attempt to take Diu from Sultan Bahadur in 1531, an anonymous Portuguese report had warned that possession of Diu "does not mean that India will no longer be in danger from the Ottomans, for they have many other ports of entry, and unless a fortress is built in the port at the gate of the straits [in Yemen], India will never be free from oppression . . . for fear of the Rumis."[52]

Less than a decade later, such fears had become a reality. Hadim Suleiman's conquest of Yemen allowed the Ottomans to build naval bases and customs houses in Aden and Mocha, giving them a permanent foothold in the Arabian Sea.[53] This Ottoman presence in Yemen also ensured continued cooperation with Hoja Safar, who despite the reverse at Diu was able to reconsolidate his position in the nearby port city of Surat, where he began to construct naval fortifications of his own (Figure 3.2).[54] Soon enough, Surat would emerge as the principal transit point for sea traffic between Gujarat and the Red Sea, rendering Portuguese control of Diu to a certain extent superfluous.[55]

By 1540, Portuguese officials were therefore painting the future of their maritime empire in the darkest of hues. The future viceroy João de Castro, for instance, wrote a letter to the king that year confirming that the Ottomans were now firmly in control of all the ports of Yemen and adding:

> It seems hardly necessary to point out just how damaging and prejudicial these new neighbors will be for us, for merely by maintaining their present position they represent such a threat, and will oblige us to undertake such enormous expenses [to provide for our own defense], that it won't take much before we are forced to abandon this land entirely.[56]

So vastly improved was the Ottomans' position following the conquest of Yemen, in fact, that some Portuguese began to speculate that it, and not Diu, had been Hadim

A View of Surat in the East Indies.
Engrav'd for Drake's Voyages.

FIGURE 3.2 A view of the fortress of Surat, constructed in the mid-sixteenth century. Between 1538 and 1573, Surat was governed by an uninterrupted series of Rumi commanders and was a center of both trade with the Ottoman Empire and pro-Ottoman political activity. Source: Edward Cavendish, *A New Universal Collection of Voyages and Travels, from the Earliest Accounts to the Present Time* (London, 1771).

Suleiman's primary objective all along.[57] True or not, the sultan in Istanbul certainly seems to have been satisfied with Hadim Suleiman's performance. Despite several fanciful accounts to the contrary by some authors from Muslim India, who insisted that the pasha was reprimanded (or even executed!) by the sultan upon his return to the capital, in truth Hadim Suleiman received a promotion—not once, but repeatedly.[58] By 1541, he was grand vizier, proving that Yemen now held the keys not only to India but to the Ottoman Empire as well.

THE FIRST OTTOMAN-PORTUGUESE PEACE NEGOTIATIONS

Hadim Suleiman's failure at Diu notwithstanding, his list of accomplishments during the 1538 campaign was substantial. The size of his armada had demonstrated a capacity to mobilize men and resources on a terrifying scale. His diplomacy, for all its flaws, had for the first time in history joined Muslims from East Africa to Southeast Asia in an active military alliance. And his conquest of Yemen secured a direct sea route from Egypt to the Indian Ocean and a permanent Ottoman military presence in the Arabian Sea. All of this left the Portuguese with no choice but to somehow come to terms with the new reality of Ottoman power. As such, 1538 witnessed not only the beginning of open warfare between Ottomans and Portuguese but also the start of the era of Ottoman-Portuguese diplomacy.

The first direct negotiations between Istanbul and Lisbon were initiated by Duarte Cataneo, an archetypal international man of mystery whose true motives and loyalties remain as impenetrable today as they did during his own lifetime. Originally, Cataneo was an Ottoman subject from the autonomous Genovese community of Chios, who seems to have become associated with Hadim Suleiman Pasha's intelligence apparatus sometime in the 1530s. Other details of his early biography are frustratingly absent, but in early 1538—only a few months before Hadim Suleiman's fleet would leave Suez for India—Cataneo somehow reached Portuguese Hormuz with a company of private merchants and, upon his arrival, demanded to speak with the Portuguese authorities about a matter of pressing importance for the Estado da Índia.[59] Once in the presence of the local governor, Cataneo explained that he had been sent to India as a spy to gather information for Hadim Suleiman's campaign, but confessed that since his conscience as a good Christian prevented him from carrying out this mission, his real hope was to help the Portuguese negotiate with the Ottomans before it was too late. Despite obvious reservations about his sincerity, the local authorities quickly sent him on to Goa. From there, the viceroy, persuaded of Cataneo's good intentions, arranged for his passage to Lisbon to speak directly with Dom João III.[60]

Cataneo arrived in Portugal in the middle of the following year, shortly after the first reports of Hadim Suleiman's siege of Diu and conquest of Yemen had reached Lisbon. In the panicked atmosphere this news provoked at court, Cataneo found a favorable audience for his soothing contention that the "real" design of the sultan was not to destroy Portuguese power in Asia but merely to obtain access to a reliable source of spices for his own market. Professing great confidence that an agreement, including a guarantee against further attacks, could be easily secured at terms acceptable to the Portuguese, he convinced the king to appoint him as part of an official Portuguese delegation to Istanbul, with wide authority to secure an armistice and negotiate a permanent settlement with the Ottomans.[61]

Since Cataneo had openly admitted being an Ottoman spy and a turncoat, it is perhaps not surprising that his role throughout the subsequent negotiation process would remain an ambiguous one. On the one hand, it is not inconceivable that Cataneo intended to negotiate in good faith and genuinely believed that an agreement was possible under the conditions he presented to the Portuguese court. But the terms that Dom João III authorized him to communicate to the sultan—including even those secret concessions that, according to Cataneo's instructions, he was to reveal only as a last resort—were far removed from anything the Ottomans would have considered a serious settlement. For this reason, it appears possible (indeed, likely) that Cataneo may have intentionally misrepresented the Ottoman position to secure for himself a lucrative appointment as ambassador, all the while continuing to act as a double agent for Hadim Suleiman.[62]

Dom João's offer consisted of the following terms: both in the Red Sea and in the Indian Ocean, the Ottomans were expected to relinquish all rights to navigation, promise to send no more armed fleets to the region, and even agree to garrison Aden with no more than the minimum number of troops needed for local defense. Meanwhile, Dom João demanded for himself virtually unlimited navigation and commercial rights, including unrestricted access for his own ships in the Red Sea and clearance for Portuguese merchants to trade freely in Aden and Jiddah under the same conditions as Muslim merchants. In exchange for all of this, Dom João declared a willingness to compromise his absolute monopoly over the pepper trade by granting the sultan permission to purchase up to three thousand quintals (roughly 130 metric tons) of Indian pepper every year. Even this concession, however, was subject to serious restrictions, including provisions that the pepper be delivered directly to Basra in Portuguese ships, that the sultan agree not to let any more pepper than this allotted amount pass through any of his ports, and that the Portuguese be given the right to police the straits of Hormuz and the Red Sea themselves to prevent any unauthorized trade. In addition, the Ottomans would be required to assist in capturing any independent Portuguese merchants who tried to sell spices in Ottoman ports without explicit permission from Lisbon. Finally, Dom João demanded access to Ottoman grain supplies for his merchants in the Mediterranean, insisting that Portuguese vessels be issued passes to purchase grain from Egypt and Syria without fear of attack from Ottoman corsairs.[63]

This offer, although the first ever presented by the Portuguese to the Ottoman sultan, was in most of its particulars consistent with agreements Lisbon had concluded with principalities throughout the Indian Ocean during the first decades of the sixteenth century, including the treaty that had been imposed on Sultan Badahur of Gujarat in 1535. Generally speaking, the tried-and-true Portuguese strategy was to offer potentially hostile land-based rulers the right to trade in a limited quantity of spices and other goods. In exchange, the crown demanded formal recognition of its sovereignty over the commerce and navigation of the sea and a pledge to cooperate in enforcing the royal spice monopoly. Clearly, Dom João hoped to somehow co-opt the Ottomans into this already established system.

But in doing so, Dom João displayed a willingness to forsake at least one fundamental cornerstone of Portuguese diplomacy in the Indian Ocean: an inveterate hostility to whatever Muslim power controlled Egypt and the Red Sea. And this in itself was a concession of no small consequence, since the Portuguese continued to imagine their imperial venture as a crusade, and insisted that the ultimate goal of their operations in the Indies was the conquest of Egypt and the liberation of the Holy Land from Muslim rule. Thus, even if the specific terms of Dom João's offer to the Ottomans appear uncompromising, the fact that the offer was made at all must have seemed, at least to the Portuguese, a dramatic break with the past. However tentatively, the Portuguese crown was adapting to the new realities of Ottoman power in the post-1538 world. By offering the sultan access to Portuguese pepper and de facto recognition of Ottoman land-based sovereignty in Egypt and Yemen, Dom João hoped to salvage what he could of Portuguese claims to sovereignty at sea.

Against this background, the Ottoman counterproposal to Dom João's offer, sent back to Lisbon with Cataneo in the summer of 1540, deserves particular attention as the earliest surviving historical source in which the Ottomans explicitly proclaimed their own ambitions in the Indian Ocean. One potentially surprising element of this proposal is therefore its indication that the Ottomans do seem to have seriously entertained at least some aspects of Dom João's offer. The sultan agreed, for example, to grant Portuguese merchants in the Indian Ocean the right to trade in Ottoman ports. He also agreed, in principle, to limit Ottoman pepper imports from India to a preestablished maximum amount, provided that this quota was raised from three thousand quintals to a slightly higher figure of four thousand quintals a year. Interestingly, however, the sultan insisted that this pepper was to be supplied not by Portuguese ships from Goa, but instead by *Muslim* ships from the independent port city of Calicut. Similarly, although the sultan also agreed to grant the Portuguese access to a supply of Ottoman grain from Egypt, he only agreed to do so indirectly, through licensed French and Venetian intermediaries, rather than allowing the Portuguese to purchase the grain directly and transport it with their own ships.[64]

Behind each of these provisions, we can detect signs of a newly emerging Ottoman strategy focused not specifically on the Portuguese pepper monopoly, but rather on the broader problem of Portuguese maritime commercial dominance in the Indian Ocean. The sultan's apparent willingness to accept Portuguese-mandated limits on pepper imports, while refusing categorically to allow Portuguese vessels to be responsible for their importation, speaks directly to this issue. Equally striking are indications that, in addressing this problem of Portuguese commercial dominance, the sultan claimed to be speaking not in defense of his own interests, but instead as the guarantor of the rights of Muslim merchants everywhere. After insisting, for example, that his pepper allotment be transported in Muslim ships, the sultan then went even further, demanding "freedom for the Muslims of India to trade in white cloths, spices, and other merchandise of that land" and requesting an explicit guarantee that the Portuguese would "favor and respect all Muslims who want to trade peacefully" in any regions under their control. Meanwhile, the sultan flatly refused to accommodate Portuguese claims to maritime sovereignty by allowing unrestricted Portuguese patrols off the Arabian coast. Instead, he called for a line of demarcation to be drawn across the sea between the Arabian Peninsula and Zeyla on the East African coast. This would be established as the naval boundary between the two states, and both sides would agree not to cross it with armed fleets of any kind.[65]

This counteroffer was clearly unacceptable to the Portuguese, since granting Muslim merchants the right to trade freely would undermine the very foundation of their system for controlling the commerce of maritime Asia. Even more alarming, the Ottoman demand for a line of demarcation at sea was rightly seen as a direct challenge to the Portuguese claim to exclusive control over oceanic navigation. In substance, the first round of negotiations between Lisbon and Istanbul thus ended with a grim recognition from both sides that their differences were close to irreconcilable. Despite some encouraging signals that an accommodation on the limited question of pepper imports was possible, the Ottomans and Portuguese were oceans apart when it came to the larger issues of freedom of commerce and maritime sovereignty.

In the post-1538 world, these two issues were destined to assume an existential importance for the Estado da Índia. As the prospect of obtaining an acceptable negotiated settlement faded away, the Portuguese were therefore left with no other choice than to resume hostilities. In 1541, hoping to catch the Ottomans by surprise before they had a chance to fully consolidate their gains, the Portuguese Viceroy Estevão da Gama led a desperate counterstrike against Ottoman positions in the Red Sea.

THE PORTUGUESE EXPEDITION TO SUEZ IN 1541

Although not quite matching the size of Hadim Suleiman Pasha's armada of 1538, the fleet commanded by Estevão da Gama in 1541 was still the largest the Portuguese had ever assembled, consisting in all of more than forty vessels large and small and some 2,300 men. With this imposing force, the viceroy intended to sail across the Indian Ocean and penetrate deep into the Red Sea. Raiding coastal settlements along the way, his ultimate objective was to attack the main Ottoman naval base in Suez, where he hoped to burn the imperial fleet and permanently destroy its arsenal and shipyard.

Had he succeeded in doing so, it is certain that the Ottomans would have been compelled to reevaluate their newfound claims in the Indian Ocean and perhaps even reconsider the peace proposal Dom João had offered them two years earlier.[66] Almost all contemporary accounts agree, however, that the list of challenges facing the Portuguese mission were so great that its sucess was never a serious possibility. First of all, having never previously sailed so far into the Red Sea, the Portuguese were dangerously unfamiliar with its daunting natural impediments to navigation, which ranged from adverse winds and treacherous shoals to lack of fresh water and extreme heat. Moreover, the success of the Portuguese mission depended almost entirely on the element of surprise, a virtual impossibility given the size of their fleet and the Ottomans' intelligence network in the region. Before ever setting sail, in fact, the Portuguese learned that Hoja Safar in Surat had been informed of their preparations and was attempting to contact the Ottomans with details about da Gama's plan of attack.[67]

Such problems were only compounded once da Gama's forces arrived in the Red Sea in late January of 1541. Heading first for the Ethiopian port of Massawa, just inside the Bab al-Mandab, the viceroy quickly realized his fleet was too large and cumbersome for the mission at hand and divided his flotilla in two. He left the larger sailing ships and a thousand of his men in Massawa under the command of another member of his clan, Manuel da Gama, and continued north toward Suez with only his smaller and more numerous oared vessels. On the way, this reduced force was obliged by lack of provisions to stop once more and raid the port of Suakin, a decision da Gama later regretted because the engagement delayed his advance and gave the local Ottoman garrison an opportunity to send an updated warning to the authorities in Egypt.

As the fleet was further slowed by contrary winds during the grueling journey north, the crew began to suffer severely from the heat and lack of fresh water. By the end of March, the situation had become so desperate that da Gama was compelled to split his fleet yet again, sending the bulk of his remaining forces back to Massawa and proceeding to Suez with only sixteen of the lightest vessels and a skeleton crew of fewer than 250 men. These finally reached the heavily guarded arsenal at Suez in late April but were hopelessly unprepared to attack, as they found the port defended by a powerful battery of guns and no fewer than two thousand Ottoman cavalry. Greeted by a heavy barrage of artillery fire and outnumbered almost ten to one, Estevão da Gama had no choice but to call for a hasty retreat without even attempting a landing on shore (Figure 3.3).[68]

The Portuguese spent another excruciating month returning to Massawa. They continued to suffer losses from the elements under the scorching May sun, only to find the situation there no less bleak than the one they had left in Suez. The port's insalubrious climate and almost total lack of provisions had taken a frighteningly heavy toll on the Portuguese left behind, and the prospect of starvation had driven more than a hundred of them to rise up in mutiny. Threatening to kill their commanding officer, Manuel da Gama, when he tried to resist them, the mutineers had fled to the deserted hinterland, where they were quickly surrounded and cut down almost to the last man by a band of local tribesmen. Those remaining in Massawa would have certainly succumbed to the elements had it not been for the arrival of a few meager provisions from the emperor of Ethiopia.

Under such circumstances, pressed to the point of desperation by both the elements and his own rebellious troops, the viceroy ordered a hasty retreat to Goa. But even this return passage brought little relief to the beleaguered Portuguese force, as several of the fleet's smaller vessels were caught in a storm during the passage home and lost at sea with all hands.[69] Estevão da Gama's expedition thus ended as a failure of spectacular proportions. Countless men had been lost, resources had been wasted, and the Ottomans' position in the region seemed more secure than ever. Indeed, several participants in the campaign (including the future viceroy João de Castro) came away from the experience convinced that the Ottoman arsenal in Suez was "impregnable" and could never be a realistic target for future Portuguese attacks.[70]

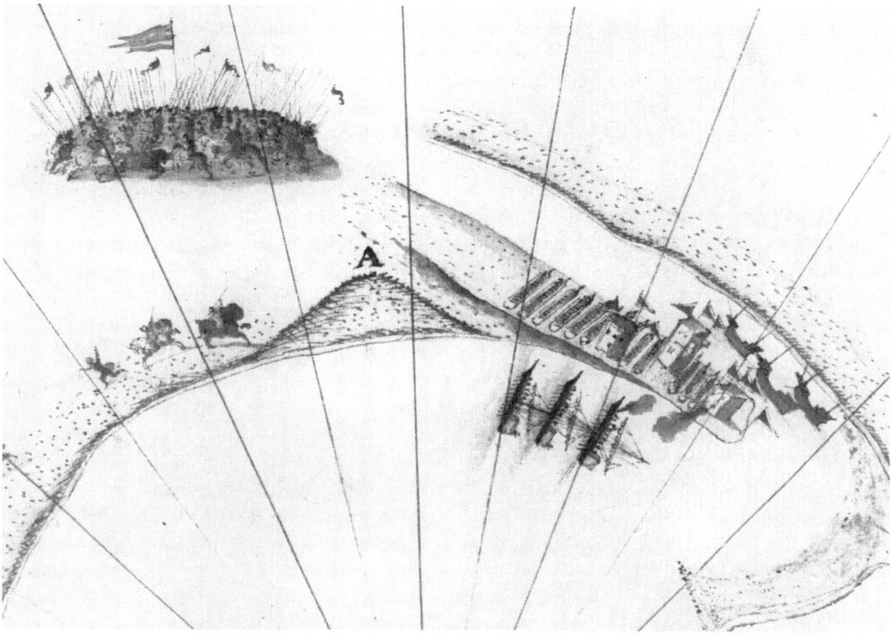

FIGURE 3.3 Three Portuguese galleys exchange gunfire with the Ottomans before the walls of Suez, while a large contingent of Sipahi cavalry waits in the background. Source: João de Castro, *Roteiro que fez Dom João de Castro da viajem que fezeram os Portugueses desde India atee Soez*, University of Minnesota James Ford Bell Library, Minneapolis, Ms. 1541 fCa, fol. 81b.

Only in distant Lisbon, where authorities had no way to receive updates from the front, was the king still banking on a Portuguese victory. From there, in anticipation of a softening in the Ottomans' stance after a successful strike on Suez, he had dispatched a second embassy to Istanbul reiterating his terms for a peace treaty. And in an act that must have come as a final ironic blow to da Gama's wounded pride, he had even issued an order to the viceroy, which awaited him upon his inglorious return to Goa, that until the crown's envoys had completed negotiations with the sultan, no further ships should be sent to south Arabia or otherwise be allowed to antagonize the Ottomans.[71]

Unfortunately for the Portuguese, the disastrous outcome of their Red Sea venture was not the only barrier to an improved negotiating climate with the Ottomans. Equally detrimental to their cause was the fact that, in the interim, Hadim Suleiman Pasha had reached a new peak of personal influence at the Ottoman court. Already promoted to the rank of second vizier upon his return to Istanbul in 1539, he was subsequently elevated to the grand vizierate in May 1541, just weeks after the final unfolding of da Gama's failed strike on Suez.[72] Predictably, his only response to the

Portuguese embassy that arrived in Istanbul that summer was to repeat the same unacceptable terms that had been offered to Duarte Cataneo in 1540.[73]

WAR SPREADS TO THE HORN OF AFRICA

While Estevão da Gama and his vanquished fleet returned to Goa to lick their wounds, a proxy war between Ottoman and Portuguese auxiliaries continued to rage in the horn of East Africa. Here, as early as 1527, the capable and ambitious Emir Ahmed Grañ al-Mujahid of Zeyla had begun to unite a considerable coalition of Muslim forces under his command and to systematically overrun territories held by Lebna Dengel, the reigning Christian emperor or "negus" of Ethiopia.[74] By the mid-1530s, thanks in part to a steady supply of firearms and artillery from Ottoman lands, Ahmed Grañ had assembled an impressive string of victories against the Ethiopians and seemed on the verge of replacing Lebna Dengel as the regional hegemon.[75] Then, in 1538, Ahmed further strengthened his hand through an open declaration of support for Hadim Suleiman Pasha as the Ottoman fleet made its way to India. As a reward for this public display of loyalty, upon the pasha's return from India, he granted Ahmed Grañ a shipment of firearms and a contingent of two hundred seasoned Ottoman musketeers from Yemen.[76] Their arrival gave the emir a decisive military advantage over his Ethiopian rivals, and within just a few months, his forces had killed one of Lebna Dengel's own sons in battle, captured another, and plundered the royal stronghold of Amba Geshen, where the accumulated wealth of the kings of Ethiopia had been held untouched for centuries.[77] Lebna Dengel himself was left a fugitive and practically bereft of forces, and province after province of his empire declared for the triumphant emir of Zeyla.

At this point, events in the Horn of Africa took a turn strangely reminiscent of those in Gujarat just a few years before, following the battlefield defeat of Sultan Bahadur at the hands of the Mughals in 1535. Just as Bahadur, pushed to the brink by "Mongols on land and infidels by sea," had been compelled to seek outside help from the Ottomans to preserve his throne, Lebna Dengel now turned to the Portuguese as the only power capable of rescuing him from the advancing Muslim armies and their terrible advantage in firearms. By means of the Portuguese cleric João Bermudez, who played a role as advisor to the Ethiopian court surprisingly similar to that played by Hoja Safar in Gujarat, Lebna Dengel sent an embassy to Lisbon offering to recognize the ecclesiastical authority of the pope in exchange for military assistance against Ahmed Grañ.[78]

The Portuguese accepted this offer and soon took concrete steps to make good their promise of support. A secondary objective of Estevão da Gama's expedition to the Red Sea in 1541, in fact, was to land troops in Massawa that would rendezvous with Lebna Dengel in the Ethiopian interior. But in yet another striking parallel to Sultan Bahadur's efforts to ally with the Ottomans, Lebna Dengel died of disease in

1540 before any Portuguese assistance could reach him. Nevertheless, Estevão da Gama dispatched a company of four hundred Portuguese musketeers under the command of his younger brother Christovão da Gama from Massawa in 1541, all of whom reached the court of Glawdewos, Lebna Dengel's son and successor, by the end of the year.

For the Portuguese, this small triumph was the only potentially positive outcome of Estevão da Gama's otherwise disastrous 1541 campaign. But the arrival of this contingent of Portuguese infantry at the Ethiopian court also held its own considerable risks by provoking a dangerous escalation of conflict in the region. Certainly Hadim Suleiman had no intention of allowing the gains of his ally Ahmed Grañ to be undermined so easily, having declared in his negotiations with the Portuguese that the Horn of Africa was an area he considered to be firmly within the Ottoman sphere of influence. And Ahmed Grañ, whose continuing success was very much dependent on access to Ottoman weapons and military expertise, was equally eager to deepen his relationship with Istanbul in order to shore up his gains in the Ethiopian highlands. At his request, within only a few weeks of the arrival of the Portuguese gunners in Ethiopia, Hadim Suleiman Pasha therefore dispatched a fleet of twelve Ottoman galleys from Suez, landing nine hundred musketeers and ten expert gunners at the African port of Beylul in August 1541.[79] In return, Ahmed Grañ agreed to formally recognize Ottoman suzerainty, pay 100,000 *okkas* of gold to the sultan, and send tribute worth another 2,000 okkas of gold annually to the Ottoman governor in Zebid, Mustafa al-Neshar.[80]

Ahmed Grañ began to reap the rewards of this strengthened alliance almost immediately, scoring a number of important victories against the combined Ethiopian and Portuguese forces during the next year. Eventually, he and his Ottoman auxiliaries faced the full strength of Emperor Glawdewos's reconstituted army and Christovão da Gama's four hundred Portuguese musketeers in a pitched battle at Wofla on August 28, 1542. This ended in lopsided victory for Ahmed Grañ and the Ottomans, in which the Ethiopian lines were broken, nearly two hundred Portuguese were killed, and Christovão da Gama and a number of his men were taken captive.[81]

At this moment of triumph, however—in a final parallel to events in Gujarat—a dispute arose between Ahmed Grañ and his Ottoman musketeers over how to deal with the Portuguese captured in the battle. The Ottomans, hoping to use these prisoners as a bargaining chip in their ongoing negotiations with Lisbon, demanded that they be handed over unharmed to the custody of provincial officials in Yemen. But Ahmed Grañ refused this request, instead executing da Gama with his own hands only hours after his capture. Enraged, the Ottoman commander and the bulk of his forces abandoned Ahmed and returned to Yemen, taking with them da Gama's decapitated head and the twelve Portuguese prisoners still alive.[82] Their departure prevented Ahmed Grañ from capitalizing on his victory, giving the Ethiopians and the remaining 120 Portuguese a chance to regroup. A year later, they staged a successful counterattack at the battle of Wayna Daga in which Ahmed Grañ was killed.[83]

In time, the armies of Zeyla would once more regroup under the leadership of Ahmed's nephew Abbas. But without the level of support from the Ottomans that his uncle had enjoyed, Abbas proved unable to extend his control much beyond the coastal lowlands around Zeyla itself. In this sense, the bloody conflict in the Horn of Africa ended in a limited victory for Glawdewos, who was able to maintain his throne and preserve the integrity of Christian rule in the Ethiopian highlands. Internationally, however, it was the Ottomans who emerged in a superior position by preventing the Portuguese from establishing a permanent military presence in Ethiopia. With Christovão da Gama dead, and most of his men either captured or killed, the Portuguese were henceforth reluctant to invest further in the region.[84] Limited ecclesiastical and mercantile exchanges between Ethiopia and Lisbon would continue in the years ahead, but Glawdewos could expect no more military assistance from the Portuguese. The Red Sea had become an Ottoman lake.

THE RISING TIDE OF OTTOMAN COMMERCIAL INFLUENCE

The Ottomans' success at stifling Portuguese adventurism in Ethiopia was indicative of the empire's rising fortunes throughout the Indian Ocean, as the consolidation of Ottoman power began to reap a series of tangible benefits far beyond the confines of the Red Sea. This trend is particularly noticeable in the commercial realm, as the early 1540s witnessed a dramatic increase in the activities of Ottoman merchants across an extensive swath of the Indian Ocean.[85] In 1542, the Portuguese chronicler Gaspar Correia recorded that the Ottomans had established a permanent factor (commercial representative) in the African port of Massawa—the same port that had been occupied by Estevão da Gama's fleet only months before.[86] In the same year, eight Ottoman vessels were sighted around the Maseira islands off the coast of southern Arabia, and the increasing prominence of Ottoman merchants was noted even in Portuguese-held Hormuz.[87] Around the same time, the Portuguese captain of Mozambique reported his fleet's destruction of an Ottoman vessel caught trading in Mogadishu, and complained of the presence of Ottoman ships up and down the Swahili Coast.[88] By 1545, the new Portuguese Viceroy João de Castro warned that merchants from the Ottoman Empire had even begun to appear in the distant trading centers of Pegu and Bengal.[89]

This mounting evidence of Ottoman commercial ascendancy eventually undermined Portuguese confidence to such an extent that, in 1545, the viceroy organized an unprecedented grand council, inviting all of the most prominent officials of the realm to discuss the possibility of unilaterally abandoning the blockade of the Red Sea in favor of a policy of free trade throughout the Indian Ocean.[90] Although the eventual outcome of this council's debate was a reaffirmation of the status quo, the fact that it was held at all was indicative, in the wake of Ottoman gains, of just how much the political and economic landscape of the Indian Ocean had changed since Hadim Suleiman Pasha's expedition to Diu in 1538.

Indeed, the extent of this change could be measured not only in the waning confidence of the Portuguese but also in a corresponding rise in Ottoman ambitions, palpably expressed by a newly grandiose nomenclature that imperial bureaucrats in the region began to employ. The Ottoman fleet stationed at Suez, for example, which had been known since the 1520s simply as the Red Sea Fleet (*Baḥr-i Aḥmer Filosu*) or Suez Fleet (*Süveys Filosu*), was grandly renamed by Hadim Suleyman Pasha as the Indian Armada (*Hind Donānması*).[91] Similarly, the admiral in charge, previously known as the Captain of Egypt (*Mıṣır Ḳaptanı*), was illustriously redubbed Admiral of the Indies (*Ḳapūdān-ı Hind*).[92] Soon enough, these semantic changes would give way to more material expressions of rising Ottoman power, although Hadim Suleiman Pasha would not remain in office long enough to oversee them.

HADIM SULEIMAN'S FALL FROM POWER AND THE OTTOMAN OFFENSIVE OF 1546

Hadim Suleiman Pasha's three-year term as grand vizier ended under the cloud of scandal in November 1544, and he died shortly thereafter. The proximate cause for his dismissal was a series of charges, leveled by his political rivals at court, of financial improprieties during his governorship of Egypt, including claims that he had misused state funds allocated for the Ottoman fleet in Suez and had seized part of Sultan Bahadur's considerable treasury for unauthorized purposes.[93] Given the pasha's demonstrable Machiavellian streak, there seems every reason to believe that these charges had at least some basis in fact. But regardless of the truth or falsehood of his alleged misconduct, Hadim Suleiman's single-minded focus on the affairs of the Indian Ocean was probably in itself an important reason for his eventual downfall. Other Ottoman power brokers, with their own bases of support in other areas of the empire, had grown tired of investing so much in the Indian Ocean theater. By 1544, they were ready to push the elderly and abrasive pasha aside and move the empire in a different direction more conducive to their own interests.

In the years to come, this change in leadership would hold serious implications for the Ottoman Age of Exploration. In the immediate term, however, the effect of Hadim Suleiman's dismissal was mitigated by the fact that virtually all of the key administrative, naval, and military posts in the frontier districts of Egypt, Yemen, the Hijaz, and even Iraq continued to be staffed by his clients and personal appointees. As a result, Ottoman policy during the years immediately following the grand vizier's removal from office displayed such a degree of continuity with the period of his greatest influence that, by 1546, his clients and allies were ready to launch a new round of attacks against the Portuguese by both land and sea. In some respects, this renewed offensive may even have benefited from the pasha's absence, allowing the

Ottomans to coordinate more effectively with far-flung Muslim allies who had been left gun-shy by Hadim Suleiman's heavy-handed diplomacy.

As in 1538, the Ottomans' most important collaborator remained Hoja Safar, who was still governor of the Gujarati port of Surat and still intent on doing everything within his power to recapture Diu from the Portuguese. With news of Hadim Suleiman's dismissal paving the way for a reorientation of Gujarati politics, Safar was therefore able to convince his sovereign, Mahmud III, of the necessity of a renewed attack on Diu.[94] Meanwhile, he also kept in constant contact with the Ottomans by means of his relative Mustafa al-Neshar, the governor of Zebid in Yemen until 1545 and, like Hoja Safar, another veteran of the 1538 campaign.

Operations began when, at Hoja Safar's urging, Mustafa al-Nashar agreed to send a shipment of artillery and five hundred janissaries directly to Diu from the Ottoman base in Mocha.[95] With the armies of Sultan Mahmud and Hoja Safar already surrounding the city, this force of Ottoman auxiliaries made a dramatic entrance into Diu's harbor on April 18, 1546, "waving Turkish flags, firing a great volley of muskets, and indulging in all of the bizarre and overbearing pageantry customary of that barbarous nation," in the words of Diogo do Couto.[96] The siege began on the very same day, and as news of the outbreak of hostilities spread, Muslim merchants up and down the coast of India began to refuse to trade with the Portuguese in anticipation of a speedy victory for Hoja Safar and his allies.[97]

Such confidence proved premature, for the second siege of Diu devolved into an even bloodier and more protracted struggle than the first had been, with fighting raging for months and casualties on both sides reaching atrocious heights. Hoja Safar himself was killed on the battlefield by an artillery bombardment, as were numerous high-ranking officers on the Portuguese side, including the viceroy's son.[98] The author of the "Arabic History of Gujarat" described the situation bluntly: "Many of the combatants were killed by gunfire; others died of putrified air; very few were left alive."[99] As the siege wore on, Muslim sappers were able to breach Diu's walls in several places, and small numbers of men even managed to briefly penetrate inside the fortress. But in the end, with both sides nearing the point of exhaustion, the Portuguese were saved by the timely arrival of a relief fleet from Goa. The second siege of Diu ended, like the first, in failure.[100]

For the Rumi elite of Gujarat, the defeat came as a crushing blow whose devastating effect was compounded by the loss of their leader, Hoja Safar. While his body still lay on the battlefield, the former galley slave-turned-governor was replaced by his son Rajab, who was given the title Rumi Khan and became the new head of Gujarat's Rumi community in his father's stead.[101] In this way, at least the integrity of Gujarat's pro-Ottoman faction was preserved. But no group had invested as much during the siege, or suffered as heavy losses, as the Rumis. Their second major defeat in eight years was both bitter and definitive. Never again would the Rumis of Gujarat directly challenge Portuguese control of Diu.

From the Ottoman imperial perspective, on the other hand, the situation was hardly as grim, for the siege still served a useful purpose even in failure. Although the Portuguese had defended their city, doing so had required an almost superhuman effort in which they had called upon every spare resource available in the Estado da Índia. And with all of their forces concentrated on Diu, they were unable to counter advances on other fronts. As a result, the Ottomans were left with a relatively free hand in what was for them an equally important theater of operations: the Persian Gulf.

Here the Ottomans launched a two-pronged assault that began just as the strength of their allies in Diu was starting to falter. Hostilities commenced in August 1546, with the departure of a small squadron of four oar-powered warships from the Ottoman naval base in Aden. This squadron headed quickly up the Arabian coast, stopping first in Shihr to help the loyal Ottoman vassal Sultan Badur capture Qishn, a neighboring port city recently allied with the Portuguese. From there, the vessels proceeded next to Qalyat, which was also attacked, and then sailed as far as the Portuguese stronghold of Muscat. Taking the Portuguese garrison stationed there by surprise, the Ottomans stormed the harbor, sacked the port, and captured a merchant vessel anchored there before finally turning around and heading back toward Aden.[102]

Meanwhile, more than a thousand miles to the east, a much larger Ottoman force was beginning to amass around Basra, a major international center of trade occupying a commanding position at the entrance to the Persian Gulf, and a prize long coveted by the Portuguese. Until the early 1540s, Basra had been ruled by Emir Rashid, a loyal Ottoman vassal who, ever since the Ottoman conquest of Baghdad in 1534, had consistently demonstrated his allegiance to the empire by reading the Friday *ḫuṭbe* and striking money in Sultan Suleiman's name.[103] After Rashid's death in 1543, however, control of the city had passed to Sheyh Yahya of the Benu Aman, an ambitious tribal leader by no means favorably disposed towards the Ottomans. By using Basra as a base to gradually extend his control up the Tigris and Euphrates rivers, Sheyh Yahya had begun to restrict the free movement of merchants between Ottoman lands and the Persian Gulf and also to make friendly overtures to the Portuguese in Hormuz.[104] With the future control of the Persian Gulf now hanging in the balance, the Ottomans therefore pounced on the opportunity to take possession of the city themselves before the Portuguese had a chance to intervene.[105]

Ayas Pasha, the governor-general of Baghdad, was the Ottoman official in charge of the campaign. He began by building a new fortress at Corna, just upriver from Basra, and then sent a letter to Sheyh Yahya demanding that the gates of the city be opened to his troops in preparation for an offensive strike against the Portuguese in Hormuz. Refusing the order, Sheyh Yahya instead forwarded this letter to Luiz Falcão, the captain of Hormuz, and offered to hand over Basra's citadel to the Portuguese in exchange for help in defending the city against the Ottomans.[106] His tribal allies in the Shatt al-Arab sent a letter of their own to Falcão with a similar request for help, ending their plea with the following warning:

> The intention of the Sultan is to seize from the Portuguese the navigation of the sea...believe this and come quickly! If the Ottomans take Basra there will be nothing left to stop them from moving against you and your territories, since the route through it is much shorter than through either Suez or Jiddah.[107]

The Portuguese in Hormuz obviously agreed. One official, writing to the viceroy in India on November 30, 1546, warned:

> Sir, these are very dangerous men and very experienced in the ways and the arts of war...they have already taken control of Mecca [and the Red Sea], and if they also build a fortress in Basra they will be able to send all the ships they possess in the other sea around to this side, an eventuality which represents the greatest possible danger for all of India.[108]

A week later, the captain of Hormuz wrote to Sheyh Yahya promising help, and then sent a letter to the viceroy asking that a fleet be sent from Goa as quickly as possible.[109] His plea, however, fell on deaf ears, for the Portuguese in India, thoroughly exhausted by the defense of Diu, were in no condition to provide help. With nothing more than local resistance to oppose him and with a force of more than three thousand troops at his disposal, Ayas Pasha easily conquered Basra and put Sheyh Yahya to flight. Almost without firing a shot, the Ottomans took possession of yet another strategic outlet onto the Indian Ocean.

BILAL MEHMED PASHA AND THE SECOND ROUND OF OTTOMAN-PORTUGUESE NEGOTIATIONS

Following the conquest of Basra, conventional wisdom throughout the Estado da Índia held that an Ottoman invasion of Hormuz was only a matter of time. But to the genuine surprise of the Portuguese, the new masters of Basra instead expressed an unprecedented willingness to negotiate with their counterparts at the opposite end of the Persian Gulf. As early as February 1547, less than two months after Ayas Pasha's conquest of the city, a letter arrived in Hormuz from Bilal Mehmed Pasha, the first Ottoman governor of the newly incorporated province of Basra. Addressed to the Portuguese Captain Luis Falcão, the letter presented a reasoned justification for the seizure of the city, explaining that Sheyh Yayha, through his unlawful attempts to impede the safe passage of merchants and merchandise between Ottoman lands and the Persian Gulf, had left the authorities with no other choice. Since the Ottoman state had been compelled to act by a responsibility to defend the principles of free trade, Bilal Mehmed went on to suggest that it was also in the state's interest to establish a peaceful trading relationship with the Portuguese. He wrote:

> For this reason, we find that it would be most beneficial to establish friendship with you, and to reach whatever kind of agreement is necessary to allow your ships and your merchants, along with their goods, to come and go under the protection of our powerful and just Sultan and without risk of damage or loss of any kind. Do not mistrust these words, or think that between them and what lies in my heart there is a discrepancy of any sort, for thus we shall be friends, both with you and with your companions in India, such that our friendship will be the envy of men to the four corners of the world.... I therefore request that you forward this letter of mine to India and to all the lands [under your possession] so that [merchants from all those parts] may come and go and trade freely and bring your wares to my lands and my wares to yours. Do this and we shall have no more cause for disagreement. Otherwise, much the contrary shall be the case.[110]

Behind the surprisingly conciliatory tone of this letter lay the foundations of a maturing Ottoman policy in the Indian Ocean—one based more than ever on a position of strength vis-à-vis the Portuguese. As in previous negotiations between Lisbon and the Ottomans, Bilal Mehmed reiterated a claim of sweeping Ottoman jurisdiction over trade-related affairs, presenting the sultan as the ultimate guarantor of commercial interests both within the borders of his own state and throughout the larger Indian Ocean world. With imperial forces now firmly in control of Basra as well as Yemen, Bilal Mehmed also made clear that the Ottomans were capable of enforcing this claim. But at the same time, the pasha's letter gave every indication that a lasting peace between his sovereign and the Portuguese was not only possible but also mutually beneficial. If the Portuguese would abandon their wasteful and ultimately futile attacks on Muslim shipping, he reasoned, they could be more than compensated for any loss of prestige through a new and profitable trading relationship with the Ottomans. The alternative was a continuation of hostilities, which the past few years had shown would bring the Portuguese only continued hardships and mounting expenses.

This proposal, framed in such thoroughly pragmatic terms, provoked widespread Portuguese soul-searching, with the viceroy calling a second grand council to debate the arguments for and against accepting it. Once again, as in 1545, Portuguese leaders ultimately decided that to abandon their established policies and embrace a system of free trade under Ottoman auspices was politically unacceptable, regardless of the benefits.[111] But this time around, there also emerged a vocal group of dissenters from within the Portuguese ranks who favored a deal despite the political costs.[112] In their view, continuing to maintain an anti-Ottoman embargo when faced with the new realities of Ottoman power in the Persian Gulf was foolhardy. Unlike the Red Sea, which was distant from Portuguese centers of trade and in any case closed to Christian merchants, they argued that Basra was close, easily accessible, and almost impossible to seal off from contact with Hormuz.[113]

Within a very short time this dissident view proved prescient, as Portuguese merchants and even high-ranking state officials soon found the temptation to trade in Basra, despite ongoing strict prohibitions from Goa, impossible to resist. Portuguese records show that Dom Manuel de Lima, who replaced Luis Falcão as the new captain of Hormuz in the spring of 1547, maintained a friendly correspondence with Bilal Mehmed Pasha throughout his term in office, even keeping a personal trading representative in Basra under the pretext of gathering intelligence about the Ottoman arsenal there.[114] By the end of his term, illicit trade between Basra and Hormuz had become so commonplace that de Lima himself sent agents to conduct business in the city on almost a weekly basis.[115]

Viceroy João de Castro made valiant attempts to stop this activity, repeatedly threatening all guilty parties with imprisonment, but the situation soon passed the point of no return.[116] By 1551, on the Ottoman side at least, it was even institutionalized: The Ottoman tax code for the Province of Basra, promulgated in that year, included a special provision that allowed the captain of Hormuz to send a factor to Basra and to buy and sell a certain quantity of goods tax-free.[117] Ottoman tax records, moreover, reveal that trade in Basra was not only booming as a result of these arrangements but was also directly benefiting the state. In 1551, the same year that the new Basran tax code was introduced, proceeds from trade-related tariffs amounted to a full two-thirds of total provincial revenues—by far the highest proportion of any Ottoman province of the Indian Ocean region.[118] Slowly but surely, the foundations of the Portuguese anti-Ottoman blockade were crumbling around them.[119]

CONCLUSION: HISTORY'S FIRST WORLD WAR

By the second half of the 1540s, relations between the Ottomans and Portuguese had, at least temporarily, acquired a certain measure of stability. But the preceding eight years, from 1538 to 1546, had been a period of bitter and almost continuous warfare between Istanbul and Lisbon, conducted across an enormous area spanning the full breadth of the Indian Ocean. On the high seas, Ottoman corsairs and their Muslim allies had faced off against the Portuguese fleet, staging coordinated attacks in theaters of operation from south India to the Arabian coast. In the Horn of Africa and in Southeast Asia, elite units of Ottoman and Portuguese musketeers—the sixteenth-century equivalent of commandoes—had locked horns in guerilla wars to prop up friendly local regimes and destabilize their rivals. And from their main bases of supply in Suez and Goa, both sides had launched massive armadas, consisting of thousands of men and dozens of ships, against each other's most important maritime redoubts in Egypt and India. Together, these violent encounters amounted to nothing less than the first truly global armed conflict the world had ever seen (Map 3.1).

What was it about the period from 1538 to 1546 that allowed war between two Mediterranean powers to be carried out on a geographic scale unimaginable only a few decades before? Technology undoubtedly counted as one important factor, as

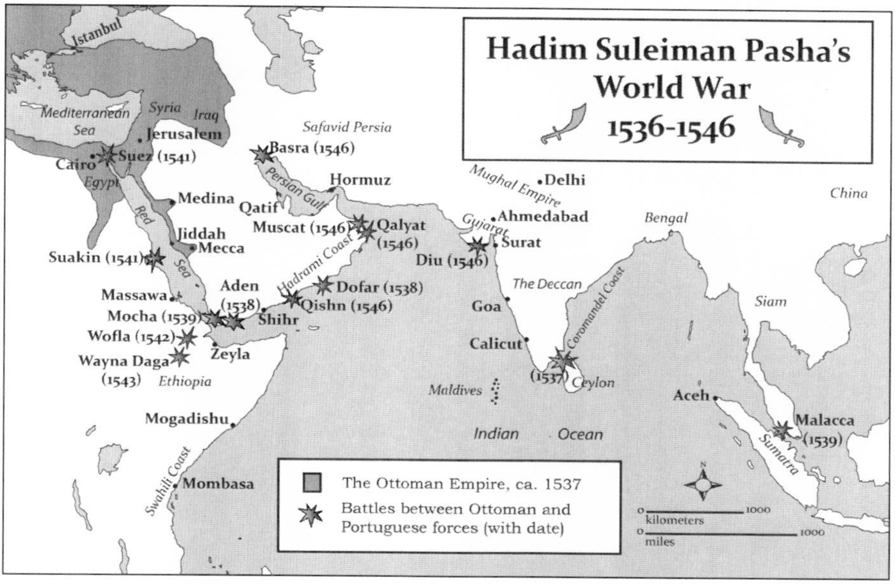

MAP 3.1 Hadim Suleiman Pasha's world war, 1536–1546

the constantly expanding range of Portuguese activities in the Indian Ocean, enabled by their advanced sailing ships and gunpowder weapons, inevitably pushed Muslims throughout the region into a closer relationship with the Ottomans. Equally important was the developing worldview of each side, since it was only in the 1530s, thanks to nearly two decades of sustained effort, that the Ottomans finally accumulated a critical mass of actionable intelligence that allowed them to think strategically on a geographic scale comparable to their Portuguese rivals. The single most critical factor in the globalization of war during this period, however, lay elsewhere, in the realm of political ideology, as Ottoman statesmen began to draw a direct link between their state's legitimacy and its ability to use sea power to protect the interests of Indian Ocean merchants. This proved a powerful motivating force for the formulation of Istanbul's policies, and even more important, it provided an ideological basis for Muslims throughout the Indian Ocean to draw a link between their own well-being and the fortunes of a distant Ottoman state. For the first time, the sultan's authority could extend across the sea lanes, rather than being limited to the land-based territories in his immediate possession.

Admittedly, this interpretation stands in stark contrast to most existing scholarship on the politics of the early modern world, which remains committed to the idea that "sovereignty over the seas" was a specifically Western concept foreign to the political thought of "Islamic land-based states." As a result, the Ottoman Empire and its allies in the Indian Ocean have been typically portrayed as states preoccupied with the acquisition of territory and, in consequence, guided by a political logic fundamentally different from the trade-oriented maritime policies of the Portuguese. Sultan Bahadur of Gujarat is said to have neatly encapsulated this general attitude in a famously pithy quotation: "Wars by sea are merchants' affairs and of no concern to the prestige of kings."[120]

But with the benefit of a detailed narrative of facts on the ground (and on the sea!) during the crucial years from 1538 to 1546, we are now in a position to assert that Ottoman policy in the Indian Ocean was anything but unresponsive to maritime commercial interests. On the contrary, Ottoman military operations consistently focused on strategic centers of maritime trade, such as Mocha, Aden, Basra, and Diu; Ottoman negotiators repeatedly demanded free trade for Muslim merchants as a precondition for any peace settlement with the Portuguese; and tax registers confirm that customs receipts were a principal source of revenue for all of the Ottoman provinces bordering on the Indian Ocean. In short, the Ottomans, like the Portuguese, viewed maritime trade as the primary resource of the Indian Ocean region.

It would be an oversimplification, however, to present this concern for maritime affairs as the exclusive result of rising customs revenues or powerful trading interests, for religion, too, had a seminal role to play in this new formulation of state ideology. By advancing a claim to supreme leadership of the Muslim world based on the twin titles of caliph (*ḫalīfe*) and protector of the holy cities (*ḫādım al-ḥaremeyn*), the Ottoman sultan assumed a sacred responsibility to keep open and safe the pilgrimage routes to Mecca and Medina—a responsibility that became an essential component of his good standing as a ruler in the eyes of the faithful.[121] And since these pilgrimage routes were also sea routes inextricably linked with the patterns of maritime trade, the sea itself became a theater in which Ottoman claims to legitimacy in the international arena would be either reaffirmed or undermined, even while retaining its importance for the more mundane concerns of the market.

This formidable convergence of religious ideology and commercial interests goes a long way toward explaining the Ottomans' preoccupation with control of the sea even in areas far removed from the borders of the empire, as can be seen in the orders that Sultan Suleiman issued to Hadim Suleiman Pasha on the occasion of his departure for India in 1538. The sultan wrote:

> You who are Governor-general of Egypt, Suleiman Pasha, as soon as this imperial edict arrives, will immediately gather weapons, supplies, and provisions and prepare for holy war in Suez; Having equipped and outfitted a fleet and mustered a sufficient quantity of troops, you will cross over to India and capture and hold the ports of India; You will free that country from the harm caused by the Portuguese infidels, who have cut off the road and blocked the path to the sacred cities of Mecca and Medina (may God almighty ennoble them!), *and you will put an end to their depredations at sea.*[122]

The fact that the sultan framed these orders to Hadim Suleiman in terms of a holy war, but one that was intended first and foremost to defend maritime pilgrimage routes, confirms that the 1538 campaign was conceived as a direct challenge to Portugal's claim to maritime sovereignty in the Indian Ocean. In this sense, Hadim Suleiman Pasha's ensuing world war must be understood not simply as a conflict over territory or resources, but as an ideologically motivated struggle for control of the sea itself. Beginning in 1538, the Ottoman sultans and the kings of Portugal thus entered into what might be termed a dialectic of maritime sovereignty, in which each side's claim reflected the other, and both states became increasingly aware that their own legitimacy would ultimately rest on an ability to control the sea at the other's expense.

But even if, at a strictly theoretical level, both sides now aimed explicitly at control of the sea, the practical implications of achieving this objective pointed the two states in very different directions: For the Portuguese, "control" implied an ability to *prevent* merchants from traveling and trading as they wished, while for the Ottomans it meant precisely the reverse. Over time, this practical difference would inevitably benefit the Ottomans, since for them state ideology and the demands of the market converged felicitously, while the Portuguese were compelled to subordinate market forces to the demands of an ideologically motivated blockade. In other words, with Hadim Suleiman as its overbearing but inspired pilot, the Ottoman ship of state was sailing toward the Indian Ocean with the economic wind at its back. But in Istanbul, as a new leader prepared to take the helm and to plot a very different course for the empire, there were ominous storm clouds gathering on the horizon.

Four

RUSTEM PASHA VERSUS THE INDIAN OCEAN FACTION

1546–1561

Throughout the middle decades of the sixteenth century, Ottoman political life was dominated by the towering figure of Rustem Pasha, a quintessential palace insider raised in the sultan's household and blessed by his favor from an early age. According to one account, he had gained his first promotion while still a palace page in early adolescence, having cavalierly thrown himself from a second-story window to retrieve an article that had accidentally fallen from the sultan's hands.[1] Other promotions followed in rapid succession, and before long, Rustem also began to benefit from the affections of the sultan's wife, Hurrem Sultan, whose many acts of patronage culminated in an offer of marriage to her only daughter, Mihrimah, in the early 1540s. These nuptials sealed Rustem's political fortune—as well as Hurrem's reputation as the empire's supreme power broker—and forged a permanent alliance between the two that proved both formidable and resilient. Nominated to the grand vizierate only shortly thereafter, upon Hadim Suleiman's dismissal in November of 1544, Rustem went on to hold the position almost continuously until his death seventeen years later.[2]

During this prolonged term in office, Rustem left a recognizable stamp on nearly every aspect of Ottoman society, as he strove to reshape the empire according to a new model of governance that can only be described as a kind of bureaucratic parochialism. Under his tutelage, Ottoman law and the structures of the state administration were centralized, codified, and standardized across the empire.[3] State-sponsored artists and architects began to articulate a distinctively Ottoman visual vocabulary of repetitive forms and predictable motifs, noticeably different from the eclectic styles of earlier decades.[4] And Ottoman intellectuals, who had previously experimented with diverse and even messianic modes of expression, now developed a self-consciously classicizing literary voice that reflected a more integrated, monolithic consciousness of both the empire's past and its present.[5] Through all of these subtle changes, Rustem tried to foster a newly coherent sense of the Ottoman Empire as a society that was both self-contained and distinct from its neighbors. In so doing, as the pace of the empire's expansion began to slow and its physical boundaries hardened, Rustem hoped to create a reinvigorated basis on which to anchor the authority of the Ottoman central administration—with himself at its head.

What implications did this new Ottoman-centric mentality hold for the Ottoman Age of Exploration? One area of especially visible change is the new way in which Ottoman intellectuals began to imagine the Indian Ocean, since it was along the empire's fluid maritime frontier to the south that the ambitions of Rustem's predecessors most openly contradicted his own more restricted and parochial vision. From very early in his tenure, Rustem therefore encouraged a different kind of scholarship that, while still relevant to the political concerns of the region, departed dramatically in intent from the exuberant imperialist tracts of previous decades.

One case in point is the "Chronicle of Rustem Pasha," a history of the Ottoman Empire attributed to the grand vizier but probably ghostwritten by the renowned historian and geographer Matrakchi Nasuh. On the one hand, this work is remarkable among contemporary Ottoman chronicles for presenting a detailed account of recent Ottoman activity in Yemen, ranking, in fact, as the earliest general Ottoman history to include this region in its narrative.[6] Surprisingly, however, it does so in a way that virtually ignores Hadim Suleiman's expedition to India or any of the connections between Yemen and maritime Asia as a whole, thereby emphasizing the province's status as an integral part of the Ottoman Empire rather than as a strategic stepping-stone to a wider world. In this manner, both as a work of history and as an expression of the Ottomans' sense of self, Rustem's chronicle reflected the receding global ambitions that characterized the grand vizier's approach to international affairs.

A very similar set of priorities can be identified in the celebrated *Mir'ātü'l-Memālik* ("Mirror of Countries"), a memoir composed by the sea captain Seydi Ali Reis and presented to Rustem in 1560, following the author's return from a four-year epic journey through India, Afghanistan, Uzbekistan, and Iran.[7] This highly original text was a groundbreaking work of Ottoman narrative prose, retaining its appeal even today as perhaps the greatest Ottoman travel narrative ever composed. Yet ironically, by constantly exploiting its exotic subject matter to accentuate the "Ottoman-ness" of its author, Seydi Ali's memoir is at the same time a uniquely poignant expression of the Ottoman-centric chauvinism characteristic of Rustem's grand vizierate.

This constantly revisited theme of Ottoman-ness—communicated in a variety of ways throughout the text—is nowhere more explicit than at the conclusion of the narrative, when the author finally returns to Ottoman territory. Overcome with emotion after so many years spent outside the confines of the empire, Seydi Ali exuberantly exclaims that "in all the world there is no country comparable to the lands of Rum, no sovereign to equal our Padishah, and no military like the victorious army of the Ottomans!"[8] Then, after recounting the last few legs of the journey back to his empire's capital city, he leaves his readers with the following exhortation:

> He who wishes to profit from this narrative, let him remember that not in vain aspirations after greatness, but in quiet and contented mind lies the secret of the true strength which perishes not. But if in God's providence he should be driven from home, and forced to wander forth into the unknown, and perchance to be caught in the turbulent waters of the sea of adversity, let him still always keep in mind that love for one's native land is next to one's faith. Let him never cease to long for the day that he shall see his native shores again, and always, whatever befall, cling loyally to his Padishah. He who does this shall not perish abroad; God will grant him his desire in this world and in the next, and he shall rejoice in the esteem and the affection of his fellow countrymen.[9]

It bears considerable emphasis that, within the context of Seydi Ali's larger narrative, such sentiments are tinged with a special sense of bitterness because of the author's experiences while abroad. This is particularly true of his sojourn in India, where most of his traveling companions—in open defiance of Seydi Ali's wishes—had elected to stay and settle among the Rumi diaspora rather than return with him to Istanbul. Thus, alongside Seydi Ali's laudable devotion to his sovereign and love for his country, this passage (and his writings generally) also betrays both hostility to the Rumis of India and a general aversion to the idea of traveling the world and settling overseas—two sentiments that, as we shall see later, Seydi Ali shared with his patron Rustem.

By comparison, most other works produced during Rustem's grand vizierate are less noteworthy for what they say than for what they leave unsaid. With the solitary exception of Seydi Ali himself (who penned, in addition to his "Mirror of Countries," a technical manual for oceanic navigation aptly titled *Kitāb al-Muḥīṭ*, or "Book of the Ocean"), other Ottoman geographers of the period appear single-mindedly focused on describing and cataloguing the lands within the confines of the empire itself, while paying consistently little attention to what lay beyond, particularly in the Indian Ocean.[10] Similarly, histories and dynastic chronicles composed under Rustem's auspices typically devote a page or two to the grand vizier's own exploits along the Arabian frontier, after which the Indian Ocean as a whole simply disappears from the narrative, as if the Ottoman Empire no longer had any contact with the region at all.[11] And predictably, this inward turn of Ottoman intellectual life was accompanied by a parallel realignment of the empire's political priorities under Rustem, a change felt most fully in the realm of trade policy.

RUSTEM'S ECONOMIC POLICIES AND THE RISE OF THE INDIAN OCEAN FACTION

Unlike his predecessor Hadim Suleiman, who had consistently sought to maximize the free flow of trade across Ottoman lands from the Indian Ocean, Rustem professed a deep-seated suspicion of foreign merchants and generally favored an economic policy that subordinated mercantile interests to the needs of supplying the army and provisioning the Ottoman capital.[12] This is not to say that Rustem was above making certain exceptions to this principle when presented with an opportunity to line his own pockets, as contemporary Venetian observers were quick to point out.[13] But overall, rather than seeing the flow of goods in and out of the Ottoman Empire as a source of wealth and a reaffirmation of Ottoman prestige, Rustem seems to have viewed international trade primarily as a threat, a drain through which the precious metals and other strategic resources of the empire were being continually sucked away.[14]

Perhaps the best known arena in which Rustem implemented a series of tangible policy initiatives based on this larger autarchic vision is the Black Sea, which under his guidance was transformed from a relatively free commercial zone into an Ottoman lake from which foreign merchants were forbidden to trade.[15] In comparison, his policies in the Indian Ocean are less well understood, having remained unexplored by modern scholars. But if anything, Rustem's attitude toward the commerce of this region seems to have been based in an even greater degree of suspicion, for here his natural inclination to restrict trade was exacerbated by another factor: the cold calculus of personal vengeance.

Having originally clawed his way to a position of influence during the grand vizierate of his predecessor, the ruthless and calculating Hadim Suleiman—with whom Rustem had never enjoyed a close relationship—the young vizier had inevitably become the target of attacks by Hadim Suleiman's supporters as his own power increased. One of his bitterest early adversaries, in fact, was Hadim Suleiman's trusted associate Daud Pasha, the governor-general of Egypt since 1538 and a rival candidate for the hand of Rustem's future wife, the Princess Mihrimah.[16] During the early 1540s, competition between the two suitors for the princess's affections had grown intense, with Daud stooping so low as to spread a rumor—slanderously corroborated by the court physician Moses Hamon—that Rustem was unfit for marriage because he suffered from syphilis. Rustem was, in the end, able to disprove the rumors and receive the sultan's blessing to marry Mihrimah, but the public affront to his honor was not to be forgotten. He began to scheme for Hadim Suleiman's removal almost immediately, and was directly responsible for arranging the financial audit that led to the pasha's disgrace and downfall in 1544.[17]

Thereafter, the lingering effects of this rancorous factional infighting would continue to be felt well into Rustem's own tenure as grand vizier, as he plotted to ensure that his political rivals would never again be able to undermine his privileged position at court. Reasoning that the empire's Indian Ocean provinces, where Hadim Suleiman's influence had always been most deeply entrenched, constituted a natural base for his enemies, he resolved to actively stifle further expansion in the region to prevent his opponents from increasing their power. To this end, he even went so far as to openly oppose Ayas Pasha's conquest of Basra in 1546, refusing to supply troops for the expedition and dismissing the port as "a ruined place... worth nothing at all."[18]

In the following year, he took a similarly dim view of Bilal Mehmed's efforts to sign a trade agreement in Basra with the Portuguese in Hormuz.[19] But as strongly as Rustem may have opposed this and other free-trade measures, he was also in a certain sense powerless to stop them. As already described in the preceding chapter, Bilal Mehmed Pasha orchestrated an unprecedented expansion in trade with Hormuz even without Rustem's consent, and by 1551, his arrangement with local Portuguese authorities was permanently enshrined in Basra's provincial tax code. Similarly, in Egypt, Rustem's archrival Daud Pasha also remained in power throughout the 1540s, where he, too, continued to pursue a protrade policy of engagement with the Indian Ocean.

Thus, rather than the definitive turning away from the Indian Ocean that Rustem Pasha may have hoped for, the years of his grand vizierate developed into a protracted tug of war between the grand vizier himself and an emerging coalition of his opponents, hereafter referred to as the "Indian Ocean faction." In this struggle, Rustem strove to contain his adversaries by transforming the border regions of the Red Sea and Persian Gulf into an integral part of the empire: limiting local administrative independence wherever possible, replacing Hadim Suleiman's appointees with his own handpicked men, and refocusing activity away from the sea and toward the hinterland. Meanwhile, the objectives of the Indian Ocean faction were almost precisely the opposite: by resisting Rustem's interference, they sought to preserve local autonomy for themselves and thereby continue the process of political and economic engagement with the larger Indian Ocean world.

Because of the overwhelmingly state-centered nature of most surviving Ottoman historical sources, we are inevitably best informed about the activities of Rustem's agents sent directly from Istanbul. Of these, the most prominent were Uveys Pasha, Piri Reis, and Seydi Ali Reis, three men who in rapid succession served as the primary instruments for implementing the policies of the central government from the late 1540s until the mid-1550s. Despite the support they enjoyed from above, however, the efforts of all three of these individuals were destined to end in dismal failure. And every step of the way, members of the Indian Ocean faction were able to capitalize on these failures to outflank Rustem and push their own agenda with relentless determination.

OZDEMIR PASHA AND THE YEMENI REVOLT OF 1547

Rustem Pasha's first major confrontation with the Indian Ocean faction, much in keeping with his bureaucratic style of leadership, came as the result of a dispute over administrative appointments in Yemen. Here, ever since Hadim Suleiman's decisive conquest of the province in 1538, the local state apparatus had been run essentially as an administrative annex of Egypt and had remained the exclusive domain of a close-knit group of veterans from Hadim Suleiman's original expedition. In 1545, however, as part of Rustem's sweeping reforms aimed at enhancing the authority of the central government, all of the Yemeni administrative districts, or *sancaḳs*, were separated from Egypt and reorganized as an independent province, or *beglerbegilik*.[20]

This move, coming just a few short months after Rustem's promotion to grand vizier, was clearly intended as an assault on his rival Daud Pasha, who continued to wield considerable authority as governor of Egypt. Daud responded to the challenge by trying to preemptively appoint his own man, Mustafa al-Neshar, as Yemen's first governor-general, or *beglerbegi*.[21] This effort failed, however, and before the year was out, Mustafa was replaced by Rustem's choice, Uveys Pasha, a former slave of Sultan Selim with close connections to the palace but no prior experience at all in Yemen.[22]

By no means suprisingly, Uveys Pasha's lack of experience led him to commit a rapid series of blunders that dangerously disrupted Yemen's fragile status quo. His first miscalculation was to threaten the Zaydi Imam Sherefeddin, a hereditary Shiite ruler who continued to govern Yemen's interior highlands as an independent emir. Learning of a smoldering dynastic dispute between Sherefeddin and his son Mutahhar, Uveys Pasha launched an attack against the Zaydi-held city of Ta'izz toward the end of 1546. Although the operation itself was a success, during the campaign Uveys began to run afoul of the old hands in the local Ottoman administration, who disparaged the newcomer's lack of judgment and resented his autocratic tendencies. When the pasha then decided, in the following months, to push even farther north and besiege the city of Sana'a, a small group from among these discontents hatched a plot against him. In the summer of 1547, with the Ottoman army already camped before the walls of Sana'a, one of their number, a Circassian named Hasan Pehlivan, assassinated Uveys as he slept in his tent after a night of drinking and debauchery.[23]

Across Yemen, chaos ensued. The main Ottoman force, paralyzed by the loss of its leader and now wracked by internal divisions, promptly lifted the siege of Sana'a and allowed the assassin to escape. Soon thereafter, the Ottoman administrative capital of Zebid was itself attacked by a group of Hasan Pehlivan's supporters and surrendered without a struggle. This, in turn, prompted a group of urban notables in Aden to likewise renounce their allegiance to Istanbul and offer their city to Ali al-Tawlaki, a tribal chieftain from Aden's hinterland. Even worse, al-Tawlaki then sent an embassy to Hormuz offering to turn over control of Aden's port and customs to the Portuguese.

Two ships under the command of Dom Paio de Noronha immediately set sail for the city, bearing a promise from Hormuz that more help was on its way.[24]

With Ottoman authority on the verge of total collapse, the fate of the province now lay in the hands of a local *beg* named Ozdemir, a man whose origins and early career were typical of many members of the empire's Indian Ocean faction. Born in Mamluk Egypt to a military family with close connections to the old pre-Ottoman regime, Ozdemir had initially entered Ottoman service during Hadim Suleiman's first tenure as Egypt's governor in the late 1520s, a time when many former Mamluks and their progeny were being reincorporated into the new provincial administration as loyal Ottoman subjects. Ozdemir spent the next decade as a mid-level provincial official in Egypt, until in 1538, he was selected by Hadim Suleiman to participate in the Ottoman expedition to Gujarat.

Little is known about Ozdemir's activities during the Gujarati campaign, but he apparently served with enough distinction that on his return from India in the fall of 1538, he received a promotion from Hadim Suleiman and was placed in command of his own small expeditionary force. Then, with orders from the pasha to reconnoiter the parched African hinterland between the Red Sea and the Nile valley, Ozdemir headed for the port of Quseyr in the winter of 1539. From there, he successfully crossed several hundred miles of desert, reached the Nile, took possession of a number of cities in Upper Egypt still outside Ottoman control, and finally returned safely to Cairo by river barge. Never before had such a mission been attempted by an Ottoman force, and its success won Ozdemir recognition as a daring and capable young commander. After a few more years of service in Egypt, he was promoted to the rank of "lord of the standard" and transferred to a prime posting in Yemen.[25]

Ozdemir was still in Yemen in the spring of 1547, and following the assassination of Uveys Pasha, he was suddenly left as the most senior Ottoman officer in the province. Facing the prospect of general insurrection, he was somehow able to restore order among the troops who remained camped outside Sana'a, and by popular acclamation, he was nominated as interim commander to replace the murdered pasha. Thereafter, he took control of affairs with astonishing speed and efficiency. Vowing revenge for Uveys's assassination, he managed to hunt down and kill Hasan Pehlivan in a matter of days; then he resumed the aborted siege of Sana'a and captured the city in less than a week. From there, he dispatched a courier to inform the authorities in Egypt of the critical condition of the province, requesting that a fleet be sent at once from Suez to help restore Ottoman control in the still rebellious strongholds of Zebid and Aden.[26]

Such help was soon forthcoming, but significantly, the response to Ozdemir's call came not from Rustem but from Daud Pasha in Egypt, who took action as soon as he received Ozdemir's dispatch without referring the matter to his superior. In a continuation of the political intrigues of previous years, Daud seems to have done this not only because of the urgency of the situation but also as a means of denying

Rustem the opportunity to select another outsider to replace the late Uveys Pasha. Daud's own choice was Solak Ferhad, a close associate with impeccable Indian Ocean credentials, having served as Hadim Suleiman's envoy to Yemen and the Hadramaut in 1537, as his chief negotiator in India in 1538, and since 1542 as admiral of the Red Sea fleet. He was now nominated by Daud Pasha to replace Uveys as the governor-general of Yemen and was dispatched immediately to Mocha, where he arrived in November 1547.[27] To assist him, Daud also ordered a substantial fleet of some sixty vessels to be prepared in Suez, and as the new admiral in command of this force he nominated Piri Reis, the renowned cartographer and navigator.[28]

Given his background, Piri Reis was by no means an illogical choice for this position. As head of the Ottoman galley squadron of Alexandria, he was at the time the most senior naval official in Egypt, and could also boast of a long record of advocacy for Ottoman expansion in the Indian Ocean.[29] But unlike Daud Pasha, Ozdemir Pasha, or Solak Ferhad, Piri was not a veteran of the Gujarati campaign and had no practical experience in the Indian Ocean prior to this appointment, meaning that he arrived in Suez in the fall of 1547 as something of an outsider. Furthermore, by this point in his career Piri was nearly ninety years old, having spent his entire life in the service of the Ottomans' Mediterranean fleet. As a result, Piri's political bearings remained firmly oriented toward Istanbul rather than Egypt, and in the end, he would emerge as a partisan not of Daud and the Indian Ocean faction, but of Rustem.[30]

These conflicted loyalties, however, would not become fully apparent until after the crisis in Yemen had been successfully averted. In the meantime, Piri set out from Suez and successfully rendezvoused with Solak Ferhad in Mocha at the beginning of December 1547. From there, the two commanders sent reinforcements overland to Ozdemir, who easily recaptured Zebid and put an end to the rebellion in the interior. Both Ferhad and Piri Reis then headed to Aden, with Ferhad arriving first with an advance force of five vessels in late December, and Piri Reis and the rest of the fleet joining him at the end of January.[31]

Once in position, their combined fleet began a massive bombardment of Aden's redoubtable defensive walls, manned by the Portuguese commander Dom Paio de Noronha and the crews of his two galleys from Hormuz. At the time, Noronha was still waiting for a larger relief force under Álvaro de Castro to arrive from India, but because of a series of delays, this fleet was still anchored in Goa and wouldn't even set sail for another two weeks. By the middle of February, with still no sign of reinforcements, Noronha finally despaired of defending the city and abandoned it. The Ottomans breached the walls and stormed Aden's citadel on the twenty-third of the month, and Álvaro de Castro, who failed to arrive off the coast of Arabia until the beginning of March, was forced to turn back without ever catching sight of Aden.[32]

The campaign thus ended in an impressive display of Ottoman military efficiency, particularly considering the extremely long distances across which the Ottomans had been forced to operate. After all, Ozdemir had been able to send his original request for help only at the end of August, meaning that his letter could not possibly have reached Daud Pasha in Egypt before the middle of September. Yet by the end of October, Daud had already outfitted an enormous fleet in Suez; by the end of November, this force had arrived safely in Yemen; by January, most of the province was pacified; and by the middle of February, Aden was recaptured—weeks before the main Portuguese force could even arrive on the scene.

None of the speed and power of this Ottoman response was lost on the Portuguese, whose confidence in their own ability to react had already been shaken by the Ottomans' lightning conquest of Basra in 1546. In the aftermath of this second major failure in as many years, the bishop of Goa gloomily advised the king about the importance of keeping better apprised of events and taking council from men of experience, "especially now that there are Ottomans in both Basra and Aden, for they are more industrious, take greater care in preparing themselves for war, and are generally better informed than we are here [in Hormuz]."[33]

Of course, by 1547, such a statement could really be made only about the Ottoman authorities in Egypt, Yemen, and the Persian Gulf and no longer about the central government in Istanbul. The speed and effectiveness of Daud Pasha's response to the crisis in Yemen had been possible only because he had bypassed the regular chain of command and acted independently of Rustem. Moreover, his intervention had been made necessary in the first place by Rustem's inappropriate appointment of Uveys Pasha, an outsider, as the head of the local administration. In the wake of this nearly averted crisis, it seems that even Rustem himself had begun, however reluctantly, to recognize this. Although he refused to reconfirm Daud's nominee Ferhad as the new governor-general of Yemen, he replaced him not with another appointee from Istanbul but instead with Ozdemir Pasha, a choice that betrayed a newfound appreciation for the importance of respecting local sensibilities and local expertise when dealing with this distant frontier region.[34]

Ozdemir would retain his position in Yemen for a full five-year term, during which he built a reputation as a competent administrator, a skillful negotiator, and a brilliant military strategist. After restoring order and punishing the last of the conspirators in the plot against Uveys (a task accomplished by early 1548), Ozdemir once again pushed north, gradually increasing the pressure on the Zaydis in the highlands and expanding Ottoman control of the interior, until by 1552, Imam Sherefeddin's son Mutahhar was forced to sue for peace. The resulting treaty, in which Mutahhar agreed to be inducted into the imperial administration as a "lord of the standard" and serve as an Ottoman official, extended Ottoman control further into the interior than ever before and removed the last pockets of local resistance to Ottoman rule.[35] By the time Ozdemir completed his term in 1554, Yemen was a rich and stable province, yielding a large annual surplus for the imperial treasury in Istanbul.[36]

Paradoxically, much of what Ozdemir accomplished during these years conformed quite closely to Rustem Pasha's original plan for the province, since

Ozdemir's efforts had transformed Yemen from a remote outpost on the shores of the Indian Ocean into an integral part of the Ottoman Empire. Because of this, Ozdemir's administration should be considered a successful early compromise between the grand vizier and the Indian Ocean faction, whereby the central government conceded a certain amount of direct control in exchange for local acquiescence in the implementation of Rustem's policies.

Unfortunately, this moment of detente would barely outlast Ozdemir's term as governor. Within a year of his leaving Yemen, the pasha would take advantage of a temporary change of leadership in Istanbul to once again redirect Ottoman expansion away from the interior and back toward the sea. And in the interim, conflict between the grand vizier and the Indian Ocean faction would continue elsewhere, with the focus of activity shifting to the Arabian Sea, and centering around a little-known colleague and contemporary of Ozdemir Pasha named Sefer Reis.

A RISING STAR IN THE EAST

It is not known when and under what circumstances Sefer Reis, or "Captain Sefer," first began his life at sea. The earliest surviving Ottoman archival document to mention him, dating from 1544, indicates that Sefer was by this time in command of a small squadron of galleys based in Suez. In this capacity, he was responsible for conducting patrols of the Red Sea as well as supplying his superiors with regular intelligence reports about the wider Indian Ocean region, suggesting that at this early date he was already a person of some stature in the hierarchy of the Ottomans' Red Sea fleet.[37] Additionally, since the year 1544 coincides with the closing months of Hadim Suleiman Pasha's grand vizierate, we can surmise that Sefer had a close connection with the Indian Ocean faction from much earlier, and like so many other members of the faction had probably been a participant in Hadim Suleiman's expedition to Gujarat in 1538. After the grand vizier's death, it seems equally likely that Sefer was involved in the general Ottoman anti-Portuguese offensive of 1546, perhaps as part of the daring raiding naval expedition that sailed up the Arabian coast as far as Muscat just before Ayas Pasha's conquest of Basra. Sefer may even have been the commander of this expedition, although we cannot be certain because there are no surviving Ottoman *mühimme* registers from these years.[38]

At any rate, by the year 1550 Sefer's name also begins to appear in Portuguese sources, and it is clear from their accounts that by this point he enjoyed a rather formidable reputation as a seafarer worth his salt. The chronicler Diogo do Couto, for example, records that in the fall of that year, a large Portuguese squadron under the command of Luiz Figueira spotted off the coast of Jor "four large and handsomely built galleots... and with them was sailing a great Muslim corsair named Sefer who had come from Mecca with the intention of sacking Muscat and raiding the ships that normally leave from Hormuz for Goa and the other ports along the coast of India."[39] Alarmed by the presence of Ottoman vessels so deep in Portuguese waters, Figueira immediately decided to give chase.

The unfolding of this first documented encounter between Sefer and the Portuguese, described extensively in Couto's chronicle, is worth recounting in some detail because it established a pattern that the corsair would repeat successfully throughout the rest of his career. As Couto tells us, Sefer's intended prey were the heavily laden and poorly defended Portuguese merchant ships that each fall crossed from Hormuz to India with the monsoon—rich prizes that must have seemed an ideal target for a corsair. At the same time, Sefer must have known that by sailing so far north and so close to the Portuguese base in Hormuz, he also ran the risk of encountering a heavily armed Portuguese patrol, which in the end is exactly what happened. But Sefer, rather than standing his ground and trying to fight Figueira directly, turned his galleys around and headed back in the direction from which he had come, moving quickly down the coast and avoiding a confrontation on the open sea. Figueira did his best to chase him down but soon realized that Sefer's light galleys were simply too fast and enjoyed too great a head start. Abandoning his futile chase, he instead set a course back to India.[40]

Almost as soon as Figueira arrived in Goa and reported the matter to his superiors, Viceroy Afonso de Noronha ordered him to arm a slightly larger fleet of four sailing ships and one oared fusta and to launch a punitive counterattack against Sefer in his home waters of the Red Sea. But because he was compelled to wait for the winter monsoon, Figueira did not reached the south Arabian coast and enter the Bab al-Mandab until January 1551—where Sefer, expecting his arrival, was lying in wait in a visible but carefully chosen location. Upon catching sight of the corsair's four galleys, Figueira, who seems to have mistaken his opponent's previous withdrawal as a sign of weakness, recklessly attacked with his own solitary oared vessel and quickly found himself surrounded. His escort of sailing ships moved in to help but realized too late that because of the shallowness of the water, they could not approach.

As they watched their commander's vessel being overwhelmed, the crews of the Portuguese sailing ships could do nothing more than fire an ineffective barrage of artillery from a distance. Before their eyes, Figueira's fusta was overrun, Figueira himself was killed, and all of his men were taken captive, forcing the remaining four Portuguese ships to flee in disgrace. Of these, one crew was so ashamed that they resolved never to return to India, instead heading for the African coast to seek refuge at the court of the Emperor of Ethiopia. The remaining three ships sailed east, adding to the disgrace of defeat during their return journey by pillaging a merchant vessel from Diu that carried a valid Portuguese license to trade.[41]

This seemingly minor encounter, involving only a handful of vessels and no direct involvement from either Istanbul or Lisbon, counted as neither the first nor most substantial Ottoman victory at Portuguese expense. Nevertheless, it appears to have been the earliest instance in which the Portuguese were bested on their own terms:

in a direct conflict at sea rather than in a siege or an amphibious assault on a land-based fortress. Even more disturbingly from the Portuguese perspective, Sefer's victory could not be attributed to overwhelming force—the Ottomans' traditional strength—but rather to a sophisticated understanding of the physical conditions of the western Indian Ocean and of the natural vulnerabilities of Portugal's maritime network.

Sefer's success came as the result of three key insights. First, he realized that there were rich opportunities for plunder in the waters between Hormuz and Gujarat, the most trafficked sea lane in all the Portuguese Indies. By using a small force of very light and fast galleys, he had a good chance of being able to run down individual merchant vessels of the Estado da Índia during the busy sailing season of the late summer and early fall. Second, although Sefer knew that his galleys were vulnerable on the open sea against armed patrols of Portuguese sailing ships, he calculated that since the monsoon winds blew consistently toward the northeast during the late summer and fall, he would always be able to evade such a force by *rowing* southwest into the wind, down the Arabian coast and back toward his base in Mocha, where the Portuguese sailing ships would be unable to follow. Third, Sefer knew that even if he failed to capture any merchant vessels while at sea, the mere appearance of his galleys around Hormuz was a provocation that would eventually lead to a counterattack by the Portuguese fleet. And since this attack could come only in the winter months, when the shifting monsoon made sailing from India to the west possible, he could prepare for their arrival in advance and lure the Portuguese into waters where fickle winds, shallows, and dangerous coral reefs would give his own galleys a deadly advantage.[42]

Over the course of the next decade, this strategy would form the basic template for almost all of Sefer's exploits at sea, which would become progressively more daring and effective with every passing year. For the time being, however, his early success would be overshadowed by the incompetence of his superiors, who were busy laying the groundwork for an unprecedented series of Ottoman defeats at sea in which Sefer was to play no part at all.

FAILURE IN HORMUZ

The stage for this embarrassing string of naval disasters was set by Rustem Pasha as a consequence of his continued meddling in the affairs of the Indian Ocean. Although Rustem and the Indian Ocean faction had negotiated a satisfactory (albeit temporary) modus vivendi in Yemen through the appointment of Ozdemir Pasha as that province's governor-general, elsewhere the grand vizier had continued to institute a series of centralizing reforms. First among these was an attempt to rein in the independence of the Ottoman fleet in the Mediterranean, accomplished with the nomination of his own brother, Sinan Pasha, as the new *ḳapūdān-ı deryā*, or grand admiral of the Ottoman navy. Like so many of Rustem's appointments, Sinan was in many ways an unfortunate choice: a man inexperienced in naval affairs whose main qualification was his reliable fraternal loyalty. In consequence, just as Uveys Pasha had run into trouble with the old military hands of Yemen, Sinan, too, soon began to antagonize the more seasoned commanders of the Mediterranean fleet. Even so, with Rustem's support he was able to retain his post for several years, and during his tenure effected permanent (if not necessarily positve) changes in the internal constitution and independence of the Ottoman navy.[43]

Then, between 1550 and 1554, Rustem appears to have applied this same centralizing logic to the much smaller and still largely autonomous Indian Ocean fleet. Despite having been forced to partially reevaluate his nominating policies as a result of Uveys Pasha's assassination, Rustem remained openly suspicious of the continuing independence of Ottoman officials in the Indian Ocean region, especially the cozy and largely unsupervised trading relationship between the Portuguese in Hormuz and the local Ottoman authorities in Basra. Moreover, he appears to have been genuinely alarmed by the Portuguese intervention in Aden in 1547, which had demonstrated that their base in Hormuz continued to pose a serious risk to the internal security of Yemen. Accordingly, Rustem set in motion an ambitious plan to expel the Portuguese entirely from the Arabian Peninsula. In so doing, he hoped to transform the Persian Gulf into an Ottoman lake which, much like the Black Sea, would be permanently sealed off from outside influence and firmly under his own control.

The centerpiece of this plan was the conquest of Hormuz, whose formidable island fortress held the keys to control of maritime access to and from the Persian Gulf. As a first step, in early 1550 he sent reinforcements to the Ottoman garrison in Basra, which under his orders took possession of the nearby port of Katif, a tributary of Hormuz and therefore under indirect Portuguese rule.[44] At the same time, he ordered the construction of a new fleet of galleys in Suez, assembling a large expeditionary force complete with artillery, infantry, and siege experts.[45] All of these men and supplies were then placed under the direct command of Piri Reis, Rustem's personal client and, since 1547, the admiral of the Indian Ocean fleet.[46]

By 1551, as a result of these preparations, Hormuz was rife with rumors of an imminent invasion, and after several local conspiracies to betray the city to the Ottomans were uncovered, the Portuguese became alarmed enough to organize a preemptive strike of their own against Basra.[47] In July of that year, the captain of Hormuz, Álvaro de Noronha, set out with 1,100 Portuguese and 3,000 local auxiliaries to Katif, which they found garrisoned by some 400 Ottoman soldiers. After several days of heavy bombardment, they compelled this garrison to abandon its position and flee, although the Portuguese elected to demolish Katif's empty fortress rather than reoccupy it. Noronha then moved on by sea toward Basra, which he hoped to surprise and capture with the help of Sheikh Yahya, the local tribal leader whom the Ottomans had forcibly ousted from Basra in 1546.[48] Unfortunately for the Portuguese, the local *beglerbegi* had received advanced warning of Noronha's movements and thereby managed, by means of an elaborate subterfuge, to convince the Portuguese that their local allies had betrayed them. Noronha ordered his fleet to turn back without attempting an attack, and Basra was saved. A few weeks later, the Ottomans reoccupied Katif as well.[49]

As all of this was taking place, Piri Reis was completing the final preparations for his fleet's departure from Suez, finally setting out with twenty-four galleys and four supply ships in April 1552. By July, an advance force commanded by his son Mehmed Reis had rounded the Arabian Peninsula and landed at the Portuguese stronghold of Muscat. Here, after an eighteen-day siege, Muscat was pillaged, its fortress was destroyed, and 128 Portuguese, along with the local commander, João de Lisboa, were taken prisoner.[50] After Piri's arrival a few days later, the armada reconstituted itself as a single fighting force and continued north, reaching Hormuz in the following week. By early August, large numbers of Ottoman troops had already been landed on the island, and gunners had dug into positions around the citadel. The siege of Hormuz, perhaps the richest prize in all of Portuguese Asia, had begun (Figure 4.1).

Up to this point, events had proceeded surprisingly smoothly for Piri Reis and his fleet. But his arrival in Hormuz marked the beginning of an almost uninterrupted series of disasters, finally ending in his own death—at Ottoman hands—within just a few short months. The earliest inklings of trouble came at the Ottomans' first arrival in Hormuz, where they learned that, by chance, a large and heavily armed Portuguese warship had reached the island just before them. This unexpected windfall had bloated

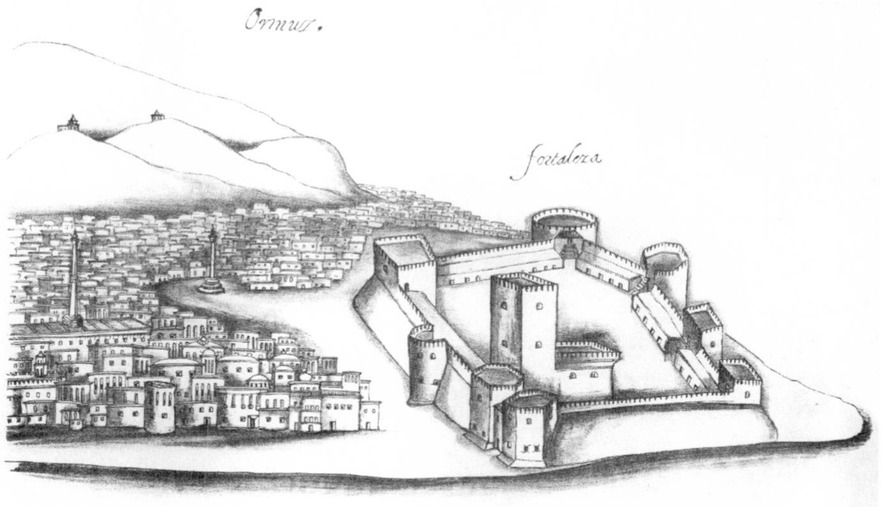

FIGURE 4.1 A mid-sixteenth-century view of the Portuguese fortress of Hormuz. *Source*: Gaspar Correia, *Lendas da Índia* (Lisbon, 1858–1864).

the number of defenders inside the fortress to the point that they nearly outnumbered the besiegers, and since the Portuguese also had an unusually large number of cannon and were well stocked with powder, they inflicted heavy losses on both the Ottoman siege troops and their ships anchored in the harbor. Meanwhile, the Ottomans' own guns proved exasperatingly ineffective against the reinforced walls of the citadel, especially since the one supply ship that had been lost during the voyage from Yemen carried a significant portion of their stores of munitions.[51]

It therefore became clear that the expensive and elaborately planned attack was hopeless, particularly after news reached the Ottomans that an additional Portuguese relief force was on its way from India. Piri Reis ordered the siege to be lifted and contented himself with looting the city's environs and capturing several richly laden merchant vessels anchored off a nearby island. Then, fearful of an encounter with the Portuguese relief force, he headed straight for Basra without even attempting a landing at Bahrain, even though his orders from Rustem had explicitly identified this island as a secondary target of attack.[52]

The situation continued to deteriorate once the fleet had arrived in Basra, where Piri seems to have suffered an acute and uncharacteristic crisis of confidence. This was possibly brought on by a combination of his advanced age (he was believed to be nearly ninety at the time), the unfamiliarity of his surroundings, and deep disappointment at his failure to take Hormuz. But whatever the reason, although safely ensconced in Basra, he was apparently seized by panic at the prospect of having his return route to Suez cut off. In direct violation of his orders, and amid vehement protests from Basra's new governor, Kubad Pasha, Piri therefore decided to load the captives and booty acquired during the campaign onto his three fastest ships and head for Suez alone, abandoning to its fate the rest of his fleet.[53] Such an act was a treasonable offense, and although Piri showed great skill in evading two separate Portuguese squadrons sent to track him during his return voyage to the Red Sea, he could not avoid the wrath of his own superiors once he arrived in Egypt.[54] Semiz Ali Pasha, who had replaced Daud Pasha as governor of Egypt in 1549, ordered Piri's arrest in Suez and shortly thereafter oversaw his execution.[55]

FURTHER DISASTERS AT SEA

With Piri Reis dead, the Ottoman fleet headless and marooned in Basra, the Portuguese still in control of Hormuz, and an enemy squadron under Pero de Taíde Inferno lurking off the coast of Yemen, the safety of the Red Sea, Jiddah, and even Suez was becoming a question of legitimate concern. But in such a moment of crisis, in many ways analogous to that following Uveys Pasha's assassination five years earlier, the Indian Ocean faction once again found an opportunity to reassert its influence. In Piri's place, interim command of the fleet in Basra was assumed by Murad Beg, a protégé of Daud Pasha and veteran of the siege of Aden who was at the time serving as administrator of the port of Katif. In July 1553, Murad selected fifteen of the best vessels from those still in Basra and attempted to escort them back to Suez, sailing as far as Hormuz before his route was cut off by a large Portuguese fleet commanded by Dom Diogo de Noronha.

The battle that ensued ranks as the largest open-sea engagement on record between Ottoman and Portuguese naval forces—and very nearly ended in a decisive victory for Murad (Figure 4.2). Taking advantage of a sudden drop in the wind that temporarily incapacitated the Portuguese sailing ships, Murad successfully sank Noronha's flagship with his artillery and then ordered all fifteen of his galleys to charge a second vessel that had separated from the main fleet. The other Portuguese captains watched helplessly as the Ottomans first destroyed the sails, rigging, and upper decks of the ship with cannon fire and then proceeded to board its foredeck, killing or capturing much of its crew. This vessel was on the verge of sinking when the wind picked up again as suddenly as it had dropped off, allowing the remaining Portuguese ships to regroup and stage a counterattack. Murad managed to save all of his galleys by seeking refuge in the shallows between the small islands off Hormuz, but his fleet sustained heavy casualties during the maneuver, and he was unable to continue on course for Suez.[56]

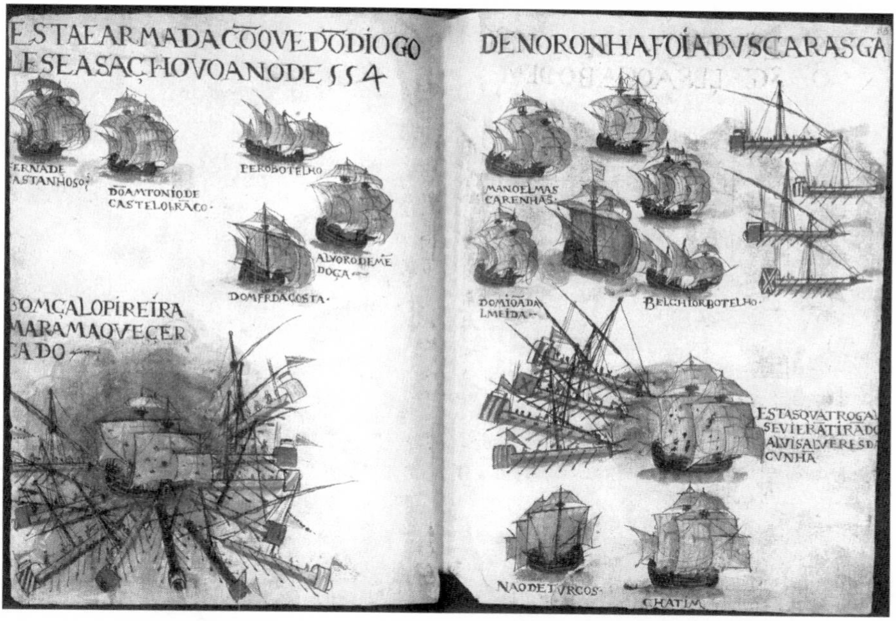

FIGURE 4.2 Two Portuguese sailing ships immobilized by the galleys of Murad Reis, as the rest of the Portuguese fleet looks on helplessly. The tongue-in-cheek caption reads: "This is the fleet with which Dom Diogo de Noronha went to look for the Ottoman galleys, and found them!" Source: Lisuarte de Abreu, *Livro de Lisuarte de Abreu*. Pierpoint Morgan Library, New York, M. 525.

Murad's subsequent return to Basra allowed Rustem Pasha once again to reassume direct control of events, as he nominated a new admiral to replace Piri Reis. His second choice for the post was Seydi Ali Reis, head of the main Ottoman arsenal in Istanbul and the progeny of a well-established family of navigators and seamen from the Black Sea (as well as the future author of the autobiographical "Mirror of Countries").[57] Like Piri Reis, Seydi Ali was an old hand of the Ottoman fleet in the Mediterranean, having participated in the conquest of Rhodes in 1522 and since then in campaigns with Hayreddin Pasha, Sinan Pasha, and other Mediterranean commanders for so many years that, in his own words, "I knew every nook and cranny of the Western Sea."[58] But also like Piri Reis, Seydi Ali accepted his new appointment without having ever previously served in the Indian Ocean, a lack of experience that would leave him similarly unprepared for the dangerous task that awaited him.

Upon receiving his commission, Seydi Ali traveled overland from Istanbul to Basra late in 1553. After overseeing repairs to the fleet during the idle months of the winter and spring of 1554, he set sail in midsummer in a renewed attempt to bring the Ottoman armada safely back to Suez.[59] During the first leg of his journey, the admiral made good progress, successfully evading the Portuguese in Hormuz and rounding the Cape of Mosandam by early August. Only upon entering the Arabian Sea did the Portuguese finally get word of his position and send a fleet in pursuit under the command of Dom Fernão de Menezes. Menezes briefly intercepted the Ottoman vessels just outside the Cape of Mosandam, but Seydi Ali managed to pull away and once more slip out of sight by hugging the coast and traveling into the wind. After rowing another fifteen days with no further sign of the Portuguese, he became convinced that contrary winds had forced them to give up the chase and return to Hormuz.[60]

This proved to be a tragic miscalculation. Rather than turning back, Menezes had instead headed into the open sea, sailing east until he was far enough from the coast to tack back across the wind and arrive in Muscat well ahead of the slow-moving Ottoman galleys.[61] He then set up an ambush, waiting with all of his sailing ships just off the coast while hiding a number of oared vessels inside the harbor of Muscat. This ensured that when Seydi Ali arrived a few days later, still heading south against the wind, he had no way to escape: since the Portuguese sailing ships, already in Muscat, were upwind from him, they could quickly overtake him if he tried to turn back; and because his path was also blocked by Portuguese oared vessels defended by artillery in Muscat, there was no way for him to avoid a confrontation by skirting the coast in waters too shallow for the Portuguese sailing ships to follow. His only remaining option was to charge headlong into Menezes's lines in the hope of breaking through. But as he did so, the heavier of his galleys soon fell behind the rest and were set upon by the Portuguese, who eventually captured six of them, enslaving their crews and seizing nearly fifty bronze artillery pieces.[62] Seydi Ali's remaining nine galleys managed to fight their way through the blockade and escape, but their crews

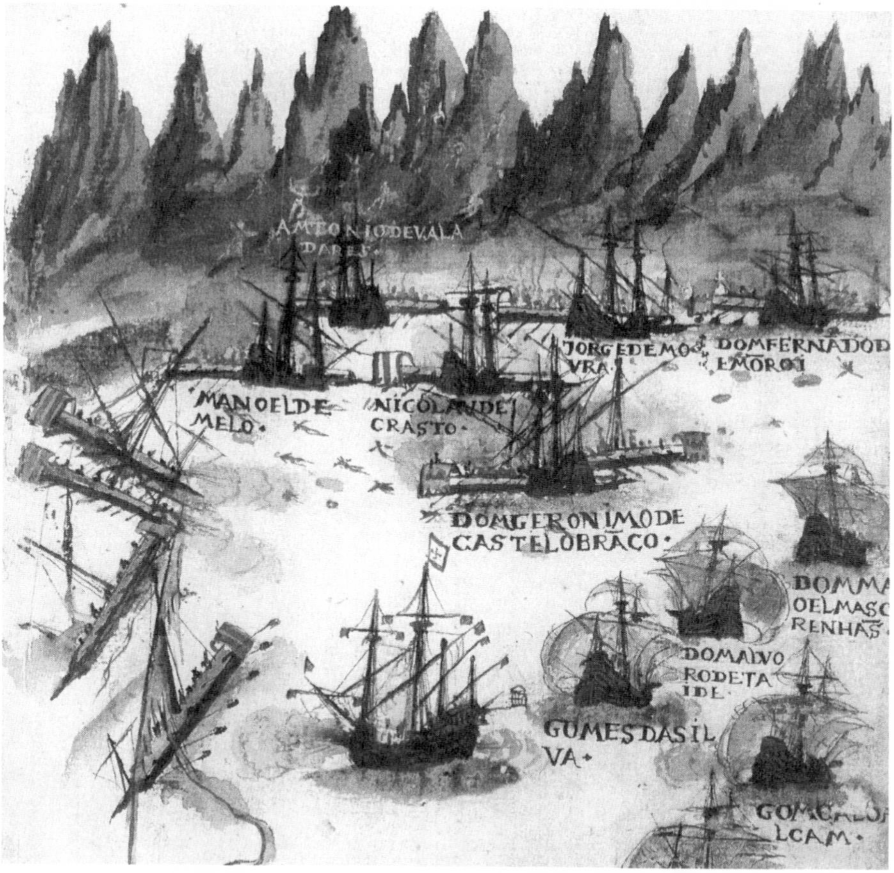

FIGURE 4.3 The fleet of Seydi Ali Reis caught in a Portuguese ambush off the coast of Muscat, August 1554. The Ottoman galleys appear to the left and in the background; Portuguese sailing ships are in the foreground and to the right. Source: Lisuarte de Abreu, *Livro de Lisuarte de Abreu*. Pierpoint Morgan Library, New York, M. 525.

were so weakened in the fray that their oarsmen lacked the strength to continue rowing, and the vessels were soon swept helplessly out to the open sea (Figure 4.3).[63]

Buffeted by storms, the admiral only now began to understand just how unprepared he was, as a Mediterranean seafarer, to confront the fierce conditions of the Indian Ocean. In his own memoir, he later wrote of the experience: "As compared to these awful tempests, the foul weather in the Western seas is mere child's play, and their towering billows are as drops of water compared to those of the Indian sea."[64] After several weeks of aimless drifting and the loss of two more galleys to violent storms, Seydi Ali finally gave up his attempt to reach the Red Sea and made instead for India, where he hoped to find a safe haven among the Ottomans' Rumi allies in

Gujarat.[65] He eventually took refuge with Hoja Safar's son Rumi Khan and son-in-law Kara Hasan and, with their help and countless further adventures, managed to return to Istanbul by means of the overland route through Afghanistan and Iran. His ships, however, were abandoned in the port of Daman and were later dismantled. Of the great fleet sent to conquer Hormuz two years before, nothing at all remained.

SEFER TO THE RESCUE

Throughout these years of unprecedented disaster, Rustem's machinations had effectively excluded Sefer Reis from any direct involvement in the operation of the Ottoman Empire's main (and now defunct) Indian Ocean fleet. Instead, while a full-blown war was raging in the Persian Gulf and along the Omani coast, the corsair had continued to conduct a series of small-scale raids against Portuguese targets elsewhere in the Arabian Sea, capturing two Portuguese merchant ships off south Arabia in 1551 and pillaging several coastal settlements in India in 1552.[66] These tiny operations, while successful, hardly compensated the Ottomans for the massive losses sustained at Hormuz and Muscat and attracted virtually no attention from the central government in Istanbul. But in Cairo, they do seem to have begun to draw the interest of Semiz Ali Pasha, Egypt's new governor-general.

Semiz ("Fat") Ali had succeeded Daud Pasha as governor of Egypt in 1549, after the extremely brief tenure of Mustafa Pasha, who served for only a few months. Since then, from this privileged vantage point, he had watched the deterioration of conditions in the Indian Ocean with a constantly increasing sense of alarm. It was Semiz Ali, in fact, who had arrested Piri Reis upon his return to Egypt and who had overseen his execution. And as a result of this experience, he seems to have developed deep misgivings about Rustem's policies, even as he began to take notice of the modest but impressive competence of Sefer Reis. Accordingly, in the summer of 1554, just as Seydi Ali was setting sail from Basra, Semiz Ali sent an order to Sefer to rendezvous with the Ottoman fleet during its return journey from the Persian Gulf and do whatever he could to escort it safely back to Suez. According to at least one contemporary account, this was because the pasha "had anticipated that Seydi Ali [would run into difficulties], and sent after him Sefer... who had better judgment than he, so that he might take the galleys over and carry out the mission that the other had originally been charged with."[67]

As he set out from the Red Sea on this dangerous mission, Sefer had under his charge nothing more than his standard fleet of four light galleots (one of them the Portuguese vessel he had captured from Luiz Figueira three years before). Although he traveled with his habitual speed to rendezvous with Seydi Ali as quickly as possible, he was still off the Omani coast somewhat to the south of Muscat when he received word of the admiral's defeat and the departure of the Portuguese for India with six captured Ottoman galleys. Devastated by this calamitous news, and suddenly alone and vastly outnumbered by the Portuguese fleet,

Sefer might have simply retreated to Mocha and awaited further orders. But instead, he sensed in the disaster a great opportunity and, as the chronicler Diogo do Couto later explained:

> Since he was by nature a corsair, and very practiced in the ways of those seas, he determined to follow in the wake of the Portuguese armada in the hopes of finding some prey to seize upon. He proceeded in this way until just before reaching the peninsula of Diu, where he came to a halt and set up a blockade, lying in wait for any vessels that might have to pass through those waters.[68]

It was an audacious plan by any measure, in which Sefer resolved to shadow a fleet that had just routed a force four times larger than his own, and then set up a blockade of Portuguese shipping—a blockade of precisely the kind the Portuguese themselves were accustomed to using against Muslim vessels heading for the Red Sea. But daring as it was, the plan worked. Within a few weeks, Sefer had captured four heavily loaded Portuguese merchant vessels and had seized, in addition to prisoners and cargo, more than 160,000 *cruzados* of gold currency. Still hoping to catch yet another particularly wealthy ship rumored to be in the vicinity, Sefer had the crews of the captured vessels bound in irons and, placing small contingents of his own men with each of them, gave them orders to return to Mocha on their own while he continued to cruise the waters around Diu.

As luck would have it, an armed Portuguese fusta under the command of Balthazar Lobato soon came across these four captured ships while on a routine patrol. When the immobilized Portuguese crew of one of the ships saw him, they staged a revolt and with Lobato's help managed to take back not only their own vessel but the other three as well, capturing their former captors and setting sail once more on a course for India. Meanwhile Sefer, who had by this time given up his attempt to catch any more vessels, by chance caught sight once more of the very same Portuguese ships and, realizing what had happened, captured them a second time. He then gave chase to Balthazar Lobato's fleeing warship, which eventually surrendered to him without a fight. All nine vessels now safely in his possession, Sefer once again set a course for Mocha, where he arrived triumphantly a few weeks later.[69]

THE CORSAIR TURNS POLITICIAN

With his coffers overflowing from the spoils of war and his only rivals for power either dead, discredited, or missing in action, Sefer's star was in the ascendant. And just as auspiciously, this moment of great personal triumph also came about in the midst of tumultuous change in Istanbul, where Rustem Pasha had just fallen victim to the same dynastic intrigues from which he had previously benefited so handsomely. The occasion for the vizier's sudden fall was his continuing alliance with the sultan's wife Hurrem, who in 1553 had used him, on false pretenses, to arrange the execution of the popular Shehzade Mustafa—the only surviving Ottoman prince who was not one of Hurrem's own sons. In the midst of popular outrage, particularly within the army, provoked by this act, Rustem was forced out of office and sent into temporary exile by an ostensibly irate sultan.

Sefer's bold response in this moment of opportunity was to leverage his new wealth to reclaim the initiative both for himself and for the Indian Ocean faction. Today, we know of these efforts thanks to an unusually detailed espionage report sent from Egypt to Portugal by João de Lisboa, a captive of the Ottomans in Cairo who had previously served as the Portuguese commander of Muscat. This report reveals that in early 1555, Sefer sent a courier with twenty thousand *cruzados* of the gold he had recently seized from the Portuguese as a gift to the sultan in Istanbul, hoping in exchange to secure a promotion to admiral of the Ottomans' Indian Ocean fleet, a post still technically held by the absent Seydi Ali. In addition, Sefer sent a second gift to the new governor of Egypt, Mehmed Pasha, asking for permission to add five additional light galleys to his fleet in Mocha. With these, he declared an intention to launch a more ambitious anti-Portuguese raid than any yet attempted by the Ottomans, by sailing as far as Ceylon to plunder Portuguese merchant ships on their way west from Malacca and Bengal. From there, he would head with the winter monsoon to East Africa, attacking Portuguese targets there as well before completing the circuit and returning to the Red Sea in the following spring.[70]

If the confidence with which Sefer presented this intrepid plan is striking, no less striking is the extent to which it appears to have been coordinated with the still powerful Rumi elites of Gujarat, who despite years of neglect by Rustem Pasha remained keenly interested in maintaining ties with the Ottoman state. From Lisboa's report, we learn that a Rumi ambassador from Gujarat arrived in Cairo at the same time as Sefer's courier, bearing several official letters including one from Rumi Khan, who was still governor of the port of Surat. According to Lisboa, who managed to meet personally with this ambassador and to discover the exact contents of his letters, the purpose of his mission was to secure a commitment from the Ottoman authorities to build no fewer than fifty war galleys in the arsenal in Suez. Rumi Khan, together with Sultan Ahmed of Gujarat, promised to cover all of the expenses associated with these galleys' construction and maintenance, as well as to build fifty more vessels of their own in Surat, and to convince the Zamorin of Calicut to provide an additional fifty. With this combined force, Rumi Khan guaranteed the conquest of Diu from the Portuguese, and upon the successful completion of this campaign also promised to hand over the city of Surat to direct Ottoman control.[71]

In essence, this proposal amounted to a full-fledged reincarnation, on an even more ambitious scale, of the coalition originally forged between Hadim Suleiman Pasha, Hoja Safar, and the Mappilla corsairs of Calicut nearly twenty years before. With Sefer Reis in command of a revamped Ottoman navy, Hoja Safar's son Rumi Khan in charge of operations in Gujarat, and cooperation from the Zamorin of

Calicut's Mappilla fleet, the power of the Indian Ocean faction could be reborn and finally fulfill its ambition of expelling the Portuguese once and for all from Diu.

João de Lisboa even suggested that this renewed alliance would be more effective than its previous incarnation, since the Rumis of Gujarat seemed to have finally gained the upper hand in their long-standing rivalry with the traditional landed gentry of the Gujarati Sultanate. In one section of his report, based on a personal conversation with a Gujarati commercial agent in Cairo, Lisboa gave details about a factional power struggle prompted by the recent death of Sultan Mahmud of Gujarat in which the Rumis had gotten the better of their rivals. In consequence, the Rumi Yusuf Khan (known in Indian sources as Imad ul-Mulk) had become the most powerful vizier at the court of the new Sultan Ahmed, and was even said to have claimed authority for himself in Gujarat on the pretext of being a "lord of the standard of the Ottoman Sultan."[72]

The extent to which this kind of appeal to the principle of Ottoman universal sovereignty continued to be a factor in Gujarat's politics—and the ease with which it could be used to revive plans for an intercontinental alliance with almost no encouragement from the Ottoman central government—serves as a testament to both the resilience of the Ottoman Empire's Indian Ocean faction and the cohesiveness of its ideology. Even so, within the Ottoman Empire there was still a limit to the ability of Sefer and his allies to direct foreign policy in the still hostile political environment left behind by Rustem Pasha. Despite his recent success, Sefer remained a marginal figure operating at the most distant fringe of the Ottoman world. And by the end of 1555, thanks to the unflinching support of the sultana Hurrem, Rustem himself was back in office as grand vizier, having weathered the political storm surrounding Prince Mustafa's execution. As a result, Rumi Khan's grandiose proposal was barely given a hearing at court, and Sefer Reis's petition for a promotion was denied. Even his modest request for five additional galleys in Mocha was scaled back: in the end, he received no more than two light galleots from the arsenal in Suez.[73]

THE HUNT FOR SEFER

If Sefer continued to be underappreciated by his superiors in Istanbul, however, he was no longer so by the Portuguese, who had by now come to view him as the single most dangerous threat to their continued prosperity in the western Indian Ocean. Already in the fall of 1554, immediately following his successful raid off the coast of Diu, the Portuguese commander Manuel de Vasconcelos had been dispatched from Goa with a major fleet, hoping to intercept Sefer while he was still loaded down with booty from his attacks. Vasconcelos reached the coast of Yemen in January 1555 but found no sign of Sefer's galleots, and after heading northeast and cruising between Hormuz and India—again with no results—he finally returned to India empty-handed.[74] The following winter, still another squadron under João Peixoto was sent out after Sefer, but this time the Portuguese found the corsair's fleet safely ensconced in his base at Mocha, which they dared not approach.[75] Further adding to their humiliation, Sefer then staged yet another raid of his own off the coast of India, seizing two Portuguese merchant vessels near the port of Chaul in the summer of 1556.[76]

João de Lisboa, writing from captivity in Cairo, gives us a taste of the extreme frustration the Portuguese experienced as a result of Sefer's ongoing success. "For what reason do you allow such thievery to continue?" he wrote to the viceroy in 1555. "[Sefer's] strength increases day by day, and Cairo grows constantly richer from spoils taken from the Portuguese. Every day his armada swells, and considering how much he was able to accomplish when he had just three vessels in his charge... how much more trouble will he give the Portuguese, and how many more riches will he send to Cairo, when he has thirty?"[77] Lisboa went on to recommend a direct strike against Sefer's base in Mocha, reporting that for the moment, the corsair had no more than four hundred men in his fleet, and Mocha itself had no walls or fortress and was defended only by a few hundred local Arab tribesmen.

By 1557, having finally despaired of the ability of their sailing ships to ever force an engagement with Sefer's oared galleys on the open sea, the Portuguese authorities in Goa were left with no option but to adopt this risky strategy. Vowing to fight fire with fire, they armed a huge force of twenty oared vessels more suited for combat in shallow waters than sailing ships, and prepared to carry out a direct assault on his home base, surprising and burning his galleys before they had a chance to escape. With intelligence that the corsair planned to winter with his fleet in Mocha, these vessels were placed under the command of Alvaro da Sylveira and dispatched late in the fall of 1557.[78]

Sylveira's fleet made slow progress, its vanguard arriving in the Red Sea only in February 1558. There the Portuguese learned that Sefer was indeed still in Mocha but preparing to leave any day for another raiding campaign, this time toward Africa's Swahili Coast to the south. Since Sylveira's forces had been partially dispersed by heavy winds during the crossing from India, some of his advisors urged him to wait and regroup before launching his attack. But the looming departure of Sefer's galleys convinced him that there was no time to lose, and he therefore charged into Mocha's narrow harbor without his fleet at full strength (Figure 4.4).

As might have been expected, Sylveira found that Sefer's forces had been warned of his approach, and almost as soon as he came within sight of the enemy, he fell under a heavy artillery bombardment by both land and sea. This fire was so intense that it damaged several of his ships and killed a dozen of his sailors within the first few minutes, forcing the Portuguese into a hasty and inglorious retreat. Sylveira's fleet lingered for several more weeks off the coast in hopes of at least capturing some merchant ships headed for Jiddah, but after this, too, failed to produce any results, Sylveira headed back to Muscat with only losses to show for his trouble.[79] Sefer had sustained a direct attack from the main Portuguese fleet and had emerged virtually unscathed.

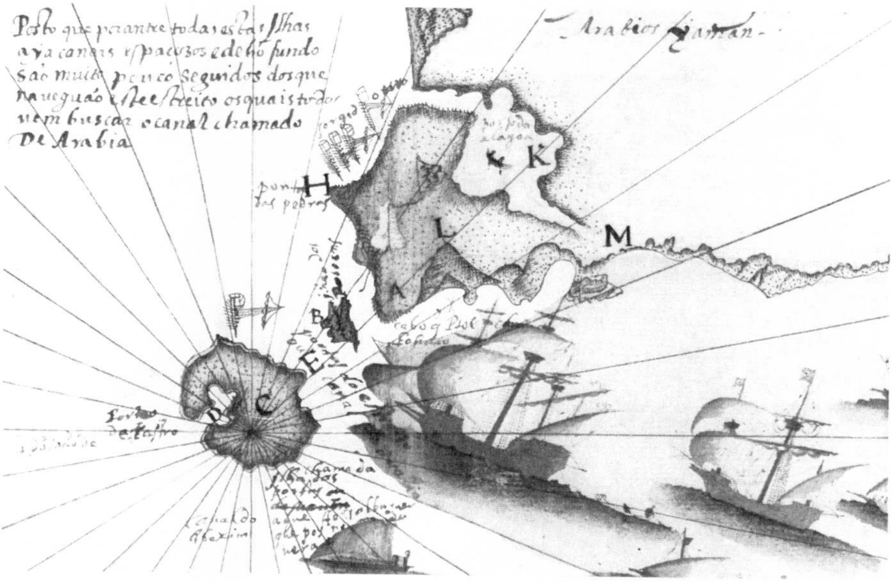

FIGURE 4.4 The port of Mocha, circa 1541. Although the image predates the earliest mention of Sefer Reis in historical sources, it is possible that the squadron of galleots pictured here (in the upper left) is under Sefer's command. The larger vessels to the lower right (not drawn to scale) are of a type similar to those used by Álvaro da Silveira in 1558. Source: João de Castro, *Roteiro que fez Dom João da Castro da viajem que fezeram os Portugueses desde India atee Soez*. University of Minnesota James Ford Bell Library, Minneapolis, Ms. 1541 fCa, fol. 81b.

OZDEMIR PASHA AND THE OTTOMAN CONQUEST OF ERITREA

During these same years, Sefer's brilliant maneuvers against the Portuguese at sea were complemented by a campaign of conquest on land in the one area of the Red Sea region still outside direct Ottoman control: Eritrea. Significantly, the mastermind of this venture was Ozdemir Pasha, who as governor of Yemen had been directly responsible for supplying Sefer Reis and his squadron during the corsair's early years of activity. Equally significantly, Ozdemir's term as governor expired in April of 1554, only a few months before the destruction of Seydi Ali's fleet at Muscat. In consequence, he was certainly aware of Sefer's preparations to lead an expedition to relieve Seydi Ali, and perhaps also of his larger ambitions to begin raids of Portuguese shipping off the coast of Gujarat. Tellingly, as Ozdemir made his way to Istanbul upon the completion of his service in Yemen, hoping to secure support for a future campaign in Eritrea, he did so at precisely the same time that Sefer was setting up his first naval blockade between Diu and Hormuz.

Ozdemir's arrival in the imperial capital also coincided with Rustem Pasha's brief exile from politics. And fortuitously, Rustem's temporary replacement, Kara Ahmed Pasha, proved a much more enthusiastic supporter of the Indian Ocean faction. In fact, thanks to Kara Ahmed's intervention on his behalf, Ozdemir had the unusual opportunity to meet face-to-face with the sultan in the private gardens of Topkapı Palace, where he presented a plan to capitalize on recent gains in Yemen by extending Ottoman influence along the Red Sea's African coast as well. The sultan found Ozdemir's case convincing, and before the year was out, he was on his way to Egypt with authorization to raise an expeditionary force of several thousand men.[80]

After a brief foray up the Nile to subdue several areas of lower Nubia still outside of Ottoman territory, Ozdemir headed for the Red Sea via Suez, from there sailing with his men to the Sudanese coastal town of Suakin. This important trading center, already under Ottoman control, he quickly reorganized as the administrative capital of the new province of Habesh, or Ottoman Eritrea.[81] He then began a rapid military offensive to the south, taking the major Eritrean port of Massawa in the fall of 1556, as well as Arkiko and the nearby island of Dahlak shortly thereafter. By the end of 1557, with the Eritrean coast fully under his control, Ozdemir was ready to turn toward the uncharted vastness of the continental interior.[82] The result, after another year of continuous fighting in the highlands, was the conquest of virtually the entire province of Tigre, including the strategic fortified hill town of Debarva.

These victories recalled the pasha's exploits of nearly twenty years before, when as a young adventurer returning from India he had blazed a trail across the desert and conquered Upper Egypt for his patron Hadim Suleiman. But as Ozdemir would soon discover, Abyssinia was not Egypt, and as he pressed on ever farther, sickness began to take an alarming toll on his troops. Eventually, as the numbers of dead and dying mounted precipitously, even Ozdemir fell victim to the region's hostile climate, finally succumbing in November 1560. His body was carried reverently back to Suakin for burial, and he was immediately replaced as governor by his only son, the future grand vizier Ozdemiroğlu ("Son of Ozdemir") Osman.

OZDEMIR PASHA AND SEFER REIS

Although Ozdemir's death forced the Ottomans to retreat from the Abyssinian interior, Ottoman gains on the coast proved lasting, and in the long run, these would constitute the most important legacy of the pasha's distinguished career. Prior to Ozdemir's conquest of these areas, particularly the strategic coastal towns of Massawa and Arkiko, the Portuguese had maintained an occasional but visible presence, and the Ottomans had in consequence never fully controlled maritime access to the Red Sea. As recently as the spring of 1556, a small fleet under João Peixoto (who was at the time searching for Sefer Reis) had used Massawa as a base to launch raids against the Ottomans as far north as Suakin.[83] Four years later, the Ottomans were for the first time able to guard the Red Sea from a commanding position on both sides of the Bab al-Mandab.

Naturally, this had an immediate effect not only on the security of the Red Sea itself but also on Sefer Reis's developing offensive tactics against the Portuguese. This became obvious in early 1560, when the corsair scored a new victory at sea, thanks to an intricate and masterfully executed deception carried out with the help of the new Ottoman authorities in Eritrea. In this encounter, Sefer's unfortunate dupe was Christovão Pereira Homem, who had been sent from India with a small squadron of three sailing ships and one oared fusta to escort a Jesuit missionary bound for Ethiopia to a safe location on the Abyssinian coast. Pereira entered the Red Sea safely and sailed as far as Massawa, which he hoped to slip by without making his presence known. But to his surprise, as he sailed past Massawa, his ships were greeted by a small skiff sent out by the local Ottoman commander, who hailed Pereira and assured him "that he was a friend of the Portuguese, and would be happy to supply them with water, provisions or anything else that they might be in need of."[84] After some deliberation, Pereira wisely declined the offer and sailed rapidly east toward the island of Kamaran, but the damage was already done. The delay had given the authorities in Massawa a chance to advise Sefer of Pereira's movements, and by the time he reached the opposite coast, the corsair had set his trap.

Arriving off Kamaran, the Portuguese caught sight of a large, solitary vessel bearing all the markings of a wealthy spice ship from Aceh, and were overcome with excitement at the prospect of capturing such rich and defenseless prey. Without hesitation, Pereira ordered his fusta to charge at full speed toward the ship, realizing too late that the vessel, far from being a spice ship, was none other than Sefer's own war galley, disguised with mock sails and riggings to bait the Portuguese into an ambush.[85] Sefer's other three light galleys then emerged from hiding places behind a nearby islet, and all four ships began to close in on Pereira's vessel at alarming speed. A frantic chase ensued, lasting the rest of the day and stretching on into the night.

By the next morning, the three sailing ships escorting Pereira had reached the African coast just outside the Bab al-Mandab and were anxiously awaiting Pereira's oared fusta when it finally appeared on the horizon just after dawn. Believing themselves free from danger, they sailed out to meet him—only to be greeted by the sight of Sefer's galleys, which had somehow divined the Portuguese position and rowed silently through the night to surprise them. As Sefer closed in on Pereira's heavily loaded fusta, its desperate crew tried to unload some men and arms onto the lightest of the Portuguese sailing ships. But this poorly conceived and even more poorly executed maneuver succeeded only in nearly capsizing Pereira's vessel. In the confusion, Sefer struck, killing or capturing everyone aboard both craft. The other two sailing ships escaped, saving their lives but returning to India in disgrace.[86]

AN OVERDUE PROMOTION

Following this victory, in the summer of 1560, an aging Rustem Pasha made one final attempt to deny Sefer Reis the recognition he deserved. He did so by trying to have his loyal client Seydi Ali, who had returned from India in 1557, reinstated in his old position as admiral—a posting that had remained vacant since the destruction of Seydi Ali's fleet in 1555. This time, however, Seydi Ali's appointment was blocked by Sufi Ali Pasha, the new governor of Egypt. In his place, Sefer Reis was finally promoted to supreme command of the empire's Indian Ocean fleet.[87]

Sefer's new appointment was accompanied by increased activity in the arsenal in Suez, where by 1560, several new warships were said to be under construction.[88] This had little effect on Sefer's strategy in the short term, for he continued to operate out of Mocha rather than Suez and, despite his newly elevated status as admiral, to carry out a familiar pattern of small-scale raids against Portuguese shipping. Nevertheless, there could be no doubt that the corsair harbored greater ambitions for the future, and that a serious reorientation of his tactics and strategy was only a matter of time. The reaction to the news of his promotion from Lourenço Pires de Távora, the Portuguese ambassador in Rome, gives some indication of the sense of foreboding with which Lisbon now looked to the future. He wrote:

> Considering the experience which that captain has of the entire Swahili Coast down to Mozambique, and in the other direction from Aden to Hormuz, it seems certain that [the Ottomans] will attempt some major undertaking along one of these two coasts, and that they have great hopes for the plan which [the new captain] has conceived and for which he has promised them great success. The Viceroy of India must stay on guard, and be prepared for every eventuality.[89]

Presentiments of this kind soon had an effect of their own, as Goa responded to Sefer's ongoing raids with a continuously escalating but always ineffective series of counterstrikes. In the fall of 1561, for example, the captain of Hormuz received intelligence that Sefer was planning once again to set up a blockade between Hormuz and Diu. In response, an armada of unprecedented size was sent against him: twenty-three oared vessels, two galleons, and "six hundred and fifty of the best soldiers of India, among them many honorable knights and gentleman" under the command of Dom Francisco Mascarenhas, himself a former viceroy.[90] This fleet set out from Goa in November 1561 and very nearly met Sefer's tiny squadron of three light galleys off the south Arabian coast, but the corsair was tipped off by local Arab sailors and in the end managed to avoid the Portuguese. Mascarenhas sailed on to Hormuz and then returned empty-handed to Goa in January 1562—while Sefer captured a Portuguese merchant vessel and returned safely to the Red Sea.[91]

A few months later, still fearing a return of Sefer with the monsoon in the spring, the Portuguese sent out yet another fleet of three galleons and several oared ships under Jorge de Moura, with orders both to search for the corsair and to patrol for

Muslim ships from Aceh, Malabar, and Cambay bound for the Red Sea.[92] During this operation, one of the ships under Moura's command did manage to engage a very large armed vessel from Aceh, although after a two-day battle, both the Portuguese ship and the Muslim ship burned and sank to the bottom.[93] The rest of Moura's fleet cruised up and down the coast of Arabia for more than a month without successfully detaining any other ships or receiving any news of Sefer, and eventually retired to Hormuz, once again frustrated. Regardless of the scale, the timing, or the methods of Portuguese efforts to confront him, Sefer was unstoppable.

SEFER REIS: INNOVATOR IN OTTOMAN NAVAL STRATEGY

Given the enormity of the Ottoman naval defeats at Hormuz in 1552 and Muscat in 1554—the only events discussed at any length by contemporary Ottoman chroniclers—it is easy to forget that the years following these reverses were a period of unprecedented Ottoman ascendancy in the Indian Ocean. At the same time that Sefer and his men were scoring success after success against Portuguese shipping, Ottoman merchants were developing a vast network of commercial relations that stretched from the Swahili Coast, to Ceylon, to Siam, often supported by freelance Ottoman corsairs operating out of Gujarat and on the Malabar coast of India.[94] As a result, traffic in pepper and luxury goods through the Red Sea and the Persian Gulf soared to new heights, not only surpassing the volumes achieved during the height of the Mamluk monopoly in the fifteenth century but also eventually outstripping the rival Portuguese trade around the Cape of Good Hope.[95]

Scholars searching for an explanation for this remarkable commercial revival have shown a mysterious reluctance to consider the policies and the activities of the Ottomans themselves. Ozdemir Pasha's operations in Eritrea, for example, are generally explained away as a "land campaign" aimed at "securing the Empire's southern frontier,"[96] and the actions of Sefer Reis, when mentioned at all, are dismissed as simple acts of piracy.[97] Meanwhile, the disintegration of the Portuguese blockade of the Red Sea and the corresponding growth in trade through the "traditional" routes controlled by the Ottomans have been attributed (with varying degrees of emphasis) to a combination of external factors: corruption within the Portuguese administration, alterations in the trade policies of the Estado da Índia, fluctuations in the global demand for spices, and the irresistible pull of "market forces."[98]

Yet the career of Sefer Reis demonstrates that the Ottomans, too, played a significant and deliberate role in altering the patterns of Indian Ocean trade. As a pioneer in the use of predatory corsair attacks directed specifically at Portuguese shipping, Sefer was the first Ottoman naval strategist to realize that the control over the seas exercised by the Portuguese was fundamentally different from anything in the Mediterranean. There, unlike in the Indian Ocean, most naval operations were essentially amphibious assaults designed to capture strongholds, or at the very least to control centers of supply that were in any case based on land.[99] Earlier Ottoman campaigns (such as Piri Reis's siege of Hormuz and even Hadim Suleiman's expedition to Diu) had clearly followed this Mediterranean pattern quite closely, and the scant success of these undertakings can in large part be explained as the result of an attempt to apply to the Indian Ocean a concept of naval warfare that was thoroughly inappropriate to its environment.

Sefer Reis was different. In stark contrast to his predecessors, he never tried to storm a fortress, transport troops, or land siege equipment. From hard years of experience, he knew that Portuguese strength lay at sea, and that their weakness lay there too. The targets of his campaigns, therefore, were not Portuguese strongholds but Portuguese ships, and his victories were measured not in hectares of conquered territory, but in captured vessels and increased customs revenues in Mocha, Jiddah, and Suez.

Meanwhile, on the Portuguese side of the ledger, the true cost of Sefer's depredations for the Estado da Índia was far greater than the actual number of ships he captured or destroyed, for his attacks represented an even more onerous drain in terms of the enormously expensive Portuguese military response they provoked. Year after year, for as long as Sefer was active, the authorities in Goa were forced to send out ever larger and costlier fleets in a fruitless attempt to hunt him down. In the process, the Portuguese also suffered a relentless erosion of their ability to control independent Muslim shipping, in part because of Sefer's strategy, and in part because, following Ozdemir's conquest of Eritrea, the Ottomans controlled both sides of the entrance to the Red Sea. This is a point made explicitly by the Portuguese chronicler Diogo do Couto, who provides an explanation for the particularly unsuccessful patrol of the Arabian Sea conducted by Jorge de Moura in 1562 in the following terms:

> While [the Portuguese] remained there [outside the Bab al-Mandab], which was for over a month, they saw more than sixty different [Muslim] vessels without ever being able to reach even one of them. This was because [the Portuguese vessels] were near the shore, and [the merchant ships] came in from the sea with the wind fully at their backs. It was therefore impossible either to catch them or to follow them inside [the mouth of the Red Sea], for [the Portuguese] dared not enter the straits for fear of risking the loss of their own ships.[100]

In other words, the main reason for the failure of de Moura's blockade was that the Portuguese were afraid to follow Muslim ships into the Red Sea—something that, in earlier decades, they would have done with impunity and to their own enormous profit. Now, however, they hesitated, and for only one reason: they were afraid of Sefer Reis.

SEFER REIS AND THE INDIGENIZATION OF OTTOMAN RULE IN THE INDIAN OCEAN

Who was Sefer Reis? With regard to his origins and family background, we are left almost totally in the dark except for two tantalizing clues: the mystery of his unusual name (spelled in Ottoman documents with a س rather than the more common ص), and a few brief passages from a cluster of very early Portuguese sources. These refer to another Ottoman corsair known to the Portuguese as Sinan the Jew (Sinão o Judeo), a predecessor of Sefer's who was based in Jiddah during the late 1530s and early 1540s, and who was almost certainly the famous corsair by the same name who had previously served with the Barbarossa brothers in North Africa.[101] In 1546, Sinan is said to have fallen ill and to have died just days before a planned departure for a raiding mission to the coast of India. And according to Portuguese sources, based on oral reports from merchants recently returned from the Red Sea, he was succeeded by his son, a sea captain based in Egypt, who was confirmed in his new position by the sultan himself.[102]

Is there a connection between Sinan and Sefer? Conclusive evidence is lacking because of the absence of surviving Ottoman archival documents from these years. But the date 1546 is significant, for it was in this year that a fleet of four Ottoman galleys first sailed from Mocha on a raid against Portuguese shipping in the Arabian Sea. These two men of the sea, Sinan and Sefer, may therefore have been nothing less than father and son, a hereditary family of Ottoman corsairs.

This possible link between Sinan and Sefer is particularly interesting given what we know about the operation of the Ottoman tax regime along the Red Sea spice route during this same period—especially in light of the possibility that Sinan was a convert from Judaism. As both Western and Ottoman sources attest, during the mid-sixteenth century the imperial customs houses in Suez and Alexandria came under the perennial control of a group of Jewish tax farmers with ties to the Iberian world.[103] This fact, combined with the possibility that the most prominent Ottoman corsairs in the region also hailed from a family of Jewish converts, suggests that members of the Iberian Jewish diaspora were able to establish themselves as agents of the Ottoman state in the Red Sea and Indian Ocean in a variety of different capacities, including even as officers in the imperial navy. This, in turn, appears to have facilitated the growth of more informal ties between the Ottoman administration of Egypt, the indigenous Jewish merchants of the Indian Ocean, and the swelling ranks of converted Portuguese "New Christians" in the Estado da Índia itself.[104]

In light of the relative weight of Red Sea customs revenues for the provincial finances of Egypt, the influence of these groups—alongside more traditional assemblages of Muslim merchants and profiteers—can help to explain why, throughout the mid-sixteenth century, Egypt's governors seem to have consistently supported the interests of traders in the Indian Ocean, regardless of the whims of the central government in Istanbul. Such merchants and tax farmers formed one link in a larger chain of both Ottoman officials and private individuals who shared a vested interest in undermining Portuguese control of trade and in pursuing a policy of continued Ottoman maritime expansion at Portuguese expense.

Before Rustem Pasha, this coalition of interests had been openly favored by the state, such that, by the end of Hadim Suleiman's term as grand vizier in 1544, this group's most prominent state representatives (including Daud Pasha, Solak Ferhad Pasha, Bilal Mehmed Pasha, Mustafa al-Neshar, and Ozdemir Pasha) seem to have more or less monopolized the entire provincial administrations of Egypt, Yemen, and the Persian Gulf. Rustem had tried to change this, replacing these officials whenever possible with his own handpicked men, and promoting his vision for a centralized and autarchic Ottoman state that left little room for independent sources of power. But in the end, Rustem's gambit was doomed to failure: Uveys Pasha was assassinated by his own men, Piri Reis was executed, Seydi Ali was defeated at sea and forced to flee to a foreign land, and even Rustem himself was for a time forced out of office.

His dismissal provided a crucial window of opportunity for members of the Indian Ocean faction to reestablish themselves, and by the time Rustem returned in 1555, the tide had turned irrevocably against him. In 1556, Ozdemir began his campaign of conquest in Eritrea, despite Rustem's return to power. In 1557, the governor of Basra, apparently without Rustem's permission, tried to renegotiate the private trade agreement with the Portuguese in Hormuz.[105] In 1559, the governor of Katif, also without the grand vizier's permission, launched an impromptu expedition to the island of Bahrain.[106] And in 1560, when Rustem attempted to reinstate Seydi Ali Reis as admiral in Suez, the grand vizier was overruled, and Sefer Reis was appointed in his place. By the following year, when Rustem himself died of infirmity, the victory of the Indian Ocean faction was complete.

CONCLUSION: A NEW GRAND VIZIER FOR A NEW ERA

Rustem was replaced as grand vizier by Semiz Ali Pasha, a changing of the guard that left the Indian Ocean faction with more reason to feel optimistic about its future than it had had for a generation. Although not necessarily a member of the faction himself, "Fat" Ali had proven, at the very least, sympathetic to its cause during his five years as governor of Egypt between 1549 and 1555. Thereafter, he had served with distinction as the empire's second vizier, earning high marks from his own colleagues and from foreign diplomats alike for his keen intellect, his amiable disposition, and his consistent openness to new ideas.[107] Even the Austrian envoy Ogier de Busbecq, an unrelenting critic of the Ottoman establishment throughout his many years in Istanbul, judged Semiz Ali to be "the only really civilized man whom I ever met among those Turkish barbarians."[108]

True to expectations, Semiz Ali began his grand vizierate by making unmistakable signs of a new direction for the empire's Indian Ocean policy. In 1562, he appointed his personal client, Dervish Ali Pasha, as the new governor of Basra and instructed him to submit a report about how best to deal with the continuing Portuguese presence in Hormuz. Dervish Ali, described in one Portuguese account as "a prudent and sagacious man," came back with an unequivocal recommendation: the grand vizier should do everything within his power to bring a permanent end to hostilities and establish once and for all a mutually beneficial trading relationship with the

Portuguese, "both as a service to the Sultan and for the sake of his own profit." To this end, a message dispatched from Basra to Hormuz invited the Portuguese to send an official embassy to the Ottoman capital to begin negotiations.[109]

Early in the following year, when the Portuguese negotiator Antonio Texeira arrived in Istanbul in response to this invitation, he was presented with a trade agreement that was both sweeping in scope and comprehensive in detail.[110] According to its terms, the Portuguese were offered the right to establish trading houses in Basra, Cairo, and Alexandria and to trade freely in all the Ottoman-controlled ports of both the Persian Gulf and the Red Sea; in return, Ottoman merchants would be granted similar freedoms throughout the Indian Ocean, including the right to establish commercial agencies of their own "in Sind, Cambay, Dabul, Calicut, and any other ports they desired."[111]

Never before had the Portuguese been offered peace with the Ottomans on such comprehensive terms. And with the Estado da Índia facing skyrocketing costs, a disintegrating trade embargo of the Red Sea and Persian Gulf, and relentless attacks against its own shipping from the likes of Sefer Reis, never before had the temptation to accept the Ottomans' terms been so great. Even before the presentation of Semiz Ali's offer, in fact, the Portuguese ambassador in Rome, Lourenço Pires de Távora, had urged the king himself to take the initiative in seeking an agreement with the Ottomans, writing:

> The prospect is worthy of serious consideration, because the volume of spices that passes through the Red Sea to Cairo and from Hormuz to Basra is enormous, and there is every reason to believe that it will continue to grow even larger before leveling off. [At the same time,] Your Majesty's expenses in India are very great, and will grow even greater if some solution is not found. It is precisely because of this, as no reasonable man would dispute, that an agreement with the Turk would be most profitable.[112]

Not everyone, however, shared this sanguine view. And in the end, despite many dissenting voices, the Portuguese authorities rejected Semiz Ali's proposal, reaffirming their long-standing conviction that to accept any Ottoman offer based on the principle of free trade simply represented too great a threat. To understand the basis of this decision, the relevant arguments of one anonymous Portuguese *fidalgo*, preserved in the chronicle of Diogo do Couto, are worth quoting here at some length:

> With regards to this [agreement], I say that if the Turks were allowed to travel freely to India, and establish factors, and trade in merchandise wherever they wished, not only would Your Majesty's own profits suffer greatly, but the rest of us would be left completely empty handed, because all of the business [handled by the Portuguese] would immediately fall to the Turks and by means of the Red Sea and Persian Gulf they would bring to India all of the principal products which we bring from this Kingdom [of Portugal], since in the Levant and other parts [of their empire] they can be acquired much more cheaply than in Portugal. In addition, the duration of their voyages, their

> transportation costs, the risks they would face and the damage they would sustain to their ships and their merchandise would be less than half of that suffered by our own ships. . . .
>
> As for [the state monopoly in] pepper and other controlled spices, this also would be threatened by allowing the Turks to establish factors in India. Even now, when they have not been allowed to openly compete against the Portuguese, it is known that they conduct a trade in secret, carrying spices to Hormuz, to Basra, and to Bengal, Pegu, China and other lands, and especially to their own markets, despite the great risks involved. Thus, [if allowed to operate freely, their ties with] local Muslims would leave them even better informed and better organized, such that by means of the [Red Sea and Persian Gulf] they could send as much [pepper] as they wanted, and become masters of the lion's share of the trade in spices.[113]

Interestingly, Diogo do Couto—who did not record these words in his own chronicle until the mid-1590s—goes on in the same passage to compare directly the threat that the Ottomans posed to Portuguese trade in the 1560s with that posed by the Dutch at century's end. Unlike the Dutch, however, it is clear from Couto's text that the Ottomans' competitive advantage was based not only on a technical ability to purchase and transport goods more cheaply but also on extensive cooperation from indigenous trading communities throughout the Indian Ocean.

If this cooperation constituted a pillar of Ottoman commercial prowess by the 1560s, it had become so as a direct result of efforts by the Indian Ocean faction. Despite Rustem Pasha's stubborn attempts to seal off the empire's borders and insulate it from outside influences, Sefer Reis, Ozdemir Pasha, and countless other like-minded frontiersmen were able not merely to preserve but to deepen and expand the ties binding the empire to the trading world of the Indian Ocean. After 1561, their activities received official sanction under the tutelage of Semiz Ali Pasha, who allowed Ottoman policies, as they had before Rustem, to support rather than thwart the empire's expanding economic reach. Before long, Semiz Ali would be succeeded by an even more ambitious successor, who would expand upon these policies to construct an entirely new model of Ottoman imperial dominion across maritime Asia.

Five

SOKOLLU MEHMED PASHA AND THE APOGEE OF EMPIRE

1561–1579

Semiz Ali Pasha's tenure as grand vizier was relatively brief, beginning in 1561 and ending with his death from natural causes only four years later in 1565. Despite this short time in office, he could be credited with decisively transforming Ottoman economic relations with the Indian Ocean, having replaced Rustem's counterproductive policies with an enlightened open border approach designed to maximize maritime trade through both the Red Sea and the Persian Gulf. But from a political rather than an economic standpoint, Ali Pasha left a more ambiguous legacy. For as a result of his enthusiasm for negotiations with the Portuguese, he had embraced a timid foreign policy that, for all its good intentions, eventually left him at odds with most members of the Indian Ocean faction.

Stated simply, Semiz Ali's strategy to entice the Portuguese into a trade agreement was to convince them, through a series of confidence-building measures, that the Ottoman Empire was a benevolent power that no longer represented a military threat. Accordingly, during his first year in office, he had recalled Sefer Reis from Mocha, postponed indefinitely his predatory corsair attacks in the Arabian Sea, and delayed preparations for Sefer's new fleet in Suez.[1] Then, once he was engaged in direct negotiations with Portuguese representatives, Semiz Ali went so far as to propose the permanent dismemberment of the Ottoman fleet in Basra.[2] As an added gesture of goodwill, in 1563 the grand vizier even allowed the retiring captain of Hormuz, Pedro de Sousa, to travel overland through Iraq and Syria with an escort of ten men, so that he could visit the holy sites of Jerusalem on his way back to Lisbon.[3]

Unfortunately, none of these measures succeeded in extracting anything concrete from the Portuguese in return. And just as important, Semiz Ali's conviction that a lasting agreement with the Portugese was both possible and desirable appeared increasingly out of touch with political currents that had begun to sweep the wider trading world of maritime Asia. Indeed, to an extent possibly unmatched by any previous period, the 1560s were characterized by a rising tide of resentment toward the Portuguese throughout the Indian Ocean—and by a tangible if still inchoate yearning among its disparate Muslim communities to transcend their differences and forge a grand pan-Islamic alliance.[4] Moreover, these bellicose sentiments among Muslims were matched by a corresponding rise in zealotry and dogmatism on the Portuguese side, manifested most visibly in a new enthusiasm for the Holy Inquisition following the arrival in Goa of the firebrand Jesuit Dom Gonçalo da Silveira in 1559. As a result of his activities, Muslims were more actively discriminated against in Portuguese ports than in the past, and ever larger numbers of influential New Christians and Iberian Jews were likewise forced to abandon Portuguese India and throw in their lot with the constantly growing ranks of Muslims inclined to organize against it.[5]

More than ever before, the Ottoman Empire emerged as the great white hope of these disparate anti-Portuguese forces, who began petitioning the sultan with rising frequency to intervene on their behalf. In 1561, for example, an Egyptian Jew known as Isaac of Cairo brought to the sultan a proposal for a bilateral alliance from Nizam al-Mulk, the ruler of Ahmadnagar in the Deccan. This was a development of no small significance, for in previous decades Nizam al-Mulk had been among the Muslim rulers of India most consistently suspicious of the Ottomans and their intentions.[6] Now, he openly proposed a joint operation to conquer from the Portuguese the port city of Chaul, where he promised that the Ottomans would find both plentiful timber and enough local logistical support to build a fleet capable of subduing all of Portuguese India.[7] Similarly, in the following year, yet another embassy arrived, this time from Ali Ala'ad-din Ri'ayat Syah, the Sultan of Aceh in distant Sumatra. Like Nizam al-Mulk, Ali Ala'ad-din submitted a request of his own for Ottoman ships, artillery, and military experts to be used in an attack on the Portuguese in Malacca.[8]

Both of these petitions fell on deaf ears, for Semiz Ali, still fully committed to peace negotiations with the Portuguese, was reluctant to do anything that would jeopardize their success. Citing the extraordinary distance between Istanbul and Sumatra, as well as the likelihood that weapons and supplies could be intercepted by the Portuguese while en route, the grand vizier granted the envoys from Aceh only ten expert cannon founders and a vague promise of more help in the future. Nizam al-Mulk's envoy, Isaac of Cairo, received nothing at all.[9]

Inaction of this kind, at such a pregnant diplomatic moment, was a bitter pill for the Muslims of the Indian Ocean to swallow, and it also served as an increasing source of frustration for members of the Ottomans' own Indian Ocean faction. Such individuals, who had originally viewed Semiz Ali Pasha's vizierate as the culmination of their efforts to reverse the policies of Rustem, had at first embraced his efforts to conclude a trade agreement with the Portuguese. But as the months passed, and negotiations with Lisbon failed to produce any tangible results, enthusiasm for Semiz Ali's policy of appeasement began to wane perceptibly. By the end of 1563, as reports filtered in from Basra and Suez that the Portuguese had once more renewed their anti-Ottoman blockade, patience was wearing thin. Sefer Reis, still held up in Suez and awaiting permission to set sail with his new fleet, was chomping at the bit.[10]

Enter Sokollu Mehmed Pasha, one of the most compelling personalities of the entire sixteenth century and the mastermind of the Ottoman Empire's last great push into the Indian Ocean. Much like his well-placed predecessors Ibrahim and Rustem, Sokollu Mehmed was a palace favorite, a member of the Imperial Divan since 1554, and a figure especially close to the sultan's son Selim, whose daughter he married in 1562. Promoted to the grand vizierate just three years later, upon the death of his aged colleague Semiz Ali, Sokollu would thereafter dominate political life in the empire as perhaps no other grand vizier ever had before. His uninterrupted tenure in office eventually spanned fifteen years and the reigns of three successive sultans before his own death in 1579.[11]

Both Mehmed's professional experience and his personal and family connections made him ideally suited to be the new leader of the Indian Ocean faction. His first major administrative posting had been as grand admiral of the Ottoman navy during the late 1540s, where he had distinguished himself as a master of logistics and planning, expanded the shipyard in Galata, and brought in Venetian shipwrights to improve the standards of Ottoman galley construction.[12] Later, as governor-general of the province of Diyarbakir, he had been responsible for the first serious attempt to develop the Ottoman arsenal in Basra, supervising the preparation of lumber in the forests of Marash and organizing supply barges to carry munitions and shipbuilding materials by river from Anatolia to the Persian Gulf.[13]

Meanwhile, Sokollu's marriage to the Princess Ismihan, who was both daughter of the future Sultan Selim II and the descendant, on her mother's side, of one of the most important noble families in Venice, placed Sokollu at the center of a vast association of financial and trading interests that stretched across the Mediterranean.[14] Other members of this circle included Michael Cantacuzenos, the fabulously wealthy heir of Byzantine aristocrats; Aron de Segura and Joseph Hamon, two of the empire's most influential Jewish courtiers; and the Venetian Bailo Marc Antonio Barbaro, with whom Sokollu maintained a lifelong friendship uninterrupted even by the outbreak of war between Venice and the Ottomans in the early 1570s.[15]

None of these personal or professional contacts, however, was as important as Sokollu Mehmed's two greatest assets: a powerful intellect and an insatiable curiosity about the world. Throughout his professional life, Sokollu proved a prodigious patron of science, art, and learning, and his cosmopolitan tastes and eclectic interests spanned the globe in a very real sense. He commissioned paintings by Veronese masters and imported fine glassware from the artisans of Venice,[16] championed the opening of the astronomer Takiyuddin Efendi's celebrated observatory in Istanbul,[17] and sponsored the translation of a world history composed by Musliheddin el-Lari, personal tutor of the Mughal Emperor Humayun.[18] Even more significantly, he worked closely with and actively bankrolled the most prominent Ottoman geographers and historians of his day. These included Feridun Ahmed Beg, who was both Sokollu's personal secretary and a prolific archivist and author; Sipahizade Mehmed, who completed the abridged Turkish version of his "Location of the Paths to the Knowledge of Kingdoms and Countries" at the grand vizier's request in 1573; and Kutbeddin Mekki, who expanded his history of the Ottoman conquests in the Indian Ocean for Sokollu in 1579.[19]

All of this meant that Sokollu Mehmed had a deeper and more nuanced understanding of world events than perhaps any other Ottoman policy maker of the sixteenth century. As such, he could draw from a bank of accumulated knowledge about the globe that allowed him to construct with unprecedented sophistication a grand strategy for imperial expansion. Sokollu's genius was to combine an appreciation of the vast rhetorical potential of Ottoman claims to universal sovereignty with an understanding of the technical prerequisites of building and maintaining a global network of communications—the principal vehicle through which these claims could be expressed. By undermining the tenuous maritime links between Portugal and its scattered colonies of the East, while at the same time facilitating travel between Ottoman lands and Muslims overseas, he hoped to turn the rising tide of pan-Islamic sentiment into a concrete manifestation of Ottoman sovereignty throughout maritime Asia.

SOKOLLU'S INFORMANT: SEYDI ALI REIS

As he began to formulate this grand imperial strategy, one of Sokollu's earliest sources of inspiration was Seydi Ali Reis's *Mir'ātü'l-Memālik* ("Mirror of Countries"). This work, as has already been argued, was commissioned by Sokollu's predecessor Rustem Pasha and reflected, at its core, the parochial and Ottoman-centric worldview that Rustem strove to promote through his intellectual patronage. Nevertheless, it was also a firsthand narrative of travel that, when placed in the right hands, counted as a uniquely useful source of information about the political climate of the contemporary Indian Ocean. Since its presentation to the sultan in 1557 closely coincided with Sokollu Mehmed's own emergence as an important figure at court, "Mirror of Countries" seems to have served, almost in spite of itself, as the initial spark for the formulation of Sokollu Mehmed's very different ideas about the Indian Ocean.

The most profound lesson that Sokollu appears to have drawn from Seydi Ali's memoir was that Ottoman prestige, despite the debacle of Seydi Ali's own mission, was at an all-time high across the region. This is a theme continually emphasized throughout the author's account of his travels, as he records vociferous expressions of *inḳıyād ve iṭāʿat* ("devotion and obedience") to the Ottoman dynasty in various Muslim ports of call from the Hadramaut to Baluchistan to Gujarat. Early in his narrative, for example, upon taking refuge with his bedraggled fleet in the Gujarati port of Daman, Seydi Ali reported an encounter with some "junks" belonging to the Zamorin of Calicut, whose captains assured him that their ruler was "waging a war night and day against the infidels in devotion and obedience to His Imperial Majesty."[20] Shortly thereafter, Seydi Ali was invited to the nearby port of Surat by Rumi Khan, the son and successor of Hoja Safar, who greeted him with the following pronouncement:

> It is most fortunate that you have arrived in Gujarat at such a time of great upheaval. Never since the days of Noah has the sea been seized by such a storm . . . but it is our hope that, God willing, the land of Gujarat will soon be joined to the protected domains of the Ottoman Empire, and the ports of India will thereby be delivered into safety from the hands of the accursed infidels.[21]

The sentiments expressed in this brief passage are striking, suggesting in no uncertain terms that the Muslims of Surat, above and beyond asking for simple military assistance from the sultan, hoped for an outright Ottoman annexation of their city. When placed together with the spy report of João de Lisboa (discussed in the previous chapter), Rumi Khan's words also provide confirmation that, during the turbulent years following the death of Sultan Mahmud of Gujarat in 1553, a reinvigorated Rumi elite had reached a position of unparalleled authority at the court of his son Sultan Ahmed, making such dreams of an Ottoman Gujarat a real possibility. By the time of Seydi Ali's arrival on the scene, this group of well-placed Rumis included, in addition to Rumi Khan himself, the powerful warlords Chingiz Khan and Kara Hasan, both of whom were veterans of the sieges of Diu with large numbers of rank-and-file Rumi soldiers in their service. Most prominent of all was Chingiz Khan's father Imad al-Mulk, the young sultan's tutor who by the late 1550s had risen to become vizier at Ahmed's court.[22]

For Seydi Ali, the extent of this group's collective influence was aptly demonstrated upon his arrival in Ahmedabad, the Gujarati capital, where the admiral was ostentatiously welcomed in a public ceremony by both Sultan Ahmed and Imad al-Mulk. Subsequently, when a Portuguese envoy arrived from Diu demanding that Seydi Ali be turned over to him, Imad al-Mulk flatly refused, saying: "We have need of the Ottoman Sultan. If our ships were unable to reach the ports of his empire, our livelihoods would suffer. And more importantly, he is the Padishah of Islam. Is it reasonable that you should ask us to surrender his admiral?"[23]

As a Rumi himself, Imad al-Mulk of course had his own self-interested reasons for proclaiming the Ottoman sultan "Padishah of Islam" and professing loyalty to him under the banner of Islamic unity. At the time of Seydi Ali's arrival, he was engaged in a high-stakes political showdown with Itimad Khan, his main rival for power at court in Ahmedabad, who represented the interests of the opposing "anti-Rumi" faction in Gujarat. By 1559, the confrontation between these groups would in fact become so bitter that Itimad Khan, having lost out to the Rumis in the contest for influence with the young sultan, would arrange for the murder of Imad al-Mulk and, in the following year, the assassination of the sultan as well.[24]

Against such a troubled local backdrop, the Rumis of Gujarat therefore had particularly concrete reasons to emphasize the transcendent authority of the Ottoman sultan and their own commitment to advancing his cause. Still, such sentiments appear to have been widespread well beyond the political circles of maritime Gujarat, to the extent that Seydi Ali would later receive very similar expressions of support even at the court of the Mughal Emperor Humayun in Delhi. Here, in fact, Seydi Ali was welcomed with truly spectacular pomp and circumstance, as an entourage of some four hundred elephants and all the magistrates of the realm greeted him as he approached the Mughal capital. During his subsequent stay at Humayun's court, he was invited into the emperor's presence on several occasions, and it is in Seydi Ali's account of these conversations with the sovereign that he reveals his most startling evidence about the truly global dimensions of Ottoman prestige. One day, when Humayun began to question him about the geographical extent of the Ottoman Empire and how it compared with the size of his own realm in India, the admiral assured him that "the seven regions over which the Great Alexander had dominion were identical with the present Empire of the Padishah of Rum." To illustrate his point, he then recounted the following story:

> I was told in the Gujarati port of Surat by the [Rumi] Muslims Hoja Bakhshi and Kara Hasan (God alone knows whether their story is true) that when the holy festival of Eid was celebrated in the lands of China, the Muslim worshippers there [of various nations] each desired to have the Friday *ẖuṭbe* read in the name of their own sovereigns. But the Rumi worshippers appealed to the Great Khan of China, saying "It is our Emperor who is the Padishah of Mecca and Medina and the Kibla." The Great Khan, although an unbeliever, understood [the justice of their appeal] and gave the order: "You shall read the *ẖuṭbe* [only] in the name of the Padishah of Mecca and Medina and the Kibla." He then ordered the Rumi preachers to be clothed in robes of honor and had them ride on an elephant through the city, and ever since the name of the Ottoman Sultan has been read whenever a religious holiday is celebrated in the lands of China. What ruler has ever before been so honored?[25]

In other words, because of Ottoman control of the holy cities of Mecca and Medina, the two Rumis (Hoja Bakhshi and Kara Hasan) claimed that the Ottoman sultan was already recognized, at least in some sense, as the de facto suzerain of Muslim communities even as far away as China—a status ostensibly confirmed by the Great Khan himself.[26] True or not, Humayun was said to be duly impressed and, turning to his nobles, exclaimed: "Surely there is no man on earth worthy of the title

'Padishah' other than his Imperial Majesty [the Ottoman Sultan]!"[27] He then issued a letter for Seydi Ali to carry back with him to Istanbul, in which he addressed Sultan Suleiman as "Caliph of the World."[28]

More than any other passage in Seydi Ali's "Mirror of Countries," this anecdotal story (and its apparent confirmation in the letter from Humayun) appears to have left a deep impression on Sokollu Mehmed. As later events would demonstrate, he became committed to the idea of increasing Ottoman authority in the Indian Ocean by encouraging precisely the kind of voluntary affiliation (*inḳıyād ve iṭā'at*) between local Muslim merchants and rulers and the Ottoman state that Seydi Ali's text suggested was already beginning to develop spontaneously.

As a result, Sokollu's vision differed substantially from that of Semiz Ali Pasha, whose reluctance, throughout the early 1560s, to engage more actively with Muslim rulers such as Nizam al-Mulk of Ahmadnagar and Ali Ala'ad-din Ri'ayat Syah of Aceh he viewed with increasing impatience. After Semiz Ali Pasha's death in 1565, Sokollu would therefore engineer a dramatic change in Ottoman policy. But even before his own accession to the grand vizierate, Sokollu was able to use indirect means to begin laying the groundwork for a new era of collaboration between the Ottomans and the Muslims of the Indian Ocean.

Early signs of Sokollu's influence are most apparent with regard to the embassy from Aceh, which in 1562 had lodged a request for Ottoman ships and artillery to be used in an attack against the Portuguese in Malacca. On this occasion, because of Semiz Ali Pasha's eagerness for a settlement with the Portuguese, his first impulse had been to refuse outright this Acehnese request and to send the envoys back to Southeast Asia empty-handed.[29] In the end, however, a compromise was reached, and Semiz Ali eventually agreed to send ten artillery experts to Sumatra, where they would assist the Acehnese in casting cannons in situ from locally available materials. This concession, a crucial first step in establishing permanent Ottoman relations with the distant Acehnese sultanate, was almost certainly the result of pressure from Sokollu, and it serves as the first concrete evidence of the future grand vizier's emerging strategy in the Indian Ocean.[30]

Just as important, the agreement to send these Ottoman cannon founders to Aceh also provided Sokollu Mehmed with the opportunity to dispatch a mysterious envoy, known to us only as "His Majesty's Servant Lutfi," as an escort on the lengthy and perilous voyage back to Sumatra. Lutfi's primary mission was to accompany the team of artillery experts to Aceh and, during his journey, gather more precise intelligence about the region in order to corroborate the information in Seydi Ali's "Mirror of Countries." At the same time, Lutfi was also under orders from Sokollu to establish contacts with local Muslims throughout the Indian Ocean and to do everything possible to incite them to rise up in a general armed rebellion against the Portuguese.

It would be hard to imagine a more elusive figure than Lutfi, a member of the sultan's *müteferriḳa re'isleri*, or private corps of sea captains, whose only extant work is a ghostwritten letter from Sultan Ali Ala'ad-din Ri'ayat Syah of Aceh, presented to the Imperial Divan upon his return to Istanbul in 1566.[31] Nevertheless, the little that is known about his activities suggests that Lutfi was a character of singular importance, playing a pivotal role in fomenting the pan-Islamic uprising that broke out across the Indian Ocean beginning in 1564. And significantly, the original flash-point for this unrest was Aceh, where Lutfi seems to have had an electrifying effect upon the local population almost as soon as he arrived sometime in the middle of that year.

AN AGENT PROVOCATEUR IN ACEH: "HIS MAJESTY'S SERVANT LUTFI"

Although the Sultanate of Aceh had served as a pole of Muslim opposition to the Estado da Índia since at least the 1520s, the Acehnese embassy sent to Istanbul in 1562 had marked a major shift in Aceh's foreign policy. Despite a long history of friendly commercial relations with the Ottoman Empire, punctuated by several instances of open military cooperation earlier in the century, there is no record of direct diplomatic contact between the Acehnese and the Ottoman court at any point during the preceding decade. Throughout these years, in fact, Aceh had remained—its bellicose reputation notwithstanding—a loyal tributary of the Portuguese, such that even as late as 1563, Portuguese ships were in the habit of occasionally visiting Aceh to trade or stock up on provisions. Moreover, despite Aceh's visibly growing aggressiveness towards its neighbors within Southeast Asia, often framed by the Acehnese in terms of a responsibility to conduct "holy war," until this date Aceh's foreign policy seems to have been directed primarily toward the conquest of Aru and Johor, two local rivals ruled by fellow Muslims.[32]

In 1564, however, at precisely the moment that Lutfi arrived in Sumatra for the first time, Portuguese crews calling at Aceh reported an abrupt change in local behavior, as their ships began to be boarded and their goods confiscated without any apparent justification. Tensions then steadily increased, until on one occasion the crew of a victimized Portuguese ship protested this treatment and "insulted an ambassador from the Grand Turk who was there [in Aceh] at that time."[33] This ambassador, undoubtedly Lutfi, professed outrage and demanded in retaliation that the entire Portuguese crew be forced to convert to Islam or be put to the sword. The Acehnese sultan agreed, and as all but two of the crew preferred martyrdom to apostasy, they were tortured and then given a grisly public execution.[34]

Almost no further details are available about this event, but if it was intended as a macabre stunt to polarize feelings against the Portuguese, it certainly had its effect. In the aftermath, Lutfi's presence in Aceh quickly began to attract the attention of an impressive series of regional power brokers both in and outside Sumatra, and during his stay, he is known to have received envoys from the Muslim communities of Calicut, Ceylon, Gujarat, and even the Maldives.[35] Moreover, within a few weeks of the execution of the Portuguese crew, the sultan of Aceh himself sent a letter to the Portuguese captain of Malacca. Within, he reminded his counterpart of the friendly relations they had enjoyed in the past but complained of being "repeatedly reprimanded by the Ottomans" for his "scandalous" failure to take up arms in defense of Muslim interests.[36] He ended with a warning that without an unequivocal gesture of friendship from Malacca, he would have no choice but to declare war.

Halfway around the world, as Sokollu Mehmed prepared to take over the reins of government in Istanbul from the rapidly aging Semiz Ali, a letter of nearly identical tone was sent from Suleiman the Magnificent to the Portuguese sovereign Dom Sebastião in Lisbon. In it, the sultan included his own terse warning that his patience for negotiations had finally reached its limits:

> It has been reported that the Muslim pilgrims and merchants coming from India by sea have been molested and abused in direct violation of the desired peace agreement between us . . . if it is truly your desire to bring peace and security to those lands, then as soon as this Imperial Ferman arrives you must cease all of your attacks at sea against merchants and pilgrims, and you must send a letter and a trusted envoy [to us] such that an agreement that will put the affairs of that region on a good footing can be concluded. If you are still set on pursuing the path of rebellion, then with the help of God Almighty we will do everything necessary to restore order to those lands, and it will no longer be of any use [for you to protest] by saying "but [we] wanted peace!" What else is there to say?[37]

With the drafting of this letter, the pace of events quickened across the Indian Ocean, as the pent-up anti-Portuguese hostility of the region's disparate Muslim communities broke out into open warfare across a formidable series of military theaters. In India's Deccan plateau, Nizam al-Mulk of Ahmadnagar and Adil Shah of Bijapur, two traditional rivals for control of the region, were able for the first time to unite forces and overthrow the neighboring Hindu kingdom of Vijayanagar, until that time a reliable Portuguese ally.[38] Further to the south, the Mappilla leader Ali Raja besieged the Portuguese fortress guarding the port of Cannanor, while his cousin Kutti Musa organized a fleet to harass the squadron of Melo da Silva off the Malabar coast.[39] And in Suez, Sefer Reis was given permission for an as yet unspecified mission against the Portuguese in the Arabian Sea.

SEFER'S LAST CAMPAIGN

The purpose of this mission—which would prove to be the last in Sefer's extraordinary life—had been the subject of speculation among Portuguese spies and diplomats since at least 1559, when the first reports of the construction of a major new fleet in Suez had begun to filter out of Egypt. Even so, his intentions were still a mystery when, toward the end of 1564, Sefer set out from Suez and advanced as far as Mocha before stopping to await further orders. He remained there throughout the following spring and summer, until Semiz Ali Pasha's death removed the last obstacle to his departure. By late fall, with the full support of the new grand vizier, Sokollu Mehmed, all ten of Sefer's galleys set sail for the south in what was intended to be the greatest and most daring campaign he had ever undertaken.[40]

According to a report sent in January 1566 by Mattias Bicudo Furtado, a Portuguese informant in Cairo, the ten ships were to be used in an entirely novel kind of attack, in which Sefer "set out with the aim of pillaging the entire Swahili coast and proceeding all the way to Mozambique, where he had great hopes of catching ships from the Royal fleet [sent annually around the Cape of Good Hope from Lisbon]."[41] Such an attack not only promised to yield an unprecedented booty of captured cargo and slaves but also threatened to virtually cut off the Estado da Índia from its capital, severing the only tenuous sea route connecting India and Portugal. Unparalleled in scope and innovative in terms of its specific target, the plan was at the same time in keeping with Sefer's fire-tested strategy, in effect recreating on a grander scale the blockade he had set up between Hormuz and Diu in 1554.

If Sefer's characteristic boldness and precision were central to the plan, however, it also bore the unmistakable imprint of Sokollu Mehmed, who among Sefer's contemporaries was the Ottoman statesman best prepared to understand, and to support, the truly global implications of such a strategy. In fact, given what we know of the grand vizier's active diplomacy during this period, it is not impossible that Sokollu actually planned the attack together with Sefer—and may even have timed the mission to coincide with a French corsair attack against the Portuguese base in Madeira, an important Atlantic way station for the annual convoy of ships sent from Lisbon to India. Suggestively, a Venetian dispatch from Madrid describing this attack, which came in the middle of 1566, also cryptically reported: "It is believed by some that these [French corsairs] have proceeded towards the Cape of Good Hope to collaborate with a ruler in those parts who is constantly at war with the King of Portugal."[42]

Unfortunately, if any such grandiose plans existed, they were undermined by Sefer's sudden and unexpected demise, reported to the Portuguese by the same Cairene informant, Mattias Bicudo Furtado, on January 18, 1566. According to Furtado, Sefer had set out from Suez late in the previous month and was a day and a half out of Mocha and headed for the island of Socotra when, without warning, he fell deathly ill. His infirmity forced him to alter his course toward the port city of Aden, and there he died just three days after his arrival.[43] Furtado's report added as an epitaph: "He was a daring thief and most practiced in [the combat] of those regions, knowing exactly how and when to strike. There is no other man such as he in all the lands of the East who we need so greatly fear."[44]

THE RETURN OF LUTFI

The timing and suddenness of Sefer's death dealt a grave blow to the cause of an Ottoman-led pan-Islamic uprising against the Portuguese. Still, although the bulk of Sefer's fleet was soon recalled to Suez, the mission was not a total loss, as a number of Sefer's crew members were apparently fitted out with new galleys in Yemen and rerouted from Mozambique to Aceh.[45] Their new mission seems to have been to provide an armed escort for the fleet of spice ships sent annually from Sumatra to the Red Sea—the first recorded instance in which an escort of Ottoman galleys was provided for an Acehnese merchant convoy.[46] In addition, these galleys were to ensure a safe return passage for Lutfi, who had attempted to make the journey home from Sumatra in the previous year but had been forced to turn back after an ambush at sea by a Portuguese patrol.[47]

Accordingly, in early 1566, the Portuguese received word that "in Aceh five galleons loaded with pepper, spices and other goods were preparing to depart for Mecca, and nine galleys were on their way [from Ottoman territory] to escort them on their journey."[48] In response, the Portuguese sent five galleons and six galleys of their own to the Maldives, in the hope of heading these ships off while still en route to the Red Sea. Upon reaching the Maldives, the Portuguese commander, Diogo Pereyra, learned that the Acehnese spice galleons and their Ottoman escort had already arrived and were waiting in a nearby channel, so he ordered his fleet to divide in two and patrol the area in an attempt to determine his enemies' exact location.

This would prove more difficult than Pereyra might have hoped, a fact lamented by the chronicler Diogo do Couto, who opined in his description of this encounter that "the Turks are daring and experienced men of war who never leave anything open to chance, as we are prone to."[49] Couto then goes on to describe how the Ottoman galley commanders, as soon as they got word of Pereyra's arrival in the area, devised a ruse to distract him. By firing off a series of bombards at different locations, they managed to convince each of the two Portuguese patrols that the other had encountered the enemy fleet. Both squadrons thus spent the better part of a day and a night looking for each other, and by the time they finally met up and realized their mistake, all of the Ottoman galleys and Acehnese spice ships had escaped.

Pereyra made a final attempt to sail to Socotra and catch up with the Ottomans there, but to no avail. Finally, after angrily looting the port of a local sheikh suspected of harboring the Ottoman vessels, Pereyra's fleet headed back to India, where it was caught in a violent storm and lost several ships with all hands on board.[50] Meanwhile, the vessels from Aceh arrived safely in Mocha, bringing with them Lutfi, a rich cargo of spices, and Hussein, the same Acehnese ambassador who had visited Istanbul in 1562.[51]

LUTFI'S REPORT

When Lutfi and Hussein reached Istanbul toward the end of 1566, they found a political climate vastly more favorable to their aims than the one they had left behind three years earlier. Not only was Sokollu Mehmed now grand vizier but also, after helping to secure the throne for his father-in-law, Selim II, following the recent death of Suleiman the Magnificent, Sokollu's position at the pinnacle of Ottoman political life was more secure than ever. In addition, this time around the Acehnese ambassador was able to appear before the Divan accompanied by Lutfi, who was prepared to present his superiors with his own firsthand account of conditions in Southeast Asia in the form of a ghostwritten letter from the sultan of Aceh.

Lutfi's letter was the most comprehensive document produced by a member of the Indian Ocean faction during these years, and its contents corroborated everything about the political situation in the Indian Ocean previously suggested by Seydi Ali's memoirs—and more. Perhaps its most striking claim was that, in Aceh, the sultan no longer wished to simply purchase arms and supplies from the Ottomans, nor even forge a temporary strategic alliance with Istanbul. Instead, Sultan Ali Ala'ad-din Ri'ayat Syah declared an intention—openly evocative of Rumi Khan's earlier proclamation recorded in "Mirror of Countries"—to have his lands formally annexed by the Ottoman state in exchange for help against the Portuguese in Malacca. In his words:

> We sincerely request that Your Imperial Majesty [the Ottoman Sultan] should no longer consider me, your servant in this land, to be an independent ruler, but instead to accept me as a poor, humble, and downtrodden slave who lives thanks to the charity of your Imperial Majesty, Refuge of the World and Shadow of God [on Earth], in no way different from the governors of Egypt and Yemen or the *begs* of Jiddah and Aden.... With God as my witness, this [city of] Aceh is one of Your Majesty's own villages, and I too am one of your servants. Your official Lutfi can personally attest to our circumstances and to our deeds, to the great endeavors we have undertaken for the sake of holy war, and to our firm and sincere longing to enter Your Imperial Majesty's service.[52]

Lutfi's letter then goes on to describe a similar level of enthusiasm for Ottoman dynastic rule in other areas of the Indian Ocean. He reports that at least one of the Rumi viziers of Gujarat, Karamanlioğlu Abdurrahman, shared the sultan of Aceh's hope to be recognized as an Ottoman *sancaḳ begi* or "Lord of the Standard," adding that he had already proven his devotion by personally transporting Lutfi in one of his own ships during his outgoing journey from Jiddah to Aceh.[53] Even more remarkably, Lutfi insisted that in addition to such members of Gujarat's Rumi elite, even the general Muslim population of various lands throughout the Indian Ocean had similarly begun to recognize the Ottoman sultan as their overlord and protector. In the Maldive archipelago, for example, he claimed that "the people... have built mosques on all of the islands, and read the *ḫuṭbe* in the noble name of your most high and blessed Imperial Majesty."[54] And in Ceylon and Calicut, although the population of these kingdoms lived under the rule of pagan sovereigns, locals had built dozens of mosques where they, too, "read the *ḫuṭbe* in the noble name of his most high and blessed Imperial Majesty, refuge of the world, and pray for the longevity and prosperity of his state."[55] Lutfi's report even suggested, presumably with a touch of hyperbole, that his activities had convinced the *rulers* of these two kingdoms to recognize Ottoman suzerainty and personally embrace Islam in exchange for military assistance from Istanbul. According to the text:

> When the rulers of Ceylon and Calicut received news that His Majesty's servant Lutfi had arrived here [in Aceh], they sent ambassadors to us who proclaimed: "We [also] are servants of His Imperial Majesty, Refuge of the World and Shadow of God [on Earth]" and then took an oath swearing that if His Imperial Majesty's propitious fleet were to journey to these lands, they themselves would come to the faith and profess the religion of Islam, and that likewise all of their infidel subjects would forsake the way of false belief for the straight path of the one true religion. God willing, with the illustrious assistance of His Imperial Majesty, all traces of the infidels in both the East and the West will be destroyed, and they will finally join the Islamic faith.[56]

With this report, Lutfi was thus able to confirm Sokollu Mehmed's greatest hope: that the Muslims of maritime Asia were ready to spontaneously adopt the concept of a universal Ottoman sultanate as a collective pan-Islamic political ideology. The grand vizier thus sensed a historic opportunity to almost effortlessly extend Ottoman influence across the Indian Ocean and responded by directing all of his considerable energy, enthusiasm, and organizational acumen toward this goal.

Sokollu's strategy for accomplishing this was, like the man himself, sophisticated and multidimensional, involving a combination of political initiatives, diplomatic maneuvers, military campaigns, market reforms, and faith-based propaganda. In the end, his record of achievement was by no means one of unmitigated success—especially with regard to the most extravagant of his plans that (beginning with the inauspicious death of Sefer in 1565) often failed to fully materialize. Even so, it must be remembered that the crux of his strategy lay not in any specific efforts to conquer territories or defeat the Portuguese at sea. Rather, his greatest aspiration was to convince Indian Ocean Muslims that the *idea* of a universal caliphate, with the Ottoman sultan at its head, was in itself meaningful and worthy of support. In this respect, even his most ostentatious failures still served his larger goals by reinforcing the idea that the Ottoman sultanate was prepared to speak—and to act—on behalf of Muslims everywhere.

PREPARATIONS FOR AN OTTOMAN EXPEDITION TO SUMATRA

In pursuing this objective, the grand vizier's first and most obvious task was to send Lutfi back to Aceh, this time in the company of a major expeditionary force. To this end, he ordered the immediate construction of a fleet in the arsenal in Suez and drew on his own long experience in naval affairs to ensure that its vessels were outfitted to perfection. Surviving records show that between September and December of 1567, Sokollu sent out literally dozens of edicts related to the expedition, in which he followed preparations down to the minutest detail. Directives sent from Istanbul during these months include an order to the governor of Egypt to identify suitable sea captains for the fleet, a request to the head cannon founder of the arsenal in Galata to select the best siege guns for the mission, and even a letter to Piyale Pasha, the grand admiral of the Ottoman navy, regarding some coils of rope required for the galleys.[57] As commander of the expedition, Sokollu selected Kurdoğlu Hizir, then captain of Alexandria, while Mahmud Reis, Sefer's recent replacement as admiral in Suez, was put in direct charge of the galleys.[58]

As 1567 drew to a close, this expeditionary force was fully equipped and ready to set sail. It consisted of a total of fifteen fully armed war galleys and was accompanied by two transport galleons loaded with "artillery pieces, muskets and other tools of war," including thirty large siege cannons.[59] The fleet was manned by seven expert gunners, a master cannon founder from the imperial artillery corps, plentiful rowers, "a sufficient quantity of troops from our victorious armies," and an unusually large number of craftsmen, including sawyers, carpenters, blacksmiths, coppersmiths, caulkers, and even three goldsmiths, all of whom received a year of advanced pay before their departure.[60] In observance of a request from the sultan of Aceh conveyed in Lutfi's letter, all participants in the expedition were also given orders, regardless of rank, to obey Sultan Ali Ala'ad-din Ri'ayat Syah's every command and not to oppose him in any way, at the risk of severe punishment.[61] And to ensure compliance with these orders, the fleet was to be accompanied by both Lutfi and the Acehnese ambassador Hussein, as well as a certain Mustafa Chavush (a member of the Imperial Messenger Corps), who was to escort the force as far as Sumatra and then return to Ottoman lands to report its safe arrival. Mustafa Chavush was also to present an imperial edict to the sultan of Aceh, acknowledging the sultan's oath of loyalty to the Ottoman state and exhorting him to make the best possible use of the assistance being sent to him. According to the text of this edict:

> You [the Sultan of Aceh] must make your best effort to carry out your responsibilities to religion and to our Imperial State. You must persevere and exert yourself, be it by conquering the strongholds of the miserable infidels, or by freeing the people of Islam from their evil and rage. With the help of God Almighty, you must cleanse those lands of the infidel filth, so that under our Imperial rule which concludes in justice, the Muslims of that land may live in a state of tranquility and, free from anxiety, may busy themselves with earning a livelihood.[62]

Finally, the sultan concluded with a promise that this initial shipment of men and weapons was only the beginning of a permanent new relationship between Istanbul and Aceh, which was to be protected and nurtured by ensuring that the lines of communication between the two distant realms remained open and secure:

> If the greatest and most noble Lord in heaven so wills it, help from our courageous armies will from now on be sent to you continuously to prevent the harm caused by those enemies of the true religion and the laws of the lord of the apostles, who have overrun the lands of the Muslims. It is hoped that it will become your habit to regularly inform our Imperial court in detail about the conditions and developments in [your] land, and to never fail in this regard.[63]

INSURRECTION IN YEMEN

With Kurdoğlu Hizir's fleet ready to sail, the stage seemed set for an unprecedented Ottoman military intervention in Southeast Asia. But in a heartbreaking blow to Sokollu's plans, the grand expedition to Aceh (like so many of the grand vizier's other most ambitious projects) was undermined at the last minute by unforeseen political developments elsewhere in the empire. In this case, the source of trouble was in the Yemeni highlands, where an uprising by the Zaydi Imam Mutahhar—the first such uprising in nearly twenty years—engulfed Yemen in turmoil, making any plans to use it as an advanced base for an expedition to Aceh a technical impossibility.

In truth, the earliest reports of this rebellion had begun to reach Istanbul as early as the summer of 1567, when the expedition to Aceh was still in its planning stages. Initially, Sokollu Mehmed downplayed the seriousness of the situation and attempted to move ahead with his naval preparations in spite of the unrest. During the following months, however, conditions in Yemen worsened at an alarming rate: the major cities of Ta'izz, Sana'a, and Aden all fell to Mutahhar's forces; the Ottoman squadron in Mocha fled to Jiddah; and even the loyalty of Sultan Badr in Shihr was coming under question.[64] By the end of 1567, only the tiny Ottoman garrison of Zebid still held out against the rebels, and the grand vizier, however reluctantly, was obliged to organize an emergency relief expedition. Koja Sinan Pasha, the new governor of Egypt, was charged with Yemen's reconquest, and Kurdoğlu Hizir and his fifteen galleys were reassigned for this purpose, postponing their departure for Sumatra indefinitely.[65]

The decision to call off the mission to Aceh, coming just two years after Sefer Reis's untimely demise, must have been a devastating disappointment to Sokollu Mehmed. But unlike the cruel coincidence of Sefer's sickness and sudden death at the outset of his mission, the inopportune timing of Mutahhar's uprising cannot be explained away as a simple case of force majeure. On the contrary, the widespread discontent in Yemen that had provoked Mutahhar's rebellion was directly connected with Sokollu Mehmed's efforts to intensify Ottoman involvement there as a prelude to his plans for expansion in the Indian Ocean.

Specifically, the numerous grievances of Mutahhar and his supporters can almost all be traced to the reckless administration of Mahmud Pasha, a compatriot of Sokollu from his home country of Bosnia who had served as the governor of

Ottoman Yemen from 1560 to 1565. Mahmud was, in addition to his ties to the grand vizier, a stolid member of the Indian Ocean faction, having originally advanced through the ranks of the Egyptian bureaucracy under Daud Pasha in the 1540s.[66] Thanks to this experience, during his subsequent tenure as Yemen's governor-general, Mahmud had proven himself to be—at least on the surface—an unscrupulous but effective administrator. His five years in office witnessed an impressive increase in provincial revenues, such that Yemen not only began to generate a large surplus for the imperial treasury but also was able to subsidize the finances of the neighboring province of Eritrea through shipments of troops and currency.[67] Eager as Sokollu Mehmed was to turn Yemen into a launching pad for further expansion, Mahmud's efforts thus met with the grand vizier's hearty approval, and after finishing his term and returning to Istanbul in 1565, the pasha was duly given a promotion to the governorship of Egypt. Only afterward, when insurrection in Yemen had already broken out, did it become clear that Mahmud Pasha's gains had been of the most ill-gotten sort.[68]

The range and extent of Mahmud Pasha's misdeeds while in office were truly impressive, even by the indulgent standards of the sixteenth century. He had begun his reign by executing the province's mint officials on groundless charges of currency debasement in order to confiscate their personal wealth for the treasury. Then, he had placed his own men in charge of the mint and shamelessly debased the currency himself, to such an extent that his soldiers were reduced to destitution and forced to sell their possessions and flee or, worse, join forces with the Zaydis.[69] Still hungry to enlarge his treasury, he then provoked a confrontation with al-Nazari, the wealthy ruler of Ta'izz, who had been granted autonomy by previous Ottoman governors. When al-Nazari fled in fright to his mountain stronghold of Habb, Mahmud managed to lure him out of the fortress with offers of clemency, only to have him arrested and promptly executed, seizing his property and demanding exorbitant tax increases throughout the region as punishment for his insubordination. Thereafter, he even had two of his own subordinates executed when they protested against his policies. Finally, upon his return to Istanbul, he used the enormous wealth gained from this and other nefarious adventures to lavish gifts on Sokollu Mehmed and the sultan and ensure his future appointment as governor of Egypt.[70] Not until a year later, when political authority in Yemen had entirely collapsed and an examination of his account books revealed the extent of his corruption, was Mahmud quietly done away with on a back street of Cairo.[71]

A SECOND WAVE OF PAN-ISLAMIC INSURGENCY

Mahmud Pasha was replaced as governor of Egypt by Koja Sinan, another of Sokollu's highest ranking protégés, and it was also Koja Sinan who was given the responsibility of organizing a relief expedition to Yemen. The long and complicated story of his subsequent reconquest of the province need not detain us here, except to say that putting down the revolt took the better part of three years and absorbed almost all of the region's available financial and military resources.[72] Before the conflict was over, Koja Sinan had requisitioned all of the spare ships stationed in Suez and the entire military reserves of both Egypt and Eritrea, in addition to Kurdoğlu Hizir's fifteen Aceh-bound galleys.

Still, even a crisis of this magnitude did not prevent the Ottomans from dispatching at least some forces in the direction of Sumatra. By the middle of 1568, Portuguese sources reported the arrival of some "500 Turks, many large bombards, abundant ammunition, many engineers and several masters of artillery" in Aceh.[73] Although specific details about this operation are lacking, these troops and supplies had presumably set sail in two galleons (*barça*) that had originally been set to depart with Kurdoğlu Hizir's fifteen war galleys in the fall of 1567. The mission of these two vessels, however, was from the start different from that of the rest of the Ottoman fleet: rather than remaining permanently in Aceh with Kurdoğlu Hizir and his men, they had instead been instructed to load a cargo of spices destined for the Ottoman treasury and to return to Yemen with the imperial messenger Mustafa Chavush.[74] Because of these separate instructions, the two ships seem to have been allowed to proceed to Aceh independently of the rest of Hizir's forces, bringing with them, in addition to Mustafa and the contingent of five hundred Ottoman mercenaries, the Acehnese ambassador Hussein, who turned up shortly thereafter in Malacca on yet another diplomatic mission.[75]

Once these forces arrived in Sumatra, the sultan of Aceh fulfilled his end of the bargain struck with Sokollu Mehmed by using his new Ottoman auxiliaries to launch a major siege of the Portuguese fortress in Malacca.[76] This attack, although ultimately unsuccessful, was accompanied by the outbreak of a new wave of hostilities throughout the Indian Ocean. In the Maldives, the corsair Kutti Musa of Calicut managed to drive out the Portuguese-installed Christian king, taking control of the archipelago for himself in 1569.[77] In the next year, on the subcontinent, Nizam al-Mulk of Ahmadnagar and Adil Shah of Bijapur once more joined forces, the former attacking the Portuguese fortress of Chaul, and the latter marching directly on Goa.[78] Both of these attempts ended in failure, as did another Acehnese assault on Malacca in 1570.[79] But with the help of Ali Raja, a kinsman of the corsair Kutti Musa, the Zamorin of Calicut then besieged the Portuguese fortress of Chaliyam, conquering it and razing it to the ground in 1571.[80]

Meanwhile, in Yemen, attempts by Mutahhar's Zaydi forces to stave off the ongoing Ottoman reconquest inspired the repetition of a series of events familiar from earlier in the century. As Koja Sinan's armies gathered outside the walls of Aden in the fall of 1568, the Zaydi commander in charge of the city's defense sent a desperate petition to the Portuguese in Hormuz, promising to turn over to them the citadel and the customs revenues of the port in exchange for help in defending against an Ottoman attack. The Portuguese dispatched a small squadron from Hormuz immediately and sent to Goa for further reinforcements. But this larger

FIGURE 5.1 The galleys of Kurdoğlu Hizir Reis chase away a Portuguese squadron off the coast of Yemen, May 1569. Source: Rumuzi, *Tārīḫ-i Feth-i Yemen*, Istanbul University Library, Ms. T.6045, fol. 87a.

fleet, which according to some accounts numbered as many as twenty vessels, arrived on the scene too late to save the city and was chased away by Kurdoğlu Hizir's galleys (Figure 5.1). Ottoman forces then converged on Aden by land and sea, recapturing it on May 19, 1569.

THE SUEZ AND VOLGA-DON CANAL PROJECTS

Although instability in Yemen had forced Sokollu Mehmed to postpone his plans for major military operations in the Indian Ocean, the indomitable grand vizier was able to use the Zaydi uprising as a pretext for promoting another of his pet projects: a revived attempt to open a canal from the Mediterranean to Suez. In early 1568, while preparations for the relief expedition to Yemen were still under way, Sokollu Mehmed had the following order sent to the governor of Egypt, in which he called for a feasibility study of the canal project:

> It has been reported that the accursed Portuguese have gained mastery over the lands of India, and the routes of the Muslims coming to visit the Holy Cities from those directions have been cut off as a result. It is intolerable that the people of Islam should be forced to live in this way under the rule of the accursed infidel. Thus, trusting in the assistance of God Almighty and taking in hand the miracle of the plentiful blessings of the Prophet (peace be upon him!), it is our intention to set out in the direction of those regions, both in the hopes of liberating the land of India from the accursed infidel, and because in the vicinity of the Holy Cities there are certain stray beasts who have separated from the flock and who need to be dealt with [i.e., the Zaydi rebels]. At present, the Imperial fleet is being readied for action in this matter, and in order for it to pass across to the port of Suez, the cutting of a canal would be most convenient. I order that:
>
> As soon as this arrives, you shall gather all of the most qualified architects and engineers of that province and send them with assistants so that they may inspect the land between the Mediterranean and the port of Suez. Once they have determined with certainty if it is possible to build a canal across it, how long it would need to be, and how many ships could pass through it, you shall report back to us, so that necessary preparations can be made and digging can begin. If God Almighty so wills it, this canal will be completed, and with His divine assistance our holy war in the path of God will come to a happy conclusion in those lands, both in clearing away the stray beasts who have separated from the flock in the area around the Holy Cities, and in conquering and subduing the Portuguese infidels in the land of India.[81]

As work began on this canal, Sokollu Mehmed swung his attention thousands of miles to the northeast, where he began to pursue a policy toward the Muslims of Central Asia conspicuously similar to that which he had first conceived of in relation to the Indian Ocean. Here, beginning in 1566, pilgrims and merchants from Samarkand, Bukhara, and Khwarazm had also begun to complain that their way to the holy cities was being obstructed, both by the Safavids in Iran and by the expansion of Ivan IV of Russia into the regions of Kazan and Astrakhan.[82] In response, Sokollu made arrangements to facilitate transportation across the Black Sea from the Crimea to the Anatolian ports of Sinop, Samsun, and Istanbul.[83] Then, in 1569, he began an even more ambitious venture to open a canal between the Don and Volga rivers far to the north.[84]

Only at this point can we begin to appreciate the truly global scope of Sokollu's imperial aspirations. Together, his twin canal projects aimed at nothing short of creating a direct maritime link between Central Asia and Mecca, allowing travelers to pass entirely by ship from Astrakhan up the Volga, then by canal to the Don, then down to the Black Sea, the Bosporus, the Dardanelles, the Aegean, and the Mediterranean, before finally crossing to Suez and into the Red Sea. Once there, such travelers would have access not only to the holy cities of Mecca and Medina but also to the far-flung communities of Muslims from the Indian Ocean who converged on the Red Sea from the opposite direction. In short, Sokollu meant to make the imagined Muslim community of the *'umma* a reality by creating a global transportation network, centered on the Ottoman Empire, that radiated out to the most distant corners of the Islamic world (Map 5.1).

In the end, neither of these canal projects was completed: in Suez, surveyors deemed the canal infeasible even before excavations had begun; and along the Don, work was abandoned after just a few weeks of digging. But at the very least, Sokollu's efforts convinced Ivan IV of Russia to reevaluate his aggressive policies and ultimately

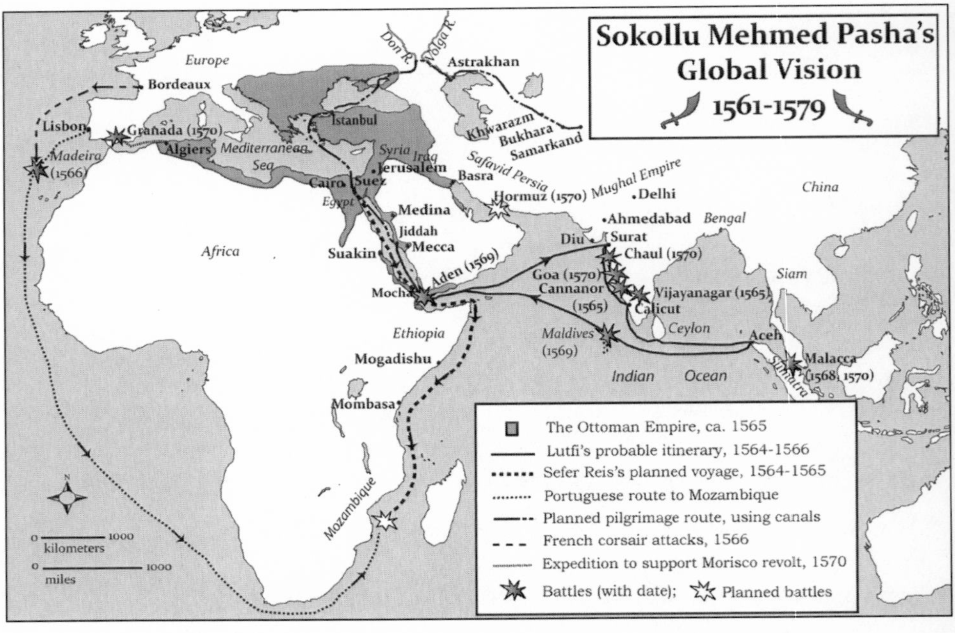

MAP 5.1 Sokollu Mehmed Pasha's global vision, 1561–1579

to sign a pledge to respect the Muslim pilgrimage routes through Kazan and Astrakhan. In this sense, even without being built, Sokollu's canals still served his goal of facilitating communications between Central Asia and the Ottoman Empire.

RENEWED PLANS FOR EXPANSION AND DISASTER AT LEPANTO

By 1569, the restoration of Ottoman authority in Yemen allowed Sokollu Mehmed to once again draw from his web of allies and informants in the Indian Ocean to prepare for a new offensive. In the middle of that year, he received a visit from yet another ambassador from Aceh, who briefed him on the outcome of Sultan Ali Ala'ad-din Ri'ayat Syah's recent siege of Malacca, as well as Aceh's intentions to renew hostilities by the following summer.[85] Similarly, by means of Jacomo d'Olivares, a New Christian who had fled Portuguese India while under threat of arrest from the Holy Inquisition, he stayed equally informed about the progress of the anti-Portuguese alliance forged between Kutti Musa, Ali Raja, Nizam al-Mulk, and Adil Shah in the Maldives, Calicut, and the Deccan.[86] Meanwhile, in the Mediterranean, he also took care to follow developments in Spain, where a violent revolt of local "Morisco" Muslims had recently broken out.[87]

By early 1570, Sokollu was taking concrete steps to provide material support for all of these groups. In April of that year, he sent an edict to the governor of Algiers to give all possible aid and comfort to the Morisco rebels of Spain, and by the summer, at least six hundred Ottoman musketeers had landed in Andalusia.[88] Around the same time, the grand vizier had another letter sent to Aceh, informing his vassals there that the uprising in Yemen had finally been suppressed and that long-awaited help from Istanbul would soon be on its way.[89] And in the Persian Gulf, where local officials learned of a bid by the Muslims of Hormuz to overthrow their Portuguese governor, the grand vizier ordered new galleys to be prepared in the arsenal of Basra in order to intervene.[90] By the end of the summer, there were even alarmed Portuguese reports filtering in from an entirely new and unexpected front: the Swahili coast of Africa, where suspicious Lutfi-like Ottoman agents were said to be inciting the local population against the Portuguese. Ottoman galleys were also reported to have been sighted as far south as the Comoro islands, uncomfortably close to the main Portuguese base in Mozambique.[91]

Andalusia, Sumatra, Hormuz, Mozambique: such were the dimensions of the chessboard upon which Sokollu Mehmed played his game of global power politics. But in this instance, as in so many others in the past, Sokollu's best-laid plans failed to fully materialize because of circumstances beyond his control. This time, the principal culprits were two of his enemies at court, Lala Mustafa Pasha and Joseph Naxi, who against the grand vizier's vehement objections managed to convince Sultan Selim II to call off the expedition to Hormuz. Instead, they moved against the Venetian island of Cyprus—a decision that not only provoked a war with Venice but also, as Sokollu had warned, led to the formation of a "Christian League" (including Spain and the Papacy) that, in the following year, handed the Ottomans at Lepanto the most crushing naval defeat in their history.[92] Sokollu came to the rescue in the aftermath of this battle, drawing from his earlier experience as head of the Ottoman arsenal to organize the construction of 150 new galleys in a single season.[93] By the next year, he had even managed to dismantle the Holy League itself, by using his friendship with the Venetian Bailo Marc Antonio Barbaro to sign a separate peace with Venice.[94] Still, the whole affair was a disaster for Sokollu, disrupting his network of contacts and preventing him from pursuing any of his own initiatives for nearly four years. Further compounding his problems, the Portuguese in Hormuz returned to the offensive in 1573, raiding Bahrain, destroying several vessels in Basra, and capturing an envoy from Laristan.[95]

This Portuguese attack provided the occasion for Sokollu's last attempt to build a grand intercontinental alliance against the Iberian powers, as he renewed ties with his informants and local supporters in Hormuz and sent two nearly identical letters to Aceh and to the Moriscos of Spain promising that help from Istanbul would be forthcoming now that the war in Cyprus was over.[96] Learning of Philip II of Spain's ongoing troubles with the Protestant rebellion in the Low Countries, he even dispatched a secret agent to Flanders, bearing a message of "friendship, compassion and favor" to the "Lutherans" of that country and vowing assistance in their struggle against "the Papists," whose religious practices they, like the Muslims, had rejected. The letter carried by this agent went on to urge the Protestants to send representatives to Istanbul as soon as possible and, in the meantime, to coordinate their activities with the Morisco rebels in Spain.[97]

At the same time, Sokollu also began to actively prepare for the invasion of Bahrain, whose conquest he hoped would protect Basra from further Portuguese incursions.[98] Accordingly, troops were moved from Basra to Katif in late 1574, and in 1575, orders were sent for the construction of eight more galleys in Basra's arsenal, bringing the total number of available ships there to twenty-two.[99] By the spring of 1576, the Ottoman governors of Lahsa, Basra, Baghdad, and Diyarbakir were all involved in supplying men, weapons, and munitions for this expedition, and by all indications, the campaign was to set sail in the fall of that year.[100]

By this point, however, the political fortunes of the grand vizier were permanently on the wane. Beginning in 1575, Sokollu became the target of a series of palace intrigues that weakened his influence and led to the systematic removal of many of his protégés from key positions both at court and in the provinces.[101] Then, in 1577, his political rivals convinced the new sultan, Murad III, to announce a full-scale invasion of Safavid Iran. In so doing, they provoked a war that would consume almost all of the empire's strength for the foreseeable future, forcing Sokollu's plans for the Indian Ocean to be permanently shelved. Even then, the grand vizier still made one valiant last effort to prove the importance of maintaining an Indian Ocean fleet, organizing a force of fifteen galleys in the arsenal of Suez that were designed to travel around the Arabian Peninsula and provide naval support off the coast of Persia for Ottoman operations.[102] But after encountering a number of technical problems, this plan, too, was abandoned, and the war against Iran was henceforth to remain strictly a land campaign.[103]

A TURN TO DIPLOMACY

Frustrated in his military ambitions, during the last years of his life the grand vizier turned once more to diplomacy to achieve his aims. Between 1578 and 1579, he signed the empire's first trade agreement with Queen Elizabeth of England, began negotiations with the Habsburgs of Spain regarding a peace treaty in the Mediterranean, and entered talks with Sarsa Dengel, the emperor of Ethiopia, concerning an armistice in the Abyssinian highlands.[104] He likewise contacted coastal communities in the Horn of Africa about the possibility of acquiring lumber for the arsenal in Mocha, and even received an embassy from Idris Alavama, the ruler of the distant Muslim kingdom of Borno in central sub-Saharan Africa.[105]

This visit by Idris Alavama's envoy paralleled in many ways the earlier embassies Sokollu had received from Aceh and Samarkand. As such, it must have been particularly satisfying for the grand vizier, since it demonstrated so clearly the cumulative rewards of his efforts to foster global pan-Islamic sentiment by facilitating travel and commerce along the traditional pilgrimage routes. According to available sources, Idris had first come into contact with the Ottomans much earlier in Sokollu Mehmed's tenure, when he had personally traveled on the hajj from Borno to Mecca by means of the Fezzan and Egypt. Then, upon his return to Borno, Idris was inspired to build his kingdom's first brick mosques and even to endow a residence in Mecca to house other hajjis from central Africa during their stay in the holy cities. The embassy that he subsequently sent to Istanbul was related to this effort, asking for guarantees from the sultan that pilgrims and traders from his kingdom would henceforth be allowed to travel freely throughout Ottoman lands. Sokollu had edicts to this effect sent to the governors of Egypt and the Fezzan, establishing a direct caravan link between the Ottoman Empire and Borno. Eventually—in addition to initiating a profitable trade across the Sahara—this link would lead to the introduction of firearms into central Africa from Ottoman lands and to Borno's emergence as a dominant regional power later in the century.[106]

SOKOLLU MEHMED AND THE ORGANIZATION OF THE OTTOMAN SPICE TRADE

Over the course of his long career, Sokollu's political and military endeavors had met with only mixed success: Sefer Reis had died unexpectedly; an uprising in Yemen had derailed the expedition to Aceh; the canal projects in Egypt and Astrakhan had been abandoned. But as the episode with Borno illustrates, the grand vizier's most significant and lasting accomplishments came not in the military arena, but in the more mundane realms of trade, finance, and diplomacy. Here, his efforts bore the fruits of a consistent attentiveness to the nuts and bolts of imperial infrastructure, especially with regard to the Indian Ocean. The numerous capital improvements to Ottoman facilities in the Red Sea and Persian Gulf carried out under his direction included expansions of the arsenals in Mocha, Suakin, and Lahsa to allow the local construction of war galleys, the establishment of a cannon foundry in Basra, and the refurbishing of fortresses to better defend the ports of Massawa and Suakin.[107] Facilities for manufacturing gunpowder were also set up in Basra and in Yemen, and an inspector was sent to Lahsa to investigate the possibility of locally mining saltpeter.[108] Additionally, the governor of Eritrea was ordered to move his military headquarters from the highlands around Debarva back to Suakin in order to better defend the coast, while in the Red Sea, regular naval patrols were established to keep the sea lanes safe.[109] In the Persian Gulf, a separate admiralty of Lahsa was created for similar purposes.[110]

All of this was related to what was perhaps Sokollu's greatest single achievement: a comprehensive reform, reorganization, and rationalization of the Ottoman spice trade. Certainly, there was nothing new during Sokollu's reign about the state's involvement in this trade per se, as the Ottomans had profited from taxation of the spice routes at least since the conquest of Egypt in 1517. But in the second half of the sixteenth century, under Sokollu Mehmed's tutelage, the Ottoman state engaged in the international spice market in an entirely novel way, profiting from it not merely through the passive collection of customs revenues but by becoming an active agent in the trade itself.

The story of Sokollu Mehmed's personal interest in spices long predates his grand vizierate, beginning with a single entry from a *mühimme defteri* ("registry of important affairs") from the year 1554. It records the following transaction arranged by Ozdemir Pasha, who at the time was the outgoing governor of Yemen:

> [Before Ozdemir Pasha left Yemen], he had forty [four] *kīselik* of spices from the annual revenues of that province sent to Egypt with [his assistant] Mustafa. He sold the above mentioned spices there [in Egypt], and from these forty-four *kīselik* of spices he sent eight hundred gold pieces to the Imperial palace for [Sokollu] Mehmed Pasha, and granted the remainder [as the salary] for the office of Chief of the Musketeers in Yemen.[111]

As unexceptional as it may seem, this document is the earliest direct archival evidence of any kind dealing with the Ottoman state's active involvement in the spice trade, which at this point seems to have been limited to an isolated transaction rather than a regularized system for exploiting revenues. The text's explicit reference to Sokollu Mehmed is therefore striking, indicating that he played a leading role in the formulation of this experimental new trade policy from the very beginning.[112] In fact, the date of this first documented shipment of state-owned spices coincides almost exactly with Sokollu's promotion to the rank of third vizier in 1554, making him an ex officio member of the Imperial Divan for the first time.[113] This suggests that Sokollu's promotion was instrumental in giving him the authority to begin using state funds to play the market in such a speculative way, effectively increasing the tax yields of Yemen by converting the local customs collected in kind from incoming spice cargoes into cash at higher Egyptian market rates.[114]

One troublesome point of ambiguity relates to the precise meaning of *kīselik* in this document, a term that translates literally as "one purse's worth" but does not correspond to a standard measure known to have been typically employed with reference to spices. Since *kīse* (usually rendered "kese") was also used as a measure of currency, it is possible that the term here refers to the actual market value of the spices rather than their quantity. Unfortunately, as a currency unit *kīse* is associated with a bewildering array of possible values, making it very difficult to draw any firm conclusions about the actual size of the transaction here described. The term is cited, for example, as equivalent to 20,000 silver *akçes* in an Ottoman source dating to 1537 and to 10,000 gold pieces in another source dating from later in the century—the latter figure being roughly thirty times higher than the value of the former according to exchange rates in the 1550s.[115] Further compounding the problem is the fact that *mühimme* documents describing similar shipments of spices in later decades give no figures at all (in *kīselik* or otherwise), leaving us in the dark about the actual margin of profit that the state could realize in this way.[116]

In any case, the document is clear about at least one fact: Sokollu Mehmed profited handsomely from the transaction (to the tune of eight hundred gold pieces), as did the chief musketeer of Yemen. And although further evidence from the second half of the 1550s is lacking because of the fragmentary conservation of contemporary *mühimme* registers, it appears that this experiment proved successful enough that it was rapidly expanded and regularized. By 1560, the year in which Sokollu's friend and ally Mahmud Pasha became governor of Yemen, that province's entire annual surplus (valued at three million *akçes* or about fifty thousand gold pieces) was sent to Egypt not in cash but as a shipment of "Calicut pepper."[117] In addition, all of Yemen's lords of the standard were given smaller allotments of spices as part of their yearly salaries, as well as passes allowing them to ship these allotments tax-free from Yemen and sell them at a profit in Egypt.[118]

This pass-based system was attractive for two reasons. First, it allowed the state to use market mechanisms to increase the real salaries of its officials in Yemen at minimal cost to the treasury. Second, it had the added advantage of functioning as a check against corruption, since the free passes issued to provincial officials had value only if the tax regime on the spice trade was judiciously enforced. For these reasons, the pass system soon became such an important part of Yemen's finances that, by 1565, the new provincial governor Ridvan Pasha was allotted spices and a pass to trade in lieu of any cash payment from the treasury for his salary.[119]

AN OTTOMAN SPICE MONOPOLY

Despite such promising beginnings, the pass-based system introduced in the 1560s was continued only until the disastrous Yemeni uprising of 1567. Thereafter, to rein in the wanton excesses that had besmirched Mahmud Pasha's tenure as governor of that province, Sokollu opted for a policy of much more centralized control of trade. Indeed, so strict was this new regime that to an outside observer such as the Veronese traveler Filippo Pigafetta, who visited the Red Sea in the early 1570s, it appeared to have all the characteristics of a bona fide trading monopoly. According to Pigafetta:

> The arsenal [in Suez] is used to construct [not only war galleys] but also merchant vessels for the Sultan, who has a monopoly. In that sea, in fact, it is strictly forbidden for anyone to own their own ships, or to contract them out privately. All belong to the Sultan, or pay fees to the Sultan, such that the Red Sea is extremely lucrative for His Majesty because of the ships and customs revenues, and it alone more than pays for the expenses of Yemen.[120]

Pigafetta's claim of an outright imperial trade monopoly is an exaggeration, for in reality we know that the operation of private merchant vessels was never discouraged. Still, if such merchants wished to engage in the transit spice trade from the Indian Ocean to Egypt, they were expected to limit their movements to a prescribed itinerary and were required to stop in Mocha, Jiddah, and Suez along the way and pay substantial transit fees at each port.[121] Meanwhile, a regular convoy of state-owned ships traveled directly from Mocha to Suez every year, carrying a cargo of spices for the imperial treasury that was exempt from any form of taxation.[122] Initially, this cargo was sold in Egypt at a profit, and the proceeds from the sale were sent on to Istanbul in cash. But over time, a combination of the huge amount of money involved and the unpredictable fluctuations of the market increasingly exposed the system to corruption, both from tax farmers (who repeatedly tried to illegally tax state-owned cargoes) and from state officials (who were eager to collect an illicit commission by selling the spices at below-market rates).[123] Because of this, after the mid-1570s, Sokollu mandated that the entire cargo of state spices be shipped all the way to Istanbul, where he could control its safe arrival and sale more directly.[124] Provincial officials, who had previously been encouraged to trade in spices as a way to augment their income, were henceforth expressly forbidden from engaging in trade of any kind.[125]

Despite these not inconsiderable changes in the regulations surrounding the sale of state spices (*mīrī bahār*), the operation of the state-owned galleys that carried them proved extremely consistent over time: throughout the 1570s and for many years thereafter, they carried spices from Mocha to Suez every year without fail, regardless of whether Yemen's provincial budget ran a surplus or a deficit. In other words, the spice galleys were not simply a way of transferring surplus funds from

Yemen to the Egyptian treasury when available, but rather an independent market-driven venture pursued for its own sake.

One important implication of this independence is that, because the spice galleys were operated separately from the provincial finances of Egypt or Yemen, details about the purchase and sale of the spices they carried do not appear in surviving budgets from either province. This makes it very difficult to draw firm conclusions about the scale or the profit margins involved in these transactions. But it also suggests that Yemen, despite the fact that its own provincial budget typically showed a deficit during the second half of the sixteenth century, nevertheless constituted a major source of reliable revenue for the Ottoman fisc.[126] As Pigafetta states quite clearly, it was the "spice monopoly" that justified Yemen's expenses.

COORDINATION BETWEEN THE RED SEA AND PERSIAN GULF

In comparison to the Red Sea, with its regime of tightly controlled and closely supervised trade, the Persian Gulf during the 1560s and 1570s was characterized by a markedly more relaxed trading environment—something that remained true even during the most acute periods of political tension with the Portuguese. In 1565, for example, as Sokollu became embroiled in an unprecedented series of anti-Portuguese provocations across the Indian Ocean (including Lutfi's mission to Sumatra and Sefer Reis's planned expedition to Mozambique), the grand vizier had nevertheless continued trade negotiations with the Portuguese in the Persian Gulf. Two years later, in October 1567, while deeply involved in preparations for his military expedition to Aceh, Sokollu had reconfirmed the captain of Hormuz's lapsed trading privileges in Basra, allowing him to establish a commercial factor in the city to buy and sell tax-free in exchange for permission to send an Ottoman agent to Hormuz with similar exemptions.[127]

Meanwhile, trade along the overland portion of this transit route, from the Levant to the Persian Gulf via Aleppo, Baghdad, and Basra was opened to merchants from any state at peace with the empire, including those of western Europe.[128] To facilitate this traffic, roads, port facilities, and caravanserais along the way were improved and expanded, ensuring that the journey was fast, safe, and comfortable.[129] Later, when renewed political instability around Bahrain in the early 1570s began to interfere with this trade, Sokollu even reduced the tax rate on transit goods collected in Basra to help traffic through the port return to its previous levels.[130] As a consequence of these measures, the overland crossing from Basra to Aleppo soon became so popular that not just merchants but even Portuguese officials began to prefer it for their most urgent correspondence with Lisbon. By 1581, this traffic had become heavy enough the Altano trading firm of Venice established a regular public courier service along the route. The firm guaranteed its clients delivery of letters from Venice to Hormuz in three months or less, and it expected its agents to travel from Aleppo to Hormuz in just forty days, charging 260 ducats for the trip with 1 ducat subtracted for every day late.[131]

Overall, this bifurcated strategy of support for free trade in the Persian Gulf, coupled with the more tightly controlled commercial system of the Red Sea, points to a comprehensive rationalization of the Ottoman state's policy toward the transit spice and luxury trade. Engineered by Sokollu Mehmed himself, it was an approach based on a sophisticated understanding both of market conditions and of the Ottomans' own strategic position, which differed substantially in these two trading zones. In the Red Sea, the empire enjoyed two distinct advantages ripe for exploitation: its control of the entire route from Yemen to Alexandria, which allowed a great degree of independence in establishing trade policies, and its "captive market" over the hajj traffic to and from Mecca, which kept the Red Sea less sensitive to taxation than other competing routes. As a result, transit trade through the Red Sea was restricted to Muslims, merchants were subjected to tight controls, and tax rates were kept very high. But in the Persian Gulf, where such a regime was impossible because of the Portuguese presence in Hormuz, Sokollu's solution was different. Here he provided a variety of incentives both to private merchants and to the Portuguese authorities in Hormuz to ensure that the sea lanes remained open to all comers, thereby maximizing revenues by increasing the *volume* of trade rather than the tax rate.[132]

In addition, as Sokollu strove to accommodate the very different trading conditions of the Red Sea and Persian Gulf, he also took care to keep these two routes relatively isolated from one another. Under his watch, pilgrims bound for Mecca who entered Ottoman territory from the Persian Gulf were expressly forbidden from taking the direct route across the Arabian desert, and were instead required to travel first to Damascus and then join the annual state-operated caravan that left for the holy cities from there.[133] In this way, Sokollu was able to protect the integrity of the Red Sea as a special region of state-supervised trade, by restricting access to certain specified (and highly taxed) entry and exit points. This, in turn, provided an ideal environment for the operation of the state spice galleys, by means of which the Ottoman state itself assumed an active role in the transit spice trade and directly competed with the Portuguese Crown's own monopolistic Carreira da Índia.

Indeed, the elegance of this system has important implications for our understanding of the Carreira da Índia, whose operation during the second half of the sixteenth century has recently attracted a good deal of attention from scholars. Their research has shown that despite a precipitous increase in the volume of spices passing through the Red Sea and Persian Gulf in the 1560s and 1570s, the rival Portuguese-controlled trade route around the Cape of Good Hope nevertheless remained more competitive than was previously believed.[134] This finding should not, however, be interpreted as evidence that the voyage around Africa was somehow a cheaper or safer way to get from the Indian Ocean to Europe, for contemporary Portuguese sources are nearly unanimous in agreeing that the shorter routes through Ottoman lands were always superior in this respect. Instead, if the more costly Portuguese route continued to be marginally profitable, its resilience can be explained only by the fact that tax rates across the Ottoman-controlled overland routes were so high that the longer trip around Africa could still remain economical.[135]

But crucially, this taxation applied only to spices carried by *private* merchants through the Red Sea and Persian Gulf. Unlike them, the state-owned cargoes of the Ottoman spice galleys were transported from Mocha to Alexandria entirely tax-free. This left the Ottoman state in an unrivaled position *as a merchant*, for among all of the various competitors for the transit spice trade, including the Portuguese Crown, it alone had the ability both to make use of the shorter and cheaper route through the Red Sea and to avoid paying taxes at any point along the way. As far as we can tell from available evidence, it was under Sokollu Mehmed that the empire began to actively exploit this competitive advantage for the first time. And although the convoys of state spice ships that regularly crossed between Mocha and Suez were the most visible manifestation of this effort, its influence stretched far beyond the confines of the Red Sea to the farthest reaches of the Indian Ocean.

THE SPICE TRADE AS AN ENGINE OF OTTOMAN FOREIGN POLICY

To varying degrees, virtually all of Sokollu Mehmed's major political initiatives in the eastern theater were somehow connected to the spice trade. But this connection is most explicit with respect to Aceh, whose relations with the Ottoman state always had about them the flavor of a moneymaking venture. Even the first Acehnese envoys to arrive in Istanbul in 1562, despite the grand rhetoric of pan-Islamic unity that they employed in their presentation to the sultan, clearly had the intention of paying for the military assistance they were requesting.[136] And when Lutfi was sent back with this embassy to Aceh, his mission was not only diplomatic but also economic. According to Lutfi's own report, before his departure from Aceh he had procured "sixteen quintals of pepper, silk, cinnamon, cloves, camphor, hisalbend, and other products from the 'Lands Below the Winds' and loaded them onto a large and famous ship known as the Samadi."[137]

Later, when he appeared before the sultan upon his return to Istanbul, Lutfi insisted that in Aceh "there is a wealth of jewels, gold and silver which is beyond reckoning, but which for a long time has fallen to the lot of the wretched infidels. If the Almighty so wills it, one day a rightful share [of these riches] will belong to the warriors of your Imperial Majesty's army of the faithful."[138] Accordingly, when Sokollu Mehmed began preparing the expedition to Sumatra in 1567, his orders to Kurdoğlu Hizir, the commander of the mission, included instructions "to load your transport ships with the spices available in those regions and send them back."[139] Although the fifteen galleys originally intended for Aceh never reached their destination, these transport vessels did make the voyage, exchanging a shipment of artillery, munitions, gunners, and five hundred Turkish mercenaries for a cargo of pepper and other spices.[140]

Ultimately, it was this type of commercial transaction, rather than any high-minded political or military cooperation, that would define relations between Aceh and the Ottoman Empire over the long haul. Official diplomatic correspondence between the two powers continued on a fairly regular basis for only about ten years, finally petering out after 1575. By comparison, trade relations proved much more lasting, such that an imperial agent engaged in buying and selling goods for the Ottoman treasury seems to have remained a permanent fixture in Aceh at least until century's end. Dutch reports from the 1590s mention the existence of such an agent, as do French visitors from as late as 1602.[141] Their observations are further confirmed by the details of an Ottoman provincial budget from Yemen in 1599, which includes under an entry for "buying and selling" a figure of 23,880 *paras* for "miscellaneous expenses of the sea captain [*nāḫudā*] who travels in the direction of India and back to the port of Mocha, exerting himself greatly for the sake of the Emperor's property."[142] This captain is almost certainly the same "Nachoda from Mecca" who, according to an early-seventeenth-century Dutch visitor to Aceh, "as part of the preliminaries of trade offers the Sultan of Aceh military assistance from his country."[143]

A text composed by the Bishop of Malacca during the mid-1580s gives us further insight into the particulars of this commerce. According to his account, Aceh was visited every year by four or five ships from "Mecca" that brought cargoes of gold and silver currency, slaves, assorted Ottoman products such as rose water, glassware, silk brocades, and woolen cloth, but most important, large quantities of valuable military supplies:

> The above mentioned ruler [of Aceh] has more than one hundred pieces of large bronze artillery and many more of iron, and has over two hundred medium-sized guns, more than four hundred small caliber pieces, and a great quantity of musketeers, for every year these arrive in the ships from Mecca, as I have already described above, and he also has abundant supplies of very good quality gunpowder and cannonballs of all different varieties.[144]

This passage highlights an important and too often overlooked aspect of trade between Aceh and the Ottoman market, which is that the cargoes of spices and other Southeast Asian products loaded by Ottoman merchants were paid for in large part with guns and ammunition. In effect, the Ottomans were therefore exporters of technology, an eminently more favorable medium of exchange than mere trade goods or even hard currency. After all, artillery was the technologically advanced and labor-intensive product par excellence of the sixteenth century, with an added value many times greater than the raw materials out of which it was produced and an almost unlimited demand overseas. Its export allowed the Ottomans to check the outflow of precious metals from their home market toward the Indian Ocean, while also providing desirable political consequences. In this way, trade with Aceh was not only a profitable venture but also a means of militarily strengthening one of the Ottomans' closest trading partners.

Was the Ottomans' partnership with Aceh an exception, or was it indicative of a larger pattern of commercial ties established throughout the Indian Ocean? This is a difficult question to answer, for even in the case of Aceh, we have almost no documentation of trade relations beyond the tangential references in Lutfi's report and in other instances of diplomatic correspondence. Documents dealing specifically with the mechanisms of trade, the maintenance of imperial factors abroad, or the technical details of how deals were financed have yet to be uncovered and quite possibly never will be.

Still, a number of clues suggest that Ottoman state-sponsored commercial activity in the Indian Ocean was significantly more widespread than is generally acknowledged. There is no question, for example, that the governor of Basra had sporadically maintained an imperial factor in Hormuz at least since the 1540s and that this practice was continued (or revived) under Sokollu Mehmed.[145] In addition, during peace negotiations with the Portuguese in the early 1560s, the Ottomans explicitly demanded the right to establish their own commercial agents "in Sind, Cambay, Dabul, Calicut, and any other ports they desired."[146] Although the Portuguese refused to accept these demands, is it possible that Sokollu established commercial factors in these ports anyway, as he had in Aceh, even without Portuguese approval? We may never know for sure, but the most likely answer seems to be yes.

OTTOMAN RELIGIOUS PROPAGANDA AND THE WORLD CALIPHATE

Even in places where only an informal network of relations connected independent merchants to the Ottoman Empire, Sokollu Mehmed still took steps to ensure that the allegiance of these merchants rested increasingly with the Ottoman sultan. This was accomplished through the creation of a new ideological and religious infrastructure based on the concept of the caliphate, a task facilitated by the work of Sokollu's contemporary Ebu's-Suud, the supreme religious authority of the Ottoman Empire since the late 1530s. Although the title of caliph was as old as Islam itself, and had certainly been invoked by Ottoman sultans before Sokollu's time, Ebu's-Suud was the first Ottoman legal scholar to systematize its use as a way of shoring up the empire's legitimacy in the midst of its ongoing struggles with the Habsburgs and Safavids. He did so by creating a clearly articulated doctrine of caliphal authority and a canonical basis in the sharia for sultanic legislation.[147]

Over time, the impact of this caliphal doctrine was felt far beyond the borders of the empire. In the Indian Ocean, it coincided with the first widespread application of the sharia in the Islamic states of Southeast Asia, as well as a noticeable increase in self-conscious conversions to Islam and the rapid propagation throughout the region of jihad as a political concept.[148] To some extent, of course, such trends should be considered part of a normal indigenous response to the pervasive and antagonistic presence of the Portuguese, as well as a natural outgrowth of the increased traffic along the pilgrimage routes to Mecca.[149] But it is also clear that the rising political tenor of religious discourse in the Indian Ocean was fostered by the missionary activities of an increasingly visible set of itinerant Muslim clerics, many of whom either were Ottomans or had been trained in Ottoman religious institutions. Contemporary Portuguese and Spanish observers repeatedly inveighed against the influence of these "false prophets," whom they consistently blamed for Islam's growing international strength. In Aceh alone, these included a Meccan cleric by the name of Abu'l-Khayr, a Yemeni known as Shaykh Muhammed, and a Shafi'i scholar from Egypt called Muhammad Azhari.[150]

Were the activities of such clerics organized by a central authority somewhere in the Ottoman Empire, or were they acting purely on their own initiative? Here the sources are again frustratingly vague, with the exception of the following remarkable reference in the *mühimme* registers from the year 1576:

> An edict to the Governor-general of Egypt:
> In times past, one hundred gold pieces [a year] were sent to the mosques of the twenty-seven cities located in the Indian port of Calicut for the Friday sermon [*ḫuṭbe*]. However, it has been reported that for the last few years only fifty gold pieces have been sent, and sometimes not even that amount. . . . Be diligent in this affair and see to it that, in fulfillment of the requirements of my orders, one hundred florins are sent every year without fail and in perpetuity from the port of Jiddah for the above-mentioned sermons. As far as any payments that have still not been made from previous years are concerned, these also should be paid in full from the revenues of Jiddah.[151]

This singular document provides a fleeting but invaluable glimpse into the bureaucratic infrastructure supporting Ottoman dynastic pretensions in the Indian Ocean. As it clearly shows, preachers in Calicut not only read the Friday sermon or *ḫuṭbe* in the name of the Ottoman sultan but also were paid to do so by regular shipments of gold from the Ottoman treasury. Unfortunately, it is impossible to tell just how widespread this practice was. No other references in the *mühimme* registers allude to similar transactions, and even this document owes its existence solely to the fact that funds earmarked for Calicut were being illegally skimmed. Still, the reference in the text to "twenty-seven mosques" is suggestive because it is conspicuously similar to a figure in Lutfi's report (from more than a decade earlier) in which he described Calicut as a city whose Muslims "have built twenty-four mosques and read the *ḫuṭbe* in the noble name of his most high and blessed Imperial Majesty." From this, we can therefore speculate that Sokollu began financing Calicut's preachers in the mid-1560s based on a specific recommendation from Lutfi. Moreover, since Lutfi also mentions in the same report the suspiciously precise figure of "fourteen mosques" in Ceylon, in addition to those on "all the islands" of the Maldives, in all likelihood this transaction represents only one small part of an extensive system of imperial financial support for "Ottoman" mosques abroad.

CONCLUSION: THE "SOFT" WORLD EMPIRE OF SOKOLLU MEHMED PASHA

The writings of Portuguese authors from the 1560s and 1570s are filled with dire and even apocalyptic warnings about the mounting strength of the Ottoman Empire throughout maritime Asia. For the most part, these warnings have appeared to later historians to be vastly out of proportion with the actual scope of Ottoman military successes in the region, suggesting to some that the Portuguese may have suffered from a kind of collective paranoia about an Ottoman menace—one that in reality did not exist.[152] Rather than dismissing outright the judgments of contemporary Portuguese observers, however, it seems reasonable to ask whether it may not be modern scholars who have failed to understand the true nature of this Ottoman threat. For even if Sokollu Mehmed's most flamboyant ventures ended in failure—either because the technological and material resources of the empire could not match his ambitions or because his plans were undermined by political rivalries and unforeseen calamities—these ventures were only one small part, the icing on the cake, of a much larger attempt to create what we might term a "soft empire" in the Indian Ocean (Map 5.2).

Certainly, the term "soft empire" today has very precise connotations rooted in the concerns of contemporary global politics.[153] But if the concept of soft power has proven useful for students of more recent empires as a way to broaden the analysis of

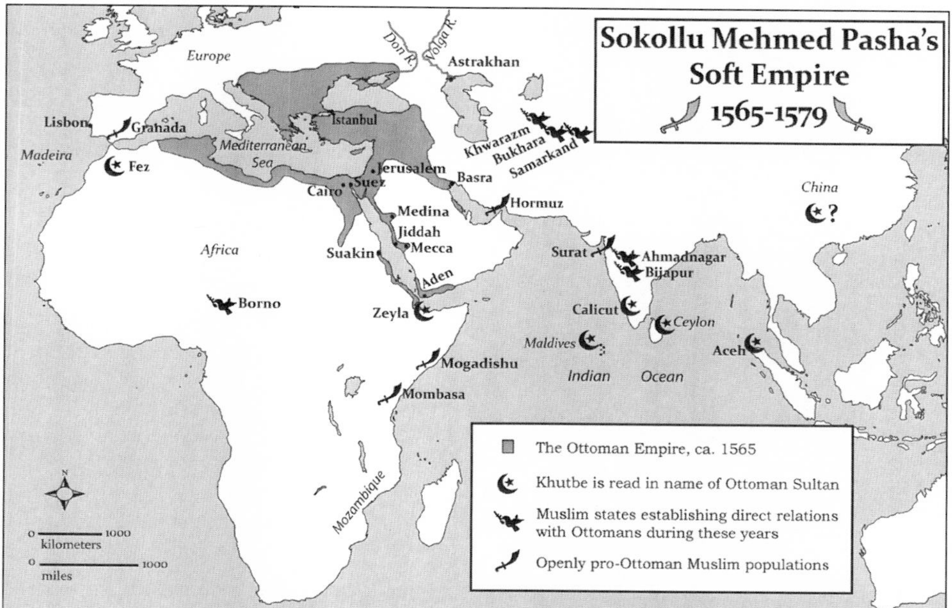

MAP 5.2 Sokollu Mehmed Pasha's soft empire, 1565–1579

imperial power beyond the traditional focus on coercive force and the acquisition of colonies, it is in this same sense that it appears most useful with regard to the sixteenth-century Ottoman Empire. In other words, the Ottoman imperial dominion in the Indian Ocean under Sokollu Mehmed was a soft empire because it was based not on territorial expansion, but instead on an infrastructure of trade, communication, and religious ideology.

If modern historians have until now failed to recognize the importance—or even the existence—of this soft power, at least part of the blame lies with a deeply entrenched scholarly tradition of defining the Ottoman Empire as a state preoccupied with territorial acquisition and agricultural revenues to the exclusion of all else. But this is a convention that was by no means shared by the Portuguese of the day, who were only too aware of Sokollu's sophisticated understanding of market forces, his formidable skills as a diplomat, and his dangerous ability to use religious ideology as an instrument of state power. A Portuguese observer from the mid-1560s, for example, offered the following perfect synopsis of the simplicity, the economy, and the hard reality of Sokollu's soft empire:

> The true intention of the Ottomans is not just to control the spice trade, but in the long run to become lords of all of the states of India...and incite them to rise up against our strongholds...and in the meantime they will be left with all of the trade in spices through both the straits [of the Red Sea and Persian Gulf] that we have forbidden. Thus, the Grand Turk will become master of all without the expense of a fleet, or the need to maintain fortresses, or the risk [of insubordination] from vassals....By controlling trade, all of the Ottomans' neighbors will side with them, such that even without investing their own resources, their allies alone will be enough to push us out and make them masters of India.[154]

When measured according to these criteria, Sokollu Mehmed's imperial strategy was inarguably successful, to the extent that his tenure as grand vizier marked the apogee of Ottoman influence in the Indian Ocean. Trade flourished, with the state itself taking a leading role. Lines of communication had never been stronger, with Ottoman envoys, trade representatives, and secret agents operating throughout maritime Asia. Most important, the Ottoman dynasty's authority as caliph of the universal community of believers was recognized on a scale never equaled before or since, receiving formal expression in the Friday sermons of Muslim houses of worship from the Horn of Africa to Indonesia.

Finally, it should be emphasized that Sokollu's imperial project was a truly global affair, and although his attention was often focused on the Indian Ocean, it was by no means limited to it. During his grand vizierate, Ottoman military operations stretched from Morocco to Sumatra and from Madagascar to Astrakhan. Diplomatic relations extended from England and Muscovy to Ceylon and Samarkand. Indeed, the global extent of Sokollu's activities can be judged favorably even by the impressive standards of his rivals in Portugal and Spain. Although these powers operated in the New World, an area that always lay beyond the horizon of Ottoman ambitions, Sokollu developed contacts in places like Transoxiana and Central Africa that were equally beyond the reach of any contemporary European power. Sokollu Mehmed and his soft empire were thus protagonists of the first order in the history of global expansion in the sixteenth century. But the newly interconnected world that he helped to create was about to confront the empire with a whole range of new and dangerous challenges.

Six

A MAN, A PLAN, A CANAL

Mir Ali Beg's Expeditions to the Swahili Coast, 1579–1589

In the year 1579, a cataclysmic and nearly simultaneous sequence of global political upheavals shook the very foundations of the Ottoman soft empire in the Indian Ocean. Most unexpectedly, the first blow was struck in the highlands of Abyssinia, where at the battle of Addi Qarro the armies of the emperor of Ethiopia handed Ottoman forces a sudden and crushing defeat, killing their governor, capturing the mountain redoubt of Debarva, and threatening Ottoman control of the Red Sea for the first time in more than two decades.[1] Meanwhile, in distant Aceh, the aging Sultan Ala'ad-din Ri'ayat Syah passed away, ushering in an extended period of political and social turmoil in Sumatra that deprived the Ottomans of their most reliable ally in Southeast Asia.[2] Then, most traumatically of all, in October 1579 Sokollu Mehmed Pasha, the grand architect of Ottoman expansion overseas, was stabbed to death by an assassin while receiving petitioners at his private court in Istanbul.[3]

The gravity of this dramatic confluence of events was further compounded by developments in North Africa, where in the preceding year the death knell of Portugal's ruling dynasty had been sounded by the reckless crusading adventurism of the Portuguese king Dom Sebastião. On August 4, 1578, on the Moroccan battlefield of al-Kasr al-Kabir, the young sovereign and the flower of the Portuguese nobility had been slaughtered, leaving Portugal without an heir and in political disarray. Abd al-Malik, the Ottoman-installed client ruler of Morocco, was also killed in the fighting and replaced by his brother and rival, Ahmed al-Mansur, a leader hostile to Istanbul and eager to establish permanent independence for his kingdom.[4] Even worse, since King Philip II of Spain was related to the Portuguese royal line on his mother's side, the prospect of Portugal's annexation by Habsburg Spain now loomed like a buzzard over Lisbon. By 1580, when this historic transfer of power was completed, the Ottomans' most dangerous adversary in the Mediterranean took control of the Estado da Índia and was poised to threaten the empire from the east as well as from the west.[5]

In the midst of all these foreboding developments, an even more ominous threat began to materialize in Mughal India, where the young Emperor Akbar was for the first time preparing to openly challenge the Ottoman dynasty. Signs of this threat had come as early as 1573, when Akbar's conquest of Surat—a city until then firmly within the Ottoman sphere of influence—had given him control of his first major outlet onto the Indian Ocean. By 1576, Akbar had begun to use this port to become actively involved in the organization and finance of the hajj: appointing a permanent official in charge of the pilgrimage, setting aside funds to pay the travel expenses for pilgrims wishing to make the trip from India, and arranging for a special royal ship to sail from Surat to Jiddah every year specifically for this purpose. By means of this ship, Akbar also distributed enormous quantities of gold and silver currency for the poor of Mecca and Medina, as well as sumptuous gifts of textiles and other luxury products for the loftier notables and religious dignitaries in the holy cities. In the first year alone, these amounted to the tremendous sum of 600,000 silver rupees and 12,000 robes of honor. In the next year, another 100,000 rupees were added to this total as a personal gift for the Sharif of Mecca.[6] In addition to this public largesse, Akbar also sent a prominent entourage of ladies from his own household, including his paternal aunt and his own wife, on an extended pilgrimage to the holy cities. These ladies arrived with his first convoy of ships in 1576 and stayed for several years, eventually performing the hajj four times and with each season dispensing alms widely in Akbar's name.[7]

None of this ostensibly pious activity was threatening to the Ottomans in and of itself. Under different circumstances, such generosity could even be interpreted as a sign of friendship or, at the very least, as a normal and innocuous component of the religious obligations of a ruler of Akbar's stature. But Akbar, unlike his father Humayun, had never shown himself to be particularly friendly toward Istanbul. On the contrary, a desire to limit Ottoman influence had been a major motivation for his original conquest of Gujarat, which had been achieved largely through the connivance of Itimad Khan, the leader of the kingdom's anti-Rumi faction. In 1568, Itimad Khan had arranged for the murder of the Rumi warlord Chingiz Khan, after the latter had installed himself in the capital of Ahmedabad and seemed on the verge of being declared Gujarat's new sultan. In the unrest that followed this assassination, Itimad Khan had then turned to the Mughals as the only way of holding the Rumis at bay and retaining his own hold on power.[8]

Under such circumstances, the Ottomans could feel justified in detecting a whiff of political opportunism in the young Mughal emperor's sudden interest in the hajj following his conquest of Surat in 1573. By 1579, their suspicions were confirmed when, in September of that year, Akbar promulgated the famous "infallibility decree" that marked his first open challenge to the Ottoman dynasty's claims to superior status as caliph and protector of the holy cities. In the months that followed this promulgation, Akbar's courtiers began, at his urging, to experiment with an increasingly syncretic, messianic, and Akbar-centric interpretation of Islam known as the *dīn-i ilāhī*.[9] Buttressed by this new theology of his own creation, Akbar then began to openly style himself as "Padishah of Islam," "Imam of Justice," and even "Caesar"—all titles closely associated with the Ottoman dynasty.[10] In a letter to Abdullah Khan of the Uzbeks, he even expressed a wish that the Friday *ḫuṭbe* in Mecca and Medina—the ultimate symbol of Ottoman protectorship over the holy cities—would one day be read in his name rather than in the name of the sultans in Istanbul.[11] Such rhetorical boasts, combined with Akbar's profuse charitable contributions and his attempts to usurp administrative control of the pilgrimage route, began to take the shape of a comprehensive strategy to replace the Ottoman Empire as the leading state of the Islamic world.

How should Istanbul respond to such an unprecedented ideological broadside, fired in the midst of so many other tumultuous and disorienting events? As a temporary measure, the Ottomans' first reaction was simply to forbid the distribution of alms in Akbar's name in Mecca (it nevertheless continued in secret for several more years) and to order the entourage of ladies from his court to return to India with the next sailing season.[12] But behind the scenes, it was clear to all concerned that a more serious reorientation of imperial policy was in order. Ottoman decision makers, particularly those with an interest in the Indian Ocean, realized that in light of the myriad challenges to their rule emerging around 1579, Sokollu's delicate system of soft empire had become untenable. Instead, a stark choice seemed to present itself: either convert this soft empire into a more traditional system of direct imperial rule in maritime Asia, or stand idly by as Ottoman influence in the region gradually eroded or disappeared entirely.

FROM SOKOLLU TO KOJA SINAN: THE RECONFIGURATION OF THE INDIAN OCEAN FACTION

During the final months of his life, Sokollu Mehmed ranked first among the Ottoman statesmen most in favor of a proactive policy to preserve Ottoman influence as the international storm clouds gathered. Unfortunately, his efforts to mobilize support for a new initiative were seriously hampered by the empire's ongoing war with Iran, a conflict that had begun, against his own wishes, in 1578. At that time, because of a chaotic dynastic crisis that had overwhelmed Iran following the death of Shah Tahmasp in 1576, the invasion of Safavid lands had been presented by Sokollu's rivals as an opportunity to expand Ottoman territory quickly, easily, and with relatively little opposition. But the grand vizier knew better, guessing correctly that the campaign would deteriorate into a bloody war of attrition that promised to consume all of the empire's reserves of men, money, and material resources for the foreseeable future.[13]

So pessimistic was Sokollu about the prospect of a swift conclusion to the conflict that, by the end of 1578, he had opened negotiations with Philip II of Spain, hoping thereby to secure a permanent, comprehensive armistice in the Mediterranean. Ostensibly, this was intended as a measure that would allow the Ottomans to focus every available resource on the Safavid front. But during his subsequent meetings with Philip's negotiator Giovanni Margliani, it soon became clear that the affairs of the Indian Ocean also remained a central part of the grand vizier's strategic thinking. According to Margliani, who personally met with Sokollu Mehmed on several occasions in 1579, a consistent sticking point throughout the negotiation process was Sokollu's adamant refusal to include Portugal and its overseas possessions in the provisions of any treaty—even after it had become clear that Portugal's annexation by Spain was all but unavoidable. When pressed for an explanation, Sokollu insisted that under no circumstances did he intend to send a fleet through the straits of Gibraltar or otherwise threaten Portugal directly. But the pasha could offer no such guarantee with regard to the Indian Ocean, declaring ominously: "God alone knows what will happen there."[14] Equally ominously, this barely veiled threat coincided with reports from Portuguese India that Sokollu was in the process of contacting indigenous communities in East Africa, apparently with the aim of securing supplies of lumber for the construction of a new fleet in Yemen.[15] Even at the eleventh hour of his career, and with a war raging in Iran, it seems the tireless grand vizier was still entertaining plans for a major new initiative in the Indian Ocean.

These efforts were brought to a grinding halt by Sokollu's assassination. With no leaders waiting in the wings able even to approach the imposing stature of the late vizier, the empire was instead left in the hands of a group of mutually suspicious and bitterly divided rivals, locked in a seemingly endless cycle of backstabbing, recriminations, and scandal. In the year following Sokollu Mehmed's death, three different contenders briefly held the rank of grand vizier, and during the next decade, several more would follow them in rapid succession. Moreover, this newly fractious political climate was accompanied by a host of other problems, all symptomatic of a much wider and deepening structural crisis in the empire. Throughout the 1580s, corruption, runaway inflation, lack of progress in the war against Iran, and a full array of other pressures, both internal and external, provoked chronic discontent, increasingly frequent episodes of unrest, and in some cases, open rebellion.[16]

Nevertheless, even in the throes of a general crisis such as this, it was still possible to identify a core group of Sokollu Mehmed's supporters and protégés who managed to retain positions of considerable influence, and who would soon form the basis of a newly reconstituted Indian Ocean faction. This diverse cast of characters included Kilich Ali Pasha, the grand admiral of the imperial fleet since his appointment by Sokollu in 1571; Hazinedar Sinan, the head of the Egyptian treasury under

Sokollu and future governor of that province; Hasan Pasha, the governor of Yemen throughout the 1580s; Hizir Beg, the captain of Suez and future governor of Eritrea; and the corsair Mir Ali Beg, a worthy successor to Sefer Reis as head of the Ottoman naval squadron in Mocha. Over the course of the following decade, all of these individuals, by closely coordinating their activities, would play a critical role in reshaping Ottoman policy in the Indian Ocean.

But in the short term, by far the most influential member of this group—and the chief standard-bearer of the imperial project of Sokollu Mehmed—was without question Koja Sinan Pasha, a close associate of the late grand vizier and a towering figure of Ottoman statecraft in his own right. Already in the 1560s and 1570s, partly as a consequence of Sokollu's patronage and partly as a result of his own competence as an administrator, Koja Sinan had occupied an unparalleled variety of prominent postings in the Indian Ocean region, including two stints as governor-general of Egypt (1567–1568 and 1571–1573) and another as governor of Yemen (1569–1570). He had also proven himself to be a capable military leader, having led the reconquest of Yemen from Mutahhar and his Zaydi insurgents in the late 1560s, as well as the Ottoman reconquest of Tunis from Spain in 1574. Throughout these long years of service, Koja Sinan had also developed a wide array of business interests, amassing in the process a vast personal fortune. Although little is known about the particulars of these commercial activities, evidence suggests that Koja Sinan regularly entered into partnerships with private merchants, particularly those active in the Indian Ocean, and may even have controlled his own fleet of ships in the Red Sea while serving as governor of Egypt.[17]

Equally important, Koja Sinan was a master in the art of using his unique combination of professional experience and private wealth as a tool for self-promotion. Taking a cue from Sokollu Mehmed, Koja Sinan went to great lengths to cultivate a reputation as the special patron of Indian Ocean merchants, investing large sums of money (both from his own pockets and from the state treasury) toward construction of warehouses, rest houses, and other merchant facilities all along the commercial route from Egypt to Yemen, as well as the pilgrimage routes from Aleppo and Damascus to the holy cities.[18] One of the most notable legacies of his governorship in Egypt, for example, was a lavish caravanserai for traders in Suez, replete with a trellised seaside promenade and shaded sitting areas along the boardwalk, described by the traveler Filippo Pigafetta as "truly the ornament of Suez."[19] Koja Sinan also shared Sokollu's fondness for canals, having been intimately involved with Sokollu's abortive attempt to cut a waterway from the Mediterranean to Suez in 1569.[20] More than a decade later, one of his first major undertakings during his own first term as grand vizier was to endorse another flamboyant canal project—although one far removed from the Red Sea—which aimed to cut an alternate sea route from the Black Sea to Istanbul by digging a channel to the Bay of Izmit via Lake Sapanca.[21]

Finally, Koja Sinan was a generous patron of Ottoman intellectuals, especially geographers, historians, and other scholars with a measure of expertise in matters related to the Indian Ocean. As in the case of his philanthropy in support of public works, this patronage seems to have been driven not only by an expansive intellectual curiosity, but also by a keen understanding of how scholarly works could be used to enhance his reputation and advance his political career.[22] In the afterglow of his triumphant expedition to Yemen, for instance, he had commissioned the first version of Kutbeddin Mekki's *Al-Barḳ al-Yemānī fī'l-Fetḥi'l-'Os̱mānī* ("The Lightning over Yemen during the Ottoman Conquest"), a history of Ottoman expansion in the Arabian Peninsula that gave Sinan's own exploits more than a prominent role in its narrative.[23] Even more blatantly sycophantic was the poet Rumuzi's *Tārīẖ-i Fetḥ-i Yemen* ("History of the Conquest of Yemen"), a work in rhyming verse commissioned by Sinan and devoted specifically to the glorification of his victories against both the Zaydis and the Portuguese during this same 1568 campaign.[24]

In short, Koja Sinan was a product of his own troubled and corrupting times rather than a carbon copy of Sokollu Mehmed. But of all the contenders for power in the post-1579 Ottoman Empire, he was also the one man most capable of reproducing Sokollu's grand imperial vision and of taking up the torch of the Indian Ocean faction. Thanks to his wealth and political acumen, he displayed a political staying power that few of his rivals could match, and he eventually served five separate terms as grand vizier (a record unmatched by any previous Ottoman statesman). It was his first term, however—a frenetic period stretching from 1580 to 1582—that had the most lasting importance for the Ottoman Age of Exploration.[25]

KOJA SINAN PASHA FLEXES HIS MUSCLES

With so many challenges facing the Ottoman state at once, Koja Sinan's most pressing priority was to restore order to the beleaguered province of Eritrea, where the local Ottoman administration was still reeling from its crushing defeat at the battle of Addi Qarro. To deal with this crisis, Sinan appointed Hizir Beg, a fellow stalwart of the Indian Ocean faction who was at the time serving as the admiral of Suez, as the province's new governor. Together with Bayram Beg, the newly commissioned captain of Mocha, Hizir Beg quickly assembled a relief force in Yemen and set sail on the short journey to Eritrea in the spring of 1581.[26]

Over the course of the next year, Hizir Beg and Bayram Beg recaptured key positions on the Red Sea coast that had recently fallen to the Ethiopians, including the strategic port towns of Arkiko and Beylul. From there, in 1582, Hizir advanced into the interior with a sizable force of seven thousand troops, eventually recapturing the fallen city of Debarva after a series of major victories in the highlands. To ensure the area's future stability, Koja Sinan then had supplies sent from Egypt for the construction of a chain of seven new fortresses along the coast from Suakin to Massawa.[27] With this mission completed, at the end of 1582 Hizir was replaced as provincial governor by one of his lieutenants, Mustafa Pasha, whose seven-year term was to prove a period of peace and even cooperation between the provincial authorities and the Christians of the interior.[28]

This land campaign in the Horn of Africa was coupled with the corsairing debut of the sea captain Mir Ali Beg, a swashbuckling figure whose sudden rise from obscurity to celebrity bears a striking resemblance to the earlier experience of Sefer Reis. Much like his predecessor, Mir Ali too was based in the Yemeni port of Mocha, and in the summer of 1581 was given the nod to launch a daring raid against Portuguese-held Muscat. For the mission—again like Sefer—the corsair had under his command only three lightly armed galleots. But through a combination of stealth, clever diversionary tactics, and cooperation from friendly local Muslims, Mir Ali managed to take Muscat by surprise, put the city to sack for six full days, and eventually return to Mocha with three captured vessels and a king's ransom in hard currency and stolen merchandise.[29] According to one Iberian chronicler, "in the opening and closing of an eye he entered the town a pauper and came out again a rich man."[30] News of this stunning success quickly spread throughout the western Indian Ocean, establishing Mir Ali's corsairing credentials and setting the stage for his future campaigns in the Swahili Coast.

KOJA SINAN'S DIPLOMATIC OFFENSIVE

Much in keeping with his predecessor Sokollu Mehmed's long-established modus operandi, Koja Sinan augmented these military operations in East Africa and Muscat with an even wider ranging diplomatic initiative. These efforts centered on a secretive delegation of renegade Portuguese Jews, who in 1581 were sent by Koja Sinan to visit both the Portuguese in Goa and the Mughal court in Agra. In Goa, their delicate mission was to seek out certain Portuguese officials who, rumored to be disillusioned with their country's recent annexation by Spain, might therefore be coaxed into an alliance with Koja Sinan as a means of maintaining their independence. According to Germigny, the French ambassador in Istanbul at the time, the envoys thus carried an open invitation to the Portuguese of maritime Asia "to come from the East Indies, from the Kingdom of Hormuz, from the islands and ports of the Orient belonging to the Kingdom of Portugal, and trade in the ports and way stations of His Majesty [the Sultan] in Egypt and Syria," where they were promised "guarantees of good treatment and every comfort and convenience."[31]

It remains unclear whether Koja Sinan expected this proposal to be seriously considered or whether, by making such an offer, he hoped merely to complicate the already traumatic transition to Spanish rule in Portuguese India. In any case, despite widespread anti-Spanish sentiment—and real concerns about the loyalty of at least some Portuguese subjects—the authorities in Goa predictably chose to remain loyal to Dom Francisco Mascarenhas, the new Habsburg-appointed viceroy, rather than taking the drastic step of throwing in their lot with the Ottomans. Shortly thereafter, in a demonstration of his new authority, Mascarenhas responded to Koja Sinan's provocation by sending a small Portuguese squadron to the Arabian Sea to raid Muslim merchant vessels bound for Jiddah—the first such raid in nearly a decade.[32]

Disappointed but undaunted by this rebuff, the Ottoman delegation headed next to the Mughal court in Agra, where they urged Akbar to renounce his anti-Ottoman policies and join with the sultan in a holy war against the Habsburgs. Here, however, Akbar had already reached an accommodation with the new regime in Goa, having recently received trading passes from Mascarenhas giving him the right to send two pilgrimage ships annually to the Red Sea.[33] The Mughal emperor thus angrily rejected the Ottoman proposal, going so far as to violate diplomatic protocol by ordering the delegation to be bound in chains and banished to confinement in Lahore. According to the testimony of a Jesuit father then resident at Akbar's court, this extreme reaction was provoked "by the arrogance both of the ambassadors themselves and of the ruler who sent them, and by the endeavor which they made to persuade him to wage war against the King of Spain and Portugal."[34]

Considering the high level of tension that already existed between Akbar and the Ottomans, the emperor's hostility to the Ottoman proposal can hardly have come as a surprise. As such, the real objective of this embassy may have been, as in Goa, to convince those unhappy with the regime—particularly in Gujarat—to break ranks with Akbar and declare their support for an Ottoman intervention. Muhammad Kilij Khan, for example, who was the Mughal governor of Surat and a regular attendee at Akbar's court, responded to the Ottoman call for an alliance in a most public fashion: when Akbar's two maritime trading passes, or "*cartazes*," arrived from the Portuguese in Goa, he brazenly declared an intention to send a ship of his own to the Red Sea—but insisted that, unlike Akbar, his *cartaz* would be "the handle of the dagger in his belt."[35] Accordingly, he ordered the construction of a mighty ship in Surat, obliging the Portuguese to blockade Surat's harbor for most of the winter to prevent his departure.[36]

This symbolic act of defiance, combined with the simultaneous activities of Mir Ali Beg at sea and Hizir Beg in the Horn of Africa, provided the catalyst for a series of similar and apparently spontaneous anti-Portuguese reactions in ports of call throughout the Indian Ocean. By the following summer, even in distant Aceh resistance was again forming against the Portuguese, as a fleet 160 sails strong (including seven galleons, eleven galleys, and a sizable contingent of Ottoman mercenaries) attacked the Portuguese fortress at Malacca.[37]

By the fall of 1582, encouraged by such developments and anticipating more concrete success in the future, Koja Sinan began trade talks with the Duke of Brabant, hoping to establish at Antwerp a great entrepôt for merchandise from India once the power of Lisbon and the Habsburgs had been permanently eclipsed.[38] And then, as a final flourish, the grand vizier capped this series of diplomatic maneuvers with a domestic initiative truly in the spirit of Sokollu Mehmed: a renewed attempt to build a Suez canal. To be sure, this idea had been tried in the past with scant success, as Koja Sinan knew only too well. But his experience told him that the project was both feasible and necessary, and had not been completed on previous occasions simply due to a lack of political will. To improve his chances of successfully lobbying for the canal, Koja Sinan resolved to make a delicate but impassioned appeal directly to the reigning sovereign, Sultan Murad III.

A MANIFESTO FOR THE INDIAN OCEAN FACTION: THE *TARIH-I HIND-I GARBI*

The unique vehicle Koja Sinan chose for this purpose was a book, the *Tārīẖ-i Hind-i Ġarbī* ("History of the West Indies"; see Figure 6.1), which was composed sometime between 1580 and 1582 and personally dedicated to Sultan Murad.[39] Today, the "History of the West Indies" is known to scholars as the first major work in Ottoman Turkish about the Spanish exploration and conquest of the New World, a topic rich with rhetorical implications for the imperial designs of Koja Sinan. More directly relevant to the question of a Suez canal, however, is the content of the work's introductory section, which deals not with the New World but instead with the contemporary Indian Ocean.

In this opening segment, the anonymous author (who was probably one of Koja Sinan's personal clients) builds a clear and articulately argued case for digging a Suez canal as part of a comprehensive new Ottoman strategy in the Indian Ocean.[40] After a brief discussion of recent advances in geographic knowledge due to the European voyages of exploration, the text describes the Portuguese discovery of the Cape route and their activities in the Indian Ocean, followed by an extended warning about the danger they continued to pose both to Muslim shipping and to the long-term safety of Mecca and Medina. Advocating immediate action to remedy the situation, but echoing views previously expressed by Sokollu Mehmed about the impracticability of launching a direct attack on Portugal itself, the text goes on to argue that a great fleet should be sent against Portuguese possessions in the Indian Ocean "to seize strongholds and conquer lands, and expel and eliminate the base unbelievers."[41] It was for this reason that a Suez canal would be necessary, so that ships and supplies might pass easily from the Mediterranean to the Red Sea and allow the superior numbers and resources of the Ottoman fleet to overwhelm its adversaries once and for all.

In making this case, the author of the "History of the West Indies" also goes to considerable lengths to anticipate and rebut any potential counterarguments to his plan. But interestingly, the manner in which he does so suggests that he expected the most serious objections to be raised on ideological and religious rather than on practical grounds. This may seem surprising considering the obvious failure of previous attempts to build a canal for strictly technical reasons. But within the context of Istanbul's ongoing factional rivalry during the early 1580s, this ideological defensiveness can be understood as the direct consequence of the canal project's explicit polit-

FIGURE 6.1 A miniature painting from the anonymous "History of the West Indies," showing Spanish explorers in an exotic landscape of the New World. Source: *Tārīḫ-i Hind-i Ġarbī* or *İḳlīm-i Cedīd,* Istanbul, Beyazıt Devlet Kütüphanesi, Ms. 4969, fol. 70v.

ical connotations, and its centrality to Koja Sinan Pasha's plan to consolidate his own hold on power.

Specifically, the canal's proponents must have known that it was a project almost certain to be denounced by the ultraconservative cleric Kadizade Ahmed Shemseddin Efendi, an intractable opponent of Sokollu Mehmed during the previous decade and, in the years since his death, a leading ideological mouthpiece for those most interested in dismantling his legacy. Indeed, shortly after Sokollu's assassination in 1579, Kadizade Ahmed had lobbied successfully for the closure of the astronomer Takiyuddin Efendi's celebrated observatory (a pet project of the late grand vizier), on the pretext that astronomy, because of its close association with the occult science of astrology, was in violation of the basic tenets of Islam.[42] Since evidence suggests that the anonymous author of the "History of the West Indies" may himself have been a former employee of this observatory, the possibility that similar arguments could be used to sway opinion against the canal loomed large in his thinking.[43] And of course, any such objections would also have wider political implications for Koja Sinan and his allies, who had all been close associates of Sokollu Mehmed and thus natural antagonists of Kadizade Ahmed and his followers.

As a result, the text of the "History of the West Indies" takes care to reassure its readers (and especially the sultan) that any possible concerns about the canal on theological grounds were unfounded. As the author points out, a channel between the Nile and the Red Sea had already been opened under the rule of the pharaohs of ancient Egypt. Later, even the great Abbasid Caliph Harun al-Rashid was said to have entertained the idea of reopening this canal, deciding against the plan only because of fears that Christian fleets might use it to cross to the Red Sea and threaten the holy cities. Now, since the Portuguese had reached the Indian Ocean by means of a different route, the time was finally ripe for undertaking the project without hesitation. According to the text:

> Thanks to God, the [Ottoman] Sultan of fortune, of majestic power and force and pomp and majesty, is stronger than the kings of the past, and he has in his retinue many wise leaders...who follow his orders in every respect. And the emirs of the Maghreb and the kings of Yemen and possibly all the kings of the time express great pleasure in serving him and find happiness in conforming to the Sublime Order. So even if only a drop was to be expended from the sea of power of the Sultan, in the shortest time it would be possible to join the two seas [the Mediterranean and the Red Sea]...thenceforth, from Well-Protected Constantinople, the place of prosperity and the abode of the throne of the Sultans, ships and their crews would be organized and sent to the Red Sea and would have the power to protect the shores of the Holy Places. And in a short time, by an excellent plan, they would seize and subjugate most of the seaports of Sind and Hind and would drive away and expel from that region the evil unbelievers, and it would be possible for the exquisite things of Sind and Hind and the

> rarities of Ethiopia and the Sudan, and the usual items of the Hijaz and Yemen and the pearls of Bahrain and Aden to reach the capital with a trifling effort.[44]

Here, in so many words, was the political program of Koja Sinan Pasha and the revamped Indian Ocean faction. Buttressed ideologically by this forceful manifesto, Koja Sinan and his supporters were ready to confront all skeptics and use the construction of a Suez canal to jump-start a new and unprecedented phase of Ottoman expansion in the Indian Ocean.

Unfortunately, the turbulent Ottoman political climate of the early 1580s made any such scheme perilously difficult to implement, and even Koja Sinan's staying power soon proved inadequate for the task. At the end of 1582, personal rivalries, intrigues at court, and military setbacks on the Iranian front pushed Koja Sinan out of office, leaving the remaining members of his faction without a leader and obliged to seriously reevaluate their strategy.

HASAN PASHA EYES THE SWAHILI COAST

With Koja Sinan out of power, initiative in the Indian Ocean faction passed from the capital to the empire's periphery, coalescing around Hasan Pasha, the governor of Yemen since 1580. From this post, Hasan was the provincial official most closely in touch with developments in the Indian Ocean, including the recent military operations in Eritrea, Mir Ali Beg's naval expedition to Muscat, and the developing responses to Ottoman diplomatic maneuvering in India. At the same time, the great physical distance separating him from Istanbul was in some ways a liability, preventing him from influencing decisions at court to the same extent as Koja Sinan. But this distance also gave him a significant amount of space to operate independently, an advantage that allowed Hasan, by making the most of the limited resources at his disposal, to lay the groundwork for a new Ottoman offensive of astonishing, if ephemeral, success.

Hasan Pasha's larger goals remained much in keeping with Koja Sinan's program, as outlined in the "History of the West Indies," of building a Suez canal and proceeding with a full-scale military invasion of Portuguese India. For the time being, however, the more limited object of Hasan's activities was the nominally Portuguese territory of Africa's Swahili Coast, an obvious choice for a number of reasons. First of all, the Swahili Coast was a region relatively familiar to the Ottomans, whose ships had sailed its length as early as the 1540s and had traded regularly with local merchants ever since. Moreover, the area was poorly defended by the Portuguese, who had no permanent bases north of Mozambique and normally maintained no more than a small number of lightly armed vessels as a local coast guard. Just as important, the few Portuguese stationed there faced almost overwhelming hostility from the area's Muslim population, obliging them to maintain control not by virtue of their own strength, but by exploiting the intense internecine rivalry that perennially divided the region's various local city-states. This they accomplished primarily through a strategic alliance with Malindi, an upstart power who used friendly relations with Goa to bully its neighbors (especially its archrival Mombasa) with the threat of Portuguese intervention.[45]

All of this meant that Hasan Pasha could anticipate substantial local support from Malindi's enemies should he choose to intervene on their behalf, a prospect with serious implications for any long-term struggle with the Portuguese for control of the wider Indian Ocean region. As he well knew, the Swahili Coast offered access to rich sources of ivory, gold, and slaves from the continental interior and had good supplies of lumber for the construction of ships—a critical resource that was chronically scarce in the Red Sea region.[46] In addition, the area was in easy striking distance of Mozambique, the naval base upon which, as Sefer Reis had shown, the entire system of communications between Portuguese India and Europe depended.[47]

In sum, the Swahili coast was an ideal place to begin converting Sokollu Mehmed Pasha's soft empire into a more concrete Ottoman dominion in the Indian Ocean. The problem that Hasan Pasha faced, however, was that without Koja Sinan's support in the capital, there was no obvious way for him to secure the resources necessary to take advantage of this opportunity. His solution was to use the two advantages provided by his distance from Istanbul—his independence and his privileged access to local information—as sources of political leverage.

An opening to do precisely this presented itself in 1583, when the fortuitous arrest of two Spanish spies in the Red Sea furnished Hasan Pasha with a perfect pretext to begin making demands of the Sultan. In subsequent reports to Istanbul about this arrest, both he and Mustafa Pasha in Eritrea included, along with information about these spies' activities, dire warnings about the general unpreparedness of Ottoman defenses in the midst of Spain's takeover of the Estado da Índia. In the words of one of these reports: "Once the accursed Spanish seize the strongholds in the lands of India and send their fleet to [the Indian] ocean, they are capable of causing [us] great harm, since none of the fortresses in any of [our] ports, from Eritrea, Yemen and the Hijaz all the way to Suez, are strong [enough to resist them]."[48]

It is impossible to say with certainty whether Hasan Pasha truly believed that the Spanish presented a threat of this magnitude (subsequent events would suggest that he did not). What is clear, however, is that Sultan Murad III duly requisitioned two armed galleots to be sent to Yemen from Suez—and that Hasan Pasha did *not* use them (as he had promised) for any purposes related to local defense.[49] Instead, he placed them under the command of Mir Ali Beg and dispatched them on a daring expedition to the Swahili Coast, apparently without informing anyone in Istanbul of his plans.[50]

MIR ALI BEG'S FIRST EXPEDITION TO EAST AFRICA

Mir Ali's mission was, at least on the surface, one of simple reconnaissance mixed with a bit of privateering, not substantially different from his strike against the Portuguese in

Muscat in 1581.[51] But in addition to these straightforward raiding activities, the corsair was also charged with a more sophisticated assignment, which involved establishing and expanding contacts with the local Muslim population of East Africa. With their help, he was to select the location for a future fortified naval stronghold that would be suitable as an advanced base for further attacks. Eventually, this base was to serve as the launching point for a genuine expedition of conquest "to expel the Portuguese from the entire coast, even as far as Mozambique and the mines of Cuamá."[52]

To accomplish all of this, as he set sail from Mocha at the end of 1585, Mir Ali had under his command only the two galleots recently delivered from Suez and a contingent of no more than 150 fighting men. During his outgoing voyage, even this meager force was reduced by half, when one of his vessels became waterlogged and was obliged to turn back. Thus, when the corsair finally reached the East African coast, his "fleet" consisted of just one war galley and perhaps eighty men.

What Mir Ali may have lacked in personnel and supplies, however, he more than made up for in swagger and reputation. In January 1586, when he sailed into Mogadishu, his first port of call, he received nothing short of a hero's welcome from the inhabitants of the city. Once informed of the reasons for Mir Ali's visit, the town notables enthusiastically swore allegiance to the sultan, voluntarily turned over money for the future expenses of the expedition, and armed twenty *pangaios*, or light coastal craft, to escort Mir Ali's galleot on its continuing voyage south.

Thus reinforced, the corsair was ready to head for the Swahili Coast proper, where over the next several weeks his experience in Mogadishu was repeated almost exactly in the towns of Brava, Jugo, and Pate. One after another, the petty rulers of all of these island ports declared for the Ottomans as soon as he arrived, swore allegiance to Mir Ali personally, and offered money, supplies, and exuberant guarantees of more in the future. In the admiring words of a later Spanish chronicler, who marveled at Mir Ali's success: "How much can be accomplished by just one man, either by luck or by pluck! Such was the fame of Mir Ali, who was held to be so vivacious, so charming and so bold... that he managed all of this not through the strength of the arms that he carried with him, but only through the promise of what he might bring in the future!"[53]

As this commentary suggests, the overwhelming local response to Mir Ali's arrival caught the Portuguese of the region completely by surprise. As a result, Captain Ruy Lopes Salgado, the sole Portuguese official responsible for the Swahili Coast's defense, chose to fortify himself in the friendly port of Malindi rather than confront the corsair—an act of cowardice that left other ships in the area unprotected and easy prey for Mir Ali. Accordingly, the twelve crewmembers of a Portuguese merchant vessel belonging to the captain of Diu soon crossed paths with the small Ottoman fleet and became its first victims, surrendering without a fight after a brief standoff. Thereafter, Mir Ali netted an even bigger prize: the warship of Malindi's outgoing Captain-Major Roque de Brito, which was handed over to the

Ottomans (along with its commander and its escort of fifteen Portuguese soldiers) by the inhabitants of the island of Lamu. Mir Ali promptly consigned these men to the docks of his galley and assumed control of their warship, rearming it with a crew of local Muslim volunteers and a few of his own sailors. Then, he used it to hunt down yet another Portuguese ship belonging to the captain of Chaul, which yielded as well after a brief exchange of artillery fire.

It was now the end of March, just a little over two months since his first arrival in Mogadishu. From virtually nothing, Mir Ali had managed to build a formidable fleet of twenty-four ships, including (in addition to his own galleot) the twenty *pangaio* auxiliaries, the small merchant ship from Diu, the vessel from Chaul, and Roque de Brito's war galley. With this armada, he spent the month of April sailing the full length of the Swahili Coast, "filling his ships to the brim with tribute in gold, amber, ivory and slaves" and securing the allegiance of every major port town in the region except Malindi, which still remained a staunch Portuguese ally.[54] Loaded down with booty valued at over 150,000 gold *cruzados*, and with nearly sixty Portuguese captives in tow, the corsair returned in triumph to his home base in Mocha with the summer monsoon. He was accompanied by ambassadors from Mombasa, Pate, and Kilifi, who were to consult with Hasan Pasha in Yemen about his plans for a second and more serious expedition to occupy the region permanently.

DEVELOPMENTS IN INDIA

Mir Ali's mission to the Swahili Coast coincided with several other major developments, as the political pulse began to quicken perceptibly on both sides of the western Indian Ocean. In early 1585, while the corsair was still in the early planning stages of his departure for East Africa, Hasan Pasha also renewed his contacts with Muhammad Kilij Khan in Surat, who attempted once more to evade Portuguese patrols in the Gulf of Cambay and send a ship to the Red Sea without a *cartaz*. The Portuguese responded by again imposing a naval blockade on Surat, but Muhammad Kilij coaxed them into reopening the port through a promise of negotiations, and then promptly launched his ship before any agreement had been reached. The vessel successfully reached Mocha some weeks later, loading a full cargo of artillery, munitions, and two hundred select Ottoman mercenaries, although its homeward voyage proceeded much less smoothly. Returning to Surat late in the summer in the midst of a heavy storm, it was greeted by several Portuguese vessels waiting in ambush. Charging through this blockade with its newly acquired Ottoman cannon firing from the gun ports, the ship missed the entrance to the harbor and was run aground by the strong winds, where it was surrounded by the Portuguese and bombarded for several days. The damaged craft survived the barage only to be broken up in another storm, although the crew and much of its military cargo did reach Surat safely.[55]

In retaliation for this coordinated act of defiance, the Portuguese sent a fleet of their own to south Arabia in the fall of 1585, with orders to attack Muslim shipping and prevent the free passage of merchants through the Bab al-Mandab. Significantly, this mission, led by Ruy Gonsalves da Camara, was the first serious Portuguese attempt to restrict access to the Red Sea in more than a decade, and with a fleet numbering some twenty-six vessels in all, it also counted as one of the largest naval forces ever sent by the Portuguese to the region.

Despite its numerical strength, however, Ruy Gonsalves da Camara's expedition proved a veritable fiasco, failing to catch even a single Muslim ship in four months of patrolling. In the process, his men lost one of their own vessels in an Ottoman coastal ambush near Aden, and nearly succumbed en masse to thirst and other privations during their homeward voyage before finally reaching Muscat in April 1586. Throughout these many months at sea, da Camara had also failed to gather any meaningful intelligence about Mir Ali, remaining completely ignorant of his expedition even though the corsair's departure for the Swahili Coast had preceded the Portuguese arrival in Mocha by only a few weeks.[56]

Only upon his return to Goa in the fall of 1586, where news of Mir Ali's exploits had reached the Portuguese authorities there by other means, did da Camara learn of Sefer's campaign, being greeted upon his arrival with "black flags and signs of mourning as if it had been a funeral."[57] Meanwhile, the scant success of da Camara's own mission was met with a grim lack of surprise by the elders of Goa, one of whom was said to have declared: "Just as the Turks are incapable of sending a fleet to India without suffering a loss, so none of our own vessels will ever travel to the straits of Mecca without meeting the same fate."[58] In Goa's harbor, da Camara heard a similar judgment from an Abyssinian pilot manning one of the Mughals' licensed trading vessels, who chided: "The only thing you have accomplished with this mission is to wake the proverbial sleeping dog!"[59]

These words proved prophetic, for da Camara's blundering was indeed to have severe consequences. Although his mission had accomplished none of its original objectives, the mere appearance of a large Portuguese fleet in the Red Sea provided the perfect occasion for Hasan Pasha in Yemen to restart his well-oiled propaganda machine. Seizing the opportunity, in the months that followed he appears to have hatched a complicated plot to advance the cause of Ottoman maritime expansion in a singularly underhanded fashion: Through a series of regular dispatches sent back to the capital, he began a calculated campaign of misinformation in which he and his factional allies intentionally exaggerated the threat posed by the Portuguese at sea, hoping thereby to secure resources and financing from Istanbul for his imperial designs in the Indian Ocean.

A PLOT IS HATCHED, AND A FACTION REBORN

The first evidence of this propaganda offensive comes in the form of several unfounded rumors about Ruy Gonsalves da Camara's expedition that began emanating from the Red Sea in the early months of 1586. Without exception, these grossly misrepresented the effectiveness of the Portuguese attack, to the extent that, by June of that year, France's ambassador in Venice was forwarding reports that the Portuguese had not only entered the Red Sea but also looted and pillaged the entire coast as far north as Tor, even suggesting that they were planning to return the following year to land troops and build a fortress near Aden.[60] Panic followed at court in Istanbul, and in the midst of this rumor-induced hysteria, the sultan appointed Hasan Pasha's ally Hazinedar Sinan as the new governor-general of Egypt to handle the "crisis"—replacing Ibrahim Pasha, the previous governor, who had tried to refute these rumors as groundless.[61] Even more suspiciously, in Hazinedar Sinan's first official dispatch following his promotion, he confirmed Istanbul's worst fears, writing that the Portuguese had indeed cut off all trade to the Red Sea, were building a permanent base on the island of Socotra, and were in the final stages of planning a direct naval assault on Jiddah and the holy cities.[62]

Since Hazinedar Sinan had already been serving in Egypt as provincial treasurer long before his appointment as governor, it is difficult, if not impossible, to imagine a scenario in which he would not have known this information to be patently untrue. His written confirmation of these spurious reports therefore demonstrates that he was not only a direct beneficiary of Hasan Pasha's campaign of misinformation but also an active collaborator. Indeed, in the interest of further advancing their cause, the two pashas seem to have agreed even to suppress information about Mir Ali's mission to the Swahili Coast during these critical months, as no information about his accomplishments in Africa appears in any surviving dispatches from either Egypt or Yemen. Instead, presumably out of a concern that the easy success of Mir Ali's mission would undermine their claims about a mounting Portuguese threat, Hasan Pasha and Hazinedar Sinan seem to have presented the ships and men the corsair had captured on the Swahili Coast (and duly forwarded on to Hazinedar Sinan in Egypt) as war matériel recovered from da Camara's fleet in the Red Sea—thereby producing physical evidence of a military encounter that had never actually taken place![63]

Duplicitous as this tactic may have been, as a ploy to swing opinion at court in the two pashas' favor it proved brilliantly effective. Almost immediately upon receipt of Hazinedar Sinan's report, in the middle of July 1586, a ferman was sent from Istanbul to Egypt authorizing the construction of twenty new war galleys in the arsenal of Suez.[64] By the end of the same month, the Venetian envoy Lorenzo Bernardo wrote from Istanbul of growing criticism of Sultan Murad "for attending to the Persian war and thus allowing Spain to reach such a pitch of power."[65] Bernardo then went on to repeat the information contained in Hazinedar Sinan's report, describing the panic it had provoked among the empire's ruling elite. He also discussed the developing Ottoman response to this challenge—which went so far as to include renewed talk of building Koja Sinan Pasha's Suez canal. According to the text of this dispatch:

> The Spaniards have fortified the island of Kamaran opposite the Kingdom of Aden. . . . This disturbs the Turks, for the possession of that island will allow the Spanish to close the spice traffic from the Indies to Cairo. This will mean the loss of half a million of gold a year which comes in from the customs dues. The Spanish fleet in the Red Sea will now be masters of the gulf of Suez, and the pilgrimage route to Mecca will be no longer safe. The Turks also remember that they have now to deal with a Sovereign very powerful at sea, who, although engaged in a war with England and with Flanders has been able to strike this blow, from which they conclude that if he sends a large armament into those waters he will make himself master without any difficulty. They hold therefore that it is absolutely necessary for them to keep a huge armament in those parts, and to accomplish this they are entertaining the idea of excavating the ancient canal constructed by the kings of Egypt, which led from the port of Damietta to our sea, through one hundred and fifty miles of land to Suez on the Red Sea.[66]

As a final note, Bernardo stated that the sultan was at present in consultation with his Divan about how best to proceed with the canal's construction and was being advised by none other than Hasan Pasha, who had recently made the trip from Yemen to Istanbul specifically for this purpose.[67]

Within weeks, Grand Admiral Kilich Ali Pasha—another accomplice in this affair with a long personal history of manipulating intelligence for political purposes—was leaking specifics about the plan to Istanbul's resident French ambassador Savary de Lanscome.[68] According to Lanscome, the admiral boasted that in light of recent provocations, Sultan Murad was determined to open a channel to Suez and send a fleet to eliminate the Habsburg threat once and for all, having already set aside for the project 25 galleys, 100,000 men, 40,000 mules, 12,000 camels, and the entire revenue of Egypt for a year, totaling some 600,000 ducats. Lanscome added as a postscript:

> This grand scheme of theirs has so inflated their already habitual arrogance, and sparked their greed and ambition to such an extent that it appears to them as if all the treasures and precious gems of India are already in their hands, and Persia ensnared in their net as well. They hold the Spanish of no account whatsoever, since they say that [in all of India] they have no more than four thousand men. And if truth be told, should their aspirations be fulfilled to build this canal, and they do send two hundred armed galleys [to India] as they say they will, then since they are already masters of Arabia they will make rapid progress with no one to stop them, and will shut the door [to India] on Lisbon and Spain.[69]

The striking similarity between the intentions outlined in this report and the previously cited passage from the "History of the West Indies" can hardly be coincidental, and demonstrates just how consistently the surviving members of the Indian Ocean faction, four full years after their leader Koja Sinan Pasha's dismissal, had been able to retain their influence and advance their agenda. Nevertheless, the construction of a Suez canal remained, even under the best of circumstances, a challenge fraught with technical difficulties. And in addition to these practical obstacles, for a state with its resources already strained by war with Iran it also ranked as an exorbitantly expensive project. In consequence, as doubts about its feasibility mounted and details were revealed about the true extent (or lack thereof) of Portuguese operations in the Red Sea, Istanbul's swell of enthusiasm for the canal quickly began to dissipate. By the end of the summer, even Grand Admiral Kilich Ali had withdrawn his support, citing the difficulties of construction in the sand and winds of the desert, as well as fears that the excavations could cause an inundation of salt water from the Red Sea into the valley of the Nile.[70] Soon enough, Sultan Murad lost his enthusiasm as well and brought to a close for the third and final time Ottoman attempts to cut a channel from the Mediterranean to the Red Sea.[71]

THE PLOT THICKENS

Frustrated but not entirely disheartened, Hasan Pasha and Hazinedar Sinan were now ready to play their final conspiratorial card in a bid to salvage what remained of their dreams of empire in the Indian Ocean. Although deprived of a canal, the two alarmists could at least console themselves with a small fleet of five galleots that was sent from Suez to Yemen during the fall of 1586 "for the defense of the coasts."[72] Encouraged by this limited but concrete success, Hasan Pasha responded by sending yet another communiqué to Istanbul in which he again raised the specter of an impending attack from Goa. Arguing that five galleots would be barely sufficient for defending the ports of Yemen should such an attack materialize, he boldly asked for another "twenty or thirty galleys" in order to "strike out at the infidels from the sea."[73]

To enhance the urgency of this request, he and Hazinedar Sinan also forwarded a simultaneous "spy report" that they claimed had been recently provided by agents returning from India. This contained information with all the makings of a diplomatic bombshell, namely that Akbar had concluded a formal alliance with Spain and that the two powers were now preparing a fleet for a joint invasion of Yemen.[74] This terrifying prospect, which played on the most deeply rooted fears of Istanbul's leadership, was probably the only imaginable scenario that could seem more immediately threatening to the empire than its ongoing war with Iran. Moreover, from the two pashas' perspectives, it mattered little if the report was actually true, provided it proved useful for political purposes.

Realistically, there was virtually no reason to believe that a joint Mughal-Portuguese operation of this kind was ever seriously considered. Although the Mughals had established a permanent embassy in Goa in 1584, there is no record in any Mughal or Portuguese source of any such proposal ever having been discussed.[75] After 1582, in fact, Akbar had cut off his annual subsidies to the Sharif of Mecca and his generous support for pilgrims traveling to the holy cities.[76] And while he continued to maintain superficially smooth relations with the Portuguese, in his correspondence with other Muslim leaders he had begun to talk openly of plans to seize for himself the important Portuguese strongholds of Diu, Chaul, and even Goa.[77]

The two pashas' spy report thus seems to have been nothing more than another conscious and manipulative distortion. But at least in the short term, their gambit proved once more to be an effective one. By January 1588, the sultan had authorized the construction of fifteen additional galleys in Suez and five more in Basra, all to be used in a future sea campaign.[78] In his accompanying instructions to Hasan Pasha, the sultan left no doubt about the gravity with which he viewed the situation, writing: "You shall act like a wolf and prevent the base infidels from ravaging my protected domains.... Do not take this matter lightly! Do not leave anything to chance! It is imperative that you make all possible efforts to ward off the danger."[79]

SPAIN AND PORTUGAL ON THE DEFENSIVE

In reality, of course, there was no real danger to be warded off, either from Akbar or from the Estado da Índia. Quite to the contrary, in the same month that this ferman was issued by the sultan in Istanbul, Philip II of Spain had sent the following directive to his viceroy in Goa:

> Since in these parts [i.e. Europe] there are many affairs deserving of attention, it will from now on be necessary for you to preserve the gains that have already been made rather than to seek out new ventures. Keep in mind that offensive wars have many disadvantages, as has been demonstrated by the armada which you sent under Ruy Gonsalves da Camara to the Red Sea which, far from resulting in any of the successes that had been hoped for, served only to provoke the Turks at great and unprofitable expense... and with much discredit to the state.[80]

Evidently, the "many affairs deserving of attention" to which Philip referred were his preparations for the Spanish Armada, which by 1588 had grown into an all-consuming enterprise for the Spanish Empire.[81] At the same time, Philip's new defensive mandate for the Indian Ocean came after a year in which the Estado da Índia had struggled to keep its own house in order following the upheaval caused by Mir Ali Beg's lightning expedition to the Swahili Coast. After Mir Ali's return to Mocha in the spring of 1586, the King of Malindi had in fact sent his Portuguese allies a panicked letter describing the full extent of the corsair's depredations and suggesting that the worst was yet to come. In his view, if the Ottomans returned with a larger fleet (as Mir Ali had promised) and were allowed to build a fortress in Mombasa (as Mombasa's king had offered), "he could threaten to destroy all of India... since from there [the Ottomans] could easily seize not only Sofala and the Mines of Cuamá but even the fortress of Mozambique itself, whence they could ambush and capture the Royal fleet from Europe."[82]

Faced with such a threat, the reigning viceroy Dom Duarte de Meneses had acted as quickly and decisively as he could, dispatching a sizable fleet to the Swahili Coast in January 1587.[83] Once there, the fleet's commander, Martim Afonso de Melo, singled out for punishment the inhabitants of the island of Pate, who were accused of having tortured and executed one of Mir Ali's Portuguese prisoners during the previous year.[84] In retribution for this act, de Melo ordered a merciless attack on the settlement, razing its houses to the ground, killing its king, massacring and enslaving its population, and even destroying its groves of date palms to prevent future inhabitants from resettling the area.[85] Then de Melo headed for Mombasa, whose terrified inhabitants abandoned their homes and property and fled, allowing de Melo to sack their town as well.

In the end, however, Martim Afonso de Melo was unable to use this emphatic show of force to reconsolidate Portuguese authority in any lasting way. Instead, records show that he was under strict orders from Philip II not to establish a permanent garrison in Mombasa and to avoid "tyrannizing or molesting the locals unnecessarily," which Philip deemed "the best and most useful remedy" against rising pro-Ottoman sentiment.[86] As an added complication, de Melo soon learned of renewed activity in the Ottoman arsenal in Basra, suggesting that Mir Ali's recent operations in East Africa had perhaps been a diversion and that the Ottomans' real objective was the much more important Portuguese base in Hormuz. Under such circumstances, de Melo was thus obliged to pacify the remaining city-states of the Swahili Coast on the cheap, demanding nothing more from their leaders than oaths of loyalty and token payments of tribute. Then he quickly set sail for Hormuz with the spring monsoon, hoping to launch a surprise attack against Basra before the Ottoman galleys under construction there could be completed.[87]

Ultimately, the strain of conducting two campaigns in a single year appears to have been too much for de Melo, who died just a few weeks later, shortly after reaching the Persian Gulf.[88] For that matter, his belated show of leniency in the Swahili Coast also failed to have its intended effect, for his severe treatment of Pate and Mombasa, followed by his hasty departure, seems to have left a much deeper impression than his clemency toward the rest of the region's Muslims. Even before his death, in fact, the same collection of city-states that he had only recently coaxed into an oath of loyalty to the king of Spain once more sent an embassy to Yemen with "letters, money and presents" for the local Ottoman authorities. Apprising Hasan Pasha of the details of de Melo's attack, these envoys pleaded with him to fulfill Mir Ali's earlier promise to return with a fleet "and take revenge upon the Portuguese for their insults, depredations and killings by casting them out of these lands once and for all."[89]

For his part, Hasan Pasha had every intention of obliging this request. But ironically, as he contemplated his next move, he found himself facing some of the same constraints as his counterparts in Portuguese India. For just as Philip II's preoccupation with the Spanish Armada had led him to discourage any new anti-Ottoman offensives in the Indian Ocean, the Ottomans' own ongoing (and intensifying) war with Iran presented a similar obstacle for Hasan Pasha. To make matters worse, Hasan's carefully crafted coalition of supporters also began to disintegrate at this critical juncture, beginning with the death of Kilich Ali Pasha in 1587 and the expiration of Hazinedar Sinan Pasha's term as governor of Egypt in early 1588.

Egypt's new governor, Kara Uveys, was an administrator openly hostile to Hasan Pasha and deeply skeptical about the sincerity of his claims. Over the course of the next year, it seems that Kara Uveys intentionally delayed the construction of Hasan's additional ships in the arsenal of Suez, while sending letters of his own back to Istanbul denying that Yemen or the Red Sea was in any immediate danger.[90] By late fall of 1588, as the sailing season approached and none of the promised reinforcements from Suez had materialized, an increasingly isolated Hasan Pasha was left with no choice but to once again take matters into his own hands and act independently of Istanbul. Gathering together Mir Ali's original galleot, the Portuguese warship captured from Roque de Brito in 1586, and three of the five galleys already delivered from Suez by Hazinedar Sinan, Hasan armed a modest fleet and placed it under the command of Mir Ali, who set sail once more for East Africa in December 1588. This time, Mir Ali's orders were to permanently occupy the island of Mombasa, thereby providing facts on the ground with which Hasan Pasha hoped to restore his fading credibility at court.[91]

MIR ALI BEG'S SECOND EXPEDITION TO THE SWAHILI COAST

Mir Ali's return to the Swahili Coast began as auspiciously as his first visit three years before.[92] Just as he had on his previous trip, he headed first for the port of Mogadishu, where he received money, supplies, and a hero's welcome from the local population. From there, he continued on to the south and once more garnered enthusiastic pledges of support from "all the cities and resting-places of the Moors of that coast."[93] The only exception, predictably enough, was Malindi, which he found garrisoned by the Portuguese captain Mateus Mendes de Vasconcelos. After stopping there for a desultory bombardment of Malindi's town walls, Mir Ali continued on to his final destination, Mombasa.

According to surviving Portuguese sources, Mir Ali had already identified Mombasa as his primary target during his first visit to the region in 1586. Of all the island city-states of the Swahili Coast, it commanded the most centrally located and easily defensible position, had a large population inveterately hostile to both Malindi and to the Portuguese, and enjoyed good access to timber and other locally available resources. Furthermore, although the total military force at Mir Ali's disposal was smaller than what he may have anticipated—a mere five light vessels as opposed to the "twenty or thirty" war galleys that Hasan Pasha had originally requested—the corsair nonetheless had a very clear strategy about how to transform Mombasa into a permanent advanced base for future operations.

The centerpiece of this strategy was artillery. Hailing as he did from the Ottoman seaport of Mocha, Mir Ali was surely familiar with his predecessor Sefer Reis's ability, with just a few oared galleots and support from heavy artillery fire, to consistently defend Mocha against direct assaults from even very large Portuguese fleets. Mir Ali's hope was clearly to export this proven tactic from Yemen to East Africa. To do so, he had brought with him, in addition to his five vessels and their escort of perhaps three hundred fighting men, a very large number of high-quality artillery pieces, including several very powerful siege cannons for use on land. With this heavy ordnance and logistical support from a friendly local population, Mir Ali aimed to build a fortified stronghold and force the Portuguese to come to him.

For this the corsair did not have long to wait, as the authorities in Goa had received advance warning of his movements from spies in Yemen. By the time Mir Ali reached East Africa, in fact, Captain-Major Tomé de Sousa Coutinho had already set out from India with a fleet of eleven oared warships, six galleons, and more than nine hundred fighting men, a force that outnumbered Mir Ali's by a ratio of more than three to one (and to which were later added two additional ships and a large number of auxiliary troops supplied by the Portuguese allies in Malindi). Still, with energetic cooperation from the population of Mombasa, Mir Ali moved ahead at an impressive pace with preparations for a defensive stand, such that, by the end of February, his men had managed to complete a fortified tower commanding the entrance to Mombasa's harbor. Inside, Mir Ali placed his heaviest siege guns to secure the port from attack by sea, and as a second line of defense, he positioned his five galleots along the shore in front of the city itself, with their bows and deck guns facing seaward to guard against an amphibious assault. This was precisely the same defensive formation that Sefer Reis had used repeatedly (and to great effect) against the Portuguese in Mocha, and it also resembled the tactics employed by Selman Reis in his heroic defense of Jiddah against the fleet of Lopo Soarez as early as 1517. Thus, with history and experience on his side, Mir Ali had every reason to approach the coming battle with confidence, despite his numeric disadvantage.[94]

The one contingency that the corsair could not possibly have prepared for was the appearance of an overwhelming force from an entirely different, indeed, unimaginable direction: a mysterious marauding horde of Zimba warriors, who emerged from the interior of Africa just as the Ottomans were making ready their final defensive positions. According to the colorful (and problematic) account of João dos Santos, whose *Etiópia Oriental* is the main surviving Portuguese source for subsequent events, these ferocious Zimba constituted a veritable army of no fewer than twenty thousand individuals, who were charged, among other atrocities, of systematic acts of mass cannibalism.[95] Whatever their true numbers and true identity—and regardless of whether their putative cannibalism was fact or a Portuguese flight of fancy—their spectacular appearance at Mombasa only days before the arrival of the Portuguese fleet was a disaster for Mir Ali. Expecting an attack by sea, the corsair had neglected to defend the narrow estuary dividing Mombasa from the mainland, which was shallow enough to wade across at low tide. Because of the untimely arrival of the Zimba, Mir Ali had no choice but to move his best artillery, two of his war galleys, and the greater part of his men to the other side of the island to prevent them from crossing over. In defense of the city itself, he left only a skeleton crew in the fortified tower and in his three remaining ships still guarding the harbor.

This was the situation when, on March 5, 1589, the Portuguese commander Tomé de Sousa Coutinho reached Mombasa at the head of his powerful Portuguese fleet. As Coutinho charged into the harbor, Mir Ali and his men set off a barrage of artillery fire, still hopeful of sinking at least some of the enemy vessels as they passed. Instead, all of the Portuguese ships avoided direct hits, and a lucky shot from their own guns silenced the Ottomans' main cannon in the fortress tower. With no more to fear from Ottoman defensive fire, the Portuguese were able to charge the three beached galleys and easily overwhelm them, putting their crews to flight and capturing the stragglers.

This accomplished, de Sousa Coutinho sent a contingent of ships around to the estuary dividing the island from the mainland, where his men found the rest of the Ottoman troops fully engaged with the Zimba and still trying to prevent them from crossing over to Mombasa. Once again the Portuguese easily overran the Ottoman positions, after some intense hand-to-hand combat forced several desperate Ottoman crewmen to jump ship and attempt to swim to safety on the mainland. These unfortunates the Zimba hacked down to the last man, prompting the rest of the Ottoman defenders to surrender as a group to the Portuguese commander. In all, nearly a hundred of their number were killed in the fray or fell to the Zimba. Another seventy were taken prisoner by the Portuguese, along with both vessels, twenty-three fine bronze artillery pieces, and six more large iron guns, one of which was described by dos Santos as "exceptionally large."[96]

His galleys and artillery lost, Mir Ali and the remainder of his men took refuge with the Mombasans in the interior of the island. Since the Portuguese were still reluctant to leave their ships and face the corsair on land, a few days of inconclusive negotiations followed. Eventually, Tomé de Sousa Coutinho was approached by an envoy from the Zimba chief, who declared common cause with the Portuguese and requested permission to cross over to the island and confront the Ottomans and Mombasans directly. The unscrupulous Portuguese commander, recognizing an opportunity to flush out Mir Ali without putting his own men at risk, immediately acquiesced. But as he did so, he simultaneously ordered the launches from his own ships to be sent to shore, so they could pick up the Ottomans and their Mombasan allies as the approaching Zimba forced them out.

Soon enough—if we are to believe João dos Santos's version of events—the Portuguese oarsmen who dutifully assumed positions along the shore were met with an almost indescribable spectacle, as throngs of terrorized islanders came running from the island's interior, calling desperately for help and making for the beach with the Zimba close at their heels. Panic ensued as the small boats were quickly filled beyond their capacity and began pulling away from the shoreline to avoid being capsized and overwhelmed. Just as the very last of these launches was about to depart, Mir Ali appeared on horseback, with the Zimba in close pursuit and a rain of arrows cascading around him. Galloping at full speed, he charged headlong into the sea, flung himself toward the Portuguese boat, and was pulled to safety at the last possible moment. Thirty of his companions were similarly saved by the boats, along with around two hundred Mombasans. A great many more, however, were left behind. From the safety of their launches, the Portuguese rowers watched as dozens of women and children hurled themselves into the waves in despair, in dos Santos's words, "preferring to drown rather than face the cruel iron of the barbarians."[97]

Once he was safely on board the Portuguese flagship, a visibly relieved Mir Ali congratulated his Portuguese counterpart and declared: "I do not lament my adverse fortune, for such is the nature of war, and I would much rather be a captive of the Christians, as I was once before in Spain, than food for the barbarous and inhuman Zimba."[98] The Portuguese captain did his best to reassure Mir Ali, telling him he had made the right choice and would no longer have anything to worry about. Nevertheless, it seems that the worst was still to come for Mir Ali and most of his companions. His men were condemned to serve as slaves in the galleys of the Estado da Índia, where many remained in servitude for the rest of their lives. The ringleaders from among his local supporters, including the king of Lamu and several prominent notables from Pate and Kilifi, were rounded up and publicly executed. The island of Mandra was also sacked in punishment for siding with the corsair, and Mombasa, once the Zimba had retreated to the mainland, was handed over to its archrival Malindi as a reward for the latter's loyalty to the Portuguese crown.

As for Mir Ali, with the next monsoon he was taken back to Goa and was received by the viceroy. There, in a thoroughly gentlemanly exchange, Mir Ali was offered kind words by his new master, who urged him to "be of good cheer and trust in God. For I also was once a captive, and of [the pirates of] Malabar, a much harsher master than yours, and yet you can see for yourself where I stand today. The same may happen to you."[99] The corsair gallantly responded: "Sir, it is true that I am a captive, but being one of Your Excellency's I consider myself a great lord."[100] Then, according to dos Santos, Mir Ali was sent to Portugal, where he converted to Christianity "and with this act restored for his soul all of the losses and injuries sustained by his body."[101]

We shall never know if this conversion was sincere or merely a ploy for leniency. But in either case, it seems to have earned him no permanent reprieve from his Portuguese captors. Archival records from as late as 1608 indicate that at this advanced date Mir Ali, now known by his Christian name, Francisco Julião, was still in captivity, languishing in the Portuguese dungeon of the Castle of S. Julião da Barra.[102]

THE HARD LANDING OF A SOFT EMPIRE

In many ways, the career of Mir Ali Beg can be read as a history of the Ottoman Age of Exploration in microcosm. Like the Ottoman Empire as a whole, Mir Ali's charisma was high, and his reputation in the western Indian Ocean widespread. His technical qualifications as a naval commander were impeccable. His military record against the Portuguese was long and distinguished. His strategic planning was sound. And his ability to inspire loyalty from far-flung Muslim communities was barely short of awe-inspiring.

With all of these advantages in his favor, what might have happened had Mir Ali and his allies managed to prevail at Mombasa in 1589? Supposing the Ottoman plan had worked, and Tomé de Sousa Coutinho and the Portuguese fleet had actually been defeated, it seems at least conceivable that Mir Ali would have eventually forced the capitulation of Malindi, Portugal's last local ally, and from there taken possession of the entire Swahili Coast. This, in turn, could have allowed Hasan Pasha to present Sultan Murad III with irrefutable evidence of the merits of continued expansion in the Indian Ocean, silencing naysayers and finally ensuring a steady stream of material support for continued campaigning in the south. In time, the Ottomans might very well have extended their rule as far as the Zambezi River (or "the mines of Cuamá" in the language of the Portuguese sources), seizing control of the lucrative trade in gold, ivory, and slaves from the African interior and depriving the Portuguese of this crucial source of revenue. Thus weakened, it is an open question whether the Portuguese could have maintained control of Mozambique, and it is even more uncertain how they could have faced the coming challenge from the Dutch in the following century. In short, under only slightly different circumstances, Mir Ali's expedition to the Swahili Coast could quite possibly have spelled the premature demise of Portuguese Asia and ushered in an entirely new era of Ottoman dominion in East Africa.

If none of this came to pass, it was due not only to the timely and ferocious intervention of the Zimba but also to certain structural limitations that Mir Ali's expedition shared with the Ottoman Empire as a whole. First and foremost, the corsair was faced with a formidable constraint of physical geography: the near total lack of timber and other strategic resources in the Ottomans' arid Indian Ocean provinces, which left them chronically starved of ships, men, and supplies. Theoretically, this was a problem with an obvious solution: a canal linking the Mediterranean to the Red Sea, which would have allowed the Ottomans to mobilize the full strength of their Mediterranean fleet. But even if such a canal was feasible from a purely technical standpoint, it was a project beyond the capacities of a perennially divided Ottoman leadership, never able to fully commit itself to the Indian Ocean because of a combination of ongoing domestic distractions and international upheavals.

As a result, Mir Ali was obliged to operate under conditions that left him only a razor-thin margin of error. The dramatic denouement of his last stand at Mombasa,

FIGURE 6.2 An early seventeenth-century view of the island of Mombasa, dominated by Fort Jesus. Source: António Bocarro, *Livro das plantas de todas as fortalezas, cidades e povoaçoens do Estado da Índia Oriental*, Évora, Biblioteca Pública, Códice CXV/2-1.

leading to his final and definitive defeat, was thus a direct consequence of the structural constraints imposed on him by geography, technology, and the political culture of his superiors. Certainly the Zimba also had a role to play in his downfall, but as a proximate cause. Much like the Zaydi revolt of 1567, the untimely death of Sefer Reis in 1565, or the assassination of Selman Reis in 1528, the Zimba intervention proved decisive because the Ottomans were already operating at the outer limit of their material, physical, and human capabilities.

Even so, Mir Ali's gamble was fruitless but by no means misguided. In fact, after his defeat and capture, the Portuguese paid him the ultimate compliment by essentially co-opting his strategy: acknowledging that Mombasa, rather than Malindi, was indeed the most strategically valuable location on the coast, they built an imposing fortress of their own at virtually the same location as Mir Ali's fortified tower—a structure that remains to this day one of Mombasa's most distinguishing landmarks.[103] Once this fortress, dubbed Fort Jesus, was completed in 1596 (Figure 6.2), it became the new headquarters of a revamped colonial administration that ruled the region for most of the next century.[104]

Meanwhile, outside of East Africa, the battle of Mombasa in 1589 marked the end of Portuguese power politics in the western Indian Ocean. As subsequent events would show, the Portuguese—now under Spanish rule—permanently lost their stomach for any further confrontation with the Ottomans, despite their victory against Mir Ali. Ruy Gonsalves da Camara's mission to the Red Sea in 1586 was, for all intents and purposes, the very last of its kind, demonstrating once and for all the futility of "waking the sleeping Ottoman dog." Henceforth, the Estado da Índia would adopt a much more practical system for taxing trade, in which the state issued official *cartazes* to anyone willing to pay for the privilege, regardless of religious or political affiliation.[105] From Goa's perspective, trade in the Indian Ocean thus lost its ideologically charged significance as a weapon in the struggle between Christianity and Islam. At the battle of Mombasa, Portugal's century-long campaign to control trade through the Red Sea finally sputtered to an end.

Seven

THE DEATH OF POLITICS

The early seventeenth century was an era of unprecedented wealth, prosperity, and power for the island sultanate of Aceh, a state that for generations had enjoyed closer links to Istanbul than almost any other in maritime Asia. Located strategically but precariously along the main trade route between Southeast Asia and the Arabian Sea, Aceh's rulers had in previous decades served as loyal but relatively humble allies of the Ottomans—humble enough to have requested the voluntary annexation of their lands by the Ottoman sultan during the heyday of Sokollu Mehmed's soft empire. But now, with a state treasury overflowing from the bounty of transoceanic trade, Aceh was poised to become an imperial power in its own right.

Beginning in 1607, under the determined leadership of its newly crowned sovereign Iskandar Muda (r. 1607–1636), Aceh amassed a mighty fleet of several hundred vessels, a powerful army replete with a famed elephant corps, and an arsenal of firearms boasting, at its height, more than two thousand units of artillery. At the head of this potent military machine, Iskandar systematically extended his rule over much of Sumatra, as well as several neighboring islands and even to outposts on the Malaysian mainland. And as his stature grew, in order to give a proper public face to his rapidly rising status as an empire builder, the young sultan also surrounded his person and household with a refined ritual of state, in many cases adopting practices and symbolic gestures of power openly evocative of the Ottoman court.[1]

Yet if Aceh's new ruler continued to look to Istanbul as a model of prestige and imperial authority, by the early seventeenth century there was no longer any reason for him to consider his state as part a larger political world actively dominated by the Ottomans. Quite to the contrary, Iskandar Muda's pretensions to an imperial status all his own were in large measure a direct response to the Ottomans' rapidly diminishing political presence in Southeast Asia.

This is a fact made explicit in the *Hikajat Atjeh* ("Story of Aceh"), a Malay-language biographical panegyric to Iskandar composed sometime toward the end of his reign in 1636. Among many episodes about the sultan's early life included within its pages, there is one in particular that speaks directly to Istanbul's changing relationship with this distant corner of the Indian Ocean. According to the tale, a Portuguese embassy arrived in Aceh in the early 1590s, a time when the young Iskandar was only a small boy. The reason for the visit was to ask Iskandar's grandfather, then the reigning sultan of Aceh, to forsake his traditional friendship with the Ottomans and hand over to the Portuguese the naval redoubt guarding his city's access to the sea. As a harbinger of this new alliance, the envoys presented the sultan with a magnificent racehorse that they claimed to be the fastest in all of Portugal, and confidently challenged him to race it against any horses he might have in his stables "from Mecca or Istanbul."

Openly scornful of both the envoys' proposal and their gift, the sultan immediately produced a prize thoroughbred recently sent to him by "his brother, the Sultan of Istanbul," which he raced several times against the Portuguese charger but always to the advantage of the latter. Duly impressed, one of the sultan's attendants then asked to ride the Portuguese horse himself but was told by the envoys that only the Portuguese were men enough to do so. When he insisted and mounted the charger anyway, he was immediately thrown to the ground and knocked unconscious.

Enraged by this shameful spectacle, the sultan then called on his grandson to salvage his honor. The young Iskandar, only ten years of age, readily agreed, but not before first ordering the saddle removed from the beast "since with such a saddle even a baby could ride a horse." Iskandar then mounted the animal and galloped comfortably around the field, embarrassing the Portuguese into trying to do the same. But as soon as the first of them climbed onto the animal, it became clear that, without the saddle, he was unable to maintain control and was almost immediately thrown to the ground. Publicly disgraced, the Portuguese embassy promptly left Aceh without daring to make any more demands.[2]

This story, almost certainly apocryphal, is nevertheless one that contains a deep historical truth about the waning years of the Ottoman Age of Exploration. Iskandar Muda's grandfather, like all the Acehnese rulers of the latter sixteenth century, had depended on a strategic partnership with the Ottomans to retain his power and keep the Portuguese threat in check. But by the early seventeenth century, such a strategy was no longer either feasible or desirable. If the young Iskandar, upon reaching maturity, truly intended to "ride the Portuguese horse," he would therefore have to do so by relying on his own resources and without expecting any help from distant Istanbul.

THE WORLD THAT TRADE CREATED

Throughout maritime Asia, the disappearance of the Ottoman Empire as a visible political presence was an undeniable reality during the decades after 1589. But as the example of Aceh shows, these same decades were also a time of booming trade and unparalleled prosperity for many Muslims across the region.[3] Meanwhile, within the Ottoman Empire itself, individual members of the Indian Ocean faction enjoyed a similarly bountiful "peace dividend" in this postideological age—even though, as a group, they ceased to exist as a cohesive political faction.

This transformation from state agency to individual entrepreneurship depended on two preconditions: externally, the end of the Portuguese threat to maritime traffic through the Red Sea and Persian Gulf and, internally, the dismantling of Sokollu Mehmed Pasha's carefully constructed system for controlling the spice trade. The first of these was accomplished, ironically enough, by the failure of Mir Ali's expedition in 1589. The second was realized more gradually, over a period of years dating back at least to the 1570s. But in an equally ironic twist of history, Sokollu's own supporters in the Indian Ocean faction played the most decisive role in bringing his trading system to an end.

Sokollu's protégé Koja Sinan Pasha was a leading protagonist in this process, having already established a precedent for mixing private trading interests with official duties during his tenure as governor of Egypt in the early 1570s.[4] In fact, in 1574, only months after Koja Sinan had completed his second term as Egypt's governor, Sokollu had issued an angry directive calling for renewed enforcement of his ban on commercial activities for the province's state representatives. The document specifically decried "infringement of the rights of the merchant class" because "the governor, the chief financial officer, and the judges, lords and other state officials have been actively engaging in trade," suggesting that Koja Sinan had not only bent the rules on his own behalf while in Egypt but also turned a blind eye to the trading activities of his underlings.[5]

Considering the leading role that Koja Sinan was destined to play in Indian Ocean politics after Sokollu Mehmed's death, his apparent excesses while his patron was still in office could hardly augur well for the future of the Ottoman spice monopoly. Indeed, as soon as Koja Sinan Pasha began his own first term as grand vizier in 1580, one of his first acts had been to permit Hasan Pasha in Yemen to sell a portion of state spices locally rather than sending them with the annual spice galley to Egypt. At the time, this was presented as a temporary emergency measure, justified by the need to subsidize Ottoman operations in Eritrea.[6] But two years later, in 1582, he relaxed central control of the spice trade even further by allowing state-owned cargoes arriving in Egypt to be sold directly to European merchants, rather than insisting that they be forwarded for sale in Istanbul.[7]

Koja Sinan was removed from office shortly thereafter, but the steady erosion of Sokollu's trade regime would continue unabated, and seemingly without regard to the faction in power in Istanbul. In 1584, for example, the new Grand Vizier Siyavush Pasha, who was not associated with the Indian Ocean faction, received complaints that private merchants in the Red Sea had begun to bypass Jiddah—a mandatory stop under Sokollu Mehmed's system—and sail directly from Mocha to Suez. Siyavush Pasha forbade the practice, but it seems to have continued regardless, apparently with the open collusion of Hasan Pasha in Yemen.[8] Subsequently, when the Sharif of Mecca demanded, in compensation for lost revenue from this illicit traffic, that ships from India be similarly allowed to bypass Yemen and sail directly to Jiddah, Siyavush Pasha had no choice but to grant the request.[9]

Thus, within just a few years of Sokollu Mehmed's death, several key elements of his trading system had already been systematically compromised. And although many factors were to blame, first among them was the enthusiasm with which high-ranking members of his own faction had become personally invested in the spice trade—and noticeably unscrupulous about keeping these activities separate from their role as servants of the state. This was a process already well under way by 1589, when Mir Ali Beg faced defeat and capture at Mombasa. But once it became clear, in the years that followed, that the Portuguese no longer posed even a minimal threat to commerce through the Red Sea and Persian Gulf, any remaining calls to maintain elements of Sokollu's soft empire were completely drowned out. Thereafter, while the trading activities of individual members of the Indian Ocean faction became continuously more extensive and lucrative, the state itself became increasingly irrelevant as a guarantor of this trade.

The subsequent careers of some of the most prominent factional members provide a clear demonstration of this process at work. Koja Sinan, who never returned to the Indian Ocean region after 1589, was nevertheless able to leverage his vast personal wealth—derived in no small part from his ongoing trading concerns in Egypt and the Red Sea—to outlast his political rivals and regain the grand vizierate four more times during the 1590s. Hasan Pasha, who remained as governor of Yemen for fifteen years after the dramatic events of 1589, similarly owed his longevity in office to a remunerative private trade in spices, carried out with a wide range of influential business partners that included the French consul in Cairo.[10] His success established a model for later Yemeni governors, as well as for officials in Egypt, Eritrea, and Jiddah, all of whom regularly took advantage of their positions to entice investors, raise capital, and buy on credit to great personal advantage.[11] Increasingly, they also expanded their trading activities into the emerging market for coffee, a new commodity with a booming international demand that was cultivated exclusively in Yemen and the Horn of Africa.[12] By the 1610s, Dutch observers noted that pashas from Istanbul might arrive in Yemen as paupers, but always returned home as rich men.[13] And yet, none of this activity ever translated into any new political or military initiatives beyond the confines of Red Sea. Through the prosperity of its individual members, the Indian Ocean faction had rendered itself superfluous.

Meanwhile, these same years also witnessed the consolidation of powerful private merchant families, who developed their own equally extensive commercial operations in an era of booming trade. Among the best known were two families based in Cairo, the Abu Taqiyya and Ibn Yagmur, whose members begin to figure prominently in surviving Egyptian court records from as early as the 1560s and 1570s, and whose activities expanded precipitously in the decades that followed. By century's end, they had assumed a dominant position in many aspects of the India trade, often entering into key partnerships with individual members of the Indian Ocean faction. And significantly, as they dealt in ever greater quantities of spices, coffee, and other goods, they also began to take over from the state a leading role in maintaining the infrastructure of trade in Egypt and the Red Sea by endowing caravanserais, warehouses, and commercial facilities for public use.[14]

Within the larger history of the Ottoman Age of Exploration, the final decades of the sixteenth century thus present themselves as a period of paradox. Beginning in the 1560s and 1570s, the success of Sokollu Mehmed's policies had prompted a steady wearing down of Portuguese power at sea and a corresponding upswing of trade through Ottoman-controlled ports. But precisely because this strategy had proved so successful, trade eventually grew to such an extent that Sokollu's system for controlling it was rendered both unsustainable and unnecessary. This, in turn, led not only to the dismantling of his spice monopoly but also to the effective end of his vision of a soft empire in the Indian Ocean.

Nevertheless, in other ways the empire's relationship with the region became richer, deeper, and more intense than ever before. In the 1580s, as the volume of merchant and pilgrim traffic bound for the Red Sea continued to grow, Ottoman commercial relationships expanded into progressively more distant areas of the Indian Ocean, most notably the Bay of Bengal, where the first regular maritime links were established between Ottoman ports and the important trading centers of Pegu and Masulipatnam.[15] In the western Indian Ocean, where the number and size of merchant vessels reached even greater heights, privately owned ships capable of carrying more than a thousand passengers became commonplace, with at least six such vessels traveling regularly between India and the ports of the Red Sea on an annual basis by the 1590s.[16] In 1602, a private trade delegation from Egypt even visited the court of the once fearsomely hostile Mughal Emperor Akbar, requesting a series of trade concessions for Ottoman merchants in ports under his control. By this point, earlier fears about the threat posed by Akbar to Ottoman dynastic legitimacy had apparently been all but forgotten.[17]

Among contemporary Ottoman observers, however, not everyone who remarked on these developments was necessarily enthusiastic about their implications. In 1581, for instance, the notoriously dour intellectual Mustafa Ali composed a text lamenting the fallen state (in his view) of Ottoman society in his day. Within, he identified one of the most appalling symptoms of this decline to be "the rich merchants who count their money, as numerous as the stars, all night until morning ... and whose associates travel to India and beyond, returning with various precious rarities with which they constantly enlarge their capital."[18] He added that in cities like Cairo, Aleppo, and Damascus, "even those among them who seemingly live in poverty and destitution are still engaged in trade with countries as far as India."[19]

One such merchant, a Damascene by the name of Ibn Kereki, who arrived in Aleppo after a sojourn of ten years in India when Mustafa Ali was himself a resident in the city, seems to have left an especially deep impression on the author. During Ibn Kereki's time abroad, "his capital had produced a multitude of goods and immeasurable profit," and upon his return to his native city, he was accompanied by "500 camels, and all these loaded with goods, and the porters and the camel-drivers alone being 300 men." His entourage and baggage train were apparently so extensive that he rented out an entire caravanserai to accommodate them—a fact initially met with enough incredulity that the author felt compelled to verify it with his own eyes.[20]

As a died-in-the-wool statist, Mustafa Ali harbored nothing but contempt for the likes of Ibn Kereki, collectively accusing this new class of merchants of shirking their responsibility to the Ottoman fisc and bemoaning the fact that "the poor suffer under the hardships of destitution while such rich blockheads thrive in pomp and power."[21] Even so, in expressing such anxieties, Mustafa Ali's writings only confirm the impression that by the 1580s the Ottomans' burgeoning trade with maritime Asia had far outstripped the state's ability to control it, becoming in the process an engine of measurable socioeconomic transformations within the empire.

DISCOVERY IN A POSTPOLITICAL WORLD

In an age such as the one described by Mustafa Ali, in which viziers were overshadowed by merchants, and state institutions were overwhelmed by the open floodgates of trade, what might be the consequences for the intellectual dimension of the Ottoman Age of Exploration? As in earlier decades of the sixteenth century, political patronage from members of the Indian Ocean faction continued to serve as an important stimulus for the collection, analysis, and dissemination of information about the world of maritime Asia. But beginning in the 1560s, in a process that would accelerate throughout the rest of the century, the steadily growing volume of trade with the Indies created a new constituency of Ottoman social groups with a direct interest in the economy, geography, and history of the Indian Ocean. As a result, during these years Ottoman discovery literature began to take on a self-reinforcing and dynamic quality for which even the most sophisticated political analysis is inadequate.

Admittedly, in a time and place with no functioning print industry, no private libraries whose collections still survive, and no firm statistics regarding literacy or the market for books, the exact connection between this intellectual trend and a market demand among the wider Ottoman reading public is difficult to establish in all its details. Nevertheless, there is enough evidence in the surviving historical record to assert an exponential increase in the production of Ottoman discovery literature during the final decades of the sixteenth century, both in terms of the variety of texts produced and their sheer numbers. And there are also enough clues—some of them provided by the texts themselves—to suggest that this was the direct result of a growing popular appetite for geography and cartography among the Ottoman literate classes.

One measurable indicator of this emerging demand is the increased availability of geographical works originally produced in much earlier periods as a result of imperial patronage. Piri Reis's "Book of the Sea," for example, presented to Sultan Suleiman in 1526, remained a unique manuscript until 1550, and there is no evidence that before this date it left the palace or was consulted by anyone outside the sultan's closest circle of advisors. Between 1560 and the end of the sixteenth century, on the other hand, the work was copied and circulated in large numbers, with at least fifteen known reproductions dating from this period that are still extant.[22] Naturally, this represents only a very small percentage of the total number available at the time, a figure that can only be guessed at but that may have reached well into the hundreds.[23] Production of this kind is simply too large to be explained by anything other than a genuine growth in demand in the literate population, particularly considering the enormous expense associated with reproducing, by hand, a work that included several dozen illustrated multicolor maps. Despite this prohibitive cost, Piri Reis's magnum opus still managed to become a virtual best seller by the standards of contemporary Ottoman manuscripts. But crucially, it did so only during the freewheeling years of booming trade in the late sixteenth century—not during the lifetime of the author himself.

Similar conclusions can be drawn from another rough index of the popularity of geographical texts among Ottoman consumers of books: the rate at which works originally composed in Arabic were translated into Turkish, thereby becoming available to a larger and more diverse body of readers. Prior to the sixteenth century, there had been almost no Turkish-language translations of Arabic geographies, and to a surprising extent this seems to have remained the case well into the 1550s.[24] But thereafter, Turkish versions of several major Arabic geographical texts began to appear, including standard works such as Istakhri's *Mesālikü'l-Memālik* ("The Paths of Kingdoms") and Ibn Zunbul's *Ḳānūnü'd-Dünyā* ("Code of the World"). Like Piri Reis's "Book of the Sea," these also exist in multiple contemporary copies, indicating a relatively wide circulation.[25]

Equally important, these same decades also witnessed the composition of the first synthetic works by Ottoman authors who were well versed in the learning of Arabic geographers but who clearly aimed to repackage this information in a manner that was both more relevant and more easily digestible for a contemporary Ottoman audience. A precocious example of this type of scholarship is Seydi Ali Reis's *Kitābü'l-Muḥīṭ* ("Book of the Ocean"), completed in 1562. Like the famous "Mirror of Countries" by the same author, the "Book of the Ocean" was inspired by Seydi

Ali's travels in India, but unlike this earlier work, it was free of any overt political implications. Instead, it was designed as a technical guide to navigation in the Indian Ocean, based on a combination of Seydi Ali's personal experiences at sea, his conversations with local navigators while abroad, and several Arabic treatises on navigating the monsoons that were previously unknown to an Ottoman audience. As its title suggests, the text was therefore intended to be a complementary work to Piri Reis's "Book of the Sea," which held a similar practical value for navigators in the Mediterranean. At the same time, it also represented an obvious attempt at scholarly one-upsmanship appropriate to an age in which Ottoman horizons had expanded far beyond the shores of the Mediterranean.[26]

Following the completion of "Book of the Ocean," a very large number of other works began to appear that shared the same basic aim of introducing Arabic geographical knowledge to a Turkish-speaking readership, but with significant variations of tone, content, and register in order to accommodate a diversity of tastes and interests. At one end of this spectrum is Mahmud al-Hatib al-Rumi's *Nevādirü'l-Ġarā'ib ve Mevāridü'l-'Acā'ib* ("Wondrous Rarities and Marvelous Blossoms"), a text, completed in 1563, with both a high entertainment value and a correspondingly large audience (with more than a dozen late-sixteenth-century copies still extant).[27] At the other extreme is Mehmed Ashik's *Menāẓirü'l-'Avālim* ("The Vantage Points of the Worlds"), an imposing tome more than a thousand pages in length that provided Turkish-speaking readers with a definitive synthesis of Arabic geographical learning. Completed in 1597, it remained a standard reference work throughout the seventeenth century.[28]

Among the most interesting examples of this developing geographical genre is Sipahizade Mehmed's *Evẓaḥü'l-Mesālik fī Ma'rifeti'l-Buldān ve'l-Memālik* ("The Location of the Paths to the Knowledge of Kingdoms and Countries"), a work that displayed an impressive bibliography of classical Arabic authors but also departed from these classical models in important ways. Its many innovations included extensively expanded sections on areas of the Ottoman state itself, updated information about the Indian Ocean, and even a small chapter about the discovery of the New World. In addition, it featured numerous schematic maps of cities, rivers, islands, and mountain ranges of a form not found in any of its cited sources, as well as an original world map of both the eastern and western hemispheres.[29]

Significantly, Sipahizade Mehmed wrote two separate versions of "The Location of the Paths," the first composed in Arabic in the 1550s for a strictly erudite audience and the second, completed in 1573, as an abridged and revised Turkish-language translation of his earlier work. This new version was presented in a small, almost pocket-sized volume, was written in an accessible style, and included margins with ample space for readers to make their own notes and additions to the material. In this popularized reincarnation, "The Location of the Paths" was thereby transformed into an eminently practical and market-savvy work, intended first and foremost to be handy, portable, and up-to-date.[30]

There were other authors, meanwhile, who shared Sipahizade's desire to write for a more popular audience but not his erudite interest in Arabic predecessors. One scholar in this category is Seyfi Chelebi, who completed a historical geography of Asia in 1582 under the strangely baroque (but descriptive) title: "History of the Rulers of the Domains of India, Sind, Cathay, Kashmir, Iran, Kashgar, Khalmuk, China, and Many Other Kingdoms, including the Descendants of the Great Genghis Khan and the Emperor of China and the Rulers of Hindustan in the Time of Sultan Murad, Son of Sultan Selim."[31] Written in simple language and organized geographically, it included several chapters dealing specifically with the recent political history of India and gave a brief description of the most important contemporary rulers on the subcontinent and in the islands of Ceylon and Sumatra, as well as separate sections on Iran, China, and Central Asia.

Seyfi Chelebi's text is particularly significant because, while composed in a popular rather than a scholarly register, it is entirely free of the sensationalistic cosmographical content typical of medieval "Wonders of Creation" literature, remaining instead firmly focused on the concerns of contemporary maritime Asia. As such, it speaks to an emerging popular hunger for information about the world that was both current and empirically verifiable, a characteristic shared in common with another down-market work, Mustafa b. Ali al-Muvakkit's *İ'lāmu'l-'İbād fi A'lāmi'l-Bilād* ("A Public Announcement of the Milestones of Countries"). In this curious little book, originally produced during the reign of Suleiman the Magnificent but circulated widely in the final decades of the century, the main text presents a simple list of one hundred important cities between Morocco and China, along with their geographical coordinates and respective distances from Istanbul. In its introduction, the author provides an excellent, if anecdotal, illustration of the general cultural atmosphere in which this work and others like it were circulated. He writes:

> Among the common people, the number of days and months it takes to travel between Istanbul and the various cities of the world has become a common topic of conversation, and even if some of the things that are said on this subject are correct, the vast majority are known to be untrue, since some people are inclined to intentionally exaggerate distances, and others simply make them up off the top of their heads.[32]

The author, as he explains, is thus setting the record straight about this important topic of contemporary debate.

MAPS AND THE MARKET: THE EVOLUTION OF THE OTTOMAN PORTOLAN CHART

Of all the surviving intellectual artifacts of this final phase of the Ottoman Age of Exploration, portolan charts provide some of the most fertile ground for exploring the relationship between trade and cultural production. This is because portolans, in use in the Ottoman Empire since the mid-fifteenth century, were designed as practical tools for navigation, meaning that they were both produced for and used by the individuals most intimately involved in the day-to-day conduct of maritime commerce.

One consequence of this practical function, however, is that portolans were required to conform to several strict technical conventions, including a crisscross network of so-called rhumb lines (by means of which pilots used a compass and ruler to plot their course) and meticulously labeled place-names at very small intervals (so that mariners could identify their exact location at any given landfall). Out of necessity, standard portolans were therefore extremely constrained geographically, since the straight rhumb lines on which their navigation system depended could not account for the curvature of the earth on larger scale maps. This explains why, as a rule, traditional portolans rarely depicted any area outside of the Mediterranean, the Black Sea, and the Atlantic coast of Europe (for an example, see Figure 1.2).[33]

How did Ottoman draftsmen, trained in the art of this sophisticated but highly conservative mapmaking tradition, respond to the challenge of adapting their craft to the new requirements of the Age of Exploration? One early answer is shown in the map of El Hajj Ebu'l-Hasan, drafted in the 1550s and today preserved in the Topkapı Palace Library (Figure 7.1).[34] Upon casual inspection, this map appears to be a conventional sea chart, in Arabic script, featuring all of the basic characteristics of a standard portolan. But a closer examination reveals a number of surprising departures from the portolans of the past. Most obviously, while the main focus of the chart is the Mediterranean basin, at its bottom margin it includes an awkward extension of the African coast all the way to the Cape of Good Hope, thereby clearly indicating the opening of a maritime route to the Indian Ocean. Somewhat mysteriously, this southern portion of the map also retains the series of labeled place-names typical of portolans, although most of these labels are unidentifiable and almost certainly imaginary. In other words, because of these modifications, the map is clearly of little use as a guide to navigation, the primary function of a standard portolan. Instead, the purpose of El Hajj Ebu'l-Hasan's creative departure seems to be not practical but didactic: to demonstrate visually the opening of the Mediterranean world and the existence of new geographical knowledge (in this case about the circumnavigability of Africa) that could not be adequately expressed through the established conventions of portolan chart making.

In subsequent decades, other Ottoman mapmakers would eagerly embrace the challenge visibly expressed in El Hajj Ebu'l-Hasan's portolan by finding new and progressively more flexible ways of using maps to represent the contemporary world. Between 1560 and the end of the sixteenth century, a greater number of Turkish-language maps and charts were produced than during any previous period in the history of the empire, including a new genre of atlas (a word that was itself first introduced into Ottoman Turkish during these years) of which several examples are still extant. As a group, these atlases share a surprising number of common features: each appears to have been designed for navigators, with carefully drawn coastlines but few (or no) terrestrial features; each contains roughly the same sequence of double-folio charts of the

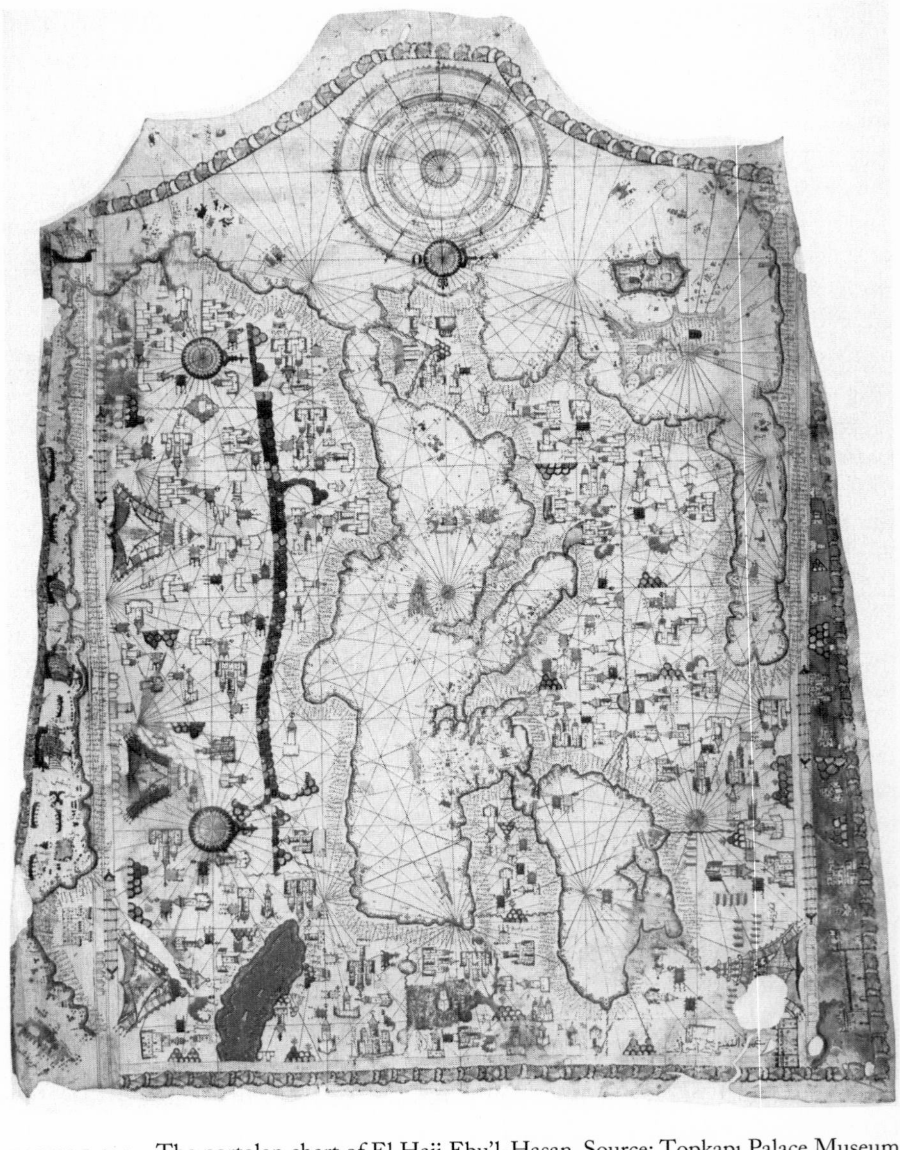

FIGURE 7.1 The portolan chart of El Hajj Ebu'l-Hasan. Source: Topkapı Palace Museum Library, Istanbul, Hazine Ms. 1822.

Black Sea, various regions of the Mediterranean, and the Atlantic coast of Europe; and each displays draftsmanship of a very similar technical and aesthetic quality.[35] These shared characteristics reveal a very high degree of standardization, suggesting that these bound volumes are the few surviving exemplars of a genre of atlas that was once extremely common and probably mass-produced according to standard templates.

At the same time, these atlases also retain certain individualized qualities that indicate an ongoing experimentation with mapmaking techniques, each including at least one or two original maps in addition to the standard sequence of Mediterranean and Atlantic charts. Of these, one example from the recently discovered *Aṭlās-ı Hümāyūn* ("Imperial Atlas"; Figure 7.2) is of particular interest because it shows roughly the same geographical area as the earlier portolan chart of El Hajj Ebu'l-Hasan.[36] Unlike its predecessor, however, this new map is plainly unconstrained even by a superficial adherence to the conventions of portolan mapmaking, having forsaken entirely both the cumbersome system of labeled place-names and the restrictive contours of a typical portolan. In so doing, it conveys a much more comprehensive picture of the extra-Mediterranean world, while avoiding the cramped distortions resorted to by El Hajj Ebu'l-Hasan.

The spartan elegance of this image is a characteristic of all of the maps in this genre of atlas and is reproduced to an even higher degree of draftsmanship in a slightly later volume, the *Deñiz Aṭlāsı* ("Sea Atlas"; Figure 7.3).[37] Like the "Imperial Atlas," this version, too, features at least one image with no known equivalent in other contemporary atlases: a full-page chart not of the

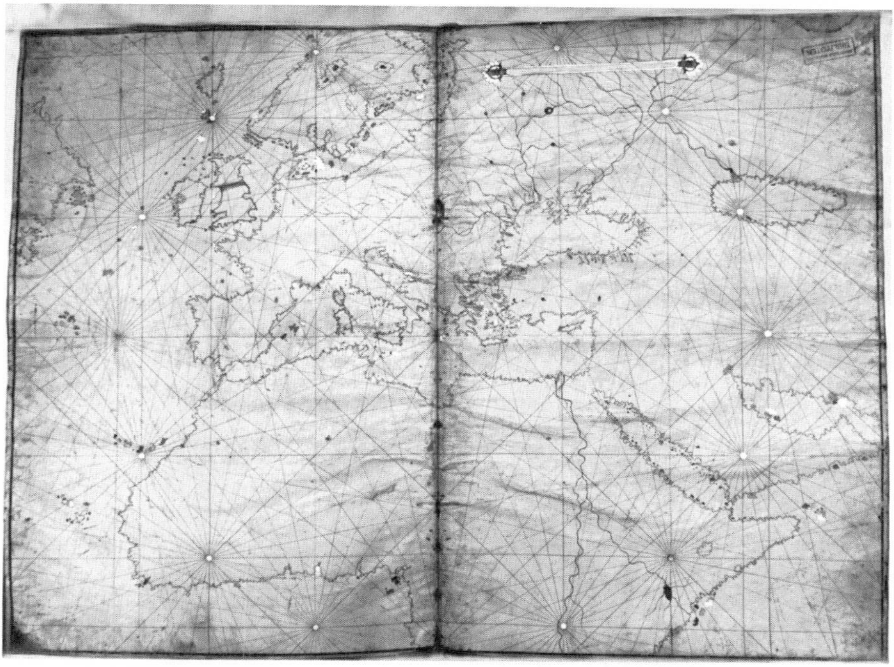

FIGURE 7.2 A map from the *Aṭlās-ı Hümāyūn* ("Imperial Atlas"). The work is undated but was probably drafted in the 1570s. Source: Istanbul Archaeology Museum, Ms. 1621, fols. 9b–10a. Photograph by Başak Tolun.

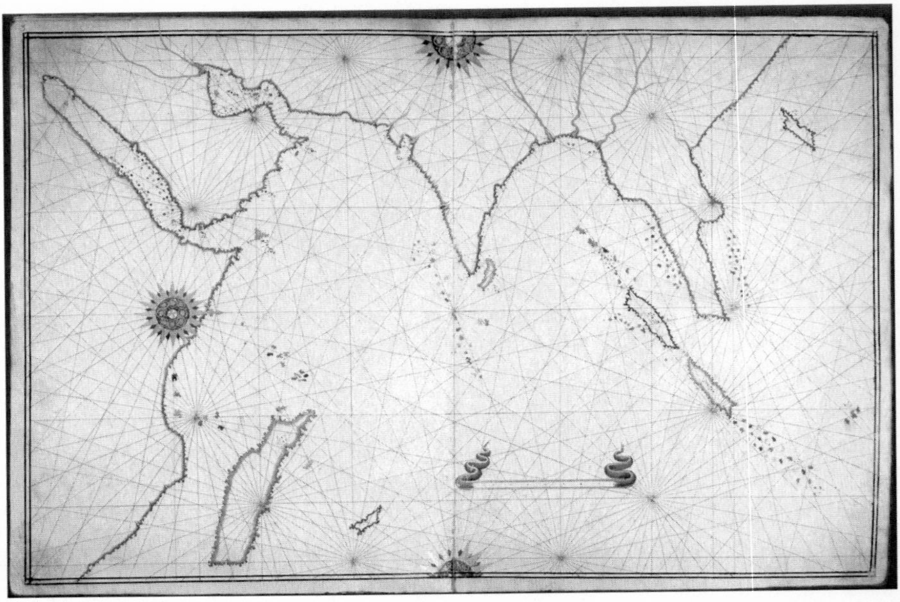

FIGURE 7.3 A map of the Indian Ocean from the *Deñiz Aṭlāsı* ("Sea Atlas"). The work is undated but was probably produced circa 1580. Source: Walters Art Museum, Baltimore, W.660, fols. 2v–3r.

Mediterranean, but of the Indian Ocean basin. In fact, it counts as the earliest known Ottoman chart of any kind to depict the Indian Ocean exclusively, rather than as part of a larger world map. Its inclusion in an atlas otherwise devoted to the Mediterranean and Europe speaks to the special importance that this part of the world had begun to occupy in the minds of a certain segment of consumers—and the flexibility with which the producers of these maps were now able to accommodate their interests.

TRADE WITH THE WEST: THE OTTOMAN MARKET FOR EUROPEAN MAPS

To what extent, if any, did these trends translate into an expanding demand for European maps in addition to an increasing desire for original Ottoman productions? Since as early as the year 1481, when the Florentine humanist Francesco Berlinghieri prepared for Mehmed the Conqueror a copy of his recently published Ptolemaic geography, it had been relatively common for Ottoman sultans and highly placed statesmen to receive Western maps as gifts, to purchase them, and in some cases, even to steal them.[38] But in a process that mirrors closely the expanding interest in indigenously produced geography and cartography, not until the latter decades of the sixteenth century were there signs of an Ottoman demand for European maps with broader socioeconomic roots.

One body of evidence for this trend is the Ottoman atlases just discussed. In many cases, their maps conform so closely to contemporary examples produced in Italy that, in the view of at least one modern scholar, they may have been the product of Italian workshops, with only their place-names added later by Ottoman draftsmen.[39] Most specialists disagree, remaining convinced that these atlases were the original work of local Ottoman cartographers—a view at least circumstantially supported by the seventeenth-century Ottoman author Evliya Chelebi, who described in a fair amount of detail the mapmakers' shops he visited in the Istanbul neighborhood of Pera.[40] But at the very least, there are enough similarities between the two types to affirm that Ottoman mapmakers were thoroughly familiar with the work of their contemporaries in Italy, a fact which suggests that by the 1560s and 1570s, Western maps had become fairly easy to obtain in the Ottoman market.

A more concrete manifestation of this trans-Mediterranean exchange is the so-called Mappamundi of Tunuslu Hajji Ahmed, a heart-shaped world map that was produced in an unknown Venetian workshop in 1559 and counts as the earliest Turkish-language map ever adapted to the printing press. Originally executed as a woodcut carved onto six planks of applewood, the work conformed to the highest technical standards of its time, with an image designed by the cartographer Oronce Finé (chair of mathematics at the Collège Royal de France until 1554) and textual reference points taken from the most recent edition of the Venetian geographer Ramusio's authoritative *Navigationi et Viaggi*.[41] The most unusual characteristic of the map, however, is its extensive companion text in Ottoman Turkish, which presents a brief history of European voyages of exploration, a politically informed overview of the contemporary world, and a summary of the recent conquests of the Ottoman Empire and its imperial rivals.[42] Intended for publication and sale on the Ottoman market, the map was a pioneering attempt to mass produce the latest Western geographical knowledge in a form relevant to a literate Ottoman audience—both as a way to facilitate the international exchange of ideas and for the more venal purpose of turning a profit. As the map's introductory text announced to its readers: "This is no mere work of art, but a tool of reference for understanding the whole world.... Verily, until the true conditions of all the lands of the earth are known, scientists and philosophers must consult with one another, and endless resources must be invested!"[43]

The map was printed in a run of 150 copies, giving an idea of the level of demand its creators believed they would find in the Ottoman Empire. But because its completion coincided with the introduction of the Holy Inquisition in Venice, its distribution was delayed by newly introduced prohibitions against printing in non-Latin alphabets (a measure originally intended to restrict the publication of books in Hebrew). Surviving records show that permission from the Venetian Council of Ten to distribute and sell the map was not granted until 1568, and it remains unclear how many of these copies were eventually sold on the Ottoman market.[44]

FIGURE 7.4 A view of Takiyuddin Efendi's astronomical observatory, showing a European terrestrial globe in the foreground. Source: Seyyid Lokman's *Şehinşāhnāme*, circa 1581, Istanbul University Library, Ms. F 1404, fol. 57a.

As a result of such difficulties, no other Turkish-language maps are known to have been published in Europe during the remaining decades of the sixteenth century (although there were subsequent publications of Arabic geographies in their original language, most of them produced in Italy).[45] Despite this, it is clear that by the 1570s and 1580s, quite a large number of untranslated Western published works were in circulation in the Ottoman market, and they could often reach an Ottoman audience surprisingly quickly after first appearing in Europe. In 1573, for example, a translator at the Ottoman court is known to have ordered and received two copies of Abraham Ortelius's famous *Teatrum Orbis Terrarum*, a collection of maps first published in the Low Countries only three years earlier, in 1570.[46]

Perhaps the most evocative record of the Ottomans' use of Western cartographical tools, however, is to be found not in any surviving collections of maps or archival records, but rather in an Ottoman miniature painting. Preserved in Seyyid Lokman's *Şehinşāhnāme* ("Book of the King of Kings"), an illuminated manuscript prepared for Sultan Murad III in 1581, the painting depicts a scene from the astronomical observatory of Takiyüddin Efendi that includes in its foreground an image of several apprentice astronomers consulting a European-style globe (Figure 7.4).[47]

FIGURE 7.5 A close-up of the globe from Takiyuddin Efendi's astronomical observatory in Seyyid Lokman's *Şehinşāhnāme*.

This image is significant on two levels. Most basically, it provides a record of the practical value that European globes held for Ottoman astronomers. But equally important, it also suggests a culture of Ottoman connoisseurship for the artistic qualities of European maps. This is implied by the manner in which the globe dominates the foreground of the painting, and even more so in the painstaking extent to which its details have been copied down. Although it is reproduced to an extremely small scale—in the original image the globe is barely two centimeters across—the main outlines of continents and oceans as well as rivers and even minor terrestrial features are all clearly visible (Figure 7.5). As an ornamental element in an illuminated manuscript, there is no obvious reason why the globe's surface should be reproduced with such care, except to indicate that, by the 1580s, a taste for the fineries of European mapmaking had developed even within the tradition-bound and discriminating circles of Istanbul's guild of master illuminators.

OTTOMAN DISCOVERY IN COMPARATIVE PERSPECTIVE

This growing and varied Ottoman appreciation for Western maps is only one of many ways in which the Ottoman Age of Exploration, during its most mature phase, developed in tandem with the intellectual world of the contemporary West. For in Europe, as well as in the Ottoman Empire, the second half of the sixteenth century proved qualitatively different from any previous period in terms of the production and circulation of geography and cartography. During earlier decades, the most widely available examples of European discovery literature had been brief pamphlets, notices, and letters printed to report the results of the latest voyages of exploration. Only later did scholars begin to tackle the problem of how to compile, organize, and synthesize this huge new body of knowledge into a coherent and usable form. The product of their collective labors, of which Ramusio's *Navigationi et Viaggi* and Mercator's *Atlas* are two of the earliest examples, did not make their grand appearance until the 1550s and 1560s—at precisely the same time that Ottoman scholars had begun to demonstrate their own emerging receptivity to new ideas about mapmaking and geography.[48]

Moreover, the eagerness with which Ottoman intellectuals engaged with and translated works from the classical corpus of Arab geography also had parallels in Europe. Like the Ottomans, Western humanists, too, combined an interest in the geography of the contemporary world with the enthusiastic rediscovery of scholarship from an earlier age (in their case, the geographical corpus of classical Greece and Rome).[49] But in addition to these classical texts, Western intellectuals could also draw direct inspiration from the same Arabic models as their Ottoman colleagues, as the second half of the sixteenth century was the first period when large numbers of Arabic geographies became widely known and available in Europe. The Venetian publisher Giovanni Battista Ramusio openly advocated adopting the Arab geographers' method of cataloguing information, which he described in the preface to his famous *Navigationi et Viaggi* as an "*ordine veramente bellissimo.*"[50] And importantly, many of the Arabic texts that reached him and other Western scholars during these years were supplied by Ottoman intermediaries.[51]

At the same time, the firsthand experiences of the Ottomans themselves could also inform the development of Western geographic knowledge. During an extended stay in Istanbul during the 1560s, for instance, the Austrian envoy Ogier Ghiselin de Busbecq recorded a conversation with "a wandering Turk who had traversed almost the whole of the East, where he said he had made acquaintance with Portuguese travelers; then, kindled with a desire to visit the city and kingdom of Cathay, he had joined some merchants who were starting hither."[52] Since China was a region about which contemporary Europeans still had very little firsthand information, Busbecq then devoted several pages to describing the Chinese portion of this adventurous itinerary.[53]

Of course, even as they strove to learn from one another, Ottoman and Western intellectuals also faced imposing barriers to the free exchange of ideas. Of these, the most obvious related to printing in Arabic script, which was banned throughout the Ottoman Empire and severely restricted in many areas of Mediterranean Europe. Unfortunately, historians are still far from a full understanding of the impact of this printing ban on the development of Ottoman literate culture.[54] And in recent years, the picture has become even murkier in comparative terms, as scholars of European history have begun to critically reexamine many long-held assumptions about the "revolutionary" character of print culture within the West itself.[55]

That said, there is little question that the absence of printing had significant consequences for the Ottoman Age of Exploration. Without dismissing the very real accomplishments of late-sixteenth-century Ottoman scholars, it seems obvious that the necessity of copying every new text by hand was, in the most literal sense, a serious handicap, rendering the mechanics of scholarly exchange exponentially more time-consuming and expensive than in the West. Over time, this had a clearly detrimental effect on the sustainability of Ottoman discovery, since the lack of easily reproducible standard texts created, particularly in later centuries, a consistent level of confusion about the kinds of information that were verifiable.[56]

In saying this, however, it is important not to unnecessarily exaggerate the boundaries that divided the intellectual worlds of the Ottoman Empire and western Europe because of the printing ban. Even in the absence of a local printing industry, there were numerous ways in which published works from the West could still have influence in the Ottoman Empire, and some Western printers—despite significant obstacles—are known to have published books specifically for the Ottoman market.[57] In 1585, for instance, the Medici Press published an original language edition of a contemporary Arabic geography, Ahmed b. Halil al-Salihi's *al-Bustān fī 'Acā'ibi'l-Arż ve'l-Buldān* ("The Garden of Wonders of the World and Its Nations").[58] And three years later, apparently in direct response to a local demand for more works of this kind, Sultan Murad III issued an imperial edict authorizing Italian merchants to import and sell without hindrance "certain printed works in Arabic, Turkish and Persian."[59]

By the same token, as the contemporary experience of Portugal clearly shows, *printing* and *discovery* were hardly synonymous even in a strictly European context. Throughout the sixteenth century, Portugal remained on the very forefront of the discoveries themselves, logging more voyages of exploration than any other Western nation. Yet despite this, the vast majority of the travel narratives, geographies, and maps produced by the Portuguese remained, like their Ottoman equivalents, unpublished manuscripts. When they did appear in print, it was more often than not in the publishing houses of Italy or the Low Countries rather than in Portugal, and in translation within larger collections that were prepared for a wider, non-Portuguese audience.[60] In some cases, these texts were printed by the same publishing houses that produced volumes in Ottoman Turkish and Arabic.

With this in mind, perhaps the best way to understand the development of Ottoman discovery literature during the final decades of the sixteenth century is to see it as part of a larger trans-Mediterranean intellectual division of labor. On the frontiers of this cultural zone, the subjects of young and vigorously expanding states, including the Ottoman Empire, as well as Portugal and Spain, physically traveled to the far-flung corners of the world and gathered information about the places they visited. Upon their return, the separate task of compiling, organizing, and publishing this information was left to the more developed printing centers of Italy and the Low Countries.

THE END OF DISCOVERY

By the end of the sixteenth century, the Ottoman Empire's era of relentless international expansion had drawn to a close. But thanks to the complex combination of political patronage, market stimuli, and intellectual cross-fertilization of the preceding decades, the Ottomans had acquired a critical mass of scholarly tools that allowed them to understand the physical and human dimensions of the world to an unprecedented degree of sophistication. In the process, they had also gained a new self-consciousness about the global role of their own empire, allowing them to look back on the grand imperial designs of Ibrahim Pasha, Hadim Suleiman, and Sokollu Mehmed with a sense of informed historical detachment. Tellingly, during the very last years of the century, a new genre of historical writing began to develop that strove to rewrite the history of the Ottoman state from an international perspective and to describe the genealogy of its relationship with other powers, particularly the rival Islamic empires of Safavid Iran and Mughal India.[61]

Inevitably, however, as the Ottomans looked ahead to an increasingly uncertain future, such discussions of the past also began to be tinged with a palpable sense of nostalgia for a world that was no longer their own. In 1603, for example, the chronicler Talikizade composed a list of the twenty most distinctive qualities of Ottoman governance, many of which were openly evocative of the halcyon days of Sokollu Mehmed's soft empire. These included, most notably, the sultan's role as protector of Mecca and Medina, which gave him supreme authority over all of the world's Muslims, as well as the fact that the *hutbe* was pronounced in the sultan's name "in each of the seven climes of the inhabitable world."[62] Equally important, and in Talikizade's view, even more uniquely Ottoman, was the empire's rule "over both the land and the sea." In his words:

> Never since the days of Adam could those sultans ruling over the sea ever control the land, nor could the lords reigning over the land ever take possession of the sea. That singular good fortune has only been bestowed by God's grace on the great lords [of the Ottoman Empire]. Indeed, because His Illustrious Majesty Suleiman [the Magnificent] was the one who achieved this honor—may God Almighty be praised—he ordered his imperial signet ring to be adorned with the following words: "The Emperor who is guided by honor along the righteous path, Sultan of the Land and of the Sea, Suleiman, son of Selim."[63]

As he composed this text, it is certainly significant that Talkizade could remember a time when, many years before, he had himself been a personal client of Sokollu Mehmed as a young man in the 1570s. As such, his words must have held a bittersweet taste, for by 1603 these heady assertions of universal Ottoman sovereignty had long lost their currency for the world in which he now lived. Instead, the Ottomans of the early seventeenth century had collectively exchanged their claims to global empire for a more tranquil life in the pursuit of commerce. And in the short term, the benefits were tangible. But at what price?

In the Indian Ocean, the day of reckoning would come sooner than most probably imagined, as a receding state and a disintegrating sense of political cohesion left the Ottomans woefully unprepared for the challenges of a rapidly changing world. Appropriately, the central drama in this story of Ottoman collapse would play itself out in Yemen, the same province that, a century before, Selman Reis had identified as "Master of the Lands of India." Here, beginning in 1626, the Zaydi Imam al-Qasim Mansur led an uprising of such intensity that, within ten years, it brought a permanent end to imperial rule in Yemen. By 1636, when the last Ottoman garrison evacuated Mocha, Ottoman circumstances were so reduced that its commander was forced to beg for passage from a visiting Indian merchant ship, having been left without a single vessel under his own charge.[64]

Elsewhere in maritime Asia, there had been even earlier signs that the Ottoman Age of Exploration was in its twilight. In 1622, a coordinated attack by Shah Abbas of Iran and a naval squadron of the upstart English East India Company had wrested control of Hormuz from the Portuguese and cut off Basra's contact with India by means of the Persian Gulf.[65] In the next year, Basra was further isolated by the Safavid occupation of Baghdad; and with its lines of communication severed, the entire province was hastily auctioned off by the Ottoman central government as a hereditary lease to a local chieftain.[66] Meanwhile, at the opposite end of the Indian Ocean, the naval power of Aceh was permanently destroyed by the Portuguese in 1629, just twelve years before Portuguese Malacca was itself conquered by the Dutch.[67] By then, the political terrain of the entire Indian Ocean region had changed completely. The principal players were now the Dutch, the English, the Safavids and the Mughals, while the Ottomans and their old network of allies (and enemies) were fading from the picture, never to return.

Inexorably, Ottoman commercial fortunes soon followed the same sinking curve, for despite the decoupling of trade and politics of the preceding decades, it was impossible for Ottoman merchants not to suffer the consequences of this comprehensive combination of political disruptions and military defeats.[68] By 1625, conditions had already deteriorated to the point that one Ottoman author, the scholar Omer Talib, offered the following grim assessment of his empire's prospects in an era of declining trade with the East:

> Now the Europeans have gained knowledge of the entire world, send their ships in every direction, and take possession of the most important ports.... Only the things they do not consume themselves reach Istanbul and the other Muslim countries, and even then are sold at five times their original price. They derive enormous profits from this trade, and it is the main reason for the scarcity of gold and silver in the lands of the Muslims today.... If nothing is done, before too long the Europeans will become lords even of the lands of Islam![69]

Views of this kind must be placed in context, for the 1620s and 1630s were a time of general malaise in Ottoman lands, when the range of problems to be faced—fiscal insolvency, endemic social unrest, a dynastic crisis, and wars on several fronts—appeared so serious as to threaten the very existence of the empire.[70] Against this background, it may therefore be tempting to see the Ottomans' souring fortunes on their distant southern frontier as merely a symptom of this more wide-ranging crisis—and Omer Talib's gloomy pessimism as an expression of a sometimes overwrought "decline consciousness" that permeated many genres of Ottoman writing from this period.[71]

It bears considerable emphasis, however, that elsewhere in the empire the Ottomans were able to survive this crisis, even to the point of beginning a new period of modest imperial expansion later in the seventeenth century. Only along the Indian Ocean frontier—in the Red Sea, the Persian Gulf, and the Horn of Africa—did the Ottomans permanently cede territory and fail to ever recover from the loss. In this sense, the end of the Ottoman Age of Exploration, like its beginning, is a story that confounds standard interpretations of Ottoman history, inviting us to reconsider some of the most basic assumptions about the empire's past and its place in the history of the early modern world.

CONCLUSION: EMPIRE LOST AND FOUND

In modern maps of the sixteenth-century Indian Ocean, the Ottoman Empire typically appears as a mass of solid color in the upper left-hand corner of the page, its control stretching seamlessly over virtually all of the Middle East, the Arabian Peninsula, and northern Africa. In contrast, the Portuguese Estado da Índia is most often represented by a scattering of simple dots, each placed strategically at a spot along the Indian Ocean's coasts and connected to the next by the region's most important corridors of oceangoing trade. To the uninitiated, such maps may therefore appear, at least at first, to present the Ottoman Empire in a comparatively favorable light, its territorial heft dwarfing the Portuguese and their paltry collection of coastal settlements. But on a deeper level, the impression left by such maps is one of Ottoman complacency rather than of Ottoman power, implying a state that was content to live off the revenues from own its vast landed estates and, in consequence, both unwilling and incapable of engaging with the dynamic political economy of the world beyond its borders.

But what if an alternate map of the empire's Indian Ocean provinces could be drawn, one based on a very different understanding of Ottoman power in the harsh physical environment of the Red Sea and Persian Gulf? This map, if placed in the hands of a gifted enough mapmaker, might convey a sense of the scarcity of locally available resources, the dependence of the local economy on the patterns of oceanic trade, and the absence of any direct maritime link with the Ottoman Mediterranean. In addition, the empire's own presence in the region might be represented as something other than solid swaths of sovereign territory, consisting instead of a series of tiny but strategic islands of authority, isolated from one another except by sea, hugging the coast, and surrounded, in most cases, by hundreds of miles of the most inhospitable deserts on earth.

Such a map, by providing a more sophisticated physical image of the Ottomans' Indian Ocean provinces, would also imply a very different kind of Ottoman state. For in an environment this forbidding, an imperial presence could be maintained only through a dogged and coordinated political commitment, involving the mobilization of human and natural resources far removed from the Red Sea and Persian Gulf, and motivated by something more sophisticated than the simple desire to accumulate territory.

In the real world of the sixteenth century, this imposing set of physical challenges provided a backdrop for almost every aspect of the Ottomans' tenacious pursuit of empire in the Indian Ocean. It explains the persistence of their efforts to gather intelligence about the region, the methodical resolve with which they constructed alliances overseas, and the brilliance of their carefully calibrated strategy to promote trade. But in terms of the sheer scale of their determination, nowhere do their labors appear more impressive than with regard to naval affairs: Throughout the sixteenth century, because of the near-total lack of locally available timber and the absence of a Suez canal, every vessel operated by the Ottomans in the Indian Ocean theater was requisitioned from Istanbul, built from wood cut in the forests of Anatolia, and then shipped over a thousand miles to its final point of construction—in most cases by sea to Egypt and from there by pack animal across another hundred miles of desert to Suez.[72]

This improbably complex and exorbitantly expensive logistical effort was without real parallel in other parts of the empire, which were connected to one another and to the imperial center by a far less tenuous network of roads, sea lanes, and caravan routes. Indeed, this fact alone goes a long way toward explaining why Ottoman rule in its Indian Ocean provinces fared so badly during the general crisis of the early seventeenth century. Elsewhere in the empire, this same crisis produced a painful but by no means catastrophic renegotiation of the balance of power between center and province, resulting in a much higher degree of local autonomy that, in many cases, provided tangible economic and fiscal benefits for the empire as a whole.[73] But along the Ottomans' southern frontier, where local authority owed its very existence to robust support from the central government, imperial rule simply could not survive a prolonged period of crisis without the coordinated political advocacy of the Indian Ocean faction. Only in the areas around Mecca and Medina, which because of their religious importance continued to be tied to the rest of the empire through the infrastructure of the hajj, was a modicum of Ottoman authority able to survive past the 1630s.[74]

However, if the Ottoman Age of Exploration owed its end to a failure of political will, it also owed its beginning to a prescient political vision. For in 1517, at the moment of their first contact with the world of the Indian Ocean, the Ottomans encountered a region whose trade-based economy was under the choke hold of Portugal's maritime blockade, meaning that only a very farsighted appreciation of its future potential could justify continued investment there. Despite this unpromising beginning, the history of the Ottoman Age of Exploration in the decades that followed is the story of a state employing progressively more determined means to realize this potential, including the massive allocation of military resources (sometimes without the prospect of any obvious territorial gains), invasive state interventions into the market (sometimes to the detriment of individual private merchants), and active support for distant allies with few natural constituencies within the empire itself. By the 1570s, these collective efforts had proven so successful that the Portuguese embargo had been brought to its knees, allowing the Ottomans to control a far larger share of the Indian Ocean spice trade than the Portuguese Crown ever had.

Yet paradoxically, all of this had been accomplished not despite the Portuguese but because of them, for it was they who had first introduced a new kind of global politics into the world of the Indian Ocean, thereby creating the conditions that allowed the Ottomans to formulate their own globally informed political response. Had it not been for the threat posed by the Portuguese to the Muslim trade and pilgrimage routes, neither the original articulation of Ottoman claims in maritime Asia nor the subsequent dedication with which members of the Indian Ocean faction defended these claims would ever have been possible. And once this Portuguese threat was removed, the Ottomans' grand imperial project quickly became an unsustainable venture.

Herein lies the most profound lesson to be drawn from the Ottoman Age of Exploration, whose history should put to rest once and for all the notion that the empire was somehow a victim of the first era of European overseas expansion. Quite to the contrary, the Ottomans were among the most direct beneficiaries of this expansion, and in the end were victims of only one thing: their own success.

NOTES

NOTES TO INTRODUCTION

1. See, for example, Deno John Geanakoplos, *Constantinople and the West: Essays on the Late Byzantine (Palaeologan) and Italian Renaissances and the Byzantine and Roman Churches* (Madison, 1989).
2. The most significant exception is the pioneering work of Salih Özbaran, whose groundbreaking use of Portuguese sources in conjunction with the riches of the Ottoman archives constitute a sine qua non of the present study. Of particular importance is his lengthy article "Osmanlı İmparatorluğu ve Hindistan Yolu: Onaltıncı Yüzyılda Ticaret Yolları Üzerinde Türk-Portekiz Rekabet ve İlişkileri," *Tarih Dergisi* 31 (March 1977): 66–146; as well as the more eclectic collection of Özbaran's articles in English published under the title *The Ottoman Response to European Expansion: Studies on Ottoman-Portuguese Relations in the Indian Ocean and Ottoman Administration in the Arab Lands during the Sixteenth Century* (Istanbul, 1994). For a more recently updated anthology of Özbaran's articles in Turkish, see also *Yemen'den Basra'ya Sınırdaki Osmanlı* (Istanbul, 2004), which includes an extensive bibliography of other scholarly contributions on the subject of the Ottomans in the Indian Ocean. Unfortunately, a more recent rearticulation of Özbaran's views in English, *Ottoman Expansion towards the Indian Ocean in the 16th Century* (Istanbul, 2009), appeared in print too late to be incorporated into this book. In addition to Özbaran, the works of Andrew Hess (discussed later) also deserve mention here, as well as three earlier narrative works in Turkish: Cengiz Orhonlu's *Osmanlı İmparatorluğu'nun Güney Siyaseti: Habeş Eyaleti* (Istanbul: 1974); Yakub Mughul, *Kanuni Devri Osmanlılar'ın Hint Okyanusu Politikası ve Osmanlı-Hint Müslümanları Münasebetleri 1517–1538* (Istanbul, 1974); and Herbert Melziğ, *Büyük Türk Hindistan Kapılarında: Kanuni Sultan Süleyman Devrinde Amiral Hadım Süleyman Paşa'nın Hind Seferi* (Istanbul, 1943).
3. On the trading world of the Indian Ocean, see George Hourani, *Arab Seafaring in the Indian Ocean in Ancient and Early Medieval Times*, 2nd ed. (Princeton, 1995); and Patricia Risso, *Merchants and Faith: Muslim Commerce and Culture in the Indian Ocean* (Boulder, 1995). On the fifteenth-century Chinese voyages of exploration, see Louise Levathes, *When China Ruled the Seas: The Treasure Fleet of the Dragon Throne, 1405–1433* (New York, 1994).

4. On the intellectual world of Columbus, see Valerie Flint, *The Imaginative Landscape of Christopher Columbus* (Princeton, 1992); and more generally, Donald Lach, *Asia in the Making of Europe, vol. 1: The Century of Discovery* (Chicago, 1965).
5. Anthony Pagden, *Lords of All the World: Ideologies of Empire in Spain, Britain and France 1500–1800* (New Haven, 1995), 29–62; on early Portuguese claims to overseas empire, see Luís Filipe Thomaz, "L'idée imperiale manueline," in *La Découverte, le Portugal et l'Europe: Actes du colloque, Paris, les 26, 27 et 28 Mai 1988* (Paris, 1990), 41.
6. For a recent synthesis of the literature, see Jan Glete, *Warfare at Sea 1500–1650: Maritime Conflicts and the Transformation of Europe* (London, 2000); also Carlo Cipolla's classic *Guns, Sails and Empires: Technological Innovation and the Early Phases of European Expansion 1400–1700* (New York, 1965); and Geoffrey Parker, *The Military Revolution: Military Innovation and the Rise of the West, 1500–1800*, 2nd ed. (Cambridge, 1996), especially chapter 3, "Victory at Sea," 82–115; on gunpowder, see Bert Hall, *Weapons and Warfare in Renaissance Europe: Gunpowder, Technology and Tactics* (Baltimore, 1997).
7. As a general introduction to this enormous subject, see Donald Lach, *Asia in the Making of Europe, vol. 2: A Century of Wonder* (Chicago, 1965); also Alfred Crosby, *The Measure of Reality: Quantification and Western Society 1250–1600* (Cambridge, 1997); and Anthony Pagden, *The Fall of Natural Man: The American Indian and the Origin of Comparative Ethnology* (Cambridge, 1982).
8. The numerous works of Andrew Hess, discussed in more detail later, present the most coherent articulation of this view. For an important historiographical discussion of the problem of viewing the Ottomans as an obstacle rather than a participant in the explorations, see Palmira Brummett, *Ottoman Seapower and Levantine Diplomacy in the Age of Discovery* (Albany, 1994).
9. On the Ottomans' use of these terms during the reign of Suleiman the Magnificent, see Colin Imber, "Suleyman as Caliph of the Muslims: Ebu's-Su'ud's Formulation of Ottoman Dynastic Ideology," in Giles Veinstein, ed., *Soliman le Magnifique et son temps* (Paris, 1992), 179–84. To date, the importance of Ottoman claims to the caliphate for political history beyond the borders of the empire during the early modern period has been largely ignored.
10. Several important works on Ottoman military history have appeared in recent years, although most have little to say about the Indian Ocean theater. See Gábor Ágoston, *Guns for the Sultan: Military Power and the Weapons Industry in the Ottoman Empire* (Cambridge, 2005); and Rhoads Murphey, *Ottoman Warfare, 1500–1700* (New Brunswick, N.J., 1999); on the Ottomans' role in the diffusion of firearms, see Halil Inalcik, "The Socio-Political Effects of the Diffusion of Firearms in the Middle East," in Halil Inalcik, ed., *The Ottoman Empire: Conquest, Organization and Economy* (London, 1978), 195–217; also Özbaran, *Ottoman Response*, 61–66.
11. On this question, see two recent works by İdris Bostan, *Osmanlılar ve Deniz: Deniz Politikaları, Teşkilat, Gemiler* (Istanbul, 2007), and *Osmanlı Denizciliği* (Istanbul, 2006); and for a magnificent collection of contemporary images of Ottoman sailing ships and oared craft, see the recent publication by the same author, *Kürekli ve Yelkenli Osmanlı Gemileri* (Istanbul, 2003); see also Colin Imber, "The Navy of Suleyman the Magnificent," *Archivum Ottomanicum* 6 (1980): 211–82.
12. The Ottoman economic relationship with the Indian Ocean remains vastly understudied. A summary of the limited scholarship that is available can be found in Halil Inalcik, *An Economic and Social History of the Ottoman Empire* (Cambridge, 1994), 1: 315–64; for a more microeconomic approach, see Nelly Hanna, *Making Big Money in 1600: The Life and Times of Isma'il Abu Taqiyya, Egyptian Merchant* (Syracuse, 1998).

13. Here my interpretation stands in contrast to most existing scholarship, which remains attached to an understanding of the "Muslim worldview" as essentially static throughout the early modern period. The standard work is still Bernard Lewis, *The Muslim Discovery of Europe* (New York, 1982); for a perspective more directly focused on the early modern Ottomans, see also the relevant sections in Nicolas Vatin, *Les Ottomans et l'Occident, XV–XVI siècles* (Istanbul, 2001); for a recent critique of Lewis, see Nabil Matar, *In the Lands of the Christians: Arab Travel Writing in the Seventeenth Century* (New York, 2003); and for a general reevaluation of the concept of curiosity in a Western context, Barbara Benedict, *Curiosity: A Cultural History of Early Modern Inquiry* (Chicago, 2001).
14. See, for example, Stephen Greenblatt, *Marvelous Possessions: The Wonder of the New World* (Chicago, 1991); Anthony Grafton, *New Worlds, Ancient Texts: The Power of Tradition and the Shock of Discovery* (Cambridge, 1992); and Anthony Pagden, *European Encounters with the New World from Renaissance to Romanticism* (New Haven, 1993).
15. For a brief sampling of the very large number of works in this category of scholarship produced over the past decade (in addition to those already cited), see Stuart Schwartz, ed., *Implicit Understandings: Observing, Reporting and Reflecting on the Encounters between Europeans and Other Peoples in the Early Modern Era* (Cambridge, 1994); Joan-Pau Rubiés, *Travel and Ethnology in the Renaissance: South India through European Eyes, 1250–1625* (Cambridge, 2000); Andrew Fitzmaurice, *Humanism and America: An Intellectual History of English Colonization* (Cambridge, 2003); and Michael Gaudio, *Engraving the Savage: The New World and Techniques of Civilization* (Minneapolis, 2008). For works specifically focused on the impact of Europe's encounter with the Ottoman world, see Deborah Howard, *Venice and the East: The Impact of the Islamic World on Venetian Architecture 1100–1500* (New Haven, 2000); Rosamund Mack, *Bazaar to Piazza: Islamic Trade and Italian Art* (Berkeley, 2001); Barbara Fuchs, *Mimesis and Empire: The New World, Islam and European Identities* (Cambridge, 2001); Nancy Bisaha, *Creating East and West: Renaissance Humanists and the Ottoman Turks* (Philadelphia 2004); and Stefano Carboni, ed., *Venice and the Islamic World* (New Haven, 2007).
16. This Eurocentric bias has been tempered in very recent years by a growing interest in non-Western examples of travel literature, cartography, and ethnography from the early modern period. See, for example, Laura Hostetler, *The Art of Ethnography: A Chinese Miao Album* (Seattle, 2007); Muzaffar Alam and Sanjay Subrahmanyam, *Indo-Persian Travels in the Age of the Discoveries* (Cambridge, 2007); and Nabil Matar, *Europe through Arab Eyes: 1578–1727* (New York, 2009). More generally, see Jerry Brotton and Lisa Jardine, *Global Interests: Renaissance Art between East and West* (Ithaca, 2000). A particularly strong recent uptick of interest in the fifteenth-century expeditions of the Ming admiral Zheng-He has been provoked by Gavin Menzies's sensationalistic *1421: The Year China Discovered America* (New York, 2004); for a critique, see Robert Finlay, "How Not to (Re)Write World History: Gavin Menzies and the Chinese Discovery of America," *Journal of World History* 15/2 (2004): 229–42.
17. A by no means comprehensive sampling of recent contributions to this type of scholarship might include Victor Lieberman, *Strange Parallels, vol. 1: Integration on the Mainland: Southeast Asia in Global Context, c. 800–1830* (Cambridge, 2003); Kenneth Pomeranz, *The Great Divergence: China, Europe and the Making of the Modern World Economy* (Princeton, 2000); Jared Diamond, *Guns, Germs and Steel: The Fates of Human Societies* (New York, 1999); Patrick Manning, *Migrations in World History* (London, 2005); and John R. McNeill and William McNeill, *The Human Web: A Bird's-Eye View of World History* (New York, 2003).

18. Sanjay Subrahmanyam's concept of connected histories suggests one way for world history to address this problem, and it has been very influential for the present study. See Subrahmanyam, "Connected Histories: Notes towards a Reconfiguration of Early Modern Eurasia," *Modern Asian Studies* 31/3 (1997): 735–762.
19. Recent studies of the use of cartography and ethnography have suggested a similar process in other areas of the non-Western world in the early modern period. For one example, see Laura Hostetler, *Qing Colonial Enterprise: Ethnography and Cartography in Early Modern China* (Chicago, 2001).
20. See, for example, Svat Soucek, "Piri Reis and the Ottoman Discovery of the Great Discoveries," *Studia Islamica* 79 (1994): 121–42.
21. Leaving aside the question of motivation, there were also formidable physical obstacles to Ottoman navigation in the Atlantic: a combination of contrary prevailing winds (from the northwest) and a powerful but unfavorable surface current (flowing from the Atlantic into the Mediterranean) meant that except for a few brief periods of the year, it was virtually impossible for a fleet of galleys to sail from the Mediterranean through the Strait of Gibraltar to the Atlantic—especially a fleet as far from its main bases of supply in the eastern Mediterranean as the Ottoman fleet. See John Pryor, *Geography, Technology and War: Studies in the Maritime History of the Mediterranean, 649–1571* (Cambridge, 1988), 12–24.
22. For a detailed study of Afonso de Albuquerque, see Geneviève Bouchon, *Albuquerque, le lion des mers d'Asie* (Paris, 1992).

NOTES TO CHAPTER I

1. See, for example, Ivana Elbl, "Man of His Time (and Peers): A New Look at Henry the Navigator," *Luso-Brazilian Review* 28/2 (1991): 73–89; P. R. Russell, *Prince Henry the Navigator: The Rise and Fall of a Cultural Hero* (New York, 1984); also Malyn Newitt, "Prince Henry and the Origins of European Expansion," in Anthony Disney, ed., *Historiography of Europeans in Africa and Asia, 1450–1800* (Brookfield, 1995), 85–111.
2. B. W. Diffie and G. D. Winius, *Foundations of the Portuguese Empire: 1415–1580* (Minneapolis, 1977), 113–22.
3. David Woodward, "Medieval Mappaemundi," in J. B. Harley and David Woodward, eds., *The History of Cartography, vol. 1: Cartography in Prehistoric, Ancient and Medieval Europe and the Mediterranean* (Chicago, 1987), 286–370.
4. Jacques Le Goff, "The Medieval West and the Indian Ocean: An Oneiric Horizon," in Anthony Pagden, ed., *Facing Each Other: The World's Perception of Europe and Europe's Perception of the World* (Burlington, 2000), 2.
5. Anthony Pagden, *European Encounters*, 12.
6. Robert Finlay, "Crisis and Crusade in the Mediterranean: Venice, Portugal and the Cape Route to India (1498–1509)," *Studi Veneziani* 28 (1994): 45–90.
7. Gerald R. Tibbetts, "The Role of Charts in Islamic Navigation in the Indian Ocean," in Harley and Woodward, *History of Cartography*, 2: 256–62.
8. See, for example, Marshall Hodgson, *Rethinking World History: Essays on Europe, Islam and World History* (Cambridge, 1993), 203.
9. For a preliminary study of late-fifteenth-century Ottoman copies of one important work, al-Istakhri's *Kitāb al-Masālik wa'l-Mamālik*, see Karen Pinto, "3 Ways of Seeing: Scenarios of the

World in the Medieval Cartographic Imagination" (PhD dissertation, Columbia University, 2002), 56–118.

10. There are two main catalogues of Ottoman geographical works (each problematic in its own way): Cevdet Türkay, *İstanbul Kütüphanelerinde Osmanlılar Devrine Ait Türkçe-Arapça-Farsça Yazma ve Basma Coğrafya Eserleri Bibliyografyası* (Istanbul, 1958); and Ekmeleddin İhsanoğlu, *Osmanlı Coğrafya Literatürü Tarihi* (Istanbul, 2000). There is no comparable guide for Ottoman map collections. For a general introduction, see Ahmet Karamustafa, "Military, Administrative and Scholarly Maps and Plans of the Ottomans," in Harley and Woodward, *The History of Cartography*, 1: 209.
11. There is one very ancient copy of Bozorg b. Shahriyar's collection of sailors' lore in the Süleymaniye Library, but no information is available about how or when this manuscript reached Istanbul. See Bozorg b. Shahriyar, *Livre des merveilles de l'Inde*, trans. Marcel L. Devic (Leiden, 1883), 9; the only known copy of al-Biruni's *al-Hind* in Istanbul is in Süleymaniye Library, Köprülü Ms. no. 1001.
12. See Türkay, *Coğrafya Eserleri*, for the extant manuscripts of this text in Turkish collections, none of which dates conclusively to before the sixteenth century.
13. The first Ottoman scholar to have had access to such maps seems to have been Piri Reis, discussed later. See Tibbetts, "Role of Charts," 256–62.
14. A. Adnan Adıvar, *Osmanlı Türklerinde İlim*, 9th ed. (Istanbul, 2000), 70.
15. This work was first introduced to an Ottoman audience in 1554, with the completion of Seydi Ali Reis's *Muḥīṭ*. See Ahmad b. Majid al-Najdi, *Arab Navigation in the Indian Ocean before the Coming of the Portuguese, Being a Translation of the Kitāb al-Fawā'id fī Usūl al Bahr wa'l-Qawā'id of Ahmad b. Mājid al-Najdī*, ed. and trans. G. R. Tibbetts (London, 1971).
16. İhsanoğlu, *Osmanlı Coğrafya Literatürü*, 1–13.
17. Even within the madrasa setting, the study of geography was limited by the fact that it was not included as one of the fields of the traditional Islamic curriculum. This may help explain why the diffusion of geographical works seems to have been so much less marked than works in other fields, such as grammar, jurisprudence, and even astronomy and mathematics, in the early centuries of Ottoman history. On intellectual life in the Ottoman Empire during the latter fifteenth century, see Franz Babinger, *Mehmed the Conqueror and His Time*, trans. Ralph Manheim (Princeton, 1978), 483–93.
18. See Tony Campbell, "Portulan Charts from the Late Thirteenth Century to 1500," in Harley and Woodward, *History of Cartography*, 1: 371–447; also David Woodward, "Maps and the Rationalization of Geographic Space," in Jay Levenson, ed., *Circa 1492: Art in the Age of Exploration* (New Haven, 1991), 83–88.
19. *T.S.M.K.* G.I.27.
20. *T.S.M.K.* H.1823.
21. Istanbul, Deniz Müzesi Kütüphanesi, no. 882.
22. G. R. Crone, *Maps and Their Makers: An Introduction to the History of Cartography*, 2nd ed. (London, 1964), 39–46; Fuat Sezgin, *The Contribution of the Arabic-Islamic Geographers to the Formation of the World Map* (Frankfurt, 1987), 40–45.
23. M. Destombes, "Fragments of Two Medieval World Maps at the Topkapı Saray Library," *Imago Mundi* 18 (1964): 240–44.
24. For examples, see Sebastiano Gentile, *Firenze e la scoperta dell'America: Umanesimo e geografia nel '400 fiorentino* (Florence, 1992).
25. Crone, *Maps*, 68–75.

26. Sezgin, *Contribution of the Arab-Islamic Geographers*, 46; on the early history of publishing maps, see Tony Campbell, *The Earliest Printed Maps* (London, 1987), 122–38.
27. For a discussion of Ottoman cartography under Mehmed and its relation to the development of cartography in the West, see Jerry Brotton, *Trading Territories: Mapping the Early Modern World* (London, 1987), 98–114.
28. *Coğrāfyā-yı Baṭlamyūs*, Istanbul, Süleymaniye Library, Ayasofya Ms. no. 2610; see also Adıvar, *Osmanlı Türklerinde İlim*, 34–37. The fact that Mehmed felt a need for his own translation of the work, which had already been translated into Arabic several times in pre-Ottoman centuries, is further evidence of Ottoman isolation from earlier Islamic geographical traditions.
29. *T.S.M.K.* G.İ. 84.
30. Berlinghieri later rededicated it to Mehmed's son, the new Sultan Bayezid II. See James Hankins, "Renaissance Crusaders: Humanist Crusade Literature in the Age of Mehmed II," *Dumbarton Oaks Papers* 49 (1995): 127; see also Sean Roberts, "Cartography between Cultures: Francesco Berlinghieri's *Geographia* of 1482" (PhD dissertation, University of Michigan, 2006).
31. Records in Italian archives, for example, reveal that Selim's grand vizier Pir Mehmed arranged for the purchase of a Venetian planisphere in 1519. See Antonio Fabris, "The Ottoman Mappa Mundi of Hajji Ahmed of Tunis," *Arab Historical Review for Ottoman Studies* 7–8 (1993): 31–37.
32. The work was originally composed in Persian and translated into Turkish later in the century. Yih-Min Liu, "A Comparative and Critical Study of Ali Akbar's Khitaynama with References to Chinese Sources," *Central Asiatic Journal* 27/1–2 (1983): 58–78; see also Mevhibe Pınar Emiralioğlu, "Cognizance of the Ottoman World: Visual and Textual Representations in the Sixteenth-Century Ottoman Empire 1514–1596" (PhD dissertation, University of Chicago, 2006), 186–90.
33. Paul Kahle, "China as Described by Turkish Geographers from Iranian Sources," in Paul Kahle, *Opera Minora I* (Leiden, 1956), 312–25.
34. Nicolas Vatin, *Sultan Djem: Un prince ottoman dans l'Europe du XVe siècle d'après deux sources contemporaines: Vakiat-ı Sultan Cem, Oeuvres de Guillaume Caoursin* (Ankara, 1997).
35. On the connection between Selim and Piri Reis, see Andrew Hess, "Piri Reis and the Ottoman Response to the Voyages of Discovery," *Terrae Incognitae* 6 (1974): 19–37. More generally, see Svat Soucek, *Piri Reis and Turkish Mapmaking after Columbus* (Oxford, 1996).
36. For a facsimile and translation of the Piri Reis map, see Piri Reis, *Piri Reis Haritası Hakkında İzahname*, ed. Yusuf Akçura (Istanbul, 1935).
37. See Erich von Daniken's *Chariots of the Gods* (New York, 1970) for an example of this less-than-scholarly scholarship.
38. The *Kitāb-ı Baḥrīye* or "Book of the Sea," completed by Piri in 1525 and discussed in greater detail later, includes a long introductory section that is essentially a textual version of his earlier world map.
39. Piri Reis, *Kitāb-ı Baḥrīye* (Ankara, 1988), 1: 43.
40. J.-L. Bacqué-Grammont and Mohammad Mokri, "Une lettre di Qâsim Širvânî à Muzaffer Sâh du Gujarat: Les premieres relations des Ottomans avec l'Inde," in Rudolf Vesely and Eduard Gambar, eds., *Zafername Memorial Volume of Felix Tauer* (Prague, 1996).
41. Adıvar, *Osmanlı Türklerinde İlim*, 74–79.
42. Piri Reis, *Kitāb-ı Baḥrīye*, 1: 43.
43. See, for example, Soucek, "Ottoman Discovery," 121–42.
44. For studies arguing against an economic motivation for Selim's conquest, see Jean-Louis Bacqué-Grammont and Anne Kroell, *Mamlouks, Ottomans et Portugais en Mer Rouge: L'affaire*

de Djedda en 1517 (Cairo, 1988), 20; Jean Aubin, "La politique orientale de Selim I," in Raoul Curiel and Rika Gyselen, eds., *Itinéraires d'Orient: Hommages à Claude Cahen* (Bures-sur-Yvette, 1994), 197–215; and Soucek, "Ottoman Discovery," 128; for the opposite, trade-oriented view, see Brummett, *Ottoman Seapower*, 2; Michael Mazzaoui, "Global Policies of Sultan Selim, 1512–1520," in Donald P. Little, ed., *Essays on Islamic Civilization Presented to Niyazi Berkes* (Leiden, 1976), 224–43; and Vitorino Magalhães Godinho, "Le tournant mondial de 1517–1524 et l'empire portugais," *Studia* 1 (Jan. 1958): 188. See also Salih Özbaran, "The Ottomans in Confrontation with the Portuguese in the Red Sea after the Conquest of Egypt in 1517," *Studies in Turkish-Arab Relations* (1986): 209.

45. On Malik Ayaz's origins, see Jean Aubin, "Albuquerque et les négotiations de Cambaye," *Mare Luso-Indicum* 1 (1971): 5.
46. Anecdotal evidence includes a contemporary source from the Hadramaut claiming that Malik Ayaz was a slave purchased from an Ottoman merchant. See R. B. Serjeant, *The Portuguese off the South Arabian Coast: Hadrami Chronicles with Yemeni and European Accounts of Dutch Pirates off Mocha in the Seventeenth Century* (Oxford, 1963), 43.
47. On the use of the term "Rumi," see Salih Özbaran, "Ottomans as 'Rumes' in Portuguese Sources in the Sixteenth Century," *Portuguese Studies* 17 (2002): 64–74; see also Giancarlo Casale, "The Ethnic Composition of Ottoman Ship Crews and the 'Rumi Challenge' to Portuguese Identity," *Medieval Encounters* 13 (2007): 124–27; On Malik Ayaz's dining habits, see E. C. Bayley, *The Local Muhammadan Dynasties: Gujarat* (London, 1886), 234.
48. M. N. Pearson, *Merchants and Rulers in Gujarat: The Response to the Portuguese in the Sixteenth Century* (Berkeley, 1976), 103.
49. On the diplomatic maneuverings of Malik Ayaz, see Aubin, "Négotiations de Cambaye," 5–15.
50. The Hadrami chronicles describe Hussein's arrival in 1515 as "the beginning of the coming of the Rumis and the cause of all the troubles," 49.
51. On these events, see Kutbeddin Mekki, *Aḫbār al-Yemānī*, Istanbul, Süleymaniye Library, Hamidiye Ms. no. 886, fols. 4–8; also Zeinu'd-Din, *Tohfut ul-Mujahideen*, trans. M. J. Rowlandson (London, 1833), 96–97; and Muhammad Hajji ad-Dabir, *An Arabic History of Gujarat*, trans. M. F. Lokhandwala (Baroda, 1970), 1: 34–44.
52. A contemporary Yemeni source, for example, insists that Sultan Selim supported operations against the Portuguese but "did not know the secret aspirations of the ruler of Egypt and his Amir Husayn as to seeking the conquest of Yemen." L. O. Schuman, *Political History of the Yemen at the Beginning of the 16th Century According to Contemporary Arabic Sources* (Amsterdam, 1961), 20.
53. There is no evidence that Selim ever corresponded directly with Malik Ayaz before his arrival in Egypt, but Malik Ayaz is known to have corresponded with Selman Reis, the leader of a contingent of volunteer Ottoman mariners serving in the Mamluk force then stationed in Yemen. See Kutbeddin Mekki, *Aḫbār al-Yemānī*, fol. 7b; also Bacqué-Grammont and Mokri, "Lettre de Qâsim Širvânî," 40.
54. Ibn Iyas, *Journal d'un bourgeois du Caire: Chronique d'Ibn Iyās*, Gaston Wiet, trans. (Paris, 1945), 2: 78 [excerpt is from the French translation].
55. Ibn Iyas, *Journal d'un bourgeois*, 2: 107 [excerpt from French translation].
56. Bacqué-Grammont and Mokri, "Lettre de Qâsim Širvânî," 35.
57. Bacqué-Grammont and Mokri, "Lettre de Qâsim Širvânî," 44 [excerpt from French translation].

58. Feridun Beg, *Mecmū'a-yı Münşe'āt-ı Selāṭīn* (Istanbul, A.H. 1264–75/A.D. 1848–1858), 1: 447. The letter is dated Nov. 23, 1518; See also Nizamuddin Maghrebi, "The Ottoman-Gujarat Relations (1517–1556): Political and Diplomatic," in P. M. Joshi, ed., *Studies in the Foreign Relations of India from the Earliest Times to 1947* (Hyderabad, 1975), 187; and Naimur Rahman Farooqi, *Mughal-Ottoman Relations: A Study of Political and Diplomatic Relations between Mughal India and the Ottoman Empire 1556–1748* (Delhi, 1989), 12. Around the same time, Malik Ayaz's suzerain, Sultan Muzaffer Shah of Gujarat, sent an enthusiastic response of his own to the Ottoman court. See Feridun Beg, *Münşe'āt-ı Selāṭīn*, 1: 446.
59. "*Com a nova dos Rumes achey a muy revolta. Ora vede senhor que serya terem nos por vezinhos afora ho credito que tem nestes partes.*" *Gavetas*, 15, 14–38.
60. "*Tem Dio com os braços apertos esperando pullos Rumes... esta Cambaya tem agora todo ho trato de Meca nam fazem nas naos senam ir e vir.*" *Gavetas*, 15, 9–11.
61. Nicolas Mirkovich, "Ragusa and the Portuguese Spice Trade," *Slavonic and East European Review* 21/56, part 1 (March 1943): 180.
62. "*Il Gran Turco desiderava l'amicitia de' Venetiani e che nel principio del nuovo imperio procurava d'accrescere i traffichi in quella provincia per particolare utilità e commodità di quei sudditi e per interesse dell'entrate publiche.*" Quoted in A. H. Lybyer, "The Ottoman Turks and the Routes of Oriental Trade," English Historical Review 30 (1915): 582.
63. Marin Sanuto, *I diarii di Marino Sanuto* (Venetia, 1879–1903), 25: 464.
64. Thomaz, "L'idée imperiale," 41.
65. See Cemal Kafadar, *Between Two Worlds: The Construction of the Ottoman State* (Berkley, 1995); for an alternate view, see Heath Lowry, *The Nature of the Early Ottoman State* (Albany, 2003).
66. António Vasconcelos de Saldanha, "Conceitos de espaço e poder e seus reflexos na titulação régia portuguesa da época da expansão," in *La Découverte, le Portugal et l'Europe: Actes du colloque, Paris, les 26, 27 et 28 Mai 1988* (Paris, 1990), 105–30.
67. Thomaz,. "L'idée imperiale," 40.
68. Saldanha, "Titulação régia," 123.
69. Saldanha, "Titulação régia," 126 [my translation from Portuguese].
70. On Selim's imperial claims, see Mazzaoui, "Global Policies." Compare also the arguments of Cornell Fleischer, who discusses Selim's use, in official documents, of the titles *ṣāḥib-ḳirān* ("Master of the Conjunction") and *żill Allah* ("Shadow of God") immediately following the conquest of Egypt. See Fleischer, "The Lawgiver as Messiah: The Making of the Imperial Image in the Reign of Suleyman," in Veinstein, *Soliman le Magnifique*, 162–63.
71. Bacqué-Grammont and Mokri. "Lettre de Qâsim Širvânī," 38.
72. Sa'deddin, *Tācu't-Tevārīḫ* (Istanbul, A.H. 1279/A.D. 1863), 2: 371–72; see also Faroqhi, *Pilgrims and Sultans: The Hajj under the Ottomans 1517–1683* (New York, 1994), 147–48.
73. Ibn Iyas, *Journal d'un bourgeois*, 2: 246.
74. Feridun Beg, *Münşe 'āt-ı Selāṭīn*, 1: 397. The tradition of acknowledging the caliph in Egypt as the symbolic superior of the ruling sultan was well established in Gujarat before the Ottoman conquest. See Sanjay Subrahmanyam, "The Trading World of the Western Indian Ocean, 1546–1565: A Political Interpretation," in A. T. de Matos and L. F. Thomaz, *A Carreira da Índia e as rotas dos estreitos: Actas do VIII seminário internacional de história indo-portuguesa* (Angra do Heroísmo, 1998), 215.
75. Hussein al-Rumi, appointed governor of Jiddah in 1519 as a replacement for Kasim Shirvani, organized an expedition to Yemen in 1520 but turned back when he heard news of Selim's death. Lutfi Pasha, *Tevārīḫ-i Āl-i 'Os̱mān* (Istanbul, A.H. 1341/A.D. 1922–23), 304–5; Kutbeddin Mekki,

Aḫbār al-Yemānī, fol. 10b. This show of force apparently dissuaded a Portuguese patrol from attempting an attack on Jiddah, as the Portuguese were "overcome by fear and cowardliness" upon hearing of Hussein's presence in the vicinity. See Serjeant, *Hadrami Chronicles*, 51.

76. See Edward Said, *Orientalism* (New York, 1978).
77. Most of these sources use the notoriously vague terms "Turk" and "Rumi" with reference to both Ottomans and Mamluks. On the problems associated with the terms in Ottoman historiography, see Salih Özbaran, *Bir Osmanlı Kimliği: 14.-17. yüzyıllarda Rūm/Rūmī Aidiyet ve İmgeleri* (Istanbul, 2004).
78. Even in the realm of diplomacy, Ottoman contact with the Indian Ocean was almost nonexistent before the sixteenth century. In the fifteenth century, only the Bahmiani sultans of the Deccan seem to have exchanged a few sporadic embassies with the Ottomans, comparable to the occasional appearance of embassies from Ethiopia at the courts of Mediterranean Europe. See Maghrebi, "Ottoman-Gujarat Relations," 185; Farooqi, *Mughal-Ottoman Relations*, 12. On pre-sixteenth-century Ottoman trade with the Indian Ocean, see Halil Inalcik, "Bursa and the Commerce of the Levant," *Journal of the Economic and Social History of the Orient* 3/2 (1960): 131–47.
79. Halil Inalcik has identified a report dating to the reign of Bayezid II from an Ottoman sea captain sent for service in the Red Sea, although it is unclear in exactly what capacity he was serving there. No evidence of such an arrangement exists from Selim's reign, however. See Inalcik, "Review: David Ayalon, *Gunpowder and Firearms in the Mamluk Kingdom*," *Belleten* 21/81–84 (1957), 500–12. Sultan Bayezid also supplied the Mamluks with copper for the casting of cannon for their Indian Ocean campaign, although the sources make clear that this copper was sold to the Mamluks at a profit. Subsequently, Bayezid began to supply free arms and supplies, ostensibly as a pious contribution to the general cause of holy war against the infidel, but probably in reality as ransom for his son Korkud, who was at the Mamluk court in 1509. See Brummett, *Ottoman Seapower*, 114–15; for other examples of Bayezid's beneficence in Mecca and Medina, see Faroqhi, *Pilgrims and Sultans*, 76–77.
80. One recent study has argued that it was not Bayezid who was primarily responsible for Ottoman naval support for the Mamluks during these years, but rather the Ottoman prince Korkud, Selim's brother and rival for the throne, who was based in the Anatolian coastal province of Manisa and had demonstrably strong links with the "Sea Gazis" of the Aegean. Since Korkud was executed by Selim upon his accession, this would explain the discontinuation of Ottoman logistical support for the Mamluks. See Nabil al-Tikriti, "Şehzāde Korkud (c. 1468–1513) and the Articulation of Early 16th-Century Religious Identity" (PhD dissertation, University of Chicago, 2004), 134–36.
81. Ibn Iyas, *Journal d'un bourgeois*, 1: 230. This arrest occurred despite the fact that Selman Reis and his men had been single-handedly responsible for the heroic defense of Jiddah against a Portuguese assault in 1517. See John Guilmartin, *Gunpowder and Galleys: Changing Technology and Mediterranean Warfare at Sea in the 16th Century* (New York, 1980), 7–13.
82. See, for instance, Hess, "Piri Reis," 31–33.
83. Even Braudel, in his classic study of the Mediterranean, argued that the Ottoman conquest of Egypt came only after the West had lost interest in it because of the discoveries. Fernand Braudel, *The Mediterranean and the Mediterranean World in the Age of Philip II*, trans. Sian Reynolds (New York, 1972), 2: 666–67. For a general discussion of this question, see also Russell R. Menard, "Transport Costs and Long-Range Trade, 1300–1800: Was There a European Transport Revolution?" in James Tracy, ed., *The Political Economy of Merchant Empires* (Cambridge, 1991), 228–75.

84. Albuquerque even dreamed of building a Suez canal once the conquest of Egypt was effected. See Thomaz, "L'idée imperiale," 54; Columbus's objectives in seeking a western route to the Indies were essentially similar. See Abbas Hamdani, "Columbus and the Recovery of Jerusalem," *Journal of the American Oriental Society* 101 (1981): 323–30.

NOTES TO CHAPTER 2

1. On these changes in Suleiman's reign, see Gilles Veinstein, ed., *Soliman le Magnifique et son temps* (Paris, 1992); and Halil Inalcik and Cemal Kafadar, eds., *Suleyman the Second and His Time* (Istanbul, 1993); on the rising importance of the imperial harem, see Leslie Peirce, *The Imperial Harem: Women and Sovereignty in the Ottoman Empire* (New York, 1993), 57–90.
2. For the life of Roxelana, see S. A. Skilliter, "Hürrem," *EI²*, 66; and Peirce, *Imperial Harem*, 57–70. On the early biography of Ibrahim Pasha, see Ebru Turan, "The Sultan's Favorite: Ibrahim Paşa and the Making of the Ottoman Universal Sovereignty in the Reign of Sultan Süleyman, 1516–1526" (Ph.D. Dissertation, University of Chicago, 2007). The account presented here has benefitted greatly from Turan's work, although my own emphasis differs from hers in some important ways.
3. The quote is from the bailo Pietro Bragadin, in Eugenio Alberi, ed., *Le relazioni degli ambasciatori veneti al senato* (Firenze, 1840–), 9: 103–4. More generally, see Turan, "The Sultan's Favorite," 138–44.
4. See Turan, "The Sultan's Favorite," 179–222. As Turan has shown, Ibrahim's bride was actually a woman from the household of his former owner, and not the sultan's sister as suggested by earlier scholarship.
5. Turan has presented evidence suggesting that Ahmed Pasha and Ibrahim may have at first been allies, and that the former rebelled only after learning that the sultan had ordered his execution. Surviving accounts, however, are far from unanimous in this regard. See Turan, "The Sultan's Favorite," 188–202.
6. In fact, the rebellion had been largely suppressed before Ibrahim even reached Egypt. See Süheyli, *Tārīḫ-i Mısır al-Cedīd* (Ḳosṭanṭiniyye, H.1142), fols. 54a–b; Kutbeddin Mekki, *Aḫbār al-Yemānī*, 19b–20b; Hasan b. Tulun, *Tārīḫ-i Mısır*. British Museum, M.S. Add. 1846, fols. 348–50.
7. Subsequently, Selim assigned Piri (who until then had served under the Barbarossa brothers in Tunis and Algiers) to the newly formed imperial sea captains corps of Alexandria. Orhonlu, "Piri Reis," 35–45.
8. On this encounter, described by Piri in his *Kitāb-ı Baḥrīye*, see Hess, "Piri Reis," 19.
9. Piri Reis, *Kitāb-ı Baḥrīye*, 47.
10. See Svat Soucek, *Piri Reis and Turkish Mapmaking after Columbus* (Oxford, 1996).
11. Marcel Destombes, "L'hemisphère austral en 1524: une carte de Pedro Reinel à Istanbul," *Comptes rendus du congrès international de géographie, Amsterdam* 2 (1938): 175–85; and from the same author, "The Chart of Magellan," *Imago Mundi* 12 (1955): 65–88.
12. Destombes, "Chart of Magellan," 68.
13. On Ibrahim's interest in geography, see Nicolas Vatin, "Sur quelques propos géographiques d'Ibrahim Pacha, grand vezir de Soliman le Magnifique (1533)," in Jean-Louis Bacqué-Grammont and Emeri Van Donzel, eds., *Comité International d'Etudes Pré-Ottomanes et Ottomanes, VIth symposium, Cambridge 1st–4th of July* 1984 (Istanbul, 1987), 141–50. See also, in the same volume, Jean-Louis Bacqué-Grammont, "Une lettre d'Ibrahim Paşa à Charles Quint," 65–88.
14. Ibrahim was well known, for example, for his friendship with Alvise Gritti, illegitimate son of the Venetian doge Andrea Gritti, an important intermediary for the Ottoman court's purchase of all kinds of products available in Venice. See Gülru Necipoğlu, "Süleyman the Magnificent and the

Representation of Power in the Context of Ottoman-Hapsburg-Papal Rivalry," *Art Bulletin* 71/3 (Sept. 1989): 401–27. See also Turan, "The Sultan's Favorite," 280–315.

15. Destombes, "Chart of Magellan," 88.
16. On Selman's adventures in Yemen, see Kutbeddin Mekki, *Aḫbār al-Yemānī*, fols. 17a–19b.
17. Kutbeddin Mekki, *Ahbār al-Yemānī*, fol. 21b.
18. Salih Özbaran, "A Turkish Report on the Red Sea and the Portuguese in the Indian Ocean (1525)," *Arabian Studies* 4 (1978): 81–88. For a transcription of the original Turkish text, see Fevzi Kurtoğlu, "Amiral Selman Reis Lāyıhası," *Deniz Mecmuası* 47/335 (1935): 67–73. The original document is in the Topkapı Palace Archives, *T.S.M.A.* E. 6455; on Ibrahim Pasha's reception of the report, see Kutbeddin Mekki, *Aḫbār al-Yemānī*, fol. 22b.
19. Özbaran. "Turkish Report," 86.
20. Kutbeddin Mekki, *Aḫbār al-Yemānī*, fols. 20b–21a.
21. For the text, see Ömer Lutfi Barkan, *XV ve XVI'ıncı Asırlarda Osmanlı İmparatorluğunda Zirai Ekonominin Hukuki ve Mali Esasları, Birinci Cilt: Kanunlar* (Istanbul, 1943), 355–87.
22. On Mamluk policies preceding the Ottoman conquest, see John Meloy, "Imperial Strategy and Political Exigency: The Red Sea Spice Trade and the Mamluk Sultanate in the Fifteenth Century," *Journal of the American Oriental Society* 123/1 (2003): 1–19; Walter Fischel, "The Spice Trade in Mamluk Egypt," *Journal of the Economic and Social History of the Orient* 1 (1958): 157–74; more generally, Carl Petry, *The Reigns of the Mamlūk Sultans al-Ashraf Qāytbāy and Qanṣūh al-Ghawrī in Egypt* (Seattle, 1993).
23. According to a contemporary Portuguese account, under Kansuh Gawri, a third of all cargoes carried between Calicut and Jiddah had to be pepper, sold to Mamluk agents at Calicut prices. If a merchant arrived in Jiddah with no pepper, a third of his cargo had to be sold locally and the proceeds used to buy pepper (at the high Jiddah prices), which was then resold to state agents at the cheaper Calicut rates. Castanheda, *História do descobrimento e conquista da Índia pelos Portugueses* (Lisbon, 1833), 2: 75.
24. Ibn Iyas reports that during the years prior to the Ottoman conquest, merchant traffic in Jiddah, Alexandria, and Damietta dropped significantly "as a result of arbitrary taxation on a large scale." Ibn Iyas, *Journal d'un bourgeois*, 2: 87; Selman Reis also relates that merchants from India preferred to trade at Suakin instead of Jiddah because of "excessive injustice at the port of Jiddah." Özbaran, "Turkish Report," 85. On Mamluk corruption, see also John Meloy, "The Privatization of Protection: Extortion and the State in the Circassian Mamluk Period," *Journal of the Economic and Social History of the Orient* 47/2 (2004): 195–212.
25. For Selman's comments on this matter, see Özbaran, "Turkish Report," 85.
26. Ömer Lütfi Barkan, "H.933–34 (M.1527–28) Mali Yılına Ait Bir Bütçe Örneği," *İktisat Fakültesi Mecmuası* 15/1–4 (Istanbul, 1954), 251–93.
27. Luís Filipe Thomaz, "A questão da pimenta em meados do século XVI," in de Matos and Thomaz, *Carreira da Índia*, 88–89.
28. For statistics on the volume of spices traded in Alexandria from the turn of the century to 1532, see Vitorino Magalhães Godinho, *Os descobrimentos e a economia mundial*, 2nd ed. (Lisbon, 1981), 3: 84–85.
29. Özbaran, "Turkish Report," 82.
30. Özbaran, "Turkish Report," 82.
31. Özbaran, "Turkish Report," 85.
32. Frédérique Soudan, *Le Yémen Ottoman d'après la chronique d'al-Mawzaʿī: al-iḥsān fī duḫūl mamlakat al-Yaman taḥt ẓill ʿadālat Āl ʿUṯḫmān* (Cairo, 1999), 54 [my translation from the French].

33. Most of these warlords, especially in Ta'izz and Zebid, professed at least nominal loyalty to the Ottoman sultan. See J. R. Blackburn, "Two Documents on the Division of Ottoman Yemen into Two Beglerbegiliks (973–1565)," *Turcica* 27 (1995): 223. For a detailed contemporary account of political strife in Yemen, see Kutbeddin Mekki, *Aḫbār al-Yemānī*, fols. 13b–19b.
34. In addition to the sources cited later, this campaign is mentioned very briefly in the seventeenth-century account of Katib Çelebi, *Tuḥfetü'l-Kibār fī Esfāri'l-Biḥār*, ed. Orhan Şaik Gökay (Istanbul, 1973), 37–38.
35. Kutbeddin Mekki, *Aḫbār al-Yemānī*, fol. 22b; M. Yakub Mughul, "The Beginning of the Ottoman Domination in the Red Sea: The Way to India." *Sind University Research Journal Arts Series: Humanities and Social Sciences* 9 (1970): 68.
36. Ibn Tulun, *Tārīḫ-i Mıṣır*, fol. 350b.
37. Süheyli, *Tārīḫ-i Mıṣır al-Cedīd*, fol. 54b; Kutbeddin Mekki, *Aḫbār al-Yemānī*, fol. 21a.
38. Kutbeddin Mekki, *Aḫbār al-Yemānī*, fols. 21b–23b.
39. Kutbeddin Mekki, *Aḫbār al-Yemānī*, fols. 25a–26b.
40. Kutbeddin Mekki, *Aḫbār al-Yemānī*, fols. 26b–27a.
41. Serjeant, *Hadrami Chronicles*, 34.
42. See the letter from Cristóvão de Mendonça in Hormuz to the King, July 11, 1528, *Gavetas*, 15, 17–22.
43. Özbaran, "Turkish Report," 84.
44. *Gavetas*, 15, 17–19.
45. Dejanirah Couto, "Trois documents sur une demande de secours ormouzi à la Porte Ottomane," *Anais de história de além-mar* 3 (2002): 469–98.
46. Dejanirah Couto, "No rasto de Hādim Seleimão Pacha: alguns aspectos do comércio do mar vermelho nos anos de 1538–40," in de Matos and Thomaz, *Carreira da Índia*, 494.
47. Geneviève Bouchon, "L'évolution de la piraterie sur la côte malabare au cours du XVIe siècle," in *Course et piraterie: Etudes présentées à la commission internationale d'histoire maritime à l'occasion de son XVe colloque internationale* (San Francisco, 1975), 749. See also Jorge Manuel dos Santos Alves, *O domínio do norte de Sumatra* (Lisbon, 1999), 160.
48. *DA*, dec. IV, bk. 3, chap. 2.
49. Kutbeddin Mekki, *Aḫbār al-Yemānī*, fols. 17a–19b.
50. Kutbeddin Mekki, *Aḫbār al-Yemānī*, fols. 27a–28a; Ḥajji ad-Dabir, *Arabic History of Gujarat*, 1: 188.
51. Kutbeddin Mekki, *Aḫbār al-Yemānī*, fol. 27b; *Gavetas*, 20, 2–21; Hajji ad-Dabir, *Arabic History of Gujarat*, 1: 188; for Mustafa's career, see M. Y. Mughul, "Türk Amirali Emir Ibn Behram Bey'in Hindistan Seferi (1531)," *İstanbul Üniversitesi Edebiyat Fakültesi Tarih Dergisi* 4–5 (August 1973–74), 247–62.
52. Özbaran, "Hindistan Yolu," 91.
53. For details on Eitor da Sylveira's campaign, see *DA*, dec. IV, bk. 6, chap. 10.
54. Serjeant, *Hadrami Chronicles*, 56.
55. Kutbeddin Mekki, *Aḫbār al-Yemānī*, fol. 25a.
56. Hajji ad-Dabir, *Arabic History of Gujarat*, 1: 188.
57. Serjeant, *Hadrami Chronicles*, 56; *DA*, dec. IV, bk. 3, chap. 6.
58. On these events, see Mughul, "Türk Amirali," 250–58; Zeinu'd-Din, *Tohfut ul-Mujahideen*, 133, 189; *DA*, dec. IV, bk. 8, chap. 3.
59. Serjeant, *Hadrami Chronicles*, 59–60.
60. Bayley, *Local Muhammadan Dynasties* 347; *DA*, dec. IV, bk. 8, chap. 3; Serjeant, *Hadrami Chronicles*, 60.

61. On Mustafa Bayram's subsequent career in the service of Humayun, see Bayley, *Local Muhammadan Dynasties*, 377–95.
62. For a discussion of this Rumi elite, see Sanjay Subrahmanyam, "The Trading World of the Western Indian Ocean," in de Matos and Thomaz, *Carreira da Índia*, 217; also Farooqi, *Mughal-Ottoman Relations*, 11.
63. "*... acciò le caravelle cariche di specie potessero venire dall'India de longo in Alessandria, et de li in Costantinopoli.*" Luigi Roncinotto, *Viaggi da Venezia alla Tana* (Venice, 1545), quoted in Agostino Gambara, "Il Canale di Suez e la Repubblica di Venezia," *Archivio Veneto* 2 (1871): 181.
64. *São Lourenço*, 1: 199–200.
65. *Gavetas*, 20, 7–15; An Ottoman accounts register dated h.937 (1530–31) shows two million akçes allotted for the construction of galleys at Suez. Istanbul, Başbakanlık Arşivi, Kamil Kepeci no. 5638. See also Salih Özbaran, "The Ottomans in Confrontation with the Portuguese in the Red Sea after the Conquest of Egypt in 1517," *Studies in Turkish-Arab Relations* (1986): 210.
66. "*Dizem que mete em cabeça todalas cousas necessarias ao Turquo pera a sua armada que va ao Mar Roxo contra Portugueses e que ele sabe muy bem a pratica daquele reino de Portugall e ho que el rey pode fazer e tudo isto muidamente de maniera que dizem que ho Turquo manda fazer mais enforço do que pensava de fazer.*" *Gavetas*, 20, 7–15.
67. "*... o que elle agora faz e mays segundo dizem por a meca que por nihuma outra cousa.*" *Gavetas*, 20, 7–15.
68. Özbaran, "Hindistan Yolu," 98.
69. See, for example, Hess, "Piri Reis," 25; also Özbaran, *Ottoman Response*, 84.
70. For the text of Husrev Pasha's report, see *T.S.M.A.* E. 8964.
71. Salih Özbaran, "The Ottoman Turks and the Portuguese in the Persian Gulf 1534–1581," *Journal of Asian History* 6/1 (Spring 1972): 48–49; also Willem Floor, *The Persian Gulf: A Political and Economic History of Five Port Cities 1500–1730* (Washington, 2006), 154.
72. Zeinu'd-Din, *Tohfut ul-Mujahideen*, 127; Özbaran, "Ottoman Turks," 50.
73. *Gavetas*, 20, 7–15.
74. "*Il re di Portogallo viene in considerazione del Signor Turco... per [le cose] dell'Indie, sì per l'aiuto che ditto re potesse fare dare al Sofì per quella via, come per l'impresa che potesse il Signor Turco fare a distruzione della navigazione di Portogallo in quelle parti.*" Alberi, *Relazioni*, 3: 22.
75. Özbaran, "Ottoman Turks," 55; Floor, *Persian Gulf*, 156.
76. Although this explanation for Ibrahim's loss of the sultan's favor is the one most commonly given in Ottoman historical narratives, recent scholarship has suggested that his downfall should also be viewed within the context of Suleiman's evolving ideology of rulership. See for example Fleischer, "Lawgiver as Messiah," 166–67.
77. Skilliter, "Hürrem," *EI²*, 5: 66a–b.
78. Gökbilgin, "Ibrāhīm Pasha," *EI²*, 3: 998a.

NOTES TO CHAPTER 3

1. On Hadim Suleiman's career, see Cengiz Orhonlu, "Khādım Süleymān Pasha," *EI²*, 4: 901a.
2. de Sacy, "Foudre du Yémen," 442.
3. On Hadim Suleiman's mapmaking, see Giancarlo Casale, "An Ottoman Intelligence Report from the Mid Sixteenth-Century Indian Ocean," *Journal of Turkish Studies* 31/1 (2007): 187.
4. For a brief biography of Hoja Safar, see Subrahmanyam, "Trading World," 217; there is also an entertaining and surprisingly informative historical novel about Hoja Safar,

unfortunately available only in Turkish. See M. Turhan Tan, *Hint Denizlerinde Türkler* (Istanbul, 1939).

5. On the death of Bahadur and Hoja Safar's role in defending him, see Bayley, *Local Muhammadan Dynasties*, 397–98; and Hajji ad-Dabir, *Arabic History of Gujarat*, 215–23.
6. Pearson, *Merchants and Rulers*, 75.
7. Dejanirah Couto, "Hādim Seleimão," 494.
8. Zeinu'd-Din, *Tohfut ul-Mujahideen*, 135.
9. On these events, see *DA*, dec. IV, bk. 9, chap. 7; also Hajji ad-Dabir, *Arabic History of Gujarat*, 214.
10. Hajji ad-Dabir, *Arabic History of Gujarat*, 219.
11. *DA*, dec. IV, bk. 9, chap. 8; Hajji ad-Dabir, *Arabic History of Gujarat*, 207; M. Y. Mughul, "The Expedition of Suleyman Pasha Al-Khadim to India (1538)," *Journal of the Regional Cultural Institute (Iran, Pakistan, Turkey)* 2/3 (Summer 1969): 146.
12. Lütfi Paşa, *Tevārīẖ-i Āl-i 'Os̱mān*, 357.
13. The original letter sent by Asaf Khan, dated 17 Zilhicce 942/June 7, 1536, is still preserved in the Topkapı Palace archives, *T.S.M.A.* E.1351; the only Ottoman source to mention by name the envoy who brought this letter to Istanbul is the anonymous *Ḳānūnnāme-i Sulṭān Süleymān Ḫān*, Istanbul, Süleymaniye Library, Veliyüddin Efendi Ms. no. 1970, fol. 14a; For a firsthand account of this embassy's visit composed by a member of the Imperial Divan at the time, see Lütfi Paşa, *Tevārīẖ-i Āl-i 'Os̱mān*, 357–58; Portuguese accounts offer a somewhat different version of events than the one here described. See *DA*, dec. V, bk. 2, chap. 6.
14. Mughul, "Expedition of Suleyman Pasha," 148–48.
15. Serjeant, *Hadrami Chronicles*, 73–74.
16. See the report of Pedro de Sousa de Távora from Rome, July 19 1537 in *CDP*, III, 396–97.
17. "*lhe pedio... que mandasse sua armada a India contra os portugueses e que viesse demandar aquella ilha de Dio, onde lhe seria muito fasil tomar aquella fortz.a para o que lhe daria elle toda ajuda necessaria. E que ficava dali a ballravento de toda a India para onde a todo o tempo que quisesse poderia partir a fazer guerra as mais fortalezas dos portugueses que lhe não poderião resistir. E assy os lanssarião fora da India e tornaria a ficar o comerssio antigo em sua liberdade como dantes e a romagem da casa de Mafamade desempedida aos romeiros della.*" *DA*, dec. V, bk. 2, chap. 8.
18. Serjeant, *Hadrami Chonicles*, 78.
19. Serjeant, *Hadrami Chonicles*, 76–77.
20. On Ottoman relations with Zeyla, see Orhonlu, *Habeş Eyaleti* (Istanbul, 1974), 1–17.
21. Pinto, *The Travels of Mendes Pinto*, ed. and trans. Rebecca D. Catz (Chicago, 1989), 28; see also Anthony Reid, "Sixteenth-Century Turkish Influence in Western Indonesia," *Journal of South East Asian History* 10/3 (December 1969), 402.
22. Pinto, *Travels*, 38.
23. See, for example, Reid, "Turkish Influence," 402; Alves, *Domínio do norte*, 142.
24. Pinto, *Travels*, 21.
25. Pinto tells us that he set out from Goa bound for Malaca on April 13, 1539, with the very first monsoon after the Ottoman retreat from Diu, and he insists that the Ottomans had already been campaigning in Sumatra for at least several months at the time of his arrival. Since any force coming from Gujarat would have presumably had to wait for the same monsoon as Pinto before making the voyage to Aceh, the Ottomans must have arrived with the monsoon of the previous year, sailing directly to Southeast Asia from the Red Sea.

26. Pinto, *Travels*, 21.
27. On relations with Pate Marakkar, see Jorge Manuel Costa da Silva Flores, *Os Portugueses e o mar de Ceilão 1498–1543: Trato, diplomacia e guerra* (Lisbon, 1998).
28. Denys Lombard, *Le Sultanat d'Atjeh au temps d'Iskandar Muda 1607–1636* (Paris 1967), 37. See also Alves, *Domínio do norte*, 162–66.
29. *DA*, dec. V, bk. 2, chap. 6. An anonymous member of one of these Venetian crews was the author of a narrative that constitutes a main historical source for the expedition. For an English translation, see "Particular Relation of the Expedition of Solyman Pacha from Suez to India against the Portuguese at Diu," in Robert Kerr, ed., *General History and Collection of Voyages and Travels* (Edinburgh, 1824), 7: 257–87.
30. For a reevaluation of the size of this early fleet, see Christopher Wake, "The Myth of Zheng He's Great Treasure Ships," *International Journal of Maritime History*, 14/1 (June 2004): 59–75.
31. On population figures for Portuguese Asia, see Sanjay Subrahmanyam, *The Portuguese Empire in Asia, 1500–1700: A Political and Economic History* (Longon, 1993), 216–24.
32. In addition to the sources here cited, a main Portuguese narrative of the siege is Lopes de Sousa Coutinho's *História do cerco de Dio* (Lisbon, 1890); see also two collections of documents by Luciano Ribeiro, "O primeiro cerco de Dio," *Studia* 1 (Jan. 1958): 201–95; and "Em torno do primeiro cerco de Diu," *Studia* 13–14 (Jan.–July 1964): 41–100; and additionally Herbert Melziğ, *Büyük Türk Hindistan Kapılarında* (Istanbul, 1943). Excepting Kutbeddin Mekki's chronicle, Ottoman narratives of the siege are frustratingly absent. One partial exception is in Katib Çelebi's *Tuḥfetü'l-Kibār*, 83–84. Hadim Suleiman's own account is missing from his collection of letters. See Fevzi Kurtoğlu, "Hadım Süleyman Paşa'nın Mektupları ve Belgrad'ın muhasara planı," *Belleten* 9 (1940): 63–73; there is a letter from Hadim Suleiman to the Gujarati Vizier Ulu Khan today preserved in Portuguese translation in the Torre do Tombo Archives. See *A.N.T.T.*, *Corpo Cronológico*, parte 3a, maço 14, doc. 44.
33. *DA*, dec. V, bk. 5, chap. 3.
34. Kutbeddin Mekki, *Aḫbār al-Yemānī*, fol. 38b; Serjeant, *Hadrami Chronicles*, 44; Soudan, *Chronique d'al-Mawzaʿī*, 55–56; Katib Çelebi, *Tuḥfetü'l-Kibār*, 83; for Hadim Suleiman's own account, see Kurtoğlu, "Hadım Süleyman," 63–66.
35. For Kutbeddin Mekki's views on this matter, see *Aḫbār al-Yemānī*, fol. 38b; See also Katib Çelebi, *Tuḥfetü'l-Kibār*, 83.
36. Pinto, *Travels*, 13.
37. *DA*, dec. V, bk. 3, chap. 6.
38. Serjeant, *Hadrami Chronicles*, 97; *DA*, dec. V, bk. 3, chap. 7; Kutbeddin Mekki, *Aḫbār al-Yemānī*, fol. 39b.
39. For Hadim Suleiman's version of events, see *A.N.T.T. Corpo Cronológico*, parte 3a, maço 14, doc. 44.
40. "*miḳdār ve ḥaddın bilmez.*" Kutbeddin Mekki, *Aḫbār al-Yemānī*, fol. 40a.
41. "*vezīr-i aʿẓamı geldükde eger ṣalb eylemiş olaydım tamām murād üzere meṣāliḥ itmām olmış idi.*" Kutbeddin Mekki, *Aḫbār al-Yemānī*, fol. 40a.
42. Kutbeddin Mekki, *Aḫbār al-Yemānī*, fol. 40a. See also Serjeant, *Hadrami Chonicles*, 97.
43. Hajji ad-Dabir, *Arabic History of Gujarat*, 227; Katib Çelebi, *Tuḥfetü'l-Kibār*, 83.
44. Hajji ad-Dabir, *Arabic History of Gujarat*, 227.
45. Hadim Suleiman was in fact warned by Hoja Safar that "the Sultan is a child and everything is in the hands of the Vizier" ["*El Rey era moço e o gozil gouvernava tudo*"], *A.N.T.T. Corpo Cronológico*, parte 3a, maço 14, doc. 44. fol. 1b.

46. *"Era tam nas maos dos ymfeis que nam conheceu a sua ley." A.N.T.T. Corpo Cronológico*, parte 3a, maço 14, doc. 44, fol. 1a.
47. Some sources even suggest that Hadim Suleiman's decision to retreat was the result of a letter forged by Hoja Safar to convince him that a major Portuguese relief force was on the way. See Anonymous, "Particular Relation," 275; Serjeant, *Hadrami Chronicles*, 97; Hajji ad-Dabir, *Arabic History of Gujarat*, 227.
48. For a version of events supporting this interpretation, see Serjeant, *Hadrami Chronicles*, 85.
49. For the original letter from Sultan Badr confirming this agreement, dated Shaban 945/June 1539, see *T.S.M.A.* N.E.6704; See also Serjeant, *Hadrami Chronicles*, 85–86.
50. For Hadim Suleiman's own account of these events, see Kurtoğlu, "Hadım Süleyman," 69–73. See also Kutbeddin Mekki, *Aḫbār al-Yemānī*, fols. 41b–43a; Anonymous, "Particular Relation," 279; *DA*, dec. V, bk. 5, chap. 4; Soudan, *Chronique d'al-Mawzaʿī*, 55–56; Katib Çelebi, *Tuḫfetü'l-Kibār*, 84.
51. J. R. Blackburn, "Two Documents on the Division of Ottoman Yemen into Two Beglerbegiliks (973–1565)," *Turcica* 27 (1995): 244; Orhonlu, "Kızıldeniz Sahilleri'nde Osmanlılar," *Tarih Dergisi* 16 (July 1961): 16; Katib Çelebi, *Tuḫfetü'l-Kibār*, 84.
52. *PM*, 6: 295.
53. On fortifications in Aden, see the letter of João de Castro, Oct. 29, 1539, in *Cartas*, 38. For Mocha, see Anonymous, "Particular Relation," 240.
54. On the rise of Surat, see Sanjay Subrahmanyam, "A Note on the Rise of Surat in the Sixteenth Century," *Journal of the Social and Economic History of the Orient* 43/1 (2000): 23–33.
55. Subrahmanyam, "Trading World," 213.
56. "*quam danosa e pergudisiall nos seja esta vizimhamça a meu ver a pouco que detriminar, porque somente com estarem quedas nos farão tamta guerra e porão em tamto gasto que não sera muito de nos porem em termos de deixar a terra.*" *Cartas*, 51.
57. See, for example, *DA*, dec. V, bk. 7, chap. 1; see also Elaine Sanceau, "Uma narrativa da expedição portuguesa de 1541 ao Mar Roxo," *Studia* 9 (Jan 1962): 226; and for a modern articulation of this view, see Dejanirah Couto, "Rasto de Hādim Seleimão," 498.
58. On the confusion in local sources about the fate of Hadim Suleiman, see Soudan, *Chronique d'al-Mawzaʿī*, 57; Hajji ad-Dabir, *Arabic History of Gujarat*, 309.
59. For the career and downfall of this intriguing character, see António da Silva Rego, "Duarte Catanho, Espião e Embaixador (1538–1542)," *Anais* serie 2, 4 (Lisbon, 1953): 123–140; and Dejanirah Couto, "L'itinéraire d'un marginal: la deuxième vie de Diogo de Mesquita," *Arquivos do Centro Cultural Calouste Gulbenkian* 39 (2000): 9–35. Couto corrects some important errors in Rego's work, which states incorrectly that Cataneo was a Venetian and that he was later executed for espionage in Lisbon (in fact, he was charged but exonerated).
60. The viceroy agreed to send Cataneo to Lisbon almost immediately, but because he had to wait for the next monsoon, he did not actually leave until after Hadim Suleiman's retreat from Diu. Rego, "Duarte Catanho," 124.
61. Rego, "Duarte Catanho," 127.
62. Three years later, after traveling to Istanbul, to India, and back to Lisbon, Cataneo was caught with compromising documents and charged with espionage. Rego, "Duarte Catanho," 139.
63. Rego, "Duarte Catanho," 130–31.
64. Özbaran, "Hindistan Yolu," 106; for the original document see *A.N.T.T. Doc. Orient.* maço 1 doc. 22. The original Portuguese translation is also preserved. See *A.N.T.T. Corpo Chronológico* 1, 3–4; and for a published version, Rego, "Duarte Catanho," 131–34.

65. Özbaran, "Hindistan Yolu," 106.
66. On this expedition, see Timothy Coates, "D. João de Castro's 1541 Red Sea Voyage in the Greater Context of the Sixteenth-Century Portuguese-Ottoman Red Sea Rivalry," in Caesar Farah, ed., *Decision Making and Change in the Ottoman Empire* (Kirksville, 1993), 263–85.
67. See the letter from João de Castro to the king, dated October 1541, in *Cartas*.
68. The principal Portuguese sources for this expedition are the previously cited accounts of João de Castro and D. Manuel de Lima; for a local Arabic account, see Serjeant, *Hadrami Chronicles*, 98–100.
69. For two firsthand accounts of events in Massawa, see R. S. Whiteway, ed. and trans., *The Portuguese Expedition to Abyssinia in 1541–1543 related by Castanhoso and Bermudas* (London, 1902), 138–47, 271–77.
70. See João de Castro, *Roteiro de Goa a Suez* (Lisbon, 1940), 178–80.
71. *DA*, dec. V, bk. 10, chap. 8.
72. See Orhonlu, "K̲h̲ādım Süleymān," 902.
73. Özbaran, "Hindistan Yolu," 107; see Couto, "L'itinéraire d'un marginal," for a detailed study of negotiations in Istanbul between 1541 and 1544 involving the Ottoman authorities, Cataneo, and his colleague and rival Diogo de Mesquita. For a full text of the last letter sent by the sultan to Lisbon in October 1544, see Özbaran, *Ottoman Response*, 111–14.
74. Even earlier, in 1525, Selman Reis had noted the growing strength of the Emir of Zeyla. See Özbaran, "Turkish Report," 85.
75. For a detailed contemporary source outlining Ahmed Grañ's rise during these years, see 'Arab Faqīh, *The Conquest of Abyssinia: Futuḥ Al-Ḥabaša*, trans. Paul Lester Stenhouse (Hollywood, 2005).
76. See João de Castro's comments on the importance of Ottoman firearms for Ahmed Grañ in *Roteiros de João de Castro*, 2 vols., ed. A. Fontoura da Costa (Lisbon, 1940), 2: 60; see also Whiteway, *Portuguese Expedition*, xxxvi.
77. For a synopsis of the reign of Lebna Dengel, see E. A. Wallace Budge, *A History of Ethiopia, Nubia and Abyssinia* (London, 1928), 1: 332–36; see also Whiteway, *Portuguese Expedition*, xxxvi.
78. Negotiations relating to the union between the churches of Ethiopia and Rome, ongoing since early in the century, reached a head in the late 1530s as a result of Ahmed Grañ's advances. See Budge, *History of Ethiopia*, 1: 335–36; Whiteway, *Portuguese Expedition*, 130–33; Orhonlu, "Kızıldeniz Sahilleri'nde Osmanlılar," 20.
79. Serjeant, *Hadrami Chronicles*, 100.
80. The introductory section of this treaty is preserved in the anonymous *Ḳānūnnāme-i Sulṭān Süleymān Ḫān*, fl. 39a; see also Orhonlu, *Habeş Eyaleti*, 26–27.
81. Whiteway, *Portuguese Expedition*, 65–68.
82. Whiteway, *Portuguese Expedition*, 69; Orhonlu, "Kızıldeniz Sahilleri'nde Osmanlılar," 21–22.
83. Whiteway, *Portuguese Expedition*, 80–88; Orhonlu, *Habeş Eyaleti*, 29.
84. The only exception came in 1544, when a small relief force of five ships bound for Massawa was sent out from Goa. But this fleet was intercepted by a squadron of nine Ottoman galleys near Aden and never reached the Abyssinian coast. See Serjeant, *Hadrami Chronicles*, 104; Orhonlu, *Habeş Eyaleti*, 29.
85. Özbaran, "Hindistan Yolu," 110; Luís de Albuquerque, "O domínio português do Índico e a resposta turca," *Vertice* 36 (1976): 12.
86. Gaspar Correia, *Lendas da Índia*, ed. M. Lopes de Almeida (Porto, 1975), 4: 343–44.
87. On the Ottoman galleys off the Maseira islands, see Correia, *Lendas*, 4: 423; on Ottoman merchants in Hormuz, see Sanceau, "Narrativa da expedição," 209.

88. *PM*, 7: 132; see also Correia, *Lendas*, 4: 525.
89. On Ottoman vessels in Siam, see Pinto, *Travels*, 35; for Castro's report, see *A.N.T.T. Corpo Cronológico* 1, 7–19; see also Özbaran, "Hindistan Yolu," 111.
90. For an in-depth study of this debate, see Luís Filipe Thomaz, "Questão da pimenta," 37–206.
91. Orhonlu, "Piri Reis," 235.
92. The first "Admiral of the Indies" was Hadim Suleiman's lieutenant Ferhad Bey, appointed to the post in 1543. Orhonlu, "Piri Reis," 236.
93. See the description of Bernardo Navagero in Alberi, *Relazioni*, 3: 99; also Orhonlu, "Khādım Süleymān," 902.
94. Hajji ad-Dabir, *Arabic History of Gujarat*, 232–34.
95. One of the numerous ships sent by Hoja Safar to the Red Sea in the run-up to hostilities, captained by another of Hoja Safar's Ottoman relatives and filled with Ottoman soldiers headed for Diu, was intercepted and captured by the Portuguese. See *Cartas*, 225–28; on Mustafa al-Neshar's shipment of men and supplies, paid for by Hoja Safar in gold, see *DA*, dec. V, bk. 11, chap. 8.
96. "*foi hum gramde esquadrão de Turcos com suas bandeiras e dando uma grande salva de arcabuzaria e com outras bizarrias e soberbas que aquela barbara nação usa.*" *DA*, dec. VI, bk. 1, chap. 7.
97. *São Lourenço*, 3: 367.
98. On Hoja Safar's death, see *DA*, dec. VI, bk. 2, chap. 3.
99. Hajji ad-Dabir, *Arabic History of Gujarat*, 233.
100. For documents related to the siege, see António Baião, ed., *História quinhentista (inédita) do segundo cêrco de Dio, ilustrada com a correspondência original, também inédita, de D. João de Castro, D. João de Mascarenhas, e outros* (Coimbra, 1925).
101. Hajji ad-Dabir, *Arabic History of Gujarat*, 234.
102. Correia, *Lendas*, 4: 525; also Luís Falcão's letter to D. J. Castro from Hormuz, 4 Nov. 1546, *São Lourenço*, 2: 123.
103. Özbaran, "XVI. Yüzyılda Basra Körfezi Sahillerinde Osmanlılar: Basra Beylerbeyliği'nin Kuruluşu," *Tarih Dergisi* 25 (Mar. 1971): 54; also Robert Mantran, "Règlements fiscaux ottomans: La province de Bassora (le moitié du XVIe s.)," *Journal of the Economic and Social History of the Orient* 10 (1967): 224.
104. Özbaran, "XVI. Yüzyılda Basra," 55.
105. As early as 1542, Duarte Cataneo had warned that the Portuguese attack on Suez would only speed up the return of Hadim Suleiman to the Indian Ocean, this time to build a fortress in Basra. See Luís de Albuquerque, "Alguns aspectos de ameaça turca sobre a Índia por meados do século XVI," *Agrupamentos de Estudos de Cartographia Antiga*, 51 (1977), 137.
106. Albuquerque, "Ameaça turca," 18.
107. "*A sua temção he defemder aos Portugueses a navegação do mar... credeme e vimde loguo, per que se tomarem Baçora nam se poderaa fazer nada e hyrem sobre vos e vossas terras e este caminho para eles he mui mais perto do que he o de Suez nem o de Juda.*" Albuquerque, "Ameaça turca," 17.
108. "*Senhor, estes omens são maos e muytos muyto usados na guerra e providos de muytos arteffícios dela; vemse cheguando a cabeça deste estreito e senhoreão o de Mequa... e se eles fizeram ffortaleza em Baçora passerem os navios que tem no outro estreyto a este, o que soçedendo asy, sera muy grando perda e dano pera toda a Imdja.*" Albuquerque, "Ameaça turca," 15.
109. Albuquerque, "Ameaça turca," 19–20.

110. "*E por esta razam achamos que nos vem muito bem sermos com vosco amigos e asemtarmos as cousas pera que venham vosos navios e vosos mercadores com vosas ffazemdas, e irão e virão sob guardia e grandeza e verdade do meu Rey, sem receberam dano nam perda duum grão; e não vos pareça que destas palavras aos corações ha deferemça alguma, e nam aja em vos descomfiança nenhuma, per que desta maneira seremos amigos, asy vos como os da Imdia, perque em mim não se acharaa outra cousa e os de todas as quatro partidas do mundo averam emveja a nosa amizidade*... *e peçovos muito que esta carta mandeis a Imdia e per todas as terras, pera que seguramente tratem e vam e venham e vos levem minhas emcomendas e me tragem as vosas, per que semdo asy nam ha hy mais que dizer, e nam semdo seraa o comtrayro.*" Albuquerque, "Ameaça turca," 21.

111. Dejanirah Potach, "The Commercial Relations between Basra and Goa in the Sixteenth Century," *Studia* 48 (1989): 155.

112. Potach, "Commercial Relations," 155.

113. For an example of one such dissident view, see Özbaran, *Ottoman Response*, 172–74.

114. See Albuquerque, "Ameaça turca," 23–26; and by the same author, "Resposta turca," 17.

115. As early as 1548, there is evidence that the Portuguese were granted "viajens de Baçora" to make a direct trip from Basra to Goa. See Potach, "Commercial Relations," 156–57; see also *PM*, 7: 274.

116. *Gavetas*, 15, 16–25.

117. Robert Mantran, "Règlements fiscaux," 242.

118. Revenues from maritime trade in Basra in 1551 amounted to 1,942,068 *paras* out of a total of 2,935,551, or 66 percent of total revenues. See Mantran, "Règlements fiscaux," 246; for comparative trade figures in Egypt, see Barkan, "Bir Bütçe Örneği," 251–93; and for Yemen, Özbaran, *Sınırdaki Osmanlı*, 214.

119. For a description of this process, see the complaint lodged with the viceroy from the vizier of Cananor on 15 September 1547, in *São Lourenço*, 3: 382.

120. With specific reference to the Ottoman Empire, such views have been most influentially expressed in a series of articles by Andrew Hess published in the early 1970s. See Hess, "The Evolution of the Ottoman Seaborne Empire in the Age of the Oceanic Discoveries 1453–1525," *American Historical Review* 75/7 (Dec. 1970): 1892–1919; "The Ottoman Conquest of Egypt and the Beginning of the Sixteenth-Century World War," *International Journal of Middle East Studies* 4/1 (Jan. 1973): 55–76; and "Piri Reis," 19–37; see also Inalcik's related arguments in *Economic and Social History*, 44–54; Michael Pearson has elaborated similar arguments with reference to the Sultanate of Gujarat and later the Mughals in sixteenth-century India. For the quote from Bahadur cited here, see Pearson, *Merchants and Rulers*, 118. In the decades since the appearance of these early works, a number of scholars (including Pearson himself) have gone on to develop more theoretical arguments about the lack of connections between ruler and merchant as a fundamental characteristic of all "Islamic land-based states." See Pearson, "Merchants and States" in James Tracy, ed., *The Political Economy of Merchant Empires: State Power and World Trade 1350–1750* (Cambridge, 1991), 41–116; K. N. Chaudhuri, *Trade and Civilization in the Indian Ocean* (Cambridge, 1985), 68; and Andre Wink, "Al-Hind: India and Indonesia in the Islamic World Economy, c. 700–1800 AD," *Itinerario* 12 (1988): 57–58; for a critique of this view, see Sanjay Subrahmanyam, "Of *Imarat* and *Tijarat*: Asian Merchants and State Power in the Western Indian Ocean, 1400 to 1750," *Comparative Studies in Society and History* 37/4 (October 1995); 750–80; as well as Brummett, *Ottoman Seapower*, 175–183; and

more generally, Huri Islamoğlu-Inan, "Oriental Despotism in World-System Perspective," in Islamoğlu-Inan, ed., *The Ottoman Empire and the World Economy* (Cambridge, 1987), 1–20.

121. Lutfi Pasha, who briefly served as grand vizier during this period, later penned a treatise on the juridical legitimacy of the Ottoman caliphate. See H. A. R. Gibb, "Lutfi Paşa on the Ottoman Caliphate," *Oriens* 15 (1962): 287–95; and for the original text, Lutfi Pasha, *Khalās al-umma fī ma'rifat al-a'immah*, ed. Majidah Makhluf (Cairo, 2001); for a review of the modern historiography of the Ottoman caliphate, see Abderrahmane el-Moudden, "Sharifs and Padishahs: Moroccan-Ottoman Relations from the Sixteenth through the Eighteenth Centuries" (PhD dissertation, Princeton, 1992), 25–32; and on the significance of the *hajj* for Ottoman foreign relations, see Suraiya Faroqhi, *Pilgrims and Sultans*, 127–46.

122. "*Senki Mıṣır Beglerbegisi Süleymān Paşasın ḥükm-i şerīfüm saña vāṣıl olduġı demden yāt ve yarāḳ ve bār ve bünyāh ḥāżır idüp ve ol Süveys'de cihād fī sebīli'llah ve ġazāvetine ḥāżır olup ve müheyyā olan gemilere zād ve zevāde ḳoyup kifāyet idecek ḳadar 'asker alup varup Hind'e giçüp ve ol Hind'üñ benderlerin alup ve żabṭ idüp Mekke'nüñ ve Medīne'nüñ şerefehümā Allahu te'ālā yolın kesüp ve tarīḳin ḳaṭ' idüp Portuḳāl kāfirüñ żararın eylerden def' idüp ve elemin deryādan ref 'idesün*" [Italics in translation are my emphasis]. Hasan b. Tulun, *Tārīḫ-i Mıṣır*, fol. 353b.

NOTES TO CHAPTER 4

1. Bernardo Navagero claimed to have heard this story from Rustem himself. See Alberi, *Relazioni*, 3: 98.
2. On the rising importance of the status of *damad*, or son-in-law of the sultan, during the lifetime of Hurrem Sultan, see Peirce, *Imperial Harem*, 65–79.
3. Imber, "Suleyman as Caliph," 179–84.
4. Gülru Necipoğlu, "A Kanun for the State, a Canon for the Arts: Conceptualizing the Classical Synthesis of Ottoman Art and Architecture," in Veinstein, *Soliman le Magnifique*, 195–216; and more generally, Necipoğlu, *The Age of Sinan: Architectural Culture in the Ottoman Empire* (London, 2005), 314–31.
5. Fleischer, "Lawgiver as Messiah," 171.
6. Rüstem Paşa, *Tevārīḫ-i Āl-i 'Os̱mān*. Cambridge University Library, Turkish OR. Ms. Gg 6.33, fols. 220–380. The section on Yemen is on folios 346–80. On Matrakçı Nasuh's probable authorship of the work, see H. Yurdaydın, "Matrakçı Nasuh'un Hayatı ve Eserleri ile İlgili Yeni Bilgiler," *Belleten* 29 (1965): 354.
7. See Seydi Ali Reis, *Mir'ātü'l-Memālik*, ed. Mehmet Kiremit (Ankara, 1999); for two recent scholarly discussions of this work, see Alam and Subrahmanyam, *Indo-Persian Travels*, 94–131; and Suraiya Faroqhi, *The Ottoman Empire and the World around It* (London, 2004), 183–85.
8. "*rūy-i zemīnde ne Vilāyet-i Rūm'a mu'ādil bir vilāyet ve ne pādişāh-ı 'alem-penāh ḥażretlerine 'adīl olur bir pādişāh vardur... ve leşker-i Rūm'a muḳābil olur leşker olmaḳ cihān içinde bir daḫī mutaṣavver degildür.*" Seydi Ali Reis, *Mir'ātü'l-Memālik*, 162–63.
9. English translation taken from Sidi Ali Reis, *The Travels and Adventures of Sidi Ali Reis in India, Afghanistan, Central Asia and Persia during the Years 1553–1556*, trans., A. Vambery (London, 1899), 107; for the original text, see Seydi Ali Reis, *Mir'ātü'l-Memālik*, 168–69.
10. A good example of this type of scholarship is Matrakçı Nasuh's *Beyān-ı Menāzil-i Sefer-i 'Irāḳeyn-i Sulṭān-ı Süleymān Ḫān*, ed. Hüseyin Yurdaydın (Ankara, 1976); for a recent scholarly discussion of this work as an attempt to define Ottoman political space, see Kathryn Ebel, "City

Views, Imperial Visions: Cartography and the Visual Culture of Urban Space in the Ottoman Empire, 1453–1603," (PhD dissertation, University of Texas–Austin, 2002).

11. One typical example is Celalzade Mustafa Çelebi's *Tabaḳāt al-Memālik fī Derecāt al-Mesālik*, Istanbul, Süleymaniye Library, Hüsrev Paşa Ms. no. 427–28. On the general scarcity of information about the Indian Ocean in Ottoman chronicles, see Özbaran, *Ottoman Response*, 79.
12. Rustem's economic policies are probably the closest approximation of what some Ottoman scholars have termed "provisionism." See Mehmet Genç, *Osmanlı İmparatorluğunda Devlet ve Ekonomi* (Istanbul, 2000); see also Inalcik, "Ottoman Economic Mind," 218; Faroqhi, *Pilgrims and Sultans*, 161.
13. Alberi, *Relazioni*, 3: 84–85.
14. For a further discussion of Rustem's economic policies in the Indian Ocean, see Giancarlo Casale, "The Ottoman Administration of the Spice Trade in the Sixteenth-Century Red Sea and Persian Gulf," *Journal of the Economic and Social History of the Orient* 49/2 (May 2006): 175–76.
15. For Rustem's policy in the Black Sea and his economic program in general, see M. Tayyib Gökbilgin, "Rüstem Paşa Hakkındaki İthamlar," *Tarih Dergisi* 11–12 (July 1955): 11–50.
16. Daud Pasha had also served as Egypt's treasurer during Hadim Suleiman's tenure as provincial governor. See Süheyli, *Tārīḫ-i Mıṣır al-Cedīd*, fol. 55a.
17. Alberi, *Relazioni*, 3: 98–9.
18. On Rustem's opposition to Ayas Pasha, see the 1547 letter of Dom Manuel de Lima from Hormuz in Özbaran, *Ottoman Response*, 143; on Rustem's refusal to supply troops for the expedition, see also Halil Sahillioğlu, ed., *Topkapı Sarayı Arşivi H.951–952 Tarihli ve E-12321 Numaralı Mühimme Defteri* (Istanbul, 2002), doc. 213.
19. Özbaran, *Ottoman Response*, 143.
20. Soudan, *Chronique d'al-Mawzaʿī*, 60.
21. Mustafa had previously served as an Egyptian *kāşif* and as the *emirü'l-ḥajj*. Kutbeddin Mekki, *Aḫbār al-Yemānī*, fol. 45a.
22. Kutbeddin Mekki, *Aḫbār al-Yemānī*, fol. 45b; Soudan, *Chronique d'al-Mawzaʿī*, 60.
23. The principal Ottoman sources for this period in Yemen's history are Kutbeddin Mekki, fols. 45–55; Rustem Pasha's *Tevārīḫ*, fols. 346–80; Seyyid Lokman's *Mücmelü't-Tūmār*, British Museum, Turkish Ms. Or. 1135, fols. 72–76; and Soudan, *Chronique d'al-Mawzaʿī*, 60–64. The present account is composed from these sources. For a review of the Ottoman and Arabic sources from the period, see J. R. Blackburn, "Arabic and Turkish Source Materials for the Early History of Ottoman Yemen 945/1538–976/1568," in Abd al-Rahman b. al-Ansary, ed., *Sources for the History of the Arabs* (Riyadh, 1982), 2: 197–210.
24. See *DA*, dec. VI, bk. 6, chaps. 1–3; see also Katib Çelebi, *Tuḥfetü'l-Kibār*, 89.
25. For a modern account of Ozdemir Pasha's early career, see Orhonlu, *Habeş Eyaleti*, 33–35.
26. For the text of this letter, see J. R. Blackburn, "The Ottoman Penetration of Yemen: An Annotated Translation of Özdemir Bey's Fethnāme for the Conquest of San'a in Rajab 954/Aug. 1547," *Archivum Ottomanicum* 5 (1980): 70–89.
27. On the intrigue surrounding Ferhad's appointment, see Blackburn, "Ottoman Penetration," 77.
28. Katib Çelebi, *Tuḥfetü'l-Kibār*, 89.
29. On Piri Reis's service as captain of Alexandria, see Alberi, *Relazioni*, 3: 59.
30. One contemporary Portuguese source explicitly states that Piri Reis became a personal client of Rustem following the death of his old patron, Hayreddin Barbaros Pasha, in 1546. See *A.N.T.T. Corpo Cronológico*, part 1, maço 89, doc. 9.

31. On these and subsequent events, see (in addition to the Ottoman sources cited previously): *DA*, dec. VI, bk. 6, chaps. 1–6; Serjeant, *Hadrami Chronicles*, 108–9; Ibrahim Peçevi, *Tārīẖ-i Peçevī*, 1: 351; and for a modern account, Cengiz Orhonlu, "Hint Kaptanlığı ve Piri Reis," *Belleten* 34/134 (1967), 235–38.
32. Noronha's decision became so notorious that, according to Diogo do Couto, years after the event, a gentleman of Goa was walking on his street and saw a young girl crying because Noronha's sons had stolen a chicken from her. He told her: "Hush girl, there's no use making a scene. If it were Aden they would gladly hand it over to you, but they have no chickens to give!" ["*cala-te filha, não te mates, se fora Adem largáram-ta; mas galinha não ta hão de dar.*"] *DA*, dec. VI, bk. 6, chap. 6.
33. "*. . . maiormente neste tempo de aguora que temos os Rumes em Baçora e em Adem, e são eles mais imdustrios e tem mais cuidado aparelhar-se pera fazer cousas de guerra e ordenadamente tem seus conselhos milhor que nos qua.*" *DP*, vol. iv, doc. 24.
34. See Soudan, *Chronique d'al-Mawzaʿī*, 62.
35. Blackburn, "Arabic and Turkish," 198; Kutbeddin Mekki, "*Aẖbār al-Yemānī*," fols. 51–52.
36. For the earliest surviving budget from Ottoman Yemen, dating from 1561 and showing a significant surplus, see Özbaran, "A Note on the Ottoman Administration in Arabia in the 16th Century," *International Journal of Turkish Studies* 3/1 (Winter 1984–85), 97.
37. See Sahillioğlu, *E-12321 Numaralı Mühimme Defteri*, doc. 119; for a discussion of this document in context, see Casale, "Ottoman Intelligence Report," 187–88.
38. See Correia, *Lendas*, 4: 525; see also Diogo Luys's letter from Muscat in *São Lourenço*, 1: 125–27. According to a report from the captain of Hormuz, the Ottomans learned during this raid that ten galleys would be enough to capture all the ships in Hormuz harbor. Since Sefer's subsequent raids were directed specifically against Portuguese merchant shipping from Hormuz, this reinforces the impression that Sefer participated in this early attack on Muscat. See *São Lourenço*, 2: 125.
39. "*Quatro galeotas grandes e formosas . . . andava nellas hum Mouro grande cossario, chamado Cafár, que tinha sahido de Meca com tenção de saquear Mascate, e saquear as náos que em Outubro haviam de partir de Ormuz pera Goa, e pera outros portos da costa da India.*" *DA*, dec. VI, bk. 8, chap. 12.
40. *DA*, dec. VI, bk. 8, chap. 12.
41. See *DA*, dec. VI, bk. 9, chap. 11; and Özbaran "Hindistan Yolu,"125.
42. Within a year of the first Ottoman raid on Muscat in 1546, Dom Manuel de Lima foresaw the effectiveness of this strategy, predicting correctly that it was only a matter of time before the Ottomans would start raiding the north Arabian Sea every year. See Albuquerque, "Resposta turca," 17.
43. On Sinan Pasha see Alberi, *Relazioni*, 3: 70.
44. Özbaran, "XVI. Yüzyılda Basra," 57–59.
45. *DA*, dec. VI, bk. 8, chap. 5.
46. On Piri's relationship with Rustem, see note 30.
47. On these conspiracies, see P. Gaspar Barzaeus's letter from Hormuz, October 24, 1550, in *Documenta Indica*, 2: 69; also see Viceroy D. Afonso de Noronha's letter to the queen, January 27, 1552, *PM*, 7: 254.
48. *DA*, dec. VI, bk. 9, chap. 4; see also *A.N.T.T.*, *Corpo Cronológico* I, mç. 89, doc. 7, fol. 2.
49. *DA*, dec. VI, bk. 9, chap. 16.
50. For a Jesuit account of the capture of Muscat, see Ludovico Frois's letter from Goa, December 1, 1552, in *Documenta Indica*, 2: 487; see also Seydi Ali Reis, *Mir'ātü'l-Memālik*, 73.

51. For the siege of Hormuz, see the three accounts by Portuguese eyewitnesses in *A.N.T.T.*, *Corpo Cronológico* 1, mç. 89, doc. 9; also *DA*, dec. VI, bk. 10, chaps. 2–5; for a contrasting view of events, see Dom Álvaro de Noronha's account, in which he insists that "if [the Ottomans] had carried on with the bombardment they would certainly have brought the whole wall down" in Özbaran, *Ottoman Response*, 162; for an Ottoman version of events, see Katib Çelebi, *Tuḥfetü'l-Kibār*, 89–90.
52. See relevant documents in Orhonlu, "Piri Reis," 250–54.
53. According to Seydi Ali, Piri Reis was provoked into abandoning the fleet by Portuguese captives who warned that a fleet from India was on its way to hunt him down (Seydi Ali Reis, *Mir'ātü'l-Memālik*, 73); some Portuguese had in fact urged such an attempt, one arguing that "to burn ten Turkish ships in Basra would do a greater service to our King than seizing Constantinople from them." See *A.N.T.T.*, *Corpo Cronológico* 1, mç. 89, doc. 9, fol. 2.
54. For details on Piri's return voyage, see *DA*, dec. VI, bk. 10, chap. 10; also Orhonlu, "Piri Reis," 244.
55. Orhonlu, "Piri Reis," 245; see also Katib Çelebi, *Tuḥfetü'l-Kibār*, 90.
56. For descriptions of this encounter, see *FS*, vol. 2: 246–47; *DA*, dec. VI, bk. 10, chap. 3; *Documenta Indica*, vol. 3, 25–26; Seydi Ali Reis, *Mir'ātü'l-Memālik*, 74–75; Katib Çelebi, *Tuḥfetü'l-Kibār*, 90–91; the battle is also the first between the Portuguese and the Ottomans to be depicted visually. See Lisuarte de Abreu, *Livro de Lisuarte de Abreu* (Lisbon, 1992), fol. 83.
57. Katib Çelebi, *Tuḥfetü'l-Kibār*, 91.
58. "*külliyen deryā-yı maġribüñ eṭrāf ve eknāf geşt olınup. . . .*" Seydi Ali Reis, *Mir'ātü'l-Memālik*, 74.
59. Seydi Ali Reis, *Mir'ātü'l-Memālik*, 75.
60. Although Seydi Ali's own account in the *Mir'āt ül-Memālik* is a main source for this encounter, in several respects his reliability is suspect. He records, for example, that a fierce battle with the Portuguese occurred as he passed by Hormuz, and he claims to have sunk a Portuguese ship and forced the rest of their vessels to retreat. See Seydi Ali Reis, *Mir'ātü'l-Memālik*, 79–81; Portuguese sources suggest that the two fleets never got close enough to exchange gunfire. See Özbaran, "Turks in the Persian Gulf," 64.
61. Seydi Ali was so convinced of having evaded Menezes that he never realized he had been outmaneuvered and believed the force waiting for him in Muscat was an entirely different fleet. Seydi Ali, *Mir'ātü'l-Memālik*, 81.
62. Here as well, Seydi Ali's own version of events portrays the encounter as a fierce struggle in which equal losses were suffered on both sides. Portuguese sources do not record any significant losses on their side and make clear that the six Ottoman galleys were not sunk (as Seydi Ali claims) but captured. See *DA*, dec. VII, bk. 1, chap. 4; and the graphic depiction of the battle in the *Livro de Lisuarte de Abreu*, fol. 85.
63. See Seydi Ali Reis, *Mir'ātü'l-Memālik*, 82–83; Katib Çelebi, *Tuḥfetü'l-Kibār*, 93–94.
64. "*Deryā-yı Maġrib'de vāḳi' olan furtūnalar anuñ yanında bir ẕerrece ve ḳilel-i cibāl gibi emvācı bunuñ ḳatında bir ḳaṭrece gelmeyüp.*" Seydi Ali Reis, *Mir'ātü'l-Memālik*, 84.
65. Seydi Ali drifted as far as Baluchistan in the north and Shihr in the south before finally reaching Gujarat. See Seydi Ali Reis, *Mir'ātü'l-Memālik*, 83–88.
66. See *A.N.T.T. Corpo Cronológico*, part 1, maço 86, doc. 120, fol. 1b; *DP*, 5: 271.
67. "*A que aguardava a Ale Chelubij, parece que esteve antevendo o Turco, porque logo enviou atrás o Zafar . . . (mais ajuizado em seu conceito) para receber dele as galeras e fazer com elas o que primeiro tinha pensado do outro.*" *FS*, 3: 259.
68. "*E como era cossario, e muito prático nas cousas daquelle mar, determinou de se ir na esteira da armada, porque sempre lhe ficaria por ella cousa que preasse. E seguindo a sua derrota, antes que chegasse à ponta*

de Dio, desemmasteou e deixou-se ficar ao mar pera esperar pelas náos que haviam ir demandar aquella paragem." *DA*, dec. VII, bk. 1, chap. 5.

69. This account is based on *DA*, dec. VII, bk. 1, chap. 5; and *FS*, 3: 259; see also the contemporary report of João de Lisboa, who claims Sefer captured only three vessels. *A.N.T.T. Corpo Cronológico*, part 1, maço 86, doc. 120, fol. 1b.
70. *A.N.T.T. Corpo Cronológico*, part 1, maço 86, doc. 120, fol. 1b.
71. *A.N.T.T. Corpo Cronológico*, part 1, maço 86, doc. 120, fol. 3a; for a corroborating Portuguese report from Chaul, see *A.N.T.T. Corpo Cronológico*, part 1, maço 100, doc. 28, fol. 2b.
72. *A.N.T.T. Corpo Cronológico*, part 1, maço 86, doc. 120, fol. 6a; a similar situation is described by Seydi Ali Reis, *Mir'ātü'l-Memālik*, 90–92.
73. *A.N.T.T. Corpo Cronológico*, part 1, maço 86, doc. 120, fol. 1a.
74. *DA*, dec. VII, bk. 1, chap. 7.
75. *DA*, dec. VII, bk. 3, chap. 3.
76. *A.N.T.T. Corpo Cronológico*, part 1, maço 100, doc. 28, fol. 2b.
77. "*para que era deixar aquella ladroeira tanto tempo em Moqua... que cada dia ya em crecimento, e aquele Cairo se faz cada dia com has presas dos Portugueses mais rico e cada dia ha de acrecetar armada quando avia tres fustas somente... quanto mais trabalho lhe avria de dar aquele Cairo com trinta armadas?*" *A.N.T.T. Corpo Cronológico*, part 1, maço 86, doc. 120, fol. 1b; for a similar recommendation from Chaul in the following year, see *A.N.T.T. Corpo Cronológico*, part 1, maço 100, doc. 28, fol. 2b.
78. *DA*, dec. VII, bk. 6, chap. 7.
79. *DA*, dec. VII, bk. 7, chap. 6.
80. Orhonlu, *Habeş Eyaleti*, 34–36; see also *A.N.T.T. Corpo Cronológico*, part 1, maço 86, doc. 120, fol. 4a–5a.
81. Orhonlu, *Habeş Eyaleti*, 37–39; see also *A.N.T.T. Corpo Cronológico*, part 1, maço 102, doc. 47, fol. 2a.
82. Orhonlu, *Habeş Eyaleti*, 43–44.
83. *DA*, dec. VII, bk. 3, chap. 3.
84. "*que elle era amigo dos Portuguezes; que se queria agua, ou mantimentos, que tudo lhe mandaria dar, e de muito boa vontade e assim tudo o mais de que tivesse necessidade.*" *DA*, dec. VI, bk. 8, chap. 8.
85. "*por não ser conhecida a sua galé lhe tinha alevantadas grandes arrombadas de esteiras e sobre o masto feito huma gavea pera parecer náo, e as outras tres galés tinha mandado affastar de si.*" *DA*, dec. VII, bk. 8, chap. 8.
86. *DA*, dec. VII, bk. 8, chap. 8; *FS*, 3: 300–1.
87. On Sefer's appointment, see *MD* 4, doc. 540, 51.
88. *CDP*, 5: 396; and for a corroborating Ottoman source, see *MD* 3, doc. 550, 195.
89. "*Pella pratica e experiencia que aquelle capitão tem de toda a costa de Melinde ate Moçambique e assi da outra de Adem ate Ormuz quererão por alguma daquelles tantar ardis e effectuar speranças que elle deve ter imaginadas e por ellas offerecido grandes e proveitosos successos. A tudo se deve prevenir e de tudo deve estar advertido o Visorrei da India.*" *CDP*, 9: 111.
90. "*seicentos e sincoenta soldados dos melhores da India, em que entravam muitos fidalgos e cavalleiros mui honrados.*" *DA*, dec. VII, bk. 10, chap. 2.
91. This encounter is recorded in the *Tarih-i Shihr*, although the text confuses Sefer with the long-dead Piri Reis. See R.B. Serjeant, *Hadrami Chronicles*, 110; also *DA*, dec. VII, bk. 10, chap. 2.
92. *DA*, dec. VII, bk. 10, chap. 2.
93. Serjeant, *Hadrami Chronicles*, 110; *DA*, dec. VII, bk. 10, chap. 3.

94. On the activities of these freelance corsairs, see *DA*, dec. VI, bk. 10, chap. 1 and dec. VII, bk. 7, chap. 2; for evidence of Ottoman influence in Siam, see *Documenta Indica*, 3: 152.
95. On this question, see the classic study of Frederick C. Lane, "The Mediterranean Spice Trade: Further Evidence for Its Revival in the 16th Century," in Brian Pullman, ed., *Crisis and Change in the Venetian Economy in the Sixteenth Century* (London, 1968), 47–58; for contemporary Portuguese descriptions of this trend, see *CDP*, 9: 136; and *A.N.T.T. Corpo Cronológico*, part 1, maço 105, doc. 139.
96. Hess, "Piri Reis," 30; similarly Subrahmanyam, "Trading World," 218.
97. Özbaran, "Hindistan Yolu," 127.
98. For a lengthier discussion of this problem, see Casale, "Ottoman Administration," 171–72.
99. For a technical analysis of sixteenth-century Mediterranean galley warfare, see Guilmartin, *Gunpowder and Galleys*, 16–41.
100. "*Em quanto ali estiveram, que foi mais de um mez, houveram vista de mais de sincoenta náos por vezes, sem lhes poderem chegar, porque como elles estavam á terra, e ellas vinham de mar em fóra enfundadas, não for possivel chegaram-lhes nem seguirem-nas pera dentro, por se não metterem com ellas no Estreito a risco de se perderem.*" *DA*, dec. VII, bk. 10, chap. 3.
101. See Salvatore Bono, *Schiavi musulmani nell'Italia moderna* (Napoli, 1999), 297.
102. There are three letters by Manuel de Vasconcelos in Cannanor on this subject. *São Lourenço*, 3: 341, 353, and 373.
103. *Mühimme* documents on the Jews of the customs house in Suez include *MD* 33, doc. 323, 169; and *MD* 33, doc. 633, 306; See also Couto, "Rasto de Hadim Suleimão," 493; and, more generally, Benjamin Arbel, *Trading Nations: Jews and Venetians in the Early Modern Eastern Mediterranean* (Leiden, 1995).
104. On relations between New Christians and the Jews of Cochin with the Ottoman Empire, see José Alberto Rodriguez da Silva Tavim, "Outras gentes em outras rotas: judeus e cristãos-novos de Cochin—entre Santa Cruz de Cochin e Mattancherry, entre o Império Português e o Médio Oriente" in Matos and Thomaz, *Carreira da Índia*, 309–42; and also by the same author, "Os Judeus e a expansão portuguesa na Índia durante o século XVI. O exemplo de Isaac do Cairo: Espião, 'lingua,' e judeu de Cochim de Cima," *Arquivos do Centro Cultural Calouste Gulbenkian* 33 (1994): 137–266; more generally, see Daviken Studnicki-Gizbert, *A Nation upon the Ocean Sea: Portugal's Atlantic Diaspora and the Crisis of the Spanish Empire, 1492–1640* (New York, 2007).
105. Maria do Rosário de Sampaio Themudo Barata de Azevedo Cruz, "A 'Questão de Baçora' na menoridade de D. Sebastião (1557–1568): A perspectiva das informações colhidas na Índia e as iniciativas do governo," *Revista da Falcudade de Letras*, 5th series, 6 (1986): 50.
106. Özbaran, "Turks in the Persian Gulf," 67; also Safvet Bey, *Tārīḫ-i 'Os̱mānī Encümeni Mecmū'ası*, 14–18 (h.1329/c.e. 1910), 1139–44.
107. Semiz Ali counted among his personal friends Daniele Barbarigo, the Venetian bailo between 1561 and 1563, whom he already knew from his time as governor of Egypt (where Barbarigo had served as consul). See *A.N.T.T. Corpo Cronológico*, part 1, maço 105, doc. 139. For a brief biography of Semiz Ali and a discussion of his architectural patronage, see Necipoğlu, *Age of Sinan*, 384–89.
108. E. S. Forster, ed. and trans., *The Turkish Letters of Ogier Ghiselin de Busbecq* (Oxford, 1968), 321.
109. For a detailed contemporary account of Dervish Ali Pasha's dealings with the Portuguese, see Maria Augusta Lima Cruz, ed., *Diogo do Couto e a década 8a da Ásia*, (Lisbon, 1994), 1: 126–27.

110. It is significant that Texeira's arrival in Istanbul caused some initial embarrassment for Ali Pasha, who had apparently begun negotiating with the Portuguese without permission from the sultan. See Couto (Cruz edition of 8th decade), 127; this is perhaps a sign that members of Rustem Pasha's faction, hostile to opening the Persian Gulf to trade with the Portuguese, remained influential at court after Rustem's death.

111. Couto (Cruz edition of 8th decade), 201; for an English translation of the actual text of the letter sent from Sultan Suleiman to Portugal, see Özbaran, "Turks in the Persian Gulf," 82–84.

112. "*O negocio he grave e de muita consideração e em ser muita a somma da speciaria que vem pello mar Roxo ao Cayro e pollo de Ormuz a Baçora e bem se podem creer segundo as cousas procedem que antes este trato hira em crescimento que em diminuição. As despesas de Vossa Alteza no negocio da India são mui grandes e não se achando a ella algum remedio, sempre serão mayores. Em as pazes com o Turco para isto [sic] serem proveitosas, e não avera quem com justa rezão o contradigua.*" *CDP*, 9: 136.

113. "*Preposto isto digo que se os Turcos podessem ir livremente à Índia, e ter feitorias e tratarem nas mercadurias ditas por onde quisessem, que alem de V.A. perder os grandes proveitos que recebe dellas na Índia ficaríamos nós não tendo laa que fazer porque todas as fazendas que disse avião logo os Turcos de negociar por suas mãos, e por via dos Estreitos de Meca e Persia levarião à Índia todas as principais mercadorias que os nossos levão nas naos deste Reyno, as quais em Levante e em outras partes onde as comprassem são muito mais baratas que em Portugal, e alem disso o tempo das viagens, fretes, riscos, danificamentos dellas e das naos em que as levassem serião mais da metade dos Mouros do que custão aos nossos... e quanto à pimenta e outras drogas defesas tambem pera isto seria mor dano e perjuizo terem os Turcos na Índia feitoras porque se aos mesmos Portugueses se não pode de todo tolher o trato dellas pois se sabe que escondidamente e a risco de lhe tomarem as fazendas as levão a Ormuz, a Baçora, e a Bengala, Pegu, China e outras partes quanto mais aos Turcos, que por isso, com os mouros da terra, teriam mores intelligencias e melhor aparelho pera por via de ambos os Estreitos ficariam assi senhores de milhor e mayor parte das especiarias.*" Couto (Cruz edition of 8th decade), 205–7.

NOTES TO CHAPTER 5

1. Lourenço Pires de Távora reported a halt to the construction of this fleet as early as May 1561. *CDP*, 9: 251–52.
2. Cruz, "Questão de Baçora," 58; the first official letter sent from the sultan to the king of Portugal dates from 1564, although an exchange of embassies had already begun several years earlier. See Özbaran, "Turks in the Persian Gulf," 82–84.
3. *MD* 6 #757, 354; *DA*, dec. VII, bk. 2, chap. 8; and John E. Mandaville, "The Ottoman Province of al-Hasā in the Sixteenth and Seventeenth Centuries," *Journal of the American Oriental Society* 90 (1970): 489.
4. See Luís Filipe Thomaz, "A crise de 1565–1575 na história do Estado da Índia," *Mare Liberum* 9 (July 1995): 486.
5. Tavim, "Judeus e expansão," 166.
6. *DA*, dec. VIII, bk. 5, chap. 4.
7. Joseph Wicki, "Duas cartas oficiais de Vice-Reis da Índia, escritas em 1561 e 1564," *Studia* 3 (Jan. 1959): 54; Cruz, "Questão de Baçora," 58.

8. The arrival of the embassy was reported by the Venetian bailo in June 1562; the earliest Portuguese report, from Nicolo Pietro Cochino, was sent on Oct. 29, 1563; for further details on this embassy, see Giancarlo Casale, "His Majesty's Servant Lutfi: The Career of a Previously Unknown Sixteenth-Century Ottoman Envoy to Sumatra Based on an Account of His Travels from the Topkapı Palace Archives," *Turcica* 37 (2005): 43–81; also Reid, "Turkish Influence," 395–414.
9. For the original text of the Ottoman response to Ali Ala'ad-din Ri'ayat Syah's request, see the *Mekâtib-i Ḫulefâ ve Selâṭîn, T.S.M.K.* R. 1959, fol. 817a–18a; for a transcription and translation, see Casale, "His Majesty's Servant Lutfi," 50; for a corroborative Venetian report, see *Gavetas*, 20,14–17.
10. For the preparations for Sefer's fleet, see *MD* 6 #256, 122 and *MD* 6 #257, 122; also Imber, "Navy of Suleyman," 272.
11. For an introduction to the life of this paragon of Ottoman politics, see the popular history by Radovan Samardjitch, *Mehmed Sokolovitch: le destin d'un grand vizir*, trans. Mauricette Begitch (Lausanne, 1994).
12. Imber, "Navy of Suleyman," 253; also Veinstein, "Sokollu Mehmed," 706–11.
13. Imber, "Navy of Suleyman," 254.
14. Ismihan's mother, Nurbanu, was said to be the daughter of the Venetian Venier Baffo. See Maria Pia Pedani, "Safiye's Household and Venetian Diplomacy," *Turcica* 32 (2000), 9–32; for an alternate view, see B. Arbel, "Nur Banu (c. 1530–1580)—A Venetian Sultana?" *Turcica* 24 (1992), 241–59. For an in-depth discussion of the artistic and architectural patronage of Sokollu Mehmed and the Princess Ismihan, see Necipoğlu, *Age of Sinan*, 331–68; also Tülay Artan, "The Kadırga Palace Shrouded by the Mists of Time," *Turcica* 26 (1994): 56–124.
15. M. Lesure, "Notes et documents sur les relations vénéto-ottomanes 1570–73," *Turcica* 4 (1972): 134–64.
16. On Ottoman portraiture commissioned by Sokollu, see N. Atasoy, "Nakkaş Osman'ın Padişah Portreleri Albümü," *Türkiyemiz* 6 (1972): 2–12; and on Sokollu's importation of Venetian glassware, which he helped to design, see Stefano Carboni, "Oggetti decorati a smalto di influsso islamico nella vertraria muranese: tecnica e forma," in Ernst Grube, ed., *Venezia e l'oriente vicino: Arte veneziana e arte islamica: Atti del primo simposio internazionale sull'arte veneziana e l'arte islamica* (Venice, 1989), 147–66.
17. A. Sayılı, "Üçüncü Murad'ın İstanbul Rasathanesindeki Mücessem Yer Küresi ve Avrupa ile Kültürel Temaslar," *Belleten* 25/99 (1961): 410–11.
18. Franz Babinger, *Osmanlı Tarih Yazarları*, 105.
19. All of these authors and works are discussed in greater detail in chapter 7. For a recent study of Sokollu's patronage, see Emine Fetvacı, "Viziers to Eunuchs: Transitions in Ottoman Patronage, 1566–1617" (PhD dissertation, Harvard University, 2005), 83–139.
20. "*Ḳalküt Pâdişâhı Sâmiri'nüñ sa'âdetlü pâdişâh ḥażretlerine inḳıyâd ve iṭâ'atın 'arż idüp rûz ve şeb Portuḳâl kâfiri ile cenk üzere olduġın.*" Seydi Ali Reis, *Mir'âtü'l-Memâlik*, 89.
21. "*Vilâyet-i Gücerât'uñ iḫtilâli zamânında gelüp mu'în oldıñuz egerçi Nûḥ zamânından berü deryâda bu maḳûle ṭufân olmamışdur... mercûdur ki inşâ'allah 'an-ḳarîbi'z-zamân Vilâyet-i Gücerât Memâlik-i 'Os̱mâniyye'ye ilḥâḳ olınup Benâdir-i Hind küffâr-ı ḫâksâruñ elinden ḫalâṣ olmaġa bâ'is̱ olına.*" Seydi Ali Reis, *Mir'âtü'l-Memâlik*, 90.
22. Ḥajji ad-Dabir, *Arabic History of Gujarat*, 1: 312–20; see also Subrahmanyam, "Trading World," 217.

23. "*Biz Pādişāh-ı Rūm'a muḥtācuz gemilerimüz anlaruñ benderlerine varmasa bizüm ḥālimüz dīger-gūn olur. Ḫuṣūṣā İslām pādişāhıdur. Anuñ ḳapudānın bizden istemek münāsib midür?*" Seydi Ali Reis, *Mir'ātü'l-Memālik*, 96.

24. For an interesting discussion of this rivalry and its relation to larger developments in southeast Asia and the Ottoman Empire, augmented by material evidence from inscriptions on surviving pieces of Acehnese artillery, see Claude Guillot and Ludvik Kalus, "Inscriptions islamiques sur des canons d'Insulinde du XVIe siècle," *Archipel* 72 (2006): 69–94.

25. "*Ḥaḳ 'ālīmdür ki Vilāyet-i Gücerāt'da Sürret nām benderde Ḫvāce Bahşi ve Ḳara Ḥasan nām sevdā-gerlerden mesmū'umdur ki Vilāyet-i Çīn'de bayram olup sevdā-gerler bayram namāzın ḳılmaḳ murād idinüp her ṭāyife kendü pādişāhları adına ḫuṭbe oḳıtmak murād idinüp Rūmī sevdā-gerleri Ḫāḳān-ı Çīn'e varup bizüm Pādişāhımuz Mekke ve Medīne ve ḳıble pādişāhıdur diyü 'arż itdükde kāfir iken inṣāf idüp Mekke ve Medīne Pādişāhı adına ḫuṭbe oḳuñ diyü ḥükm idüp Rūmī sevdā-gerler ḫaṭībe ḫil'at giydürüp ve fīle bindürüp şehri gezdürüp ba'dehu bayram namāzın ḳılup Vilāyet-i Çīn'de Pādişāh-ı Rūm adına ḫuṭbe oḳınup bu maḳūle aḥvāl kimün haḳḳında olmışdur.*" Seydi Ali Reis, *Mir'ātü'l-Memālik*, 116.

26. For a fascinating historical precedent for this kind of trade-based network of allegiance [*ṭā'a*] from the medieval Indian Ocean—including a similar reference to China—see Elizabeth Lambourn, "India from Aden: Khutba and Muslim Urban Networks in Late Thirteenth-Century India," in K. Hall, ed., *Secondary Cities and Urban Networking in the Indian Ocean Realm, c. 1000–1800* (Lanham, 2008), 55–97.

27. "*Ḥaḳ budur ki rū-yi zemīnde pādişāhlıḳ nāmı devletlü ḫündigāruñ ḥaḳḳıdur özgeniñ degüldür.*" Seydi Ali Reis, *Mir'ātü'l-Memālik*, 116.

28. See İsmail Hakkı Uzunçarşılı, "Hind Hükümdarı Hümayun Şah'ın Kanuni'ye Gönderdiği bir Mektup," *Yedigün* 8/202 (1937): 5–27.

29. On this question, see the letter of Gaspar and João Ribeiro, written from Venice August 27, 1564. *A.N.T.T. Corpo Cronológico*, part 1, maço 107, doc. 9.

30. On this point, see Casale, "His Majesty's Servant Lutfi," 57–59.

31. For the original document, see *T.S.M.A.* E. 8009; and for a detailed analysis, transcription, and full English translation, see Casale, "His Majesty's Servant Lutfi," 43– 81; see also Razaulhak Şah, "Açi Padişahı Sultan Alāeddin'in Kanuni Sultan Süleyman'a Mektubu," *Tarih Araştırmaları Dergisi* 5/8–9 (1967): 373–409; Lutfi is also mentioned in several documents from the *mühimme defterleri: MD* 7 #233, 86; #234, 87; and #236, 86.

32. See Alves, *Domínio do norte*, 166.

33. "*fizerão uma descortezia a hum embaixador do Turco que ali estava.*" *Documenta Indica* 7: 89.

34. On these events, see two letters from Lourenço Peres in *Documenta Indica* 7: 34 and 89.

35. These contacts are attested to in Lutfi's own ghostwritten report, discussed previously. See Casale, "His Majesty's Servant Lutfi," 64–67.

36. According to Diogo do Couto's summary of the letter: "*por esta amisade fui muytas vezes reprehendido dos Turcos, porque não fazia guerra aos Portugueses, tendo-me tantas vezes escandalizado.*" *DA*, dec. VIII, bk. 3, chap. 6.

37. "*Ḥālā murād olunan ṣulḥa muġāyir diyār-ı Hind'den deryā ṭarafi ile gelen ḥuccāc-ı müslimīne ve tüccāra daḫl ve tecāvüz olındugı istimā' olınur . . . fi'l- ḥaḳīḳa ol ṭaraflaruñ ṣulḥ ve ṣalāḥı murādıñuz ise deryā ṭaraflarından ḥuccāc ve tüccāra tecāvüzden el çeküp mektūbıñuzla i'timād olınur ādemleriñüz gönderile ki ol diyāruñ aḥvāl-i intiẓāmına müteferri' olan umūr ne ise muḳarrer ola ve eger ol cānibüñ iḫtilāline sālik olursan bi-ınāyeti'llāhi te'ālā bu cānibden muḳtežī olan umūr ne ise tedārük olınur. Soñra ṣulḥ murād olınmışdı dimek müfīd olmaz. Ziyāde ne dimek lāzımdur.*" *MD* 6 #355, 166.

38. Anthony Reid, "Islamization and Christianization in Southeast Asia: The Critical Phase 1550–1650," in Anthony Reid, ed., *Southeast Asia in the Early Modern Era: Trade, Power and Belief* (Ithaca, 1993), 165.
39. G. Bouchon, "Sixteenth-Century Malabar and the Indian Ocean," in Ashin das Gupta and Michael Pearson, eds., *India and the Indian Ocean 1500–1800* (Calcutta, 1987), 162–184.
40. *MD* 6 #256, 122; also *MD* 6 #257, 122; *MD* 6 #270, 128; and Imber, "Navy of Suleyman," 224.
41. "*Affirmão me levava em proposito meter a sacco toda a costa de Melinde e cheguar ainda a Moçambique com sperancas muito grandes d'encontrar alguma nao do Regno.*" *PM*, 8: 154.
42. "*Si crede da alcuni che essi siano andati verso il Capo de Buona Speranza per accordarsi forse con un Re in quei paesi, il quale ha guerra continua con il Re di Portogallo.*" Antonio Tiepolo to the Venetian Senate, Dec. 1, 1566, in Julieta Teixeira Marques de Oliveira, ed., *Fontes documentais de Veneza referentes a Portugal* (Lisbon, 1996), 21–22.
43. *PM*, 8: 152; see also Serjeant, *Hadrami Chronicles*, 110–11.
44. "*Era o ladrão ouzado e pratico naquellas partes sabia bem como e quando avia de armar suas redas. Não há homem destes que naquellas nossas partes possamos temer.*" *PM*, 8: 152.
45. See Furtado's report in *PM*, 8: 152; the nine galleys discussed later seem to have been supplied to them by Mahmud Pasha in Yemen, as in 1565 there were at least six galleys stationed in Mocha. See *MD* 5 #272, 118 and *MD* 6 #382, 177.
46. According to the Hadrami chonicles, a rendezvous with "the Jiddah trade fleet coming from the island of Aceh" was in fact a part of Sefer's original mission. Serjeant, *Hadrami Chronicles*, 110–11.
47. Casale, "His Majesty's Servant Lutfi," 65–66.
48. "*No Achem ficavão sinco galeões carregando de pimenta, drogas e outras fazendas pera partirem pera Meca e que se aprestavão nove gales pera irem em sua guarda.*" *DA*, dec. VIII, bk. 2, chap. 8; see also the report of Lourenço Peres from Malacca in *Documenta Indica*, 7: 34.
49. "*Os turcos... como são homens de guerra e ardilosos, não deixão cousa alguma às occasiões do tempo como nós.*" *DA*, dec. VIII, bk. 2, chap. 8.
50. *DA*, dec. VIII, bk. 2, chap. 8.
51. Casale, "His Majesty's Servant Lutfi," 51–53.
52. "*Ol Dergāh-ı mu'allāya ricā-yı vāsıḳumuz olur ki bu bendelerini sāyir pādişāhlar a'dādından saymayup kendü ḳullarından diyār-ı Mısır beglerbegisi ve yāḫūd Yemen beglerbegisi veya Cidde ve 'Aden begleri kulları a'dādından Pādişāh-ı 'ālem-penāh-ı ẓıll Allāh ḥażretlerinüñ eṭrāf-ı vilāyetlerinde ṣadaḳa yiyen ġarīb ve miskīn ve ḥazīn ḳulları a'dādından ma'dūd buyuralar... v'allahi'l-'aẓīm işbu Açī daḫī Pādişāh-ı 'ālem-penāh ḥażretlerinüñ köylerinden bir köydür bu bendeleri daḫī ḫizmetkārlarından ḫizmetkārım... Lutfi ḳulları cemī'-i aḥvālimüze ve ef'ālimüze ve ġazā uġruna cedd ü cehdümüze Pādişāh-ı 'ālem-penāh ḥażretlerinüñ ḫizemāt-ı şerīflerine i'tiḳādumuza ve iḫlāṣumuza şāhid ve vāḳıfdur.*" Casale, "His Majesty's Servant Lutfi," 76.
53. Casale, "His Majesty's Servant Lutfi," 79.
54. "*ol cezāyirüñ ahālisi... her cezīrelerinde cāmi'ler binā idüp Pādişāh-ı 'ālem-penāh zıll Allāh ḥażretlerinüñ mübārek ve 'ālī ism-i şerīflerine ḫuṭbe oḳuyup.*" Casale, "His Majesty's Servant Lutfi," 73.
55. "*Pādişāh-ı' ālem-penāh ḥażretlerinüñ mübārek ve 'ālī ism-i şerīflerine ḫuṭbe oḳuyup izdiyād-ı 'ömr ve devletleri içün Fātiḥa oḳurlar.*" Casale, "His Majesty's Servant Lutfi," 75.
56. "*Lutfī ḳulları bu cānibe vuṣūl bulduḳlarında Seylān ve Ḳālīḳūt pādişāhlarına ḫaber olundukda anlar bu cānibe elçiler gönderüp 'arż eylediler ki biz Pādişāh-ı 'ālem-penāh-ı ẓıll Allāh ḥażretlerinüñ ḫizmetkārlarından olup 'ahd ve mīsāḳları olundı kim inşallāhü'l-'aliyyi'l-'alā Pādişāh-ı'ālem-penāh ḥażretlerinüñ mübārek donānma-yı hümāyūnları bu diyārlara*

ʿubūr bulduḳlarında kendüleri imāna gelüp şehādet getüreler ve kendü vilāyetlerinde olan küffār reʿāyāları daḫī cemiʿā imāna getürüp dīn-i bāṭıldan dīn-i ḥaḳḳā ṭoğrı yola giderler. Inşallāhüʾlʿaliyyi Pādişāh-ıʿālem-penāḥ ḥażretlerinüñ ʿulyā himmetleri ile maşraḳdan mağribe degin cümle-i küffar āsārları maḥv olup İslām dīnine gireler." Casale, "His Majesty's Servant Lutfi," 75–76.

57. *MD* 7 #474, 146; #481, 179; #571, 208; #597, 218; #610, 219.
58. *MD* 7 #236, 88, #586, 213.
59. *MD* 7 #234, 87.
60. *MD* 7 #887, 311.
61. *MD* 7 #234, 87.
62. "*Siz daḫī dīn bābında ve devlet-i hümāyūnumuza müteʿalliḳ olan umūrda bezl-i maḳdūr eyleyüp küffār-ı ḫāḳsāruñ eger ḳalʿaların fetḥ itmekde eger ehl-i İslām üzerlerinden şerr u şūrların defʿ itmekde saʿy ve iḳdām eyleyüp ʿināyet-i ḥaḳḳ celle ve āʿlā ile ol diyārı televvüsāt-ı küfürden taṭhīr ve pāk eyleyesiz ki eyyām-ı saʿādet-encām-ı ḫüsrevānemüzde ol diyāruñ ehl-i İslāmı daḫī āsūde-ḥāl olup ferāġ-ı bāl ile kār ve kisblerine meşġūl olalar.*" *MD* 7 #244, 93; an abbreviated version of this letter is in *MD* 7 #233, 86.
63. "*Inşāʾallāhüʾl-ʿassüʾl-ekrem ol cāniblerde daḫī memālik-i İslāmiyyeʾye daḫī müstevlī olan aʿdā-yı dīn-i mübīn ve düşmenān-ı āyīn-i seyyidüʾl-mürselīnüñ ʿaleyhiʾṣ-ṣalātüʾs-selām defʿ-ı mażarrāt u delāletleri içün ʿasākir-i cerrār-ı nuṣret-şiʿārımuzdan dāyimā ol cānibe irsāl olunur. Her zamānda ḳāʿide-i müstemirreñüz üzerine meʾmūldür ki ol diyāruñ aḥvāl ve mācerāsı mufaṣṣal ve meşrūḥ ʿatebe-i ʿālem-penāhımuz cānibine inbā olunmaḳdan ḫālī olunmaya.*" *MD* 7 #244, 93.
64. See Richard Blackburn, "The Collapse of Ottoman Authority in Yemen 968/1560–976/1568," *Die Welt des Islams*, n.s. 19/1–4 (1980): 120–27. For a rescript complaining that Sultan Badr of Shihr was collaborating with the Portuguese, see *MD* 5 #1699, 612.
65. For a ferman to Hussein, the ambassador from Aceh, explaining this decision, see *MD* 7 #708, 255; also for orders to the governors of Egypt and Yemen and Kurdoğlu Hizir, see *MD* 7 #611, 220; #614, 224; and #616, 224; more generally, see Caesar Farah, "Organizing for the 2nd Conquest of Yemen," *X. Türk Tarih Kongresi, Ankara 22–26 Eylül, 1986* (Ankara, 1993), 6: 1150–59.
66. Blackburn, "Collapse of Ottoman Authority," 123; also Blackburn, "Two Documents," 229.
67. For the provincial budgets of Yemen from these years, see Özbaran, "Note on Ottoman Arabia," 95–98; see also Blackburn, "Collapse of Ottoman Authority," 124–27.
68. On Mahmud's promotion to governor of Egypt, see Selānikī Mustafa Efendi, *Tārīḫ-i Selānikī* (Istanbul, 1989), 1: 13; Kutbeddin Mekki, *Aḫbār al-Yemānī*, fols. 59a–61a.
69. Blackburn, "Collapse of Ottoman Authority," 124–26; Kutbeddin Mekki, *Aḫbār al-Yemānī*, fols. 61a–62a.
70. Selānikī, *Tārīḫ-i Selānikī*, 1: 13; Mekki, *Aḫbār al-Yemānī*, fols. 62a–66b.
71. Blackburn, "Collapse of Ottoman Authority," 123; Farah, "Organizing for the 2nd Conquest," 1159; Kutbeddin Mekki, *Aḫbār al-Yemānī*, fol. 67.
72. See Blackburn, "Collapse of Ottoman Authority," and Farah, "Organizing for the 2nd Conquest," for detailed accounts of these events; the campaign is also treated at length by Kuttbeddin Mekki in *Aḫbār al-Yemānī*, and is the subject of more than one work commissioned by Sinan Pasha to glorify his own role in reconquering the province, most notably Rumuzi's *Tārīḫ-i Fetḥ-i Yemen*. See Hulusi Yavuz, ed., *Yemen'de Osmanlı İdaresi ve Rumuzi Tarihi* (Ankara, 2002).

73. *DA*, dec. VIII, bk. 3, chap. 6; Reid, "Turkish Influence," 406; C. R. Boxer, "A Note on Portuguese Reactions to the Revival of the Red Sea Spice Trade and the Rise of Atjeh 1540–1600," *Journal of South East Asian History* 10/3 (Dec. 1969): 421.
74. Mustafa was also to retrieve the artillery left behind in Gujarat by Seydi Ali Reis in 1554. See *MD* 7 #616, 224.
75. For a description of this agreement between the Ottomans and the Sultan of Aceh, see the letter of Joán Baptista de Ribera from Macau in October 1568, in *Documenta Indica* 7: 514; see also *DA*, dec. VIII, bk. 3, chap. 6; on the later career of the Acehnese ambassador Hussein, see *DA*, dec. VIII, bk. 3, chap. 7.
76. See the letter of Lourenço Peres from Malacca, Dec. 3, 1568, in *Documenta Indica* 7: 519; see also P.-Y. Manguin, "Of Fortresses and Galleys: The 1568 Acehnese Siege of Melaka, after a Contemporary Bird's-eye View," *Modern Asian Studies* 22 (1988): 607–28.
77. Bouchon, "Sixteenth-Century Malabar," 179.
78. *Documenta Indica*, 7: 156–57; on the Ottoman mercenaries serving with Nizam al-Mulk's forces in this siege, see *FS*, 4: 98.
79. Reid, "Turkish Influence," 406.
80. Bouchon, "Sixteenth-Century Malabar," 179.
81. *MD* 7 #721, 258.
82. *MD* 7 #667, 240; see also Faroqhi, *Pilgrims and Sultans*, 139–42.
83. *MD* 7 #667, 240; *MD* 7 #671, 241; *MD* 7 #2228, 812; *MD* 7 #2723, 985.
84. See Halil Inalcik, "The Origins of the Ottoman-Russian Rivalry and the Don-Volga Canal 1569," *Les Annales de l'Université d'Ankara* 1 (1946–47): 47–106; and A. Kurat, "The Turkish Expedition to Astrakhan and the Problem of the Don-Volga Canal," *Slavonic and East European Review* 40 (Dec. 1961): 7–23.
85. See the letter to D. Francisco da Costa from Cochin, Jan. 10, 1569, in Alves, *Domínio do norte*, 273; see also a contemporary report from the Archbishop of Goa in Joseph Wicki, "Duas relações sobra a situação da Índia Portuguesa nos anos 1568 e 1569," *Studia* 8 (July 1961): 208–9.
86. On the embassy of Jacomo d'Olivares, see Tavim, "Outras gentes," 325–26.
87. See Hess, *The Forgotten Frontier: A History of the Sixteenth-Century Ibero-African Frontier* (Chicago, 1978), 87–89.
88. A. Temimi, "Le gouvernement ottoman face au problème morisque," *Revue d'Histoire Maghrébine* 23–24 (1989): 258–62; Hess, *Forgotten Frontier*, 89.
89. The text of this letter is preserved in the *Mekātib-i Ḫulefā ve Ṣelāṭīn, T.S.M.K.* R.1959, fols. 820b–821b.
90. Özbaran, "Basra Körfezi," 63.
91. Francisco de Monclaro, from Moçambique, Aug. 1, 1570, in *Documenta Indica* 8: 294.
92. For a technical analysis of this battle, see Guilmartin, *Gunpowder and Galleys*, 236–64.
93. Veinstein, "Sokollu Mehmed," 709.
94. Lesure, "Notes et documents," 138–50.
95. MD 22 #631, 317; #636, 320; #638, 322; MD 23 #426, 201; and Özbaran, "Basra Körfezi," 63.
96. On Hormuz, see MD 22 #631, 317–18; #636, 320–21; #639, 322. The letters to Spain and Aceh are preserved in the *Mekātib-i Ḫulefā ve Selāṭīn, T.S.M.K.* R.1959. Spain is on fols. 824a–825b, and Aceh on fols. 881a–883b.
97. Andrew Hess, "The Moriscos, an Ottoman Fifth Column in Sixteenth-Century Spain," *American Historical Review* 74/1 (1968): 20.

98. Instructions were also sent to Egypt that two galleys should be forwarded to Mocha, considered to be under threat of Portuguese attack following the successful raid of Bahrain. See MD 23 #134, 46.
99. MD 24 #913, 397; MD 27 #433, 190; see also *DA*, dec. VIII, bk. 5, chap. 4.
100. Özbaran, "Basra Körfezi," 63; for an in-depth study of the administration of the Ottoman province of Lahsa, bordering on Bahrain, see Mandaville's "Ottoman Province of Al-Hasâ," 486–513.
101. Veinstein, "Sokollu Mehmed," 710.
102. MD 32 #151, 72; #155, 75; #156, 75.
103. MD 34 #454, 216.
104. On relations with Elizabethan England, see İsmail Hakkı Uzunçarşılı, "Türk-İngiliz Münasebetlerine Dair Vesikalar," *Belleten* 14 (1950): 27–40; on negotiations with the Habsburgs, see Chantal de la Veronne, "Giovanni Margliani et la trève de 1580 entre l'Espagne et la Turquie," *Arab Historical Review for Ottoman Studies* 3–4 (Dec. 1991): 70–75; on negotiations with Ethiopia, see the letter of Gomez Vaz from Goa, Oct. 20, 1579, in *Documenta Indica*, 11: 282.
105. On Sokollu's dealings with the Horn of Africa, see the letter of Ruy Vicente from Goa, Nov. 13, 1579, in *Documenta Indica*, 11: 704.
106. On Ottoman-Borno relations, see Cengiz Orhonlu, "Osmanlı-Borno Münasebetine Ait Belgeler," *Tarih Dergisi* 23 (March 1969): 111–31.
107. For Mocha, see MD 10 #437, 437; for Suakin, MD 33 #83, 39; for Lahsa, MD 31 #708, 319; and MD 16 #599, 318–19; and on Basra's gun foundry, MD 21 #611, 254; and MD 27 #206, 510.
108. For Basra, MD 26 #144, 55; for Lahsa, MD 16 #207, 105–6.
109. MD 33 #85, 24; also Orhonlu, *Habeş Eyaleti*, 50–61.
110. MD 27 #190, 75; see also Mandaville, "Ottoman Province of Al-Hasâ," 490. Sokollu's private endowments along the hajj route, particularly in Aleppo and the holy cities of Mecca and Medina, were also substantial. See Necipoğlu, *Age of Sinan*, 345–48.
111. "*Müşārün-ileyh mektūb gönderüp bu bendeleri Yemen'de iken vilāyet-i mezbūre maḥṣūlinden Muṣṭafā ile Mıṣır'a ḳırḳ* [*dört*] *kīselik bahār irsāl olunup meẕkūr ẕikr olunan bahārı satup ḳırḳ dört kīselik bahārdan Meḥmed Paşa içün sekiz yüz altun alup Āsitāneye irsāl idüp bāḳīsi üzerinde iken Vilāyet-i Yemen'de tüfengciler aġalıḳ ṣadaḳa olunup*." MD 2 #1243, 124.
112. Interestingly, a slightly later entry in a *mühimme* register from the mid-1560s records another example of Sokollu's creative use of the market in combination with his own trading concerns. On this occasion, to fund one of his several pious endowments in Mecca (which included a public bath, a hospital, and a lunatic asylum), he had one of his own ships sold, and then obtained a promise from the sultan that the provincial treasury of Egypt would lend him enough money to make up the difference in the necessary funds to a total of ten thousand gold pieces. See Faroqhi, *Pilgrims and Sultans*, 106–7.
113. Veinstein, "Sokollu Mehmed," 707.
114. For a more detailed discussion of this market mechanism, although with an interpretation that differs somewhat from the argument presented here, see Casale, "Ottoman Administration of the Spice Trade," 170–98.
115. For these figures, see İsmail Hakkı Uzunçarşılı, *Osmanlı Devletinde Merkez ve Bahriye Teşkilâtı* (Ankara, 1948), 354, note 2; By the seventeenth century, there was also an "Egyptian *kīse*" [*kīse-i Mıṣrī*] worth half as much (in silver) as the "Anatolian *kīse*" [*kīse-i Rūmī*]. On these

measures, on conversion rates between silver and gold in the sixteenth century, and for a more general discussion of the problems of working with currencies in Ottoman Egypt, see Şevket Pamuk, *A Monetary History of the Ottoman Empire* (Cambridge, 2000), 95–99.

116. If *kīselik* does in fact refer here to a monetary unit rather than to a quantity of spices, it is possible that the discrepancy between the two figures given in the document (forty *kīselik* in the first instance and forty-four in the second) indicates the difference between the original value of the spices in Yemen and their market rate at the final point of sale in Egypt (rather than resulting from a simple copyist error, as I have suggested in my translation). This would indicate that the price differential between Yemen and Egypt was only 10 percent, which for reasons discussed later in this chapter seems far too low. But if we take the figure of 20,000 *akçes* per *kīse* and work through the numbers, a profit of 4 *kīses*, or 80,000 silver *akçes*, calculates to around 1,300 gold pieces, which seems in line with the "800 gold pieces" for Mehmed Pasha and the unspecified amount for the chief musketeer mentioned in our document.

117. According to a provincial budget from Yemen in 1561, Yemen's *irsāliye* or provincial surplus in that year was 2,028,000 *paras* out of a total of 24,955,164 (one *para* being equivalent to 1.5 *akçes*). Özbaran, *Ottoman Response*, 36. A fragmentary *mühimme* document from this same period confirms that the practice of sending the province's surplus in spices was started by Mahmud Pasha. MD 5 #1702, 613; see also Blackburn, "Collapse of Ottoman Authority," 132.

118. This system was described in the *mühimme defterleri* after the Sharif of Mecca tried to illegally collect transit fees from the allotted spices of Ottoman officials. See MD 3 #1493, 502; #1499, 502.

119. MD 6 #707, 336; #710, 337; and Blackburn, "Collapse of Ottoman Authority," 133.

120. "*Nell'arsenale si fabbricano anche le navi mercantili per conto del sultano, che ne ha il monopolio. In quel mare infatti non è permesso ad alcuno aver navi proprie o noleggiarle da privati, ma tutte le navi sono del sultano, o pagano gran parte del nolo del sultano, sicchè il mar rosso per le navi e le gabelle rende assai al Gran Signore; anzi da qualche tempo se ne recava già tanto da supplire alle spese che si fanno per l'Jemen.*" Alberto Magnaghi, ed., "Il Golfo di Suez e il Mar Rosso in una relazione inedita de Filippo Pigafetta (1567–77)," *Bolletino della società geografica italiana* 11, part 1, and 47, part 1 (1910): 303–4.

121. MD 27 #75, 26.

122. MD 33 #633, 306; #437, 214.

123. MD 26 #780, 272; MD 27 #75, 26; MD 31 #131, 51; MD 33 #338, 169; MD 35 # 750, 296; MD 39 #109, 47; #110, 47; #506, 259.

124. MD 33 #755, 369; MD 35 # 197, 81; MD 36 #691, 323; This practice should not be confused with the small quantity of spices sent annually from Egypt (along with other foodstuffs) for the imperial kitchens, which were always kept separate from the state spices sold for profit. See Casale, "Ottoman Administration of the Spice Trade," 184.

125. MD 27 #164, 263.

126. On budget deficits in Yemen, see Özbaran, *Sınırdaki Osmanlı*, 212–15, 236–37.

127. For a detailed description of this arrangement, see MD 7 #370, 144; also *Gavetas*, 15, 2–5.

128. For contemporary accounts of travel along this route, see the letter of Francisco Pasio in *Documenta Indica*, 11: 365; and also the account of Ralph Fitch in Richard Hakluyt, *Voyages* (London, 1907), 3: 281–300.

129. See Cengiz Orhonlu, *Osmanlı İmparatorluğunda Şehircilik ve Ulaşım Üzerine Araştırmalar* (Izmir, 1984), 121–23.

130. The tax on spices in Basra was accordingly reduced to just over 7 percent from a previous rate of 10.5 percent, and the tax on luxury goods was reduced to 5 percent from 6.67 percent. See Mantran, "Règlements fiscaux ottomans," 227.
131. Anthony Disney, "The Gulf Route from India to Portugal in the Sixteenth and Seventeenth Centuries: Couriers, Traders and Image Makers," in Thomaz and Matos, *Carreira da Índia*, 535–37.
132. Casale, "Ottoman Administration of the Spice Trade," 185–90.
133. MD 27 #271, 115; for a broader discussion of this restriction, see Faroqhi, *Pilgrims and Sultans*, 135–37.
134. See, for example, the arguments of Subrahmanyam in "Trading World," based in part on research by C. H. H. Wake, "The Changing Pattern of Europe's Pepper and Spice Imports ca. 1400–1700," *Journal of European Economic and Social History*, 8/2 (1979): 362–63.
135. Although precise figures are lacking, total taxes and fees along the Red Sea route must have well exceeded 50 percent and may have been as high as 100 percent. Casale, "Ottoman Administration of the Spice Trade," 188. Along the Persian Gulf route from Basra to Aleppo (not including considerable Portuguese levies in Hormuz), total taxes on spices were just over 42 percent before 1575 and 38 percent after 1575. See Potach, "Commercial Relations," 151.
136. See the letter of Nicolo Pietro Cochino from Rome, Oct. 29, 1563, in *Gavetas*, 20, 14–17.
137. "*Ṣamadī demekle maʿrūf meşhūr ve ʿaẓīm ve büyük gemi bu diyārdan on altı ḳanṭar fülfül ve ibrişīm ve dārçīn ve ḳaranfīl ve ḥiṣālben ve sāyir Taḥta'r-rīh metāʿlarından yüklenüp.*" Casale, "His Majesty's Servant Lutfi," 74.
138. "*Nice cevāhir ve altun ve gümüş ve maʿādenleri bi-ḥesāb bulunur. Bunca zamāndan berü küffār-ı ḫāksārlara naṣīb olunur. İnşāʾallahu'l-ḳadīr anlar Pādişāh-ı ʿalem-penāh ḥażretlerinüñ ʿasākir-i mücāhidīn ve ġuzzāt-ı muvāḥḥidīn ḳullarına naṣīb ve ḳısmet olacaḳdur.*" Casale, "His Majesty's Servant Lutfi," 76.
139. "*ve barçalar, ol cevānibde bahār vardur anı taḥmīl idüp getüreler.*" MD 7 #234, 87.
140. *DA*, dec. VIII, bk. 3, chap. 6. Similarly, see Cristóvão da Costa's letter from Malacca, Dec. 6, 1568, in *Documenta Indica* 7: 530.
141. Lombard, *Sultanat d'Atjeh*, 118; see also Inalcik, *Economic and Social History*, 347.
142. "*bahā-yi ḥilāṭhā berāy-i naḫūda ki ʿan cānib-i Hind āmedend ve ilā bender-i Muḫa ezān sebeb ki ʿan māl-ı pādişāhī sa'y-i belīġ kerdend.*" Halil Sahillioğlu, "Yemen'in 1599–1600 Yılı Bütçesi," in *Yusuf Hikmet Bayur'a Armağan* (Ankara, 1985), 318.
143. Anthony Reid, "Islamization and Christianization," 156.
144. "*E terá o dito rei mais de cem peças grossas de artelharia de metal e assi tem mais algumas grossas de ferro, e de artelharia mea terā duzentas pessas, e de meuda terā perto de quatrocentas, e tem grande número de espingardas, porque todos os anos lhe vem de Mequa como acima fica dito e tem muita pólvera feita, e boa, e grande soma de pelouros de toda a sorte.*" João Ribeiro Gaio, *Roteiro das cousas do Achem: um olhar português sobre o norte de Sumatra em finais do século XVI*, ed. Jorge Manuel dos Santos and Pierre-Yves Manguin (Lisbon, 1997), 97.
145. MD 7 #370, 144.
146. Couto (Cruz edition of eighth decade), 201; for an English translation of the letter sent from Sultan Suleiman to Portugal, see Özbaran, "Turks in the Persian Gulf," 82–84.
147. Imber, "Suleyman as Caliph," 179–84; more generally, see Imber's *Ebu's-Su'ud: The Islamic Legal Tradition* (Palo Alto, 1997), 74

148. See Reid, "Islamization and Christianization," 155–76; and Pearson, *Pilgrimage to Mecca*, 62–74. The late-sixteenth-century text *Tohfut ul-Mujahideen* by Zeinu'd-din, glorifying jihad at sea against the Portuguese infidels, is an example of a Muslim ideological treatise composed in this milieu.
149. For a recent anthropological study of this process, see Engseng Ho, *The Graves of Tarim: Genealogy and Mobility across the Indian Ocean* (Berkeley, 2006).
150. Reid, "Islamization and Christianization," 162; also Alves, *Domínio do norte*, 223.
151. *"Mıṣır Beglerbegisine ḥükm ki Vilāyet-i Hind'e tābi' Bender-i Ḳālīḳūt'da yigirmi yedi şehirde vāḳi' cevāmi'de olan ḫutbeye ḳadīmden yüz altun irsāl olunduḳdan soñra Cidde'den elli altun gönderilüp gelüp ba'żı yıllarda ol daḫī irsāl olunmaduġı i'lām olunmaġın... bu ḫuṣūṣa muḳayyed olup emrüm mūcebince her seneye müstemirr[an] yüz filūrī Bender-i Cidde'den ẕikr olunan ḫutebāya bi-ḳuṣūr irsāl itdürüp şimdiye degin ḳalmış vaẓifeleri daḫī var ise bi't-tamām Cidde maḥṣūlātından gönderesin."* *MD* 28 #331, 139.
152. See, for example, the arguments of Subrahmanyam in "Trading World" and "Matter of Alignment"; see also Alves, *Domínio do norte*, 166–68.
153. The term was coined by the political scientist Joseph Nye in *Bound to Lead: The Changing Nature of American Power* (New York, 1990), a work devoted to the analysis of American power in the late twentieth century.
154. *"O intento dos Turcos não he sò este das drogas; mais adiante passa que he pretenderem faserem-se senhores de todos os estados da India... e incita-los a se levantarem contra todas as fortalezas... e então lhe ficaria a elles a negoceação de todas as drogas pera ambos os estreitos que lhe nós temos defesos. E assi ficaria o Turco senhor de tudo sem despezas de armadas, sem gastos de fortalezas... de maniera que ainda que os turcos não mettessem mais cabedal elles sos bastariam pera nos deitarem fora e se fazerem senhores da India."* Couto (Cruz edition of eighth decade), 209–11.

NOTES TO CHAPTER 6

1. Orhonlu, *Habeş Eyaleti*, 61.
2. In the decade following Ala 'ad-din Ri'ayat Syah's death, six different sultans would accede to the throne of Aceh. Alves, *Domínio do norte*, 176.
3. Veinstein, "Sokollu Mehmed," 711.
4. On Ottoman-Moroccan relations in the late sixteenth century, see El Moudden, "Sharifs and Padishahs," 58–156; see also Richard Smith, *Ahmad al-Mansur: Islamic Visionary* (New York, 2005).
5. See Geoffrey Parker, *The Grand Strategy of Philip II* (New Haven, 1998), 167–69.
6. Farooqi, *Mughal-Ottoman Relations*, 114–16.
7. Farooqi, *Mughal-Ottoman Relations*, 18–21.
8. For an overview of these events, see Guillot and Kalus, "Inscriptions Islamiques," 85–87.
9. On religion under Akbar, see John F. Richards, *The New Cambridge History of India: The Mughal Empire* (New York, 1993), 34–40.
10. Subrahmanyam, "Matter of Alignment," 467.
11. Farooqi, *Mughal-Ottoman Relations*, 190–92.
12. See Naimur Rahman Farooqi, "Six Ottoman Documents on Mughal-Ottoman Relations during the Reign of Akbar," *Journal of Islamic Studies* 7/1 (1996): 32–48.

13. On events related to this protracted conflict, see Bekir Kütükoğlu, *Osmanlı-İran Siyasi Münasebetleri* (Istanbul, 1962).
14. "*il detto signor Maometto Pascia rispuose et promisse che non mandrianno l'armata del Gran Signore a danni del detto re di Portogallo per il mare biancho ne per la parte del estreto de Gibilterra, ma per la parte del mare rosso, che Iddio sa quello sara.*" Quoted in Chantal de la Veronne, "Giovanni Margliani et la trève de 1580 entre l'Espagne et la Turquie," *Arab Historical Review for Ottoman Studies* 3–4 (Dec. 1991): 72–73.
15. See the letter of Ruy Vicente from Goa, Nov. 13, 1579, in *Documenta Indica*, 11: 704.
16. For a general overview of this period of crisis, see Suraiya Faroqhi's "Crisis and Change 1590–1699," in Inalcik and Quataert, *Economic and Social History*, 2: 411–623.
17. Hanna, *Making Big Money*, 107.
18. See Jean Sauvaget, "Les caravansérails syriens du hadjdj de Constantinople," *Ars Islamica* 4 (1937): 98–121; Hanna, *Making Big Money*, 34.
19. Pigafetta, *Relazione*, 304.
20. Pigafetta, *Relazione*, 299.
21. Safvet Bey, "Ḳara Deñiz-İzmit Körfezi Ḳānāli," *Tārīḫ-i ʿOs̱mānī Encümeni Mecmūʿası*, 13–8 (A.H.1328/A.D.1909), 948–56.
22. For a general discussion of Koja Sinan's politically motivated artistic patronage, see Emine Fetvacı, "Viziers to Eunuchs," 140–202.
23. This is the title of the original Arabic-language version of the text, later translated into Ottoman Turkish under the title *Aḫbār al-Yemānī fi'l-Fetḥi'l-ʿOs̱mānī* (a primary source for the present work). For an English translation of the section relating Koja Sinan's campaign in Yemen, see Clive Smith, *Lightning over Yemen: A History of the Ottoman Campaign of 1569–71* (London, 2002).
24. The original manuscript of Rumuzi's *Tārīḫ-i Fetḥ-i Yemen* is in the library of Istanbul University, T.Y. 6045.
25. On the rising importance of private households in Ottoman politics, see Metin Kunt, *The Sultan's Servants: Transformation of Ottoman Provincial Government, 1550–1650* (New York, 1983).
26. Orhonlu, *Habeş Eyaleti*, 61–63.
37. Forty thousand gold pieces and eleven hundred troops were dispatched from Egypt for this purpose. *MD* 43 #339, 186.
28. Orhonlu, *Habeş Eyaleti*, 63.
29. For accounts of this assault, see *DA*, dec. X, bk. 1, chap. 11; *FS*, 4: 204; and Serjeant, *Hadrami Chronicles*, 111; a document in the Ottoman archives also makes reference to the incident, *MD* 35 #743, 293.
30. "*Quasi num abrir e fechar de olhos entrou arrebetado e saiu rico.*" *FS*, 4: 204.
31. "*des Indes orientales, du Royaume d'Ormuz, isles et ports du levant despendans du Royaume de Portugal, à venir trafiquer aux ports et échelles de sa Hautesse, en Egypte et Sorie, leur offrant tout bon traitement et accueil où il consentiraient*," dispatch of Sept. 30, 1581, quoted in F. Charles-Roux, "L'isthme de Suez et les rivalités européennes au XVIe siècle," *Revue de l'histoire des colonies françaises* (1924): 173.
32. Farooqi, *Mughal-Ottoman Relations*, 21.
33. Father Monserrate, *The Commentary of Father Monserrate on His Journey to the Court of Akbar*, trans. J. S. Hoyland and S. N. Banerjee (Calcutta, 1922), 205.

34. The fleet failed to capture any ships and returned to Hormuz empty-handed. *DA*, dec. X, bk. 2, chap. 10.
35. Pearson, *Merchants and Rulers*, 57.
36. Pearson, *Merchants and Rulers*, 57–58.
37. The principal contribution of these Ottoman mercenaries to this siege was to construct a kind of floating mine from bales of cotton stuffed with gunpowder, meant to be towed upstream from the Portuguese galleons, released, and set ablaze. Only last-minute heroics by a certain Bartholomeu Fernandes managed to save the Portuguese ships from certain disaster. *DA*, dec. X, bk. 3, chap. 3.
38. Charles-Roux, "Isthme de Suez," 172.
39. For a modern translation and critical analysis of this text, see Thomas Goodrich, *The Ottoman Turks and the New World: A Study of Tarih-i Hind-i Garbi and Sixteenth-Century Ottoman Americana* (Wiesbaden, 1990).
40. The text is commonly attributed to Hasan al-Su'udi, but according to Goodrich, al-Su'udi was probably only the scribe who prepared the 1583 illuminated copy presented to Sultan Murad III. Goodrich proposes 1580 or 1581 as the most likely date of composition. See Goodrich, *Ottoman Turks and the New World*, 19.
41. Goodrich, *Ottoman Turks and the New World*, 86.
42. See Aydın Sayılı, *The Observatory in Islam and Its Place in the General History of the Observatory* (Ankara, 1988), 292.
43. Goodrich, *Ottoman Turks and the New World*, 19.
44. Goodrich, *Ottoman Turks and the New World*, 100.
45. On Portugal's relations with the Swahili Coast, see Michael Pearson, *Port Cities and Intruders: The Swahili Coast, India and Portugal in the Early Modern Era* (Baltimore, 1998).
46. On the resources available to the Ottomans on the Swahili Coast, see *DA*, dec. X, bk. 7, chaps. 8–9.
47. For contemporary Portuguese warnings about the threat to Mozambique, see the letter of Francesco Pasio from Goa, Nov. 30, 1578, *Documenta Indica*, 11: 341; and a similar warning from 1582 in *DA*, dec. X, bk. 5, chap. 2.
48. "*İspanya-yı la'īn Hindistān vilāyetlerinde ḳal'eleri żabt idüp deryāya gemiler çiḳarur ise Yemen ve Ḥabeş ve Ḥicāz cāniblerinden Süveyş'e varınca bendelerüñ cümlesinde bir muḥkem ḳal'e olmayup.*" *MD* 48 #977, 333.
49. For the ferman requisitioning two galleots for Yemen, see *MD* 49 #86, 23.
50. No contemporary Ottoman documents mention Mir Ali's expedition to East Africa, but Portuguese documents record his arrival in the Swahili Coast in early 1586.
51. The most important sources for the Mir Ali expedition are the early seventeenth-century chronicle of João dos Santos, *Etiópia Oriental*, ed. Luís de Albuquerque (Lisbon, 1989); and Couto's *Da Ásia*. The later chronicle of Faria e Sousa is based for the most part on these earlier sources; the account presented here is based on a combination of these sources. For a modern reconstruction of events, see also Charles Boxer and Carlos de Azevedo's *Fort Jesus and the Portuguese in Mombasa 1593–1729* (London, 1960), 16–23.
52. "*... lançar os Portuguezes fóra dalli, e ainda de Moçambique e das Minas de Cuamá.*" *DA*, dec. X, bk. 7, chap. 8.
53. "*Tanto pode ou o calor, ou a sorte de um só homem! Tal era o mouro Mir Alibet que, tido por vivaz, atrevido e arrebatado... tudo isto foi obrado menos com a armada que trazia do que com a que proclamava trazer.*" *FS*, 5: 64–66.

54. "*Encendo-se de ouro, ambar, marfim, e escravos em que gastou até todo Abril, e tratou com todos aquelles reys que mandassem offerecer vassallagem ao Turco, o que os demais delles fizeram.*" *DA*, dec. X, bk. 7, chap. 16.
55. Pearson, *Merchants and Rulers*, 60.
56. For a detailed account of the mission, see *DA*, dec. X, bk. 7, chaps. 15–16.
57. "*com velames, bandeiras e sinaies de luto, entrou com todos os adornos de um exécito.*" *FS*, 5: 178.
58. "*Sabei que assim como não póde vir a Índia armada de Turcos que se não perça, assim não pode ir nenhuma nossa ao estreito de Meca que não tenha o mesmo fim*" *DA*, dec. X, bk. 7, chap. 16.
59. "*Não fizestes mais com esta vinda que acordar o cão que está dormindo!*" *DA*, dec. X, bk. 7, chap. 17.
60. Charles-Roux, "Isthme de Suez," 174.
61. On the conflicting accounts of Ibrahim Pasha and Hazinedar Sinan, see *DA*, dec. X, bk. 7, chap. 17.
62. For the text of this report, see Selaniki, *Tārīḫ-i Selānikī*, 1: 171.
63. For the two pashas' reports of this incident, see *MD* 61 #239, 99 and #240, 99–100; the Portuguese captives were subsequently handed over to the custody of Kilich Ali Pasha, who also seems to have been an accomplice in this affair. See Selaniki, *Tārīḫ-i Selānikī*, 1: 185.
64. *MD* 61, #107, 40.
65. The report is dated July 23, 1586. See *Calendar of State Papers*, vol. 8, doc. 385.
66. *Calendar of State Papers*, vol. 8, doc. 385.
67. "The Bey of Jemen is here and has received, among other orders, instructions to make a survey of the ancient Suez canal." *Calendar of State Papers*, vol. 8, doc. 385.
68. On Kilich Ali's previous machinations in the western Mediterranean, see Hess, *Forgotten Frontier*, 101.
69. "*Le beau dessein leur a déjà tellement enflé leur vanité accoutumée, et attisé leur ambition et avarice, qu'il leur semble qu'ils ont déjà les trésors et pierreries de l'Inde, et qu'ils ont mis dans un rets le Perzien; il ne mettent en aucun compte l'Espagnol, car ils disent qu'ils n'y a que 4,000 hommes. A la vérité, si leur désir et espérance réunissait à faire ce canal, y mettant deux cent galères armées, qu'ils disent, ayant l'Arabie comme ils ont et y tournant la tête sans être empêchés d'ailleurs, ils fermeront la porte à Lisbonne et Espagne de ce côté, et seront pour agrandir et enrichir grandement cet empire.*" Charles-Roux, "Isthme de Suez," 176–77.
70. *Calendar of State Papers*, vol. 8, doc. 409, Sept. 17, 1586.
71. See Charles-Roux, "Isthme de Suez," 179.
72. *MD* 62 #304, 137.
73. *MD* 62 #393, 177.
74. *MD* 62 #457, 205.
75. Farooqi, *Mughal-Ottoman Relations*, 22.
76. Farooqi, *Mughal-Ottoman Relations*, 116.
77. Farooqi, *Mughal-Ottoman Relations*, 149.
78. *MD* 62 #393, 177; *MD* 62 #457, 205.
79. *MD* 62 #457, 205; for a full translation of this document, see Farooqi, "Six Ottoman Documents," 43–44.
80. "*Como nesas partes ha tantas cousas a que acudir, sempre será mas necessario tratarse de conservar o ganhado que de procurar novas ympresas atento que a guerra ofemsiva tem muytos ymcomvenientes, como se vio na armada em que mandastes por capitão mór Ruy Gonçalves da Camara ao Estreito, que alem de não ter os bons efeitos e socesos que se esperavão, não servio mays esta tão*

grande e ymfrutuosa despesa que de espertar os turcos ... com tanto discredito deste estado." *APO*, fasc. 3, 120.

81. Parker, *Grand Strategy*, 179–207.
82. "*O que faria total destruição da Índia ... porque dalli se haviam logo de fazer senhores da mina de Cuamá, e Sofala, e ainda da fortaleza de Moçambique, onde podiam esperar as náos do Reyno e tomallas.*" *DA*, dec. X, bk. 9, chap. 2.
83. *DA*, dec. X, bk. 8, chap. 10.
84. This unfortunate and nameless individual was wounded in combat and handed over to local custody by Mir Ali to give him a chance to convalesce. Instead, the locals had tormented him with demands that he abandon Christianity, and when he refused, they tortured and finally killed him. *DA*, dec. X, bk. 9, chap. 1.
85. *DA*, dec. X, bk. 9, chap. 1.
86. See Philip II's letter to this effect in *APO*, fasc. 3, 146.
87. See Philip II's letter to the viceroy, dated March 29, *APO*, fasc. 3, 293.
88. *DA*, dec. X, bk. 9, chap. 2.
89. "*pera os vingar das affrontas, perdas e mortes que tinham recebido dos Portugueses, e lançallos pera sempre daquellas terras.*" *DA*, dec. 11, chap. 26.
90. *MD* 64, #499, 195.
91. There is no indication that Hasan ever informed Uveys Pasha or the sultan in Istanbul of his plans. His last dispatch before Mir Ali's departure reported only that "there has not yet been any sign of the ships of the miserable infidels." [*küffār-i ḫāksār gemilerinden nām u nişān olmaduğın bildirüp*], *MD* 64 #499, 195.
92. Virtually the only source for Mir Ali's second voyage to the Swahili Coast is the chronicle of João dos Santos. The Portuguese archives probably contain important information on the campaign that has yet to be uncovered, but for the time being, the earliest known archival reference is a very brief account in *APO*, fasc. 3, 273; the present narrative is based almost exclusively on dos Santos.
93. "*recebêram com muito contentamento ... todas as cidades e lugares de Mouros daquella costa.*" dos Santos, *Etiópia Oriental*, 1: 27.
94. For a technical analysis of this tactical combination of good logistical support, a strong coastal fortress, war galleys, and heavy artillery, which John Guilmartin has described as "a virtually unbeatable" defensive position, see Guilmartin, *Gunpowder and Galleys*, 13.
95. For a discussion of the reliability of the chronicle of dos Santos, see Giancarlo Casale, "Global Politics in the 1580s: A Canal, Twenty Thousand Cannibals, and an Ottoman Plot to Rule the World," *Journal of World History* 18/3 (Nov. 2007), 273–76.
96. "*entre estas huma assas grande.*" dos Santos, *Etiópia Oriental*, 1: 41.
97. "*escolhendo antes a morte da água, que a do ferro cruel dos barbaros.*" dos Santos, *Etiópia Oriental*, 45.
98. "*Não me espanto de minha adversa fortuna, porque são sucessos de guerra, e mais quero ser cativo de cristãos, de quem já outra vez fui em Espanha, que ser comido dos Zimbas bárbaros e desumanos.*" dos Santos, *Etiópia Oriental*, 1: 37.
99. "*Alegrai-vos e esperai em Deus, que já eu fui cativo de pior senhor do que vós sois, que foi o Malabar, e agora estou neste estado que vedes; assim vos pode seceder a vós.*" dos Santos, *Etiópia Oriental*, 1: 242.
100. "*Senhor, verdade é que eu sou cativo, mas sendo-o de V. Senhoria, me tenho por grande senhor.*" dos Santos, *Etiópia Oriental*, 1: 242.

101. "*Mirale Beque foi mandado para Portugal, onde se converteu e se fez cristão, no que restaurou para a sua alma todas as perdas e quebras que tinha recebido no corpo.*" dos Santos, *Etiópia Oriental*, 1: 242.
102. For the document, see *Filmoteca Ultramarina Portuguesa* no.16, p. 692, quoted in Fernand Braudel, *The Mediterranean and the Mediterranean World in the Age of Philip II*, trans. Siân Reynolds (New York, 1972), 2: 760.
103. Boxer and de Azevedo, *Fort Jesus*, 23.
104. For the subsequent history of Portuguese involvement in the Swahili Coast, see Pearson, *Port Cities and Intruders*, 129–54.
105. Pearson, *Merchants and Rulers*, 49–51, 112–13; also Thomaz, "Crise de 1565–1575," 495.

NOTES TO CHAPTER 7

1. On the reign of Iskandar Muda, see Amirul Hadi, *Islam and State in Sumatra: A Study of Seventeenth-Century Aceh* (Leiden, 2004); see also Lombard, *Sultanat d'Atjeh*.
2. For a full French translation of this passage from the *Hikajat Atjeh*, see Lombard, *Sultanat d'Atjeh*, 227–33.
3. On the Indian Ocean's economy during the seventeenth century, see R. J. Barendse, *The Arabian Seas: The Indian Ocean World of the Seventeenth Century* (London, 2003).
4. See Hanna, *Making Big Money*, 107.
5. *MD* 27 #164, 263
6. *MD* 43 #328, 180.
7. *MD* 48 #617, 220. This followed bitter complaints from Istanbul in 1581 that the governor of Egypt had not sent any of the 1,100 bales of spices expected that year. See *MD* 46 #187, 99.
8. *MD* 53 #127, 65.
9. *MD* 53 #177, 66.
10. Egyptian court records indicate that in 1596 Hasan Pasha's agent in Cairo sold the French consul a cargo of spices valued at no less than 10,000 dinars. Hanna, *Making Big Money*, 108.
11. According to Egyptian court records, such men included Ibrahim Pasha of Egypt, Bayram Pasha and Fazli Pasha of Yemen, and Ahmed Pasha of Eritrea. See Hanna, *Making Big Money*, 107–9.
12. See Michel Tuchscherer, "Commerce et production du café en Mer Rouge au XVIe siècle," in Michel Tuchscherer, ed., *Le commerce du café avant l'ère des plantations coloniales: espaces, réseaux, société, XVe–XIXe siècle* (Cairo, 2001), 69–90.
13. C. G. Brouwer and A. Kaplanian, *Early Seventeenth Century Yemen, Dutch Documents Relating to the Economic History of Southern Arabia* (Leiden, 1988), 137, 166, 223.
14. Hanna, *Making Big Money*.
15. For Masulipatnam, see Sanjay Subrahmanyam, "Persians, Pilgrims and Portuguese: The Travails of Masulipatnam Shipping in the Western Indian Ocean 1590–1665," *Modern Asian Studies* 22/3 (1988): 505; for Pegu and the Red Sea, see Manuel de Abreu Mousinho, *Breve discurso em que se conta a conquista do reino do Pegu na Índia oriental*, ed. Maria Paula Caetanto (Lisbon, 1990), 60–61.
16. Pearson, *Pilgrimage to Mecca*, 56.
17. Pierre du Jarric, *Akbar and the Jesuits*, C. H. Payne, trans. (London, 1926), 178; also Farooqi, *Mughal-Ottoman Relations*, 23.
18. Andreas Tietze, ed. and trans., *Mustafa Âli's Counsel for Sultans of 1581* (Vienna, 1982), 2: 37.
19. Tietze, *Mustafa Âli*, 2: 38.

20. Tietze, *Mustafa Âli*, 2: 39.
21. Tietze, *Mustafa Âli*, 2: 36.
22. These figures are taken from İhsanoğlu, *Osmanlı Coğrafya Literatürü*, 23–25. Similar data from the same reference work indicate increased reproduction and circulation during the late sixteenth century of other earlier works, such as Kazvini's "Wonders of Creation" and Mustafa al-Muvakkit's "A Public Announcement of the Milestones of Countries." For a list of surviving manuscripts for these and other texts mentioned in the following sections, see İhsanoğlu, *Osmanlı Coğrafya Literatürü*, 5–49; for a general overview of Ottoman geographical literature, see also Fr. Taeschner, "Djughrāfiyā VI: The Ottoman Geographers," *EI²*, 2: 587–90.
23. By comparison, the geography by Ahmed b. Halil al-Salihi published in Rome in 1585 (the first Arabic-language geography to be published in movable type) exists today in only two copies, although it was originally printed in a run of several hundred. See Olga Pinto, "Una rarissima opera araba stampata a Roma nel 1585," in *Studi bibliografici: Atti del convegno dedicato alla storia del libro italiano nel V centenario dell'introduzione dell'arte tipografica in Italia, Bolzano, 7-8 ottobre, 1965* (Firenze, 1967), 47.
24. One partial explanation for the Ottomans' relative lack of familiarity with these Arabic texts is the fact that geography was not part of the standard curriculum of the *medrese*. See İhsanoğlu, *Osmanlı Coğrafya Literatürü*, xxxi–xli.
25. Adıvar, *Osmanlı Türklerinde İlim*, 93–94; see also İhsanoğlu, *Osmanlı Coğrafya Literatürü*, 28–29.
26. Seydi Ali Reis, *Kitāb al-Muḥīt*, ed. Fuat Sezgin (Frankfurt, 1997); M. Guadefroy-Demombynes, "Les sources arabes du Muhit turc," *Journal Asiatique*, 2nd series, 20 (1912): 347–50.
27. İhsanoğlu, *Osmanlı Coğrafya Literatürü*, 64.
28. Mehmet Aşık, *Menâzırü'l-Avâlim*, 2 vols., ed. Mahmut Ak (Istanbul, 2007); for the original manuscript, *T.S.M.K.*, R. 1667.
29. Istanbul, Süleymaniye Library Veliyüddin Efendi 2337; see also İhsanoğlu, *Osmanlı Coğrafya Literatürü*, 66.
30. *T.S.M.K.* R. 1642; see also Adıvar, *Osmanlı Türklerinde İlim*, 93; İhsanoğlu, *Osmanlı Coğrafya Literatürü*, 67.
31. "*Kitāb-ı tevārīḫ-i pādişāhān-ı vilāyet-i Hindū ve Ḫitāy ve Keşmīr ve vilāyet-i 'Acem ve Kaşġār ve Kalmuk ve Çin ve sā'ir pādişāhān-i pīşīn ez evlād-ı Cingiz Hān ve Ḫāḳān ve fağfūr ve pādişāhān-ı Hindūstān der zamān-ı Sulṭān Murād b. Sulṭān Selīm Ḫān.*" See Jospeh Matuz, ed. and trans., *L'ouvrage de Seyfi Çelebi* (Paris, 1968).
32. "*Halḳ mā beyninde eṭrāf-ı 'ālemde şehirlerüñ İstanbūl şehrinden bu'dı ve kaç aylıḳ ve kaç günlük yol olduġı ḥıyānā ba'żı mecālisde söylenmede 'ādet-i vāḳı'-yı evvelī gelmişdür ve söylenen aḫbāruñ daḫī ba'żısı ṣaḥīḥ olursa ekṣeri ġayr-i ṣaḥīḥ olduġı daḫī ma'lūmdur zīrā kim mübālaġa ḳasḍ idüp vaḳı' olan bu'ddan ziyāde ẕikr idüp ve ba'żı daḫī bir sabīl taḥmīn ve taḳrīr idüp.*" *T.S.M.K.* K. 893, fol. 91a.
33. See Campbell, "Portulan Charts," 371–447.
34. *T.S.M.K.* H. 1822.
35. The four known Ottoman atlases of this genre are the atlas of Ali Macar Reis, *T.S.M.K.* Ms. H.644; the anonymous atlas of the Biblioteque Nationale in Paris, Ms. A.Y. 2978; the *Atlas-ı Hümāyūn* of the Istanbul Archaeology Museum, Ms. no. 1621; and the *Deniz Atlası* of the Walters Art Gallery in Baltimore, no. W. 660.
36. The map was discovered by Thomas Goodrich in 1984. For a full description, see Thomas Goodrich, "Atlas-ı Hümayun: A Sixteenth Century Ottoman Maritime Atlas Discovered in 1984," *Archivum Ottomanicum* 10 (1985): 84–101.

37. Thomas Goodrich, "The Earliest Ottoman Maritime Atlas: The Walters Deniz Atlası," *Archivum Ottomanicum* 11 (1986): 25–44.
38. The 1550s were a particularly active period for this kind of exchange, as several competing Ottoman princes ordered world maps from Venice. See Benjamin Arbel, "Maps of the World for Ottoman Princes? Further Evidence and Questions concerning 'The Mappamondo' of Hajji Ahmed," *Imago Mundi* 54 (2002): 24–26.
39. See Svat Soucek, "The 'Ali Macar Reis Atlas' and the Deniz Kitabı," *Imago Mundi* 25 (1971): 27.
40. See, for example, Goodrich, "Atlas-ı Hümayun," 88.
41. For an extensive bibliography on the map, see Arbel, "Maps of the World," 19–20; for a discussion of the possible identity of the map's ostensible author, "Tunislu Hajji Ahmed," see See V. L. Ménage, "The Map of Hajji Ahmed and Its Makers," *Bulletin of the School of Oriental and African Studies* 21(1958): 291–314.
42. For a full transcription of the original Turkish text, see B. Şehsuvaroğlu, "Kanuni Devrinde Yazılmış ve Şimdiye Kadar Bilinmeyen bir Coğrafya Kitabı," in *Kanuni Armağanı* (Ankara, 1970), 207–25.
43. "*El-ḥāṣıl bu muṣannefetde olan resim degül cihānüñ nümūnesi ve kernāmesidür . . . li'ennehüm dünyāda vāki' olan memleket ve vilāyetlerüñ ṣaḥīḥ aḥvālerin ve ḫaberin alıncaya degin nice feylesoflar ve ehl-i 'ilmüñ ma'rifetlerin ve meşveretlerin gerek ve bī-nihāye māl ḥarc eylemesin lāzım olur.*" Şehsuvaroğlu, "Bilinmeyen bir Coğrafya," 225.
44. Antonio Fabris, "Ottoman Mappa Mundi," 31–37.
45. Robert Jones, "The Medici Oriental Press (Rome 1584–1614) and the Impact of Its Arabic Publications on Northern Europe," in G. A. Russell, ed., *The "Arabick" Interest of the Natural Philosophers in Seventeenth-Century England* (Leiden, 1994), 88–108.
46. Gabor Ágoston, "Information, Ideology, and the Limits of Imperial Policy: Ottoman Grand Strategy in the Context of Ottoman-Habsburg Rivalry," in Virginia Aksan and Daniel Goffman, eds. *The Early Modern Ottomans: Remapping the Empire* (Cambridge, 2007), 87.
47. See Aydın Sayılı, "Üçüncü Murad'ın İstanbul Rasathanesi," 397. The manuscript of Lokman's *Şehinşāhnāme* is today preserved in Istanbul University Library, M.S. 1404. On the office of *şehnāmeci* occupied by Lokman, see Christine Woodhead, "An Experiment in Official Historiography: The Post of *Şehnameci* in the Ottoman Empire, c. 1555–1605," *Wiener Zeitschrift für die Kunde des Morgenlandes* 75 (1983): 157–82.
48. On the development of European discovery literature, see (for the Spanish case) Ricardo Padrón, *The Spacious Word: Cartography, Literature and Empire in Early Modern Spain* (Chicago, 2003); and for a similar treatment of the Dutch, Benjamin Schmidt's *Innocence Abroad: The Dutch Imagination and the New World, 1570–1670* (Cambridge, 2001); see also W. D. C. Randles, "La diffusion dans l'Europe du XVIe siècle des connaissances géographiques dues aux découvertes portugaises," in *La Découverte, le Portugal et l'Europe: Actes du colloque, Paris, les 26, 27 et 28 mai 1988* (Paris, 1990), 269–78; for a more general approach, including the Ottoman perspective, see Jerry Brotton and Lisa Jardine, *Global Interests: Renaissance Art between East and West* (Ithaca, 2000).
49. On Western humanism in the Age of Exploration, see Pagden, *Fall of Natural Man*; and Sebastiano Gentile, ed., *Firenze e la scoperta dell'America: Umanesimo e geografia nel '400 fiorentino* (Firenze, 1992); on humanists' engagement with classical texts more generally, see James Hankins, *Plato in the Italian Renaissance* (New York, 1991).

50. See Justin Stagl, "The Methodising of Travel in the 16th Century: A Tale of Three Cities," in Pagden, *Facing Each Other*, 123–50.
51. See, for example, Fabris, "Ottoman Mappa Mundi," 31–37.
52. Busbecq, *Turkish Letters*, 205–7.
53. For a similar example from the seventeenth century, see Paul Kahle, "China as Described by Turkish Geographers from Iranian Sources," in Paul Kahle, *Opera Minora I* (Leiden, 1956), 312–25.
54. For a recent attempt to address this problem, see Nelly Hanna, *In Praise of Books: A Cultural History of Cairo's Middle Class, Sixteenth through the Eighteenth Centuries* (Syracuse, 2003).
55. See, for example, Adrian Johns, *The Nature of the Book: Print and Knowledge in the Making* (Chicago, 1998); see also Joseph Dane, *The Myth of Print Culture: Essays on Evidence, Textuality, and Bibliographical Method* (Toronto, 2003); for the older view on the "printing revolution," see Elizabeth Eisenstein, *The Printing Press as an Agent of Change: Communications and Cultural Transformation in Early Modern Europe* (Cambridge, 1979).
56. For a more in-depth consideration of the seemingly static nature of world maps in Islamic geographies, see Karen Pinto, "3 Ways of Seeing," 147–352.
57. On the Arabic-script publications of the Medici Press, see Jones, "Medici Oriental Press," 88–108; see also Geoffrey Roper, "Early Arabic Printing in Europe," in Eva Hanebutt-Benz, Dagmar Glass, and Geoffrey Roper, eds., *Middle East Languages and the Print Revolution: A Cross-Cultural Encounter* (Westhofen, 2002), 129–50.
58. Venice, Biblioteca Marciana, Ms. Or. 98; see Olga Pinto, "Rarissima opera araba," 47–51; see also Yousuf Alian Serkis, *Dictionary of Arabic Printed Books from the Beginning of Arabic Printing until the End of 1337 A.H.-1919 A.D.* (Cairo, 1928), 1: 1037.
59. Selim Nüzhet, *Türk Matbaacılığı* (Istanbul, 1928), 11; on the Arabic-script publications of the Medici Press, see Jones, "The Medici Oriental Press."
60. Vitorino Magelhães Godinho, "The Portuguese 'Carreira da India' 1497–1810," in Jaap Bruijn and Femme Gaastra, eds., *Ships, Sailors and Spices: East India Companies and Their Shipping in the 16th, 17th, and 18th Centuries* (Amsterdam, 1993), 36.
61. The most famous example of this scholarship is Mustafa Âli's *Künhü'l-Aḫbār* ("Essence of Histories"), completed in 1594. See Cornell Fleischer, *Bureaucrat and Intellectual in the Ottoman Empire: The Historian Mustafa Ali 1541–1600* (Princeton, 1986). Other examples include Mustafa Cenabi's *al-Ḥāfil al-Vasīt ve'l-'Aylam al-Zāḫir al-Muḥīṭ*, Süleymaniye Library, Hamidiye Ms. No. 896.
62. For a related discussion of Talikizade's text, see Necipoğlu, *Age of Sinan*, 29–30.
63. "*Devr-i Ādemden berü baḥre mālik olan selāṭīn berri żabt, ve berri ḳabża-i ḳabżına olan ḫavā ḳīn baḥri ḥavze-ı teshīre getürimemişlerdi. Bu devlet-i 'uẓmā bu 'uẓemā-yı devlete müyesser olmışdur. Ḥattā, Sulṭān-ı Ṣāḥib-ḳirān Süleymān Ḫān ḥażretleri bu şerefe nā'il olduḳlarına—şükran li'Allahi'l-āliye—mühür-i şerīflerin bu 'unvān ile tezyīn buyurmışlardı: Şahī ki ez şeref şüde ber şer' müstāḳīm Sulṭān-ı berr-ü-baḥr Süleymān ibn-i Selīm.*" Christine Woodhead, *Ta'līḳī-zāde's Şehnāme-i hümāyūn: A History of the Ottoman Campaign into Hungary 1593–94* (Berlin, 1983), 118.
64. On the loss of Ottoman Yemen, see Jane Hathaway, *A Tale of Two Factions: Myth, Memory and Identity in Ottoman Egypt and Yemen* (Albany, 2003).
65. Charles Boxer, "Anglo-Portuguese Rivalry in the Persian Gulf, 1615–1635," in Boxer, *Portuguese Conquest and Commerce in Southern Asia 1500–1750* (London, 1985).

66. Rudi Matthee, "Between Arabs, Turks and Iranians: The Town of Basra, 1600–1700," *Bulletin of the School of Oriental Studies*, 16/1 (2006): 53–78.
67. On Dutch Malacca, see Dianne Lewis, *Jan Compagnie in the Straits of Malacca 1641–1795* (Athens, 1995).
68. In 1627, for instance, no spices at all reached Egypt as a result of the Yemeni revolt, forcing Ottoman merchants to import them from Europe to meet domestic demand. See Inalcik, *Economic and Social History*, 1: 334. More generally, recent scholarship on the wider economy of the Indian Ocean in the seventeenth century has stressed the continued vitality of Ottoman trade with maritime Asia despite the political crisis within Ottoman lands. But it still seems beyond question that most of this trade slipped out of the hands of Ottoman merchants and into the control of merchants from India, Yemen, and other regions of the Indian Ocean. For an introduction to this scholarship, see Barendse, *Arabian Seas*, as well as the discussion in Inalcik, *Economic and Social History*, 1: 338–55; and Faroqhi, *Pilgrims and Sultans*, 158–60.
69. Quoted in W. Barthold and M. Fuad Köprülü, *Islam Medeniyeti Tarihi* (Istanbul, 1963), 230.
70. In addition to the very large literature on the question of "Ottoman decline," there has recently been a renewed interest in the question of the "general crisis" of the seventeenth century as a global phenomenon. See the recent forum in the *American Historical Review*, particularly the article by Geoffrey Parker, "Crisis and Catastrophe: The Global Crisis of the Seventeenth Century Reconsidered," *American Historical Review* 113/4 (October 2008): 1053–79, which raises the question of environmental change as a unifying factor in this crisis.
71. See Cemal Kafadar, "The Myth of the Golden Age: Ottoman Historical Consciousness in the Post-Süleymanic Era," in Kafadar and Inalcik, *Suleyman the Second*, 37–48.
72. Even more basic materials such as pitch, nails, and fuel were similarly lacking and had to be brought in from areas far removed from the Red Sea. In Suez, a local source of drinking water was also absent. See Faroqhi, *Pilgrims and Sultans*, 41, 71–72, 94–95; see also the more general discussion of the geography of port cities in the Indian Ocean world in Barendse, *Arabian Seas*, 13–86.
73. For an introduction to the scholarship on this question, see Daniel Goffman, *The Ottoman Empire and Early Modern Europe* (Cambridge, 2002), 123–28.
74. See Faroqhi, *Pilgrims and Sultans*, 80–91.

WORKS CITED

UNPUBLISHED OTTOMAN MANUSCRIPT SOURCES

Abdi Efendi. *Ḳānūnü'd-Dünyā.* Topkapı Sarayı Müzesi Kütüphanesi, Ms. Revan 1639.

Anonymous. *Ḳānūnnāme-i Sulṭān Süleymān Ḫān.* Süleymaniye Kütüphanesi, Ms. Veliyüddin Efendi 1970.

———. *Mekātib-i Ḫulefā ve Selāṭīn.* Topkapı Sarayı Müzesi Kütüphanesi, Ms. Revan 1959.

Aşık, Mehmed. *Menāẓirü'l-Avālim.* Topkapı Sarayı Müzesi Kütüphanesi, Ms. Revan 1667.

Cenabi, Mustafa. *Ḥafil al-Vaṣīṭ ve'l-'Aylam al-Zāḫir al-Muḥīṭ,* Süleymaniye Kütüphanesi, Ms. Hamidiye 896.

Lokman, Seyyid. *Zübdetü't-Tevārīḫ.* Topkapı Sarayı Müzesi Kütüphanesi, Ms. Hazine 1321.

———. *Mücmelü't-Ṭūmār.* British Museum, Turkish Ms. Or. 1135.

———. *Şehinşāhnāme.* İstanbul Üniversitesi Kütüphanesi, Ms. 1404.

Al-Mar'aşi, Mehmed. *İḳlīmnāme.* Topkapı Sarayı Müzesi Kütüphanesi, Ms III. Ahmed 2844.

Mekki, Kutbeddin. *Aḫbāru'l-Yemānī.* Translated into Ottoman Turkish and expanded by Haci Ali. Süleymaniye Kütüphanesi, Ms. Aya Sofya 3091.

al-Muvakkit, Mustafa b. 'Ali. *İ'lāmu'l-'İbād fī A'lāmi'l-Bilād.* Topkapı Sarayı Müzesi Kütüphanesi, Ms. Koğuşlar 893.

al-Rumi, Mahmud al-Hatib. *Nevādirü'l-Ġarā'ib ve Mevāridü'l-'Acā'ib.* Süleymaniye Kütüphanesi, Ms. Esad Efendi 2051.

Rumuzi. *Tārīḫ-i Fetḥ-i Yemen.* İstanbul Üniversitesi Kütüphanesi, Ms. 6045.

Rüstem Paşa *Tevārīḫ-i Āl-i 'Oṣmān.* Cambridge University Library, Turkish OR. Ms. Gg 6.33.

Sipahizade Mehmed. *Evẓaḥü'l-Mesālik fī Ma'rifet'il-Buldān ve'l-Memālik.* Topkapı Sarayı Müzesi Kütüphanesi, Ms. Revan 1642.

al-Su'udi, Hasan. *Tārīḫ-i Hind-i Ġarbī* or *İḳlīm-i Cedīd.* Beyazıt Devlet Kütüphanesi, Ms. 4969.

Tulun, Hasan b. *Tārīḫ-i Mıṣır.* British Museum, Ms. Add. 1846.

PUBLISHED OTTOMAN, ARABIC, AND PERSIAN SOURCES

'Arab Faqih, *The Conquest of Abyssinia: Futuḥ Al-Ḥabaša.* Translated by Paul Lester Stenhouse. Hollywood, Calif.: Tsehai, 2005.

Aşık, Mehmet. *Menâzirü'l-Avâlim*. 2 vols. Edited by Mahmut Ak. Istanbul: Türk Tarih Kurumu, 2007.

Bacqué-Grammont, Jean-Louis, ed. and trans. *La première histoire de France en turc ottoman: Chroniques des padichas de France*. Paris: L'Hattaman, 1997.

Barkan, Ömer Lütfi, ed. *XV ve XVI'ıncı Asırlarda Osmanlı İmparatorluğunda Zirai Ekonominin Hukuki ve Mali Esasları, Birinci Cilt: Kanunlar*. Istanbul: Burhaneddin Matbaası, 1943.

Bayley, E. C., ed. and trans. *The Local Muhammadan Dynasties: Gujarat*. London: W. H. Allen, 1886.

Blackburn, J. R., ed. *Journey to the Sublime Porte: The Arabic Memoir of a Sharifian Agent's Diplomatic Mission to the Ottoman Imperial Court in the Era of Suleyman the Magnificent*. Beirut: Oriental Institute, 2005.

Bozorg b. Shariyar. *Livres des merveilles de l'Inde par le captaine Bozorg fils de Chahriyār de Rāmhormoz*. Translated by Marcel L. Devic. Leiden: E. J. Brill, 1883.

ad-Dabir, Muhammad al-Makki al-Asafi al-Ulughkhani Hajji. *Zafar ul-Wālih bi Muzaffar wa Ālihi—An Arabic History of Gujarat*. Translated by M. F. Lokhandwala. Baroda, India: Oriental Institute, 1970.

Feridun, Ahmed Beg, *Mecmū'a-yı Münşe'āt-ı Selāṭīn*. 2 vols. Istanbul, A.H. 1264–1275/A.D. 1848–1858.

Goodrich, Thomas. *The Ottoman Turks and the New World: A Study of Tarih-i Hind-i Garbi and Sixteenth-Century Ottoman Americana*. Wiesbaden: Otto Harrassowitz, 1990.

Ibn Iyas. *Journal d'un bourgeois du Caire: Chronique d'Ibn Iyās*. 2 vols. Translated by Gaston Wiet. Paris: Libraire Armand Colin, 1945.

Katib Çelebi, *Tuḥfetü'l-Kibār fī Esfāri'l-Biḥār*. Edited by Orhan Şaik Gökyay. Istanbul: Milli Eğitim Basımevi, 1973.

Kutbeddin Mekki (a.k.a. al-Nahrawali, Muhammad ibn Ahmad). *al-Barḳ al-Yamānī fī al-Fatḥ al-'Uṯẖmānī*. Edited by Hamad Jasir. Riyad: Dar al-Yamamah, 1967.

———. "La foudre du Yémen, ou conquête du Yémen par les Othomans." Translated by Silvestre de Sacy. *Notes et extraits des manuscrits de la Bibliothèque Nationale* 4 (1788): 412–504.

Lutfi Pasha, *Khalās al-Umma fī Ma'rifat al-A'immah*. Edited by Majidah Makhluf. Cairo, 2001.

———. *Tevārīḫ-i Āl-i 'Os̱mān*. Istanbul A.H. 1341 /D.C. 1922–1923.

Matrakçı Nasuh. *Beyān-ı Menāzil-i Sefer-i 'Irāḳeyn-i Sulṭān-ı Süleymān Ḫān*. Edited by Hüseyin Yurdaydın. Ankara: Türk Tarih Kurumu, 1976.

al-Najdi, Ahmad b. Majid. *Arab Navigation in the Indian Ocean before the Coming of the Portuguese, Being a Translation of the Kitāb al-Fawā'id fī Usūl al-Bahr wa'l-Qawā 'id of Ahmad b. Mājīd al Najdī*. Edited and Translated by G. R. Tibbetts. London: Royal Asiatic Society of Great Britain and Ireland, 1971.

Peçevi, Ibrahim. *Tārīḫ-i Peçevī*. 2 vols. Istanbul: Maṭba'a-ı Âmīre, A.H. 1283/A.D. 1866.

Piri Reis. *Kitāb-ı Baḥrīye*. 4 vols. Ankara: Türk Tarih Kurumu, 1988.

———. *Kitāb-ı Baḥrīye*. Edited by Fevzi Kurtoğlu. Istanbul: Türk Tarihi Araştirma Kurumu, 1935.

———. *Piri Reis Haritası Hakkında İzahname*. Edited by Yusuf Akçura. Istanbul: Türk Tarihi Araştirma Kurumu, 1935.

Sa'deddin, Mehmed. *Tācü't-Tevārīḫ*. Istanbul, A.H. 1279/A.D. 1863.

Sahillioğlu, Halil. *Topkapı Sarayı Arşivi H.951–952 Tarihli ve E-12321 Numaralı Mühimme Defteri*. Istanbul: IRCICA, 2002.

Schuman, L. O., ed. and trans. *Political History of the Yemen at the Beginning of the 16th Century according to Contemporary Arabic Sources*. Amserdam: Djambatan, 1961.

Selaniki Mustafa Efendi, *Tārīḫ-i Selānikī*. 2 vols. Edited by Mehmed İpşirli. Istanbul: Türk Tarih Kurumu, 1989.

Serjeant, R. B. *The Portuguese off the South Arabian Coast: Hadrami Chronicles with Yemeni and European Accounts of Dutch Pirates off Mocha in the Seventeenth Century*. Oxford: Clarendon Press, 1963.

Seydi Ali Reis. *Mir'ātü'l-Memālik: İnceleme, Metin, İndeks*. Edited by Mehmet Kiremit. Ankara: Türk Dil Kurumu, 1999.

———. *Kitāb al-Muḥīṭ*. Edited by Fuat Sezgin. Frankfurt: Institut *für* Geschichte der Arabisch-Islamischen Wissenschaften, 1997.

———. *The Travels and Adventures of Sidi Ali Reis in India, Afghanistan, Central Asia and Persia during the Years 1553–1556*. Translated by A. Vambery. London: Luzac, 1899.

Seyfi Çelebi. *L'ouvrage de Seyfi Çelebi*. Edited by Joseph Matuz. Paris: Maisonneuve, 1968.

Süheyli Efendi. *Tārīḫ-i Mıṣır al-Cedīd*. Kostantiniyye: Müteferrika, A.H. 1142/A.D. 1729.

Smith, Clive, ed. and trans. *Lightning over Yemen: A History of the Ottoman Campaign 1569–71*. London: I. B. Tauris, 2002.

Soudan, Frédérique. *Le Yémen Ottoman d'après la chronique d'al-Mawzaʿī: al-iḥsān fī duḫūl mamlakat al-Yaman taḥt ẓill ʿadālat Āl ʿUṯmān*. Cairo: Institut Français d'Archéologie Orientale, 1999.

Süreyya, Mehmed. *Sicill-i Osmanī*. 6 vols. Edited by Nuri Akbayar and Seyit Ali Kahraman. Istanbul: Tarih Vakfı, 1996.

Tietze, Andreas, ed. and trans. *Mustafa Âli's Counsel for Sultans of 1581*. 2 vols. Vienna: Verlag der Österreichischen Akademie der Wissenschaften, 1978, 1982.

Vatin, Nicolas. *Sultan Djem: Un prince ottoman dans l'Europe du XVe siècle d'après deux sources contemporaines: Vakiat-ı Sultan Cem, Oeuvres de Guillaume Caoursin*. Ankara: Türk Tarih Kurumu, 1997.

Christine Woodhead, ed. *Ta'līḳī-zāde's Şehnāme-i Hümāyūn: A History of the Ottoman Campaign into Hungary 1593–94*. Berlin: Klaus Schwarz, 1983.

Yavuz, Hulusi, ed. *Yemen'de Osmanlı Idaresi ve Rumuzi Tarihi*. 2 vols. Ankara: Türk Tarih Kurumu, 2002.

Zeinu'd-Din. *Tohfut ul-Mujahideen*. Translated by M. J. Rowlandson. London: Oriental Translation Fund, 1833.

PORTUGUESE AND OTHER EUROPEAN PRIMARY SOURCES

Abreu, Lisuarte. *Livro de Lisuarte de Abreu* [Facsimile edition]. Lisbon: Comissão Nacional para as Comemorações dos Descobrimentos Portugueses, 1992.

Alberi, Eugenio, ed. *Le relazioni degli ambasciatori veneti al senato*. 18 vols. Florence: Società Editrice Fiorentina, 1839–1863.

Anonymous. "Particular Relation of the Expedition of Solyman Pacha from Suez to India against the Portuguese at Diu, Written by a Venetian Officer Who Was Pressed into Turkish Service on That Occasion." In *General History and Collection of Voyages and Travels*, 22 vols., edited by Robert Kerr, 7: 257–87. Edinburgh: William Blackwood, 1824.

Arquivo Nacional da Torre do Tombo. *As Gavetas da Torre do Tombo*. 8 vols. Lisbon: Centro de Estudos Históricos Ultramarinos, 1960–1977.

Baião, António, ed. *História quinhentista (inédita) do segundo cêrco de Dio, ilustrada com a correspondência original, tambem inédita, de D. João de Castro, D. João de Mascarenhas, e outros*. 2 vols. Coimbra: Imprensa da Universidade, 1925.

Bocarro, António. *Livro das plantas de todas as fortalezas, cidades e povoaçoens do Estado da Índia Oriental*. Evora, Biblioteca Pública, Códice CXV/2–1.

Busbecq, Ogier Ghiselin de. *The Turkish Letters of Ogier Ghiselin de Busbecq, Imperial Ambassador at Constantinople 1554–1562*. Translated by Edward Seymour Forster. Oxford: Clarendon Press, 1968.

Castanheda, Fernão Lopes de. *História do descobrimento e conquista da Índia pelos Portugueses*. 8 vols. Lisbon: Typographia Rollandiana, 1833.

Castro, João de. *Cartas de D. João de Castro*. Edited by Elaine Sanceau. Lisbon: Agencia Geral do Ultramar, 1955.

———. *Roteiros de João de Castro*. Edited by A. Fontoura da Costa. 2 vols. Lisbon: Agencia Geral das Colónias, 1940.

———. *Primeiro roteiro da costa da Índia; desde Goa até Dio: narrando a viagem que fez o vice-rei D. Garcia de Noronha em soccorro desta ultima cidade, 1538–1539*. Porto: Typographia Commercial Portuense, 1843.

———. *Roteiro que fez Dom João de Castro da viajem que fezeram os Portugueses desde India atee Soez*. University of Minnesota James Ford Bell Library, Ms. 1541 fCa.

Cavendish, Edward. *A New Universal Collection of Voyages and Travels, from the Earliest Accounts to the Present Time*. London: Cooke, 1771.

Corpo Diplomatico Portuguez. 15 vols. Paris: J. P. Aillaud, 1846.

Correia, Gaspar. *Lendas da Índia*. 4 vols. Edited by M. Lopes de Almeida. Lisbon: Academia Real das Ciências de Lisboa, 1858–1864.

Coutinho, Lopes de Sousa. *História do cerco de Diu*. Lisbon: Typographia do Comercio de Portugal, 1890.

Couto, Dogo do. *Diogo do Couto e a década 8a da Ásia*. 2 vols. Edited by Maria Augusta Lima Cruz. Lisbon: Imprensa Nacional-Casa da Moeda, 1994.

———. *Da Ásia*. Lisbon: Régia Officina Typografica, 1777. [vols. 10–24 of the 24-volume work *Da Ásia de João de Barros e de Diogo do Couto*.]

Documentação Ultramarina Portuguesa. Lisbon: Centro de Estudos Históricos Ultramarinos da Junta de Investigação do Ultramar, 1960–1973.

dos Santos, João. *Etiópia Oriental*. 2 vols. Edited by Luís de Albuquerque. Lisbon: Alfa, 1989.

Faria e Sousa, Manuel de. *Ásia Portuguesa*. 6 vols. Translated by Isabel Ferreira do Amaral Pereira de Matos. Porto: Biblioteca Histórica, 1956.

Fitch, M. Ralph. "The Voyage of M. Ralph Fitch, Merchant of London." In *Voyages*. 8 vols. Edited by Richard Hakluyt, 3: 281–300. London: J. M. Dent and Sons, 1907.

Gaio, João Ribeiro. *Roteiro das cousas do Achem: um olhar português sobre o norte de Sumatra em finais do sèculo XVI*. Edited by Jorge Manuel dos Santos Alves and Pierre-Yves Manguin. Lisbon: Sociedade Histórica de Independência de Portugal, 1997.

Jarric, Pierre du. *Akbar and the Jesuits*. Translated by C. H. Payne. London: Harper, 1926.

Monserrate, S.J. *The Commentary of Father Monserrate on His Journey to the Court of Akbar*. Translated by J. S. Hayland and S. N. Banerjee. New Delhi: Asian Education Services, 1992.

Mousinho, Manuel de Abreu. *Breve discurso em que se conta a conquista do reino do Pegu na Índia oriental*. Edited by Maria Paula Caetanto. Lisbon: Mem Martins, 1990.

Oliveira, Julieta Teixeira Marques de, ed. *Fontes documentais de Veneza referentes a Portugal*. Lisbon: Imprensa Nacional-Casa da Moeda, 1996.

Pigafetta, Filippo. "Il Golfo di Suez e il Mar Rosso in una relazione inedita de Filippo Pigafetta (1567–77)." Edited by Alberto Magnaghi. *Bolletino della società geografica italiana*. Ser. 4, 47/11, part 1 (1910): 264–312.

Pinto, Fernão Mendes. *The Travels of Mendes Pinto*. Edited and translated by Rebecca D. Catz. Chicago: University of Chicago Press, 1989.

Public Records Office. *Calendar of State Papers and Manuscripts Relating to English Affairs Existing in the Archives and Collections of Venice, and in Other Libraries of Northern Italy*. 38 vols. Great Britain: Public Records Office, 1939–1947.

Rego, António da Silva, ed. *Documentação para a história das missões do padroado português do oriente*. 12 vols. Lisbon: Ministério das Colónias, 1948–.

Rego, António da Silva, and T. W. Baxter, eds. *Documentos sobre os portugueses em Moçambique e na Africa central, 1497–1840*. 9 vols. Lisbon: Centro de Estudos Históricos Ultramarinos, 1962–1989.

Rivara, J. H. da Cunha, ed. *Archivo Portuguez-Oriental*. 6 vols. in 10 parts. Nova Goa: Imprensa Nacional, 1857–1877.

Rycaut, Paul. *Present State of the Ottoman Empire*. London: Starkey and Brome, 1668.

Sanceau, Elaine, ed. *Collecção de São Lourenço*. 3 vols. Lisbon: Centro de Estudos Históricos Ultramarinos, 1973–1983.

Sanuto, Marin. *I diarii di Marino Sanuto*. Edited by Rinaldo Fulin, Federico Stefani, and Marco Allegri. 58 vols. Venetia: Deputazione Veneta di Storia Patria, 1879–1903.

Whiteway, R. S., trans. and ed. *The Portuguese Expedition to Abyssinia in 1541–1543 Related by Castanhoso and Bermudas*. London: Hakluyt Society, 1902.

Wicki, Joseph, ed. *Documenta Indica*. 11 vols, Roma: Institutum Historicum Societatis Iesu, 1948–1994.

SECONDARY SOURCES

Adıvar, Adnan. *Osmanlı Türklerinde İlim*. 9th ed. Istanbul: Remzi Kitabevi, 2000.

Ágoston, Gábor. "Information, Ideology, and the Limits of Imperial Policy: Ottoman Grand Strategy in the Context of Ottoman-Habsburg Rivalry." In *The Early Modern Ottomans: Remapping the Empire*, edited by Virginia Aksan and Daniel Goffman. Cambridge: Cambridge University Press, 2007, 75–102.

———. *Guns for the Sultan: Military Power and the Weapons Industry in the Ottoman Empire*. Cambridge: Cambridge University Press, 2005.

Ak, Mahmut. "Menâzirü'l-Avâlim." *Akademik Araştırmalar Dergisi* 2/4–5 (2000): 291–306.

Akdağ, Mustafa. *Türkiye'nin İktisadî ve Ictimaî Tarihi*. 2 vols. Ankara: Türk Tarih Kurumu, 1971.

al-Aidarous, Mohamed Hasen. "The Ottoman-Portuguese Conflict in the Arabian Gulf during the Second Half of the Sixteenth Century." *Arab Historical Review for Ottoman Studies* 1–2 (Jan. 1990): 15–43.

Alam, Muzaffar, and Sanjay Subrahmanyam. *Indo-Persian Travels in the Age of the Discoveries*. Cambridge: Cambridge University Press, 2007.

Albuquerque, Luís de. "Alguns aspectos de ameaça turca sobre a Índia por meados do século XVI." *Agrupamentos de Estudos de Cartographia Antiga* 51 (1977).

———. "O domínio português do Índico e a resposta turca." *Vertice* 36 (1976): 6–18.

Alkanderei, Faisal. "Selman Reis and his Report of 931/1525." *Arab Historical Review for Ottoman Studies* 7–8 (1993): 103–26.

Allen, W. E. D. *Problems of Turkish Power in the Sixteenth Century*. London: Central Asian Research Center, 1963.

Al-Tikriti, Nabil. "Şehzāde Korkud (c. 1468–1513) and the Articulation of Early 16th-Century Religious Identity." PhD dissertation, University of Chicago, 2004.

Alves, Jorge Manuel de Santos. *O Domínio do norte de Sumatra*. Lisbon: Sociedade Histórica da Independência de Portugal, 1999.

Arasaratnam, S. "Recent Trends in the Historiography of the Indian Ocean 1500–1800." *Journal of World History* 1/2 (1990): 225–48.

Arbel, Benjamin. "Maps of the World for Ottoman Princes? Further Evidence and Questions concerning 'The Mappamondo' of Hajji Ahmed." *Imago Mundi* 54 (2002): 19–29.

———. *Trading Nations: Jews and Venetians in the Early Modern Eastern Mediterranean*. Leiden: E. J. Brill, 1995.

———. "Nur Banu (c. 1530–1580)—A Venetian Sultana?" *Turcica* 24 (1992): 241–59.

Artan, Tülay. "The Kadırga Palace Shrouded by the Mists of Time." *Turcica* 26 (1994): 54–124.

Atasoy, N. "Nakkaş Osman'ın Padişah Portreleri Albümü." *Türkiyemiz* 6 (1972): 2–12.

Aubin, Jean. "La politique orientale de Selim I." In *Itinéraires d'Orient: Hommages à Claude Cahen*, edited by Raoul Curiel and Rika Gyselen. Bures-sur-Yvette, 1994, 197–215.

———. "Merchants in the Red Sea and the Persian Gulf at the Turn of the 15th and 16th Centuries." In *Asian Merchants and Businessmen in the Indian Ocean and the China Sea*, edited by Denys Lombard and Jean Aubin. Oxford: Oxford University Press, 1988, 79–86.

——— "Albuquerque et les négotiations de Cambaye." *Mare Luso-Indicum* 1 (1971): 3–63.

Ayalon, David. "Memlukler ve Deniz Kuvvetleri." *Tarih Dergisi* 25 (March 1971): 39–50.

———. *Gunpowder and Firearms in the Mamluk Kingdom*. London: Vallentine Mitchell, 1956.

Babinger, Franz. *Osmanlı Tarih Yazarları ve Eserleri*, 3rd ed. Translated by Coşkun Üçok. Ankara: Türk Kültür Bakanlığı, 2000.

———. *Mehmed the Conqueror and His Time*. Translated by Ralph Manheim. Princeton, N.J.: Princeton University Press, 1978.

Bacqué-Grammont, Jean-Louis. "Une lettre d'Ibrahim Pacha à Charles Quint." In *Comité Internationale d'Études Pré-Ottomanes et Ottomanes, VIth Symposium, Cambridge 1st–4th of July 1984*, edited by J.-L. Bacqué-Grammont and Emeri Van Donzel. Istanbul: IFEA, 1987.

———. "Les affaires mogholes vues par un ambassadeur özbek à Istanbul vers 1550." In *Passé turco-tatar, présent soviétique: Études offertes á Alexandre Bennigsen*, edited by Ch. Lemercier-Quelquejay, G. Veinstein, and S. E. Wimbush. Paris: Peeters, 1986, 165–73.

Bacqué-Grammont, Jean-Louis, and Anne Kroell. *Mamlouks, Ottomans et Portugais en Mer Rouge: L'affaire de Djedda en 1517*. Cairo, 1988.

Bacqué-Grammont, Jean-Louis, and Mohammad Mokri. "Une lettre de Qâsim Širvânî à Muzaffer Šâh du Gujarat: Les premieres relations des Ottomans avec l'Inde." In *Zafername: Memorial Volume of Felix Tauer*, edited by Rudolf Vesely and Eduard Gambar. Prague, 1996, 35–49.

Barendse, R. J. *The Arabian Seas: The Indian Ocean World of the Seventeenth Century*. London: East Gate, 2003.

Barkan, Ömer Lütfi. "H.933–34 (M.1527–28) Mali Yılına Ait Bir Bütçe Örneği." *İktisat Fakültesi Mecmuası* 15/1–4 (1954): 251–93.

Barthold, W., and M. Fuad Köprülü. *Islam Medeniyeti Tarihi*. Istanbul: Türk Tarih Kurumu Basımevi, 1963.

Beckingham, C. F. "The Red Sea in the Sixteenth Century." *Journal of the University of Manchester Egyptian and Oriental Society* 25 (1947–1953): 28–36.

Beller-Hann, Ildikó. "Ottoman Perceptions of China." In *Comité International d'Études Pré-Ottomanes et Ottomanes, VIth Symposium, Cambridge 1st–4th of July 1984*, edited by J.-L. Bacqué-Grammont and Emeri Van Donzel. Istanbul: IFEA, 1987.

Benedict, Barbara. *Curiosity: A Cultural History of Early Modern Inquiry*. Chicago: University of Chicago Press, 2001.

Bisaha, Nancy. *Creating East and West: Renaissance Humanists and the Ottoman Turks*. Philadelphia: University of Pennsylvania Press, 2004.

Blackburn, J. Richard. "Two Documents on the Division of Ottoman Yemen into Two Beglerbegiliks (973–1565)." *Turcica* 27 (1995): 223–36.

———. "Arabic and Turkish Source Materials for the Early History of Ottoman Yemen 945/1538—976/1568." *Sources for the History of the Arabs, Part 2/2*, edited by Abd Al-Rahman b. Al-Ansary. Riyadh, 1986, 197–210.

———. "The Ottoman Penetration of Yemen: An Annotated Translation of Özdemir Bey's Fethnāme for the Conquest of San'a in Rajab, 954/Aug 1547." *Archivum Ottomanicum* 5 (1980): 70–89.

———. "The Collapse of Ottoman Authority in Yemen 968/1560–976/1568." *Die Welt des Islams*, New Series 19, 1–4 (1979): 119–76.

Bloss, J. F. E. "The Story of Suakin." *Sudan Notes and Records* 19, part 2 (1936): 71–100.

Bono, Salvatore. *Schiavi musulmani nell'Italia moderna*. Napoli: Edizioni Scientifiche Italiane, 1999.

Bostan, İdris. *Osmanlılar ve Deniz: Deniz Politikaları, Teşkilat, Gemiler*. Istanbul: Küre, 2007.

———. *Osmanlı Denizciliği*. Istanbul: Kitap, 2006.

———. *Kürekli ve Yelkenli Osmanlı Gemileri*. Istanbul: Bilge, 2003.

Bouchon, Geneviève. *Albuquerque, le lion des mers d'Asie*. Paris: Editions Desjonquères, 1992.

———. "Sixteenth-Century Malabar and the Indian Ocean." In *India and the Indian Ocean 1500–1800*, edited by Ashin Das Gupta and M. N. Pearson. Calcutta: Oxford University Press, 1987, 162–84.

———. "L'évolution de la piraterie sur la côte malabare au cours du XVIe siècle." In *Course et piraterie: Etudes présentées à la Commission Internationale d'Histoire Maritime à l'occasion de son XVe colloque international*. San Francisco, 1975, 744–65.

Boxer, C. R. *Portuguese Conquest and Commerce in Southern Asia 1500–1750*. London: Variorum, 1985.

———. "A Note on Portuguese Reactions to the Revival of the Red Sea Spice Trade and the Rise of Atjeh 1540–1600." *Journal of South East Asian History* 10/3 (Dec. 1969): 416–510.

Boxer, Charles, and Carlos de Azevedo. *Fort Jesus and the Portuguese in Mombasa 1593–1729*. London: Hollis and Carter, 1960.

Braudel, Fernand. "The Expansion of Europe and the 'Longue Durée." In *Expansion and Reaction*, edited by H. L. Wesseling. Leiden: Leiden University Press, 1978, 17–28.

———. *The Mediterranean and the Mediterranean World in the Age of Philip II*. 2 vols. Translated by Sian Reynolds. New York: Harper and Row, 1972.

Brotton, Jerry. *Trading Territories: Mapping the Early Modern World*. London: Reaktion, 1987.

Brotton, Jerry, and Lisa Jardine. *Global Interests: Renaissance Art between East and West*. Ithaca, N.Y.: Cornell University Press, 2000.

Brouwer, C. G., and A. Kaplanian. *Early Seventeenth-Century Yemen, Dutch Documents Relating to the Economic History of Southern Arabia*. Leiden: E. J. Brill, 1988.

Brummet, Palmira. "What Sidi Ali Saw." *Portuguese Studies Review* 9/1–2 (2002): 232–53.

———. "The Ottomans as a World Power: What We Don't Know about Ottoman Seapower." *Oriente Moderno*, 2nd Ser., 20/1 (2001): 1–21.

———. *Ottoman Seapower and Levantine Diplomacy in the Age of Discovery*. Albany: State University of New York Press, 1994.

———. "Foreign Policy, Naval Strategy and the Defence of the Ottoman Empire in the Early Sixteenth Century." *International History Review* 11/4 (Nov. 1989): 613–28.

Budge, E. A. Wallace. *A History of Ethiopia, Nubia and Abyssinia*. 2 vols. London: Methuen, 1928.

Cahen, Claude. "Douane et commerce dans les ports méditerranéens de l'Egypte médiévale d'après le *Minhâdj* d'Al-Makhzūmī." *Journal of the Economic and Social History of the Orient* 7/3 (Nov. 1964): 218–313.

Campbell, Tony. *The Earliest Printed Maps*. London: British Library, 1987.

———. "Portulan Charts from the Late Thirteenth Century to 1500." In *The History of Cartography, Vol. 1: Cartography in Prehistoric, Ancient and Medieval Europe and the Mediterranean*, edited by J. B. Harley and David Woodward. Chicago: University of Chicago Press, 1987, 371–447.

———. "Census of Pre-Sixteenth-Century Portolan Charts." *Imago Mundi* 38 (1986): 67–94.

Carboni, Stefano, ed. *Venice and the Islamic World*. New Haven, Conn.: Yale University Press, 2007.

———. "Oggetti decorati a smalto di influsso islamico nella vertraria muranese: tecnica e forma." In *Venezia e l'Oriente vicino: Arte veneziana e arte islamica: Atti del Primo Simposio Internazionale sull'Arte Veneziana e l'Arte Islamica*, edited by Ernst J. Grube. Venice, 1989, 147–66.

Casale, Giancarlo. "Ottoman *Guerre de Course* and the Intercontinental Spice Trade." *Itinerario* 32/1 (Spring 2008): 59–79.

———. "The Ethnic Composition of Ottoman Ship Crews and the 'Rumi Challenge' to Portuguese Identity." *Medieval Encounters* 13 (2007): 122–44.

———. "An Ottoman Intelligence Report from the Mid Sixteenth-Century Indian Ocean." *Journal of Turkish Studies* 31/1 (2007): 181–88.

———. "Global Politics in the 1580s: A Canal, Twenty Thousand Cannibals, and an Ottoman Plot to Rule the World." *Journal of World History* 18/3 (Nov. 2007): 267–96.

———. "The Ottoman 'Discovery' of the Indian Ocean in the Sixteenth Century." In *Seascapes: Maritime Histories, Littoral Cultures and Trans-Oceanic Exchanges*, edited by Jerry Bentley, Renate Bridenthal, and Karen Wigen. Honolulu: University of Hawaii Press, 2007, 87–104.

———. "The Ottoman Administration of the Spice Trade in the Sixteenth-Century Red Sea and Persian Gulf." *Journal of the Economic and Social History of the Orient* 49/2 (May 2006): 170–98.

———. "His Majesty's Servant Lutfi: The Career of a Previously Unknown Sixteenth-Century Ottoman Envoy to Sumatra Based on an Account of His Travels from the Topkapı Palace Archives." *Turcica* 37 (2005): 43–81.

Charles-Roux, F. "L'isthme de Suez et les rivalités européenes au XVIe siècle." *Revue de l'histoire des colonies françaises* (1924): 174–85.

Chaudhuri, K. N. *Trade and Civilization in the Indian Ocean: An Economic History from the Rise of Islam to 1750*. Cambridge: Cambridge University Press, 1985.

Cipolla, Carlo. *Guns, Sails and Empires: Technological Innovation and the Early Phases of European Expansion 1400–1700*. New York: Pantheon, 1965.

Çizakça, Murat. "Ottomans and the Mediterranean: An Analysis of the Ottoman Shipbuilding Industry as Reflected by the Arsenal Registers of Istanbul 1529–1650." In *Le genti del mare mediterraneo*, edited by Rosalba Ragosta. 2 vols. Naples: Lucio Pironti, 1981, 2: 773–88.

Coates, Timothy J. "D. João de Castro's 1541 Red Sea Voyage in the Greater Context of the Sixteenth-Century Portuguese-Ottoman Red Sea Rivalry." In *Decision Making and Change in the Ottoman Empire*, edited by Caesar E. Farah. Kirksville, Mo.: Thomas Jefferson University Press, 1993, 263–85.

Couto, Dejanirah. "Trois documents sur une demande de secours ormouzi à la Porte Ottomane." *Anais de História de Além-Mar* 3 (2002): 469–98.

———. "L'itinéraire d'un marginal: la deuxième vie de Diogo de Mesquita." *Arquivos do Centro Cultural Calouste Gulbenkian* 39 (2000): 9–35.

———. "No rasto de Hādim Seleimão Pacha: Alguns aspectos do comércio do mar vermelho nos anos de 1538–40." In *A Carreira da Índia e as rotas dos estreitos: Actas do VIII Seminário Internacional de História Indo-Portuguesa*, edited by Artur Teodoro de Matos and Luís Filipe Thomaz. Angra do Heroísmo, 1998, 485–508.

———. "L'espionage portugais dans l'empire ottoman au XVIe siècle." In *La Découverte, le Portugal et l'Europe: Actes du Colloque, Paris les 26, 27 et 28 Mai 1988*. Paris: Fondation Gulbenkian, 1990, 243–67.

Crone, G. R. *Maps and Their Makers: An Introduction to the History of Cartography*, 2nd ed. London: Hutchinson, 1964.

Crosby, Alfred W. *The Measure of Reality: Quantification and Western Society 1250–1600*. Cambridge: Cambridge University Press, 1997.

Cruz, Maria Augusta Lima. "Notes on Portuguese Relations with Vijayanagara." In *Sinners and Saints: The Successors of Vasco da Gama*, edited by Sanjay Subrahmanyam. Delhi: Oxford University Press, 1998, 13–39.

Cruz, Maria do Rosário de Sampaio Themudo Barata de Azevedo. "A 'Questão de Baçora' na menoridade de D. Sebastião (1557–1568): A perspectiva das informações colhidas na Índia e as iniciativas do governo." *Rivista da falcudade de letras*, 5th series, 6 (1986): 103–38.

Dames, Longworth. "The Portuguese and the Turks in the Indian Ocean in the 16th Century." *Journal of the Royal Asiatic Society* 1 (Jan. 1921): 1–28.

Dane, Joseph. *The Myth of Print Culture: Essays on Evidence, Textuality, and Bibliographical Method*. Toronto: University of Toronto Press, 2003.

Das Gupta, Arun. "The Maritime Trade of Indonesia: 1500–1800." In *India and the Indian Ocean 1500–1800*, edited by Ashin Das Gupta and M. N. Pearson. Calcutta: Oxford University Press, 1987, 240–76.

de la Veronne, Chantal. "Giovanni Margliani et la trève de 1580 entre l'Espagne et la Turquie." *Arab Historical Review for Ottoman Studies* 3–4 (Dec. 1991): 70–75.

Desai, Z. A. "Relations of India with the Middle Eastern Countries during the 16th-17th Centuries." *Journal of the Oriental Institute* 23 (1973–1974): 75–106.

Destombes, M. "Fragments of Two Medieval World Maps at the Topkapı Saray Library." *Imago Mundi* 18 (1964): 244–54.

———. "The Chart of Magellan." *Imago Mundi* 12 (1955): 77–88.

———. "L'Hemisphère austral en 1524: une carte de Pedro Reinel à Istanbul." *Comptes rendus du Congrès International de Géographie, Amsterdam 1938*, 2 vols. Leiden: E. J. Brill, 1938.

Diffie, Bailey, and George D. Winius. *Foundations of the Portuguese Empire 1415–1580*. Minneapolis: University of Minnesota Press, 1977.

Diamond, Jared. *Guns, Germs and Steel: The Fates of Human Societies*. New York: Norton, 1999.

Disney, Anthony. "The Gulf Route from India to Portugal in the Sixteenth and Seventeenth Centuries: Couriers, Traders and Image Makers." In *A Carreira da Índia e as rotas dos estreitos: Actas do VIII Seminário Internacional de História Indo-Portuguesa*, edited by Artur Teodoro de Matos and Luís Filipe Thomaz. Angra do Heroísmo, 1998, 535–37.

Ebel, Kathryn. "City Views, Imperial Visions: Cartography and the Visual Culture of Urban Space in the Ottoman Empire, 1453–1603." PhD dissertation: University of Texas, Austin, 2002.

Eisenstein, Elizabeth L. *The Printing Press as an Agent of Change: Communications and Cultural Transformation in Early Modern Europe*. 2 vols. Cambridge: Cambridge University Press, 1979.

Elbl, I. "Man of His Time (and Peers): A New Look at Henry the Navigator." *Luso-Brazilian Review* 28/2 (1991): 73–89.

Emiralioğlu, Mevhibe Pınar. "Cognizance of the Ottoman World: Visual and Textual Representations in the Sixteenth-Century Ottoman Empire (1514–1596)." PhD dissertation: University of Chicago, 2006.

Fabris, Antonio. "The Ottoman Mappa Mundi of Hajji Ahmed of Tunis." *Arab Historical Review for Ottoman Studies* 7–8 (1993): 31–37.

Farah, Caesar E. "Organizing for the 2nd Conquest of Yemen." In *X. Türk Tarih Kongresi, Ankara 22–26 July, 1986*, vol. 6, 1150–59.

Farooqi, Naimur Rahman. "Six Ottoman Documents on Mughal-Ottoman Relations during the Reign of Akbar." *Journal of Islamic Studies* 7/1 (1996): 32–48.

———. *Mughal-Ottoman Relations: A Study of Political and Diplomatic Relations between Mughal India and the Ottoman Empire 1556–1748*. Delhi: IAD, 1989.

———. "Moguls, Ottomans, and Pilgrims: Protecting the Routes to Mecca in the 16th and 17th Centuries." *International History Review* 10 (1988): 198–220.

Faroqhi, Suraiya. *The Ottoman Empire and the World around It*. London: I. B. Tauris, 2004.

———. *Pilgrims and Sultans: The Hajj under the Ottomans 1517–1683*. New York: I. B. Tauris, 1994.

———. "Crisis and Change 1590–1699." In *Economic and Social History of the Ottoman Empire, 1300–1914, Vol. 2*. Edited by Halil Inalcik and Donald Quataert. Cambridge: Cambridge University Press, 411–623.

———. "Trade, Controls, Provisioning Policies and Donations: The Egypt-Hijaz Connection During the 2nd Half of the 16th Century." In *Suleyman the Second and His Time*, edited by Halil Inalcik and Cemal Kafadar. Istanbul: Isis, 1993.

Fetvacı, Emine. "Viziers to Eunuchs: Transitions in Ottoman Manuscript Patronage, 1566–1617." PhD dissertation: Harvard University, 2005.

Finlay, Robert. "How Not to (Re)Write World History: Gavin Menzies and the Chinese Discovery of America." *Journal of World History* 15/2 (2004): 229–42.

———. "Crisis and Crusade in the Mediterranean: Venice, Portugal and the Cape Route to India (1498–1509)." *Studi Veneziani* 28 (1994): 45–90.

———. "Portuguese and Chinese Maritime Imperialism: Camões's Lusiads and Loo Maodeng's Voyage of the San Bao Eunuch." *Comparative Studies in Society and History* 34/2 (1992): 225–41.

———. "The Treasure Ships of Zheng-He: Chinese Maritime Imperialism in the Age of Discovery." *Terrae Incognitae* 23 (1991): 1–12.

Fischel, Walter J. "The Spice Trade in Mamluk Egypt." *Journal of the Economic and Social History of the Orient* 1 (1958): 157–74.

Fitzmaurice, Andrew. *Humanism and America: An Intellectual History of English Colonization*. Cambridge: Cambridge University Press, 2003.

Fleischer, Cornell. "The Lawgiver as Messiah: The Making of the Imperial Image in the Reign of Suleyman." In *Soliman le Magnifique et son temps*, edited by Gilles Veinstein. Paris, 1992, 163–79.

———. *Bureaucrat and Intellectual in the Ottoman Empire: The Historian Mustafa Ali (1541–1600)*. Princeton, N.J.: Princeton University Press, 1986.

Flint, Valerie. *The Imaginative Landscape of Christopher Columbus*. Princeton, N.J.: Princeton University Press, 1992.

Floor, Willem. *The Persian Gulf: A Political and Economic History of Five Port Cities 1500–1730*. Washington, D.C.: Mage, 2006.

Flores, Jorge Manuel Costa da Silva. "The Straights of Ceylon, 1524–1539: The Portuguese Mappilla Struggle over a Strategic Area." In *Sinners and Saints: The Successors of Vasco da Gama*, edited by Sanjay Subrahmanyam. Delhi: Oxford University Press, 1998, 57–74.

———. *Os Portugueses e o mar de Ceilão 1498–1543: Trato, diplomaçia e guerra.* Lisbon: Cosmos, 1998.

Frank, Andre Gunder. *ReOrient: Global Economy in the Asian Age.* Berkeley: University of California Press, 1998.

Fuchs, Barbara. *Mimesis and Empire: The New World, Islam and European Identities.* Cambridge: Cambridge University Press, 2001.

Gambara, Agostino. "Il Canale di Suez e la Repubblica di Venezia." *Archivio veneto* 2 (1871): 175–213.

Gaudefroy-Demombynes, M. "Les souces arabes du Muhit." *Journal asiatique*, 2nd series, 20 (1912): 547–50.

Gaudio, Michael. *Engraving the Savage: The New World and Techniques of Civilization.* Minneapolis: University of Minnesota Press, 2008.

Geanakoplos, Deno John. *Constantinople and the West: Essays on the Late Byzantine (Palaeologan) and Italian Renaissances and the Byzantine and Roman Churches.* Madison: University of Wisconsin Press, 1989.

Genç, Mehmet. *Osmanlı İmparatorluğu'nda Devlet ve Ekonomi.* Istanbul: Ötüken, 2000.

Gentile, Sebastiano, ed. *Firenze e la scoperta dell'America: Umanesimo e geografia nel '400 fiorentino.* Firenze: Olschki, 1992.

Gibb, H. A. R. "Lutfi Paşa on the Ottoman Caliphate." *Oriens* 15 (1962): 287–95.

Glete, Jan. *Warfare at Sea 1500–1650: Maritime Conflicts and the Transformation of Europe.* London: Routledge, 2000.

Godinho, Vitorino Magelhães. "The Portuguese 'Carreira da Índia' 1497–1810." In *Ships, Sailors and Spices: East India Companies and their Shipping in the 16th, 17th and 18th Centuries*, edited by Jaap Bruijn and Femme Gaastra. Amsterdam: Neha, 1993, 1–47.

———. *Os descobrimentos e a economia mundial.* 2nd ed. 4 vols. Lisbon, 1981.

———. "Le tournant mondial de 1517–1524 et l'empire portugais." *Studia* 1 (Jan. 1958): 184–200.

Goetz, Herman. "Ottoman Turkish Art in India: The Architect of the Gol Gumbaz at Bijapur." In *Studies in the Foreign Relations of India (from the Earliest Times to 1947)*, edited by P. M. Joshi. Hyderabad: State Archives Press, 1975, 522–26.

Goffman, Daniel. *The Ottoman Empire and Early Modern Europe.* Cambridge: Cambridge University Press, 2002.

Gökbilgin, Tayyib. "Rüstem Paşa Hakkındaki İthamlar." *Tarih Dergisi* 11–12 (July 1955): 11–50.

———. "Ibrāhīm Pasha," *The Encyclopaedia of Islam, New Edition.* Leiden: E.J. Brill, 1954–, vol. 3, 998a.

Goodrich, Thomas. "Some Unpublished Sixteenth-Century Ottoman Maps." In *Comité International d'Études Pré-Ottomanes et Ottomanes, VIth Symposium, Cambridge 1st–4th of July 1984*, edited by J.-L. Bacqué-Grammont and Emeri Van Dunzel. Istanbul: IFEA, 1987, 99–103.

———. "The Earliest Ottoman Maritime Atlas: The Walters Deniz Atlası." *Archivum Ottomanicum* 11 (1986): 25–44.

———. "Atlas-ı Hümayun: A Sixteenth-Century Ottoman Maritime Atlas Discovered in 1984." *Archivum Ottomanicum* 10 (1985): 84–101.

Grafton, Anthony. *New Worlds, Ancient Texts: The Power of Tradition and the Shock of Discovery.* Cambridge, Mass.: Harvard University Press, 1992.

Greenblatt, Stephen. *Marvelous Possessions: The Wonder of the New World.* Chicago: University of Chicago Press, 1991.

Guillot, Claude, and Ludvik Kalus. "Inscriptions islamiques sur des canons d'Insulinde du XVIe siècle." *Archipel* 72 (2006): 69–94.

Guilmartin, John. *Gunpowder and Galleys: Changing Technology and Mediterranean Warfare at Sea in the 16th Century*. New York: Cambridge University Press, 1980.

Hadi, Amirul. *Islam and State in Sumatra: A Study of Seventeenth-Century Aceh*. Leiden: E. J. Brill, 2004.

Hall, Bert S. *Weapons and Warfare in Renaissance Europe: Gunpowder, Technology and Tactics*. Baltimore: Johns Hopkins, 1997.

Hamdani, Abbas. "Ottoman Response to the Discovery of America and the New Route to India." *Journal of the American Oriental Society* 101/3 (July 1981): 323–30.

———. "Columbus and the Recovery of Jerusalem." *Journal of the American Oriental Society* 101 (1981): 323–30.

Hankins, James. "Renaissance Crusaders: Humanist Crusade Literature in the Age of Mehmed II." *Dumbarton Oaks Papers* 49 (1995): 111–207.

———. *Plato in the Italian Renaissance*. 2 vols. New York: Brill, 1991.

Hanna, Nelly. *In Praise of Books: A Cultural History of Cairo's Middle Class, Sixteenth through the Eighteenth Centuries*. Syracuse, N.Y.: Syracuse University Press, 2003.

———. *Making Big Money in 1600: The Life and Times of Isma'il Abu Taqiyya, Egyptian Merchant*. Syracuse, N.Y.: Syracuse University Press, 1998.

Hathaway, Jane. *A Tale of Two Factions: Myth, Memory, and Identity in Ottoman Egypt and Yemen*. Albany: State University of New York Press, 2003.

Hess, Andrew G. *The Forgotten Frontier: A History of the Sixteenth-Century Ibero-African Frontier*. Chicago: University of Chicago Press, 1978.

———. "Piri Reis and the Ottoman Response to the Voyages of Discovery." *Terrae Incognitae* 6 (1974): 19–37.

———. "The Ottoman Conquest of Egypt and the Beginning of the Sixteenth-Century World War." *International Journal of Middle East Studies* 4/1 (Jan. 1973): 55–76.

———. "The Evolution of the Ottoman Seaborne Empire in the Age of the Oceanic Discoveries 1453–1525." *American Historical Review* 75/7 (Dec. 1970): 1892–1919.

———."The Moriscos: An Ottoman Fifth Column in Sixteenth-Century Spain." *American Historical Review* 74/1 (1968): 1–25.

Ho, Engseng. *The Graves of Tarim: Genealogy and Mobility across the Indian Ocean*. Berkeley: University of California Press, 2006.

Hodgson, Marshall D. *Rethinking World History: Essays on Europe, Islam and World History*. Edited by William Burke III. Cambridge: Cambridge University Press, 1993.

Hostetler, Laura. *The Art of Ethnography: A Chinese Miao Album*. Seattle: University of Washington Press, 2007.

———. *Qing Colonial Enterprise: Ethnography and Cartography in Early Modern China*. Chicago: University of Chicago Press, 2001.

Hourani, George. *Arab Seafaring in the Indian Ocean in Ancient and Early Medieval Times*. Princeton, N.J.: Princeton University Press, 1995.

Howard, Deborah. *Venice and the East: The Impact of the Islamic World on Venetian Architecture 1100–1500*. New Haven, Conn.: Yale University Press, 2000.

İhsanoğlu, Ekmeleddin. *Osmanlı Coğrafya Literatürü Tarihi*. 2 vols. Istanbul: IRCICA, 2000.

Imber, Colin. *Ebu's-Su'ud: The Islamic Legal Tradition*. Palo Alto: Stanford University Press, 1997.

———. "Suleyman as Caliph of the Muslims: Ebu's-Su'ud's Formulation of Ottoman Dynastic Ideology." In *Soliman le Magnifique et son temps*, edited by Gilles Veinstein. Paris, 1992, 179–84.

———. "The Navy of Suleyman the Magnificent." *Archivum Ottomanicum* 6 (1980): 211–82.

Inalcık, Halil. *An Economic and Social History of the Ottoman Empire 1300–1914, Vol. 1: The Ottoman State, Economy and Society 1300–1600*. Cambridge: Cambridge University Press, 1994.

———. "The Socio-Political Effects of the Diffusion of Firearms in the Middle East." In *The Ottoman Empire: Conquest, Organization, and Economy*, edited by Halil Inalcik. London: Variorum, 1978, 195–217.

———. "The Ottoman Economic Mind and Aspects of Ottoman Economy." In *Studies in the Economic History of the Middle East*, edited by M. A. Cook. London: Oxford University Press, 1970, 207–18.

———. "Bursa and the Commerce of the Levant," *Journal of the Economic and Social History of the Orient* 3/2 (1960): 131–47.

———. "Review: David Ayalon, *Gunpowder and Firearms in the Mamluk Kingdom*," *Belleten* 21/81–84 (1957): 500–12.

———. "The Origins of the Ottoman-Russian Rivalry and the Don-Volga Canal 1569." *Les annales de l'Université d'Ankara* 1 (1946–1947): 47–106.

İslamoğlu-İnan, Huri. "Introduction: Oriental Despotism in World-System Perspective." In *The Ottoman Empire and the World Economy*, edited by Huri Islamoğlu-Inan. Cambridge: Cambridge University Press, 1987, 1–24.

Johns, Adrian. *The Nature of the Book: Print and Knowledge in the Making*. Chicago: University of Chicago Press, 1998.

Jones, Robert. "The Medici Oriental Press (Rome 1584–1614) and the Impact of Its Arabic Publications on Northern Europe." In *The "Arabick" Interest of the Natural Philosophers in Seventeenth-Century England*, edited by G. A. Russell. Leiden: Brill, 1994, 88–108.

Kafadar, Cemal. *Between Two Worlds: The Construction of the Ottoman State*. Berkeley: University of California Press, 1994.

———. "The Myth of the Golden Age: Ottoman Historical Consciousness in the Post-Süleymanic Era." In *Suleyman the Second and His Time*, edited by Halil İnalcık and Cemal Kafadar. Istanbul: Isis Press, 1993, 37–48.

———. "A Death in Venice: Anatolian Muslim Merchants Trading in the Serenissima." *Journal of Turkish Studies* 13 (1990): 191–218.

Kagay, Donald G. "Columbus as Standardbearer and Mirror of the Spanish Reconquest." *Neptune* 53/4 (Winter 1993): 254–59.

Kahle, Paul. "China as Described by Turkish Geographers from Iranian Sources." In *Opera Minora I*, edited by Paul Kahle. Leiden, 1956, 312–25.

Karamustafa, Ahmet. "Introduction to Ottoman Cartography." In *The History of Cartography, Vol. 2, Book 1: Cartography in Traditional Islamic and South Asian Societies*, edited by J. B. Harley and David Woodward. Chicago: University of Chicago Press, 1987, 206–8.

———. "Military, Administrative, and Scholarly Maps and Plans." In *The History of Cartography, Vol. 2, Book 1: Cartography in Traditional Islamic and South Asian Societies*, edited by J. B. Harley and David Woodward. Chicago: University of Chicago Press, 1987, 209–27.

Kearney, Milo. *The Indian Ocean in World History*. London: Routledge, 2004.

Kissling, Hans-Joachim. "Şah Ismail I, la nouvelle route des Indes, et les Ottomans." *Turcica* 6 (1975): 89–102.

Kosal, Nejat. *Hind Yolu ve Osmanlı İmparatorluğu*. Istanbul, 1936.

Kunt, Metin. *The Sultan's Servants: Transformation of Ottoman Provincial Government, 1550–1650*. New York: Columbia University Press, 1983.

Kurat, A. N. "The Turkish Expedition to Astrakhan and the Problem of the Don-Volga Canal." *Slavonic and East European Review* 40 (Dec. 1961): 7–23.

Kurtoğlu, Fevzi. "Hadım Süleyman Paşa'nın Mektupları ve Belgrad'ın Muhasara Planı," *Belleten* 9 (1940): 53–87.

———. "XVI. Asırda Hind Okyanusunda Türkler ve Portekizler." In *II. Tarih Kongresi*. Istanbul, 1937.

———. *Ali Macar Reis Atlası*. Istanbul, 1935.

———. "Amiral Selman Reis Lâyıhası." *Deniz Mecmuası* 47/335 (1935): 67–73.

Kütükoğlu, Bekir. *Osmanlı-İran Siyasi Münasebetleri*. Istanbul: Edebiyat Fakültesi Matbaası, 1962.

Lach, Donald. *Asia in the Making of Europe*. 2 vols. Chicago: University of Chicago Press, 1965.

Lambourn, Elizabeth. "India from Aden: Khutba and Muslim Urban Networks in Late Thirteenth-Century India." In *Secondary Cities and Urban Networking in the Indian Ocean Realm, c. 1000–1800*, edited by K. Hall. Lanham, Md.: Lexington, 2008, 55–97.

Lane, Frederick C. "The Mediterranean Spice Trade: Further Evidence for Its Revival in the 16th Century." In *Crisis and Change in the Venetian Economy in the Sixteenth Century*, edited by Brian Pullman. London: Methren, 1968, 47–58.

Le Goff, Jacques. "The Medieval West and the Indian Ocean: An Oneiric Horizon." In *Facing Each Other: The World's Perception of Europe and Europe's Perception of the World*, edited by Anthony Pagden. Burlington, Vt.: Variorum Press, 2000, 1–19.

Lesure, M. "Notes et documents sur les relations vénéto-ottomanes 1570–73." *Turcica* 4 (1972): 134–64.

Levathes, Louise. *When China Ruled the Seas: The Treasure Fleet of the Dragon Throne, 1405–1433*. New York: Oxford University Press, 1994.

Lewis, Bernard. *The Muslim Discovery of Europe*. New York: George J. Mcleod, 1982.

Lewis, Dianne. *Jan Compagnie in the Straits of Malacca 1641–1795*. Athens: Ohio University Center for International Studies, 1995.

Lieberman, Victor. *Strange Parallels: Vol. 1, Integration on the Mainland: Southeast Asia in Global Context, c. 800–1830*. Cambridge: Cambridge University Press, 2003.

Liu, Yih-Min. "A Comparative and Critical Study of Ali Akbar's Khitaynama with References to Chinese Sources." *Central Asiatic Journal* 27/1–2 (1983): 58–78.

Lo, Jung-Pang. "The Decline of the Early Ming Navy." *Oriens Extremis* 5/2 (Dec. 1958): 149–68.

Lombard, D. "L'Empire ottoman vu d'Insulinde." In *Passé turco-tatar, présent soviétique: Études offertes á Alexandre Bennigsen*, edited by Ch. Lemercier-Quelquejay, G. Veinstein, and S. E. Wimbush. Paris: Peeters, 1986, 157–64.

———. *Le sultanat d'Atjeh au temps d'Iskandar Muda 1607–1636*. Paris: Presses Universitaires de France, 1967.

Lowry, Heath. *The Nature of the Early Ottoman State*. Albany: State University of New York Press, 2003.

Lybyer. A. H. "The Ottoman Turks and the Routes of Oriental Trade." *English Historical Review* 30 (1915): 577–88.

Mack, Rosamund. *Bazaar to Piazza: Islamic Trade and Italian Art*. Berkeley: University of California Press, 2001.

Maghrebi, Nizamuddin. "The Ottoman-Gujarat Relations (1517–1556): Political and Diplomatic." In *Studies in the Foreign Relations of India (from the Earliest Times to 1947)*, edited by P. M. Joshi. Hyderabad: State Archives Press, 1975, 184–93.

Mandaville, Jan E. "The Ottoman Province of Al-Hasâ in the Sixteenth and Seventeenth Centuries." *Journal of the American Oriental Society* 90 (1970): 486–513.

Manguin, Pierre-Yves. "Of Fortresses and Galleys: The 1568 Achehnese Siege of Melaka, after a Contemporary Bird's-Eye View." *Modern Asian Studies* 22 (1988): 607–28.

Manning, Patrick. *Migrations in World History*. London: Routledge, 2005.

Mantran, Robert. "L'Empire ottoman et le commerce asiatique aux 16e et 17e siècles." In *Islam and the Trade of Asia*, edited by D. S. Richards. Philadelphia: University of Pennsylvania Press, 1970, 169–79.

———. "Règlements fiscaux ottomans: la province de Bassora (la moitié du XVIe s.)." *Journal of the Economic and Social History of the Orient* 10 (1967): 224–77.

Matar, Nabil. *Europe through Arab Eyes: 1578–1727*. New York: Columbia University Press, 2009.

———. *In the Lands of the Christians: Arab Travel Writing in the Seventeenth Century*. New York: Routledge, 2003.

———. *Turks, Moors, and Englishmen in the Age of Discovery*. New York: Columbia University Press, 1999.

Matthee, Rudi. "Between Arabs, Turks and Iranians: The Town of Basra, 1600–1700." *Bulletin of the School of Oriental Studies*16/1 (2006): 53–78.

Mazzaoui, Michael M. "Global Policies of Sultan Selim, 1512–1520." In *Essays on Islamic Civilization Presented to Niyazi Berkes*, edited by Donald P. Little. Leiden: Brill, 1976, 224–43.

Mcintosh, Gregory C. "Christopher Columbus and the Piri Reis Map of 1513." *Neptune* 53/4 (Winter 1993): 280–94.

McNeill, John R., and Willam McNeill. *The Human Web: A Bird's-Eye View of World History*. New York: Norton, 2003.

McNeill, William. *The Age of Gunpowder Empires 1450–1800*. Washington, D.C.: American Historical Association, 1989.

Meloy, John. "The Privatization of Protection: Extortion and the State in the Circassian Mamluk Period." *Journal of the Economic and Social History of the Orient* 47/2 (2004): 195–212.

———. "Imperial Strategy and Political Exigency: The Red Sea Spice Trade and the Mamluk Sultanate in the Fifteenth Century." *Journal of the American Oriental Society* 123/1 (2003): 1–19.

Melziğ, Herbert. *Büyük Türk Hindistan Kapılarında: Kanuni Sultan Süleyman Devrinde Amiral Hadım Süleyman Paşa'nın Hind Seferi*. Istanbul: Selami Sertoğlu, 1943.

Ménage, V. L. "The Map of Hajji Ahmed and Its Makers." *Bulletin of the School of Oriental and African Studies* 21(1958): 291–314.

Menard, Russell, "Transport Costs and Long-Range Trade, 1300–1800: Was There a European Transport Revolution?" In *The Political Economy of Merchant Empires*, edited by James Tracy. Cambridge: Cambridge University Press, 1991, 228–75.

Menzies, Gavin. *1421: The Year China Discovered America*. New York: Harper Perennial, 2004.

Mirkovich, Nicolas. "Ragusa and the Portuguese Spice Trade." *Slavonic and East European Review* 21/56, part 1 (March 1943): 174–87.

el-Moudden, Abderrahmane. "Sharifs and Padishahs: Moroccan-Ottoman Relations from the Sixteenth through the Eighteenth Centuries." PhD dissertation: Princeton University, 1992.

Mughul, M. Yakub. *Kanuni Devri Osmanlılar'ın Hint Okyanusu Politikası ve Osmanlı-Hint Müslümanları Münasebetleri 1517–1538*. Istanbul: Fetih Yayınevi, 1974.

———. "Türk Amirali Emir Ibn Behram Bey'in Hindistan Seferi (1531)." *İstanbul Üniversitesi Edebiyat Fakültesi Tarih Dergisi* 4–5 (Aug. 1973–1974): 247–62.

———. "The Beginning of the Ottoman Domination in the Red Sea: The Way to India." *Sind University Research Journal Arts Series: Humanities and Social Sciences* 9 (1970): 54–76.

———. "The Expedition of Suleyman Pasha Al-Khadim to India (1538)." *Journal of the Regional Cultural Institute (Iran, Pakistan, Turkey)* 2/3 (Summer 1969): 146–51.

———. "Early Relations of the Osmanlı Sultans with the Muslim Rulers of the Indo-Pakistan Subcontinent." *Sind University Research Journal: Arts Series, Humanities and Social Science* 4 (1967): 147–58.

———."Portekizlilerle Kızıldeniz'de Mücadele ve Hicaz'da Osmanlı Hakimiyeti'nin Yerleşmesi Hakkında Bir Vesika." *Türk Tarih Belgeleri Dergisi* 2/3–4 (1965): 223–40.

Murphey, Rhoads. *Ottoman Warfare, 1500–1700*. New Brunswick, N.J.: Rutgers University Press, 1999.

Necipoğlu, Gülru. *The Age of Sinan: Architectural Culture in the Ottoman Empire*. London: Reaktion, 2005.

———. "A Kanun for the State, a Canon for the Arts: Conceptualizing the Classical Synthesis of Ottoman Art and Architecture." In *Soliman le Magnifique et son temps*, edited by Gilles Veinstein. Paris, 1992, 195–216.

———."Süleyman the Magnificent and the Representation of Power in the Context of Ottoman-Hapsburg-Papal Rivalry." *Art Bulletin* 71/3 (Sept. 1989): 401–27.

Newitt, Malyn. "Prince Henry and the Origins of European Expansion." In *Historiography of Europeans in Africa and Asia, 1450–1800*, edited by in Anthony Disney. Brookfield: Variorum, 1995, 85–11.

Nüzhet, Selim. *Türk Matbacılığı*. Istanbul, 1928.

Orhonlu, Cengiz. *Osmanlı İmparatorluğu'nda Şehircilik ve Ulaşım Üzerine Araştırmalar*. İzmir: Ege Üniversitesi Edebiyat Fakültesi Yayınları, 1984.

———. *Osmanlı İmparatorluğu'nun Güney Siyaseti: Habeş Eyaleti*. Istanbul: Türk Tarihi Kurumu, 1974.

———. "Seydi Ali Reis." *Tarih Enstitüsü Dergisi* 1 (Oct. 1970): 39–56.

———. "Osmanlı-Borno Münasebetine Aid Belgeler." *Tarih Dergisi* 23 (March 1969): 111–31.

———. "1559 Bahreyn Seferine Ait bir Rapor." *Tarih Dergisi* 17/22 (1967): 1–17.

———. "Hint Kaptanlığı ve Piri Reis." *Belleten* 34/134 (1967): 235–54.

———. "Osmanlılar'ın Habeşistan Siyaseti." *Tarih Dergisi* 15/20 (March 1965): 39–54.

———. "XVI. Asırın İlk Yarısında Kızıldeniz Sahilleri'nde Osmanlılar." *Tarih Dergisi* 16 (July 1961): 1–24.

———. "Khādım Süleymān Pasha," *EI*², 4: 901–902.

Özbaran, Salih. *Ottoman Expansion towards the Indian Ocean in the 16th Century*. Istanbul: Bilgi University Press, 2009.

———. *Portuguese Encounters with the World in the Age of the Discoveries: The Near and Middle East*. London: Ashgate, 2008.

———. *Yemen'den Basra'ya Sınırdaki Osmanlı*. Istanbul: Kitap Yayınevi, 2004.

———. *Bir Osmanlı Kimliği: 14.–17. Yüzyıllarda Rūm/Rūmī Aidiyet ve İmgeleri*. Istanbul: Kitap Yayınevi, 2004.

———. "Ottomans as 'Rumes' in Portuguese Sources in the Sixteenth Century." *Portuguese Studies* 17 (2002): 64–74.

———. *The Ottoman Response to European Expansion: Studies on Ottoman-Portuguese Relations in the Indian Ocean and Ottoman Administration in the Arab Lands during the Sixteenth Century*. Istanbul: Isis, 1994.

———. "The Ottomans in Confrontation with the Portuguese in the Red Sea after the Conquest of Egypt in 1517." *Studies in Turkish-Arab Relations* (1986): 207–13.

———. "A Note on the Ottoman Administration in Arabia in the 16th Century." *International Journal of Turkish Studies* 3/1 (Winter 1984–1985): 93–99.

———. "Bahrain in 1559—A Narrative of Turco-Portuguese Conflict in the Gulf." *Journal of Ottoman Studies* 3 (1982): 91–104.

———. "Two Letters of Dom Alvaro de Noronha from the Hormuz-Turkish Activities along the Coast of Arabia: 1550–1552." *İstanbul Üniversitesi Edebiyat Fakültesi Tarih Dergisi* 9 (1978): 241–92.

———. "A Turkish Report on the Red Sea and the Portuguese in the Indian Ocean (1525)." *Arabian Studies* 4 (1978): 81–88.

———. "Osmanlı İmparatorluğu ve Hindistan Yolu: Onaltıncı Yüzyılda Ticaret Yolları Üzerinde Türk-Portekiz Rekabet ve Ilişkileri." *Tarih Dergisi* 31 (March 1977): 66–146.

———. "The Ottoman Turks and the Portuguese in the Persian Gulf 1534–1581." *Journal of Asian History* 6/1 (Spring 1972): 45–88.

———. "XVI. Yüzyılda Basra Körfezi Sahillerinde Osmanlılar: Basra Beylerbeyliği'nin Kuruluşu." *Tarih Dergisi* 25 (March 1971): 51–73.

———. "Portekiz Devlet Arşivi 'Torre do Tombo'nun XVI. Yüzyıl Osmanlı Tarihi İçin Önemi." *Tarih Enstitüsü Dergisi* 1 (Oct. 1970): 57–62.

———. "Osmanlı Tarihi Bakımından XVI. Yüzyılda Portekizli Tarihçiler." *Tarih Dergisi* 23 (March 1969): 75–82.

Özdemir, Kemal. *Osmanlı Deniz Haritaları—Ali Macar Reis Atlası*. Istanbul: Marmara Bankası, 1992.

Padrón, Ricardo. *The Spacious Word: Cartography, Literature and Empire in Early Modern Spain*. Chicago: University of Chicago, 2003.

Pagden, Anthony, ed. *Facing Each Other: The World's Perception of Europe and Europe's Perception of the World*. Burlington, Vt.: Variorum Press, 2000.

———. *Lords of All the World: Ideologies of Empire in Spain, Britain and France 1500–1800*. New Haven, Conn.: Yale University Press, 1995.

———. *European Encounters with the New World: From Renaissance to Romanticism*. New Haven, Conn.: Yale University Press, 1993.

———. *The Fall of Natural Man: The American Indian and the Origins of Comparative Ethnology*. Cambridge: Cambridge University Press., 1982.

Pamuk, Şevket. *A Monetary History of the Ottoman Empire*. Cambridge: Cambridge University Press, 2000.

Parker, Geoffrey. "Crisis and Catastrophe: The Global Crisis of the Seventeenth Century Reconsidered." *American Historical Review* 113/4 (Oct. 2008): 1053–79.

———. *The Grand Strategy of Philip II*. New Haven, Conn.: Yale University Press, 1998.

———. *The Military Revolution: Military Innovation and the Rise of the West, 1500–1800*, 2nd ed. Cambridge: Cambridge University Press, 1996.

Pearson, M. N. *The Indian Ocean*. London: Routledge, 2003.

———. *Port Cities and Intruders: The Swahili Coast, India, and Portugal in the Early Modern Era*. Baltimore: John Hopkins, 1998.

———. *Pilgrimage to Mecca: The Indian Experience 1500–1800*. Princeton: Marcus Wiener, 1996.

———. "Merchants and States." In *The Political Economy of Merchant Empires: State Power and World Trade 1350–1750*, edited by Jim Tracy. Cambridge: Cambridge University Press, 1991, 41–116.

———. *Merchants and Rulers in Gujarat: The Response to the Portuguese in the Sixteenth Century*. Berkeley: University of California Press, 1976.

Peirce, Leslie. *The Imperial Harem: Women and Sovereignty in the Ottoman Empire*. New York: Oxford University Press, 1993.

Petry, Carl. *The Reigns of the Mamlūk Sultans al-Ashraf Qāytbāy and Qānṣūh al-Ghawrī in Egypt*. Seattle: University of Washington Press, 1993.

Pinto, Karen. "3 Ways of Seeing: Scenarios of the World in the Medieval Cartographic Imagination." PhD dissertation: Columbia University, 2002.

Pinto, Olga. "Una rarissima opera araba stampata a Roma nel 1585." In *Studi bibliografici: Atti del convegno dedicato alla storia del libro italiano nel V centenario dell'introduzione dell'arte tipografica in Italia, Bolzano, 7-8 ottobre, 1965*. Firenze: Leo S. Olschki, 1967, 47–51.

Pomeranz, Kenneth. *The Great Divergence: China, Europe and the Making of the Modern World Economy*. Princeton, N.J.: Princeton University Press, 2000.

Potach, Dejanirah. "The Commercial Relations between Basra and Goa in the Sixteenth Century." *Studia* 48 (1989): 142–62.

Pryor, John. *Geography, Technology and War: Studies in the Maritime History of the Mediterranean, 649–1571*. Cambridge: Cambridge University Press, 1988.

Randles, W. G. L. "La diffusion dans l'Europe du XVIe siècle des connaissances géographiques dues aux découvertes portugaises." In *La Découverte, le Portugal et l'Europe: Actes du Colloque, Paris, les 26, 27 et 28 Mai 1988*. Paris: Fondation Gulbenkian, 1990, 269–78.

———. "From the Mediterranean Portulan Chart to the Marine World Chart of the Great Discoveries: The Crisis in Cartography in the 16th Century." *Imago Mundi* 40 (1988): 115–20.

Rego, Antonio da Silva. "Duarte Catanho, espião e embaixador (1538–1542)." *Anais*, serie 2, 4 (Lisbon, 1953): 123–40.

Reid, Anthony. "Islamization and Christianization in Southeast Asia: The Critical Phase 1550–1650." In *Southeast Asia in the Early Modern Era: Trade, Power and Belief*, edited by Anthony Reid. Ithaca, N.Y.: Cornell University Press, 1993, 151–79.

———. *Southeast Asia in the Age of Commerce 1450–1680, Vol. 1: The Lands below the Winds*. New Haven, Conn.: Yale University Press, 1988.

———. "Sixteenth-Century Turkish Influence in Western Indonesia." *Journal of South East Asian History* 10/3 (Dec. 1969): 395–414.

Ribeiro, Luciano. "Em torno do primeiro cerco de Diu." *Studia* 13–14 (Jan.–July 1964): 41–100.

———. "O primeiro cerco de Diu." *Studia* 1 (Jan. 1958): 201–95.

Richards, John F. *The New Cambridge History of India: The Mughal Empire*. New York: Cambridge University Press, 1993.

Rispoli, Adelia. ed., *İstanbul Topkapı Sarayı Müzesi ve Venedik Correr Müzesi Koleksiyonlarından XIV–XVIII. Yüzyıl Portolan ve Deniz Haritaları*. Istanbul: İtalyan Kültür Merkezi, 1994.

Risso, Patricia. *Merchants and Faith: Muslim Commerce and Culture in the Indian Ocean*. Boulder, Colo.: Westview, 1995.

Roberts, Sean. "Cartography between Cultures: Francesco Berlinghieri's *Geographia* of 1482." Ph.D. dissertation: University of Michigan, 2006.

Roper, Geoffrey. "Early Arabic Printing in Europe," In *Middle Eastern Languages and the Print Revolution: A Cross-Cultural Encounter*, edited by Eva Hanebutt-Benz, Dagmar Glass, and Geoffrey Roper. Westhofen: WVA-Verlag Skulima, 2002, 129–50.

Ross, E. Denison. "The Portuguese in India and Arabia, 1517–38." *Journal of the Royal Asiatic Society of Great Britain and Ireland* 54 (January 1922): 1–18.

Rubiés, Joan-Pau. *Travel and Ethnology in the Renaissance: South India through European Eyes, 1250–1625*. Cambridge: Cambridge University Press, 2000.

———. "New Worlds and Renaissance Ethnology." In *Facing Each Other: The World's Perception of Europe and Europe's Perception of the World*, edited by Anthony Pagden. Burlington, Vt.: Variorum Press, 2000, 81–121.

Russell, P. R. *Prince Henry the Navigator: The Rise and Fall of a Cultural Hero*. Oxford: Oxford University Press, 1984.

Safvet Bey. "Bahreyn'de bir Vaḳ'a." *Tārīḫ-i 'Os̱mānī Encümeni Mecmū'asi* 14–18 (h.1329/c.e. 1910): 1139–44.

———. "Bir Osmanlı Filosu'nun Sumatra Seferi." *Tārīḫ-i 'Os̱mānī Encümeni Mecmū'ası* 7–12 (h.1328/ c.e. 1909): 604–16 and 678–81.

———."Ḳara Deñiz-İzmit Körfezi Ḳānāli." *Tārīḫ-i 'Os̱mānī Encümeni Mecmū'ası* 14–18 (h.1328/c.e. 1909): 948–56.

Şah, Razaulhak. "Açi Padişahı Sultan Alâeddin'in Kanunî Sultan Süleyman'a Mektubu." *Tarih Araştırmaları Dergisi* 5/8–9 (1967): 373–409.

Sahillioğlu, Halil. "Yemen'in 1599–1600 Yılı Bütçesi." In *Yusuf Hikmet Bayur'a Armağan*. Ankara: Türk Tarih Kurumu, 1985, 287–319.

Said, Edward. *Orientalism*. New York: Random House, 1978.

Saldanha, António Vasconcelos de. "Conceitos de espaço e poder e seus reflexos na titulação régia portuguesa da época da expansão." In *La Découverte, le Portugal et l'Europe: Actes du Colloque, Paris, les 26, 27 et 28 Mai 1988*. Paris: Fondation Gulbenkian, 1990, 105–30.

Salinari, Marina Emiliani. "An Atlas of the 15th Century Preserved in the Library of the Former Serail in Constantinople." *Imago Mundi* 8 (1951): 101–2.

Samardjitch, Radovan. *Mehmed Sokolovitch: le destin d'un grand vizir*. Translated by Mauricette Begitch. Lausanne: L'Age d'homme, 1994.

Sanceau, Elaine. "Uma narrativa da expedição portuguesa de 1541 ao Mar Roxo." *Studia* 9 (Jan. 1962): 199–234.

Sarınay, Yusuf. *Ottoman Archives and Ethio-Ottoman Relations*. Ankara: Başbakanlık Genel Müdürlüğü, 2001.

Sarkar, Jagadash Narayan. "Indian Merchants in the Red Sea Ports, 1611." *Journal of Indian History* 27/1 (April 1949): 109–20.

Sauvaget, Jean. "Les caravansérails syriens du hadjdj de Constantinople." *Ars Islamica* 4 (1937): 98–121.

Sayılı, Aydın. *The Observatory in Islam and Its Place in the General History of the Observatory*. Ankara: Türk Tarih Kurumu, 1988.

———. "Üçüncü Murad'ın İstanbul Rasathanesindeki Mücessem Yer Küresi ve Avrupa ile Kültürel Temaslar." *Belleten* 25/99 (1961): 397–445.

Schmidt, Benjamin. *Innocence Abroad: The Dutch Imagination and the New World, 1570–1670*. Cambridge: Cambridge University Press, 2001.

Schwartz, Stuart, ed. *Implicit Understandings: Observing, Reporting and Reflecting on the Encounters between Europeans and Other Peoples in the Early Modern Era*. Cambridge: Cambridge University Press, 1994.

Şehsuvaroğlu, Bedi. "Kanuni Devrinde Yazılmış ve Şimdiye Bilinmeyen Bir Coğrafya Kitabı." In *Kanuni Armağanı*. Ankara: Türk Tarih Kurumu, 1970, 207–25.

———. "Türkçe Çok İlginç bir Coğrafya Yazması." *Belgelerle Türk Tarihi* 2 (1967): 63–72.

Serjeant, Robert Bertram. "Yemeni Merchants and Trade in Yemen: Thirteenth and Sixteenth Centuries." In *Asian Merchants and Businessmen in the Indian Ocean and the China Sea*, edited by Denys Lombard and Jean Aubin. Oxford: Oxford University Press, 1988, 79–86.

———. "The Yemeni Coast in 1005/1579: An Anonymous Note on the Flyleaf of Ibn al-Mujawir's Tarikh al-Mustahsir." *Arabian Studies* (1985):187–91.

Serkis, Yousuf Alian. *Dictionary of Arabic Printed Books from the Beginning of Arabic Printing until the End of 1337 A.H.-1919 A.D.* 2 vols. Cairo, 1928.

Sezgin, Fuat. *The Contribution of the Arabic-Islamic Geographers to the Formation of the World Map.* Frankfurt: Institut *für* Geschichte der Arabisch-Islamischen Wissenschaften, 1987.

Skilliter, S. A. "The Sultan's Messenger Gabriel Deferens: An Ottoman Master Spy of the 16th Century." *Wiener Zeitschrift für die Kunde des Morgenlandes* 68 (1976): 47–59.

———. "Hürrem," *The Encyclopaedia of Islam, New Edition*. Leiden: E. J. Brill, 1954–55: 66a–b.

Smith, Richard. *Ahmad al-Mansur: Islamic Visionary*. New York: Longman, 2005.

Soucek, Svat. *Piri Reis and Turkish Map Making after Columbus*. Oxford: Oxford University Press, 1996.

———. "Piri Reis and the Ottoman Discovery of the Great Discoveries." *Studia Islamica* 79 (1994): 121–42.

———. "The 'Ali Macar Reis Atlas' and the Deniz Kitabı: Their Place in the Genre of Portolan Charts and Atlases." *Imago Mundi* 25 (1971): 117–27.

Stagl, Justin. "The Methodising of Travel in the 16th Century: A Tale of Three Cities." In *Facing Each Other: The World's Perception of Europe and Europe's Perception of the World*, edited by Anthony Pagden. Burlington, Vt.: Variorum Press, 2000, 123–50.

Steensgaard, Niels. "The Indian Ocean Network and the Emerging World Economy c. 1500–1750." In *The Indian Ocean: Explorations in History, Commerce and Politics*, edited by Satish Chandra. New Delhi: Sage, 1987, 125–50.

———. *The Asian Trade Revolution of the Seventeenth Century*. Chicago: University of Chicago Press, 1973.

Studnicki-Gizbert, Daviken. *A Nation upon the Ocean Sea: Portugal's Atlantic Diaspora and the Crisis of the Spanish Empire, 1492–1640*. New York: Oxford University Press, 2007.

Subrahmanyam, Sanjay. *Explorations in Connected History: Mughals and Franks*. New York: Oxford University Press, 2005.

———. "A Note on the Rise of Surat in the Sixteenth Century." *Journal of the Social and Economic History of the Orient* 43/1 (2000): 23–33.

———. "The Trading World of the Western Indian Ocean, 1546–1565: A Political Interpretation." In *A Carreira da Índia e as rotas dos estreitos: Actas do VIII Seminário Internacional de História Indo-Portuguesa*, edited by Artur Teodoro de Matos and Luís Filipe Thomaz. Angra do Heroísmo, 1998, 207–29.

———. *The Career and Legend of Vasco da Gama*. Cambridge: Cambridge University Press, 1997.

———. "Connected Histories: Notes towards a Reconfiguration of Early Modern Eurasia." *Modern Asian Studies* 31/3 (1997): 735–62.

———. "A Matter of Alignment: Mughal Gujarat and the Iberian World in the Transition of 1580–1581." *Mare Liberum* 9 (July 1995): 461–80.

———. "Of *Imarat* and *Tijarat*: Asian Merchants and State Power in the Western Indian Ocean, 1400 to 1750," *Comparative Studies in Society and History* 37/4 (Oct. 1995): 750–80.

———. *The Portuguese Empire in Asia, 1500–1700: A Political and Economic History*. London: Longman, 1993.

———. *The Political Economy of Commerce: Southern India 1500–1650*. Cambridge: Cambridge University Press, 1990.

———. "Persians, Pilgrims and Portuguese: The Travails of Masulipatnam Shipping in the Western Indian Ocean 1590–1665." *Modern Asian Studies* 22/3 (1988): 503–30

Taeschner, Fr. "Djughrāfiyā VI: The Ottoman Geographers," EI^2. 1954, 2: 587–90.

Tan, M. Turhan. *Hint Denizlerinde Türkler*. Istanbul: Kanaat Kitabevi, 1939.

Tavim, José Alberto Rodrigues da Silva. "From Setubal to the Sublime Porte: The Wanderings of Jácome de Olivares, New Christian and Merchant of Cochin (1540–1571)." In *Sinners and Saints: The Successors of Vasco da Gama*, edited by Sanjay Subrahmanyam. Delhi: Oxford University Press, 1998, 94–134.

———. "Outras gentes em outras rotas: judeus e cristãos-novos de Cochin—entre Santa Cruz de Cochin e Mattancherry, entre o Império Português e o Médio Oriente." In *A Carreira da Índia e as rotas dos estreitos: Actas do VIII Seminário Internacional de História Indo-Portuguesa*, edited by Artur Teodoro de Matos and Luís Filipe Thomaz. Angra do Heroísmo, 1998, 309–42.

———. "Os Judeus e a expansão portuguesa na Índia durante o século XVI. O exemplo de Isaac do Cairo: espião, 'lingua,' e judeu de Cochim de Cima." *Arquivos do Centro Cultural Calouste Gulbenkian* 33 (1994): 137–266.

Tekindağ, S. "Süveyş'te Türkler ve Selman Reis'in Arzası." *Belgelerle Türk Tarihi Dergisi* 9 (1968): 77–89.

Temimi, A. "Le gouvernement ottoman face au problème morisque." *Revue d'Histoire Maghrébine* 23–24 (1989): 258–62.

Theunissen, Hans. "Ottoman-Venetian Diplomatics—the Ahdnames." *Electronic Journal of Oriental Studies* 1 (1998): 1–698.

Thomaz, Luís Filipe F. R. "A questão da pimenta em meados do século XVI." In *A Carreira da Índia e as rotas dos estreitos: Actas do VIII Seminário Internacional de História Indo-Portuguesa*, edited by Artur Teodoro de Matos and Luís Filipe Thomaz. Angra do Heroísmo, 1998, 37–206.

———. "A crise de 1565–1575 na história do Estado da Índia." *Mare Liberum* 9 (July 1995): 481–519.

———. "L'idée imperiale manueline." In *La Découverte, le Portugal et l'Europe: Actes du Colloque, Paris, les 26, 27 et 28 Mai 1988*. Paris: Fondation Gulbenkian, 1990, 35–103.

Thrower, J. W. *Maps and Civilization: Cartography in Culture and Society*. Chicago: University of Chicago, 1999.

Tibbetts, Gerald R. "The Role of Charts in Islamic Navigation in the Indian Ocean." In *The History of Cartography, Vol. 2, Book 1: Cartography in Traditional Islamic and South Asian Societies*, edited by J. B. Harley and David Woodward. Chicago: University of Chicago Press, 1987, 256–62.

Tuchscherer, Michel. "Commerce et production du café en Mer Rouge au XVIe siècle." In *Le commerce du café avant l'ère des plantations coloniales: espaces, réseaux, société, XVe-XIXe siècle*, edited by Michel Tuchscherer. Cairo: Institut français d'archéologie orientale, 2001.

Turan, Ebru. "The Sultan's Favorite: Ibrahim Paşa and the Making of the Ottoman Universal Sovereignty in the Reign of Sultan Süleyman, 1516–1526." Ph.D. Dissertation, University of Chicago, 2007.

Türkay, Cevdet. *Osmanlı Türklerinde Coğrafya*. Istanbul: Maarif Basımevi, 1959.

———. *İstanbul Kütüphanelerinde Osmanlılar Devrine Ait Türkçe-Arapça-Farsça Yazma ve Basma Coğrafya Eserleri Bibliografyası*. Istanbul: Maarif Basımevi, 1958.

Uzunçarşılı, İsmail Hakkı. "Türk-İngiliz Münasebetlerine Dair Vesikalar," *Belleten* 14 (1950): 27–40.

———. *Osmanlı Devletinde Merkez ve Bahriye Teşkilâtı*. Ankara: Türk Tarih Kurumu, 1948.

———. "Hind Hukumdarı Hümayun Şah'ın Kanuni'ye Gönderdiği bir Mektup." *Yedigün* 8/202 (1937): 5–27.

Vatin, Nicolas. *Les Ottomans et l'Occident (XVe-XVIe Siècles)*. Istanbul: İsis, 2001.

———. "Sur quelques propos géographiques d'Ibrahim Pacha, grand vizir de Soliman le Magnifique (1533)." In *Comité International d'Etudes Pré-Ottomanes et Ottomanes, VIth Symposium, Cambridge 1st–4th of July 1984*, edited by J.-L. Bacqué-Grammont and Emeri Van Donzel. Istanbul, 1987.

Vaughan, Dorothy M. *Europe and the Turk: A Pattern of Alliances 1350–1700*. Liverpool: AMS Press, 1954.

Veinstein, G. "Sokollu Mehmed Pasha." *The Encyclopaedia of Islam, New Edition*. Leiden: E. J. Brill, 1954–, 706–11.

Vinaver, Verk. "Mercanti e bastimenti di Ragusa in India: Una leggenda." In *Méditerranée et Océan Indien: Travaux du Sixième Colloque International d'Histoire Maritime, Venice 1962*, edited by Christine Villain-Gandossi and Manlio Cortelazzo. Paris, 1970, 170–190.

Wake, C. H. H. "The Changing Pattern of Europe's Pepper and Spice Imports ca. 1400–1700." *Journal of European Economic and Social History* 8/2 (1979): 361–403.

Wake, Christopher. "The Myth of Zheng He's Great Treasure Ships." *International Journal of Maritime History* 14/1 (June 2004): 59–75.

Wicki, Joseph, ed. "Duas relações sobre a situação da Índia Portuguesa nos anos 1568 e 1569." *Studia* 8 (July 1961): 133–235.

———. "Duas cartas oficiais de vice-reis da Índia, escritas em 1561 e 1564." *Studia* 3 (Jan. 1959): 36–89.

Wills, John E. "Maritime Asia 1500–1800: The Interactive Emergence of European Domination." *American Historical Review* 98/1 (Feb. 1993): 83–105.

Winius, George. "Iberian Historiography on European Expansion since World War II." In *Reappraisals in Overseas History Writing*, edited by P. C. Emmer and H. L. Wesseling. Leiden: Brill, 1979, 101–21.

Wink, Andre. "Al-Hind: India and Indonesia in the Islamic World Economy, c. 700–1800 AD." *Itinerario* 12 (1988): 33–72.

Woodhead, Christine. "An Experiment in Official Historiography: The Post of Şehnameci in the Ottoman Empire c. 1555–1605." *Wiener Zeitschrift für die Kunde des Morgenlandes* 75 (1983): 157–82.

Woodward, David. "Maps and the Rationalization of Geographic Space." In *Circa 1492: Art in the Age of Exploration*, edited by Jay Levenson. New Haven, Conn.: Yale University Press, 1991.

———. "Medieval Mappaemundi." In *The History of Cartography, Vol. 1: Cartography in Prehistoric, Ancient and Medieval Europe and the Mediterranean*, edited by J. B. Harley and David Woodward. Chicago: University of Chicago Press, 1987, 286–370.

Yurdaydın, H. "Matrakçı Nasuh'un Hayatı ve Eserleri ile İlgili Yeni Bilgiler." *Belleten* 29 (1965): 329–54.

Zachariadou, Elizabeth, ed. *The Kapudan Pasha: His Office and His Domain*. Rethymnon: Crete University Press, 2002.

INDEX

Boldface type indicates pages with illustrations.